D0086837

WESTWARD
EXPANSION

WESTWARD EXPANSION

Sara E. Quay

American Popular Culture Through History
Ray B. Browne, Series Editor

Greenwood Press
Westport, Connecticut · London

HOUSTON PUBLIC LIBRARY

RO1275 97536

Library of Congress Cataloging-in-Publication Data

Quay, Sara E.
   Westward expansion / by Sara E. Quay.
      p.   cm.—(American popular culture through history)
   Includes bibliographical references and index.
   ISBN 0–313–31235–4 (alk. paper)
      1. West (U.S.)—Civilization—19th century.   2. West (U.S.)—Social life and
   customs—19th century.   3. Pioneers—West (U.S.)—History—19th century.   4.
   Pioneers—West (U.S.)—History—19th century—Sources.   5. Frontier and pioneer
   life—West (U.S.)   6. Frontier and pioneer life—West (U.S.)—Sources.   7. Popular
   culture—West (U.S.)—History—19th century.   8. Popular culture—United
   States.   9. West (U.S.)—In mass media.   I. Title.   II. Series.
   F593.Q39   2002
   978'.02—dc21   2001054546

British Library Cataloguing in Publication Data is available.

Copyright © 2002 by Sara E. Quay

All rights reserved. No portion of this book may be
reproduced, by any process or technique, without the
express written consent of the publisher.

Library of Congress Catalog Card Number: 2001054546
ISBN: 0–313–31235–4

First published in 2002

Greenwood Press, 88 Post Road West, Westport, CT 06881
An imprint of Greenwood Publishing Group, Inc.
www.greenwood.com

Printed in the United States of America

The paper used in this book complies with the
Permanent Paper Standard issued by the National
Information Standards Organization (Z39.48–1984).

10 9 8 7 6 5 4 3 2 1

To my fathers

Contents

Series Foreword

Popular culture is the system of attitudes, behavior, beliefs, customs, and tastes that define the people of any society. It is the entertainments, diversions, icons, rituals, and actions that shape the everyday world. It is what we do while we are awake and what we dream about while we are asleep. It is the way of life we inherit, practice, change, and then pass on to our descendants.

Popular culture is an extension of folk culture, the culture of the people. With the rise of electronic media and the increase in communication in American culture, folk culture expanded into popular culture—the daily way of life as shaped by the *popular majority* of society. Especially in a democracy like the United States, popular culture has become both the voice of the people and the force that shapes the nation. In 1782, the French commentator Hector St. Jean de Crèvecoeur asked in his *Letters from an American Farmer*, "What is an American?" He answered that such a person is the creation of America and is in turn the creator of the country's culture. Indeed, notions of the American Dream have been long grounded in the dream of democracy—that is, government by the people, or popular rule. Thus, popular culture is tied fundamentally to America and the dreams of its people.

Historically, culture analysts have tried to fine-tune culture into two categories: "elite"—the elements of culture (fine art, literature, classical music, gourmet food, etc.) that supposedly define the best of society— and "popular"—the elements of culture (comic strips, best-sellers, pop music, fast food, etc.) that appeal to society's lowest common denominator. The so-called educated person approved of elite culture and scoffed at popular culture. This schism first began to develop in western

Europe in the fifteenth century when the privileged classes tried to discover and develop differences in societies based on class, money, privi-
lege, and lifestyles. Like many aspects of European society, the debate
between elite and popular cultures came to the United States. The upper
class in America, for example, supported museums and galleries that
would exhibit the finer things in life, that would elevate people. As the
twenty-first century emerges, however, the distinctions between popular
culture and elitist culture have blurred. The blues songs (once denigrated
as "race music") of Robert Johnson are now revered by musicologists;
architectural students study buildings in Las Vegas, Nevada, as examples
of what Robert Venturi called the "kitsch of high capitalism"; sports-
writer Gay Talese and heavyweight boxing champ Floyd Patterson were
co-panelists at a 1992 State University of New York–New Paltz sympo-
sium on literature and sport. The examples go on and on, but the one
commonality that emerges is the role of popular culture as a model for
the American Dream, the dream to pursue happiness and a better, more
interesting life.

   To trace the numerous ways in which popular culture has evolved
throughout American history, we have divided the volumes in this series
into chronological periods—historical eras until the twentieth century,
and the decades between 1900 and 2000. In each volume, the author
explores the specific details of popular culture that reflect and inform
the general undercurrents of the time. Our purpose, then, is to present
historical and analytical panoramas that reach both backward into America's past and forward to her collective future. In viewing these panoramas, we can trace a very fundamental part of American society. The
"American Popular Culture Through History" series presents the multifaceted parts of a popular culture in a nation that is both grown and
still growing.

Ray B. Browne
Secretary-Treasurer
Popular Culture Association
American Culture Association

Preface

Writing a book is something like being a pioneer. Despite the best travel guides, the path veers from its charted course and the journey takes on a life of its own. In the end, as many of the pioneers represented in this book discovered, the trip's success depends as much on the people with whom it is taken as on arriving at the final destination.

Many people traveled with me during the course of writing of this book. Dr. Beverly Dolinsky, Dean of Arts & Sciences at Endicott College, generously encouraged my completion of the manuscript, helping me carve out time to write despite the demands of work and everyday life. Betty Roland, Reference Librarian in Endicott's Fitz Memorial Library, spent countless hours tracking down sources for me, most of which she kindly renewed—without being asked—before I was inundated with overdue notices. Debby Adams, the acquisitions editor at Greenwood Press, provided quick and constructive feedback on my chapters and was kindly flexible during critical moments of the venture. Cynthia B. Ricciardi edited chapters, sharing her wealth of knowledge on frontier popular culture. My mother, Joy Mills, was an unwavering advocate whose questions and comments about the writing process made me feel that what I do is important, if to no one else but her. Grant Rice graciously sacrificed countless opportunities for adventure while I stayed home to write. He helped me to celebrate the book's completion with a trip to the Wind River Mountains where we saw traces of the Oregon Trail winding their way over the hills of South Pass, Wyoming. Other people who provided support throughout the project include William, Virginia, and Garrett Rice, who introduced me to the glory of the Utah Mountains;

Mark Kuhn, who solved a serious computer problem; and Amy Damico, who kept me in touch with the joys of teaching.

Finally, like those who made the rigorous trip west during the nineteenth century, I lost people who were close to me during the journey of this book. The first was my father, William H. Quay, who made his own westward journey. The second was my grandfather, Arthur G. Carlson who encouraged me to make time to write, every day, if only for an hour. And finally, my stepfather, Lewis H. Mills, who always saw where I was going. This book is dedicated to each of them.

Introduction

Popular culture is so deeply connected to the symbols of westward expansion that virtually no area of twenty-first century America remains uninfluenced by the West. Cigarettes are marketed through the quintessential cowboy figure of the Marlboro Man. Car advertisements are set in the rugged terrain of the western mountain ranges. Fast-food chains, like Roy Rogers and Taco Bell, borrow directly from the West in both their advertising and food selections. Levi's jeans and Stetson hats, the inspiration of early frontiersmen, remain fashion staples in contemporary culture. Successful musicians, like Shania Twain, adopt seductive western clothing styles to capture the attention of MTV audiences. Even the gun manufacturer Smith & Wesson has expanded its market by producing its own barbecue sauce and clothing. Whatever the arena, icons of the frontier saturate American life.

This book examines the deeply resonant relationship between popular culture and the period of westward expansion. The chapters focus on specific areas of frontier society and discuss the fads that occurred within them, including covered wagon graffiti, gold rush songs, and grasshopper pans. The roots of such trends, and their significance, are explored in the context of the historical moment in which the trends existed, providing readers with an overview of the cultural motifs and agendas that defined the frontier experience.

The years covered in the volume range from the first gold rush of 1849 to approximately 1890 when, in the sentiment expressed by Frederick Jackson Turner, the frontier was declared "closed."[1] Patterns in popular culture are not always contained by strict timelines, however. The infamous Donner expedition took place three years before the 1849 rush for gold, yet the Donner party's misfortune captivated Americans well into the 1850s and beyond. The dates are only a guide, in other words, for the westward expansion period in general. The events discussed may stray outside of those parameters.

In part because the time period covered in the book is so vast, and in part because frontier existence varied so greatly from region to region, the volume strives to provide an overview of the common trends of westward expansion, rather than to be a definitive encyclopedia on the topic. The popular culture found in a Nevada mining town was necessarily distinct from that experienced in a Nebraska farming community, and the ideas and activities in each were markedly different. There were also fads that spread from one region to another with remarkable speed, as, for instance, in the addictive gambling game monte, or in the anticipation of receiving Montgomery Ward's mail-order catalog. Such diffusion created a common language throughout the West that was expressed through widely known children's games, innovative recipes, and home-design styles. Encompassing both forms of mass culture, the book draws broad brushstrokes of the most common western trends while recording local fads as well.

The other objective the book pursues is to trace the roots of frontier popular culture throughout the nineteen hundreds and into the first decade of twenty-first century America. Toward the end of the nineteenth century, when the frontier was more settled than not, the historical events that had defined westward expansion came to an end. At the same time, the West increasingly began to appear in fictional mediums that blurred the boundaries between the realities and the myths of the region's history. Early Wild West Shows, for instance, featured individuals like Geronimo who had been actual participants in the events of westward expansion. While Geronimo's presence in Wild West Shows served to make the performances more "authentic" representations of the Old West, by taking part in them Geronimo also helped to create his own legend as a frontier character. As the twentieth century got under way, the West became even more mythologized through movies, radio programs, and the tourist industry, each of which represented an era that was at once historically past and culturally present. The development of sites like Disneyland's Frontierland theme park only further mixed the facts of westward expansion with the fiction of its enduring myths. The book follows these developments through many of their transformations, examining the historical relevance held by new versions of the same story.

Finally, and most important, this volume of the American Popular Culture Through History series offers readers a resource for additional exploration of the western symbols that appear in American society. The chapters are meant to enrich the reader's knowledge of those symbols so that allusions to the frontier stand out from the cultural landscape in provocative and compelling ways. Whether the reader's goal is to understand the historical roots of an icon like the cowboy, or to interpret that icon as it was reinvented in twenty-first-century culture, the book aims to serve, in the words used by participants in westward expansion, as a jumping-off place for further study.

Timeline of Westward Expansion

1823

Natty Bumppo appears in *The Pioneers*, the first novel in James Fenimore Cooper's Leatherstocking series.

1835

Sam Colt is issued a patent for the Colt revolver, a popular gun in the West.

1846

The Donner party sets out on what will become one of the most publicized, mythologized, and grisly journeys of the westward expansion period.

1847

Mormon emigrants found Deseret, by the Great Salt Lake, in what is now Salt Lake City.

1848

January 24. Gold is discovered in Coloma, California.

1849

Francis Parkman publishes *The Oregon Trail*.

The gold rush begins when the discovery of gold in California is confirmed.

1853

May. Lola Montez arrives in San Francisco, where she captures audiences with her spider dance.

1854

John A. Stone publishes *Put's Original California Songster*, creating a compendium of western songs.

1855

The U.S. Army brings camels to Texas to test their effectiveness as pack animals.

1859

The Indian Head Penny is minted.

1860

April 3. The Pony Express makes its inaugural trip.

1862

May 27. The Homestead Act offers free farmland to western settlers.

1865

Stetson hats, known as "The Hat of the West," are designed by John B. Stetson.

1869

May 10. The golden spike joins the Central and Union Pacific railroads at Promontory Point, Utah.

1872

Montgomery Ward introduces its product line, initiating the trend in mail-order catalogs.

1873

May 20. Levi Strauss and Jacob Davis are granted a patent for "Improvement of Pocket Openings."

Barbed wire is invented by Joseph Glidden, giving rise to the saying "Don't fence me in."

Cable cars start to run in San Francisco.

Arbuckle Brothers Company trademarks its Ariosa brand of coffee, targeting the West as its primary market.

1876

Fred Harvey changes the face of railroad cuisine when he opens the first in his chain of Fred Harvey Houses featuring high-quality food served by waitresses called Harvey Girls.

Mark Twain publishes *Tom Sawyer*.

1878

Deadwood Dick on Duck; or, Calamity Jane, the Heroine of Whoop-Up is published.

1881

October 25. In Tombstone, Arizona, Wyatt Earp memorializes the O.K. Corral when he kills cattle ranchers.

1882

Oscar Wilde tours the West.

1883

Buffalo Bill starts his Wild West Show.

1886

January 9. Frederic Remington's name and picture appear on the cover of *Harper's Weekly* magazine.

xx Timeline of Westward Expansion

1888

The Schoolchildren's Blizzard strands snowbound children in schools throughout the Midwest. The popular song "Thirteen Were Saved, or, Nebraska's Fearless Maid" is written to commemorate the event.

1889

April 22. The Oklahoma land rush starts.

PART ONE

LIFE AND YOUTH DURING WESTWARD EXPANSION

1

Everyday Life

> After all, there is something fascinating in the thought of the opening
> up of a new life, a change so complete as this will be.
> Mollie Dorsey Sanford[1]

Everyday life during the period of westward expansion varied dramatically from region to region, town to town, and year to year. At the same time, between 1849 and 1890, widespread beliefs, activities, and objects influenced the daily existence of western emigrants. The "rush" mentality adopted by gold, silver, and land seekers classified life in economic terms. The result was a culture determined by the boom-and-bust realities of population surges and declines, financial successes and failures. Widespread beliefs about health, medicine, and religion were impacted by that culture, and specific figures captured the essence of the era. The outlaw, for instance, who encapsulated the region's struggle with law and order, created ambiguous heroes out of men like Billy the Kid and Jesse James, heroes who have been the mainstay of popular conceptions of the frontier ever since the eighteen hundreds. In contrast to the infamous men and women of the West, who helped to define the region's unique character, frontier citizens participated in the events that influenced the nation as a whole, including presidential elections and national, as well as international, wars. Registering the West's impact on American culture, the songs and souvenirs used to mark those campaigns and battles drew on the frontier's rich symbolism for their meaning.

By the end of the nineteenth century, the movement west had slowed and daily life on the frontier was less uniquely "western" than generally American. At the same time, the myth surrounding the region known as the "wild, Wild West" flourished, leaving its mark on many aspects of American society. Whether used as a frame of reference for other historical, social, or cultural developments, or evoked in political campaigns, the West has been and continues to be an important symbol in the daily life of U.S. popular culture.[2]

FEVERS, RUSHES, AND THE WILD, WILD WEST

Throughout the eighteen hundreds, each report of gold and silver initiated a new wave in western emigrants, creating an atmosphere of recurrent rushes to lands west of the Mississippi. Major rushes for gold and silver took place in California (1849), Pikes Peak (1859), Idaho and Montana (1860–1862), White Pine, Nevada (1868–1869), and Alaska (1896). In each instance, hopeful miners traveled to the promising location as quickly as possible, bringing with them a culture that was frequently compared to a fever. The news that gold could be gathered quickly and easily, transforming lives from rags to riches overnight, caught the public's attention, infecting, as the word "fever" suggests, people as fast as the stories could travel. In the West, everyday life was marked by the financial gains and losses that determined the successes and failures of individuals and communities alike.

From Boom to Bust

The boom mentality perpetuated the belief that the West was a land of plenty, a place of excess. Some of these beliefs actually turned out to be true. At least early on, gold could be found without excessive labor. Whether or not the reports of seventy-pound tomatoes and foot-long beets were exaggerated, the perception of the West as a region of abundance—in gold, soil, or produce—captured the imagination of Americans and foreigners alike. Tales of oversized fruits, vegetables, fish, and livestock became commonplace, and those individuals seeking to reap the rewards of such bounty brought a steady flow of western travelers throughout the second half of the nineteenth century. Money, too, was considered to be plentiful and it was spent as quickly as it was acquired, especially at the local gambling tables that sprung up all over the region.

The gold rush mentality also produced an economy heavily driven by inflation, a trend that resulted in basic goods such as eggs, sugar, and boots being available only at outlandish cost. Keeping up with the rapid rise in prices seemed simple as long as the gold was plentiful, and, at least initially, westerners took inflation in their stride, adjusting to price changes as necessary and expending their newfound riches with little thought about whether—or how—future income would be available.

Just as westward expansion was defined by booms, rushes, and speculation, it was also characterized by busts, or crashes, in the economy and a decline in the availability of goods. The downside of the economic boom that followed gold and silver rushes, including the high cost involved in meeting daily needs, eventually caught up with most westerners who were faced with a fluctuating economy and inconsistent sources of income from one day to the next. Dramatic variations in success only complicated matters, as some emigrants experienced great wealth while others lost everything.

The Rush for Land

Like the gold and silver rushes, land rushes, or runs, also centered around the prospect of easy acquisition. The difference lay in the object being acquired, and the pioneers who took advantage of the Homestead Act (1862), or the opening of Oklahoma, were in search of inexpensive, if not free, land, and lots of it. When President Benjamin Harrison opened unsettled land to white emigrants on April 22, 1889, somewhere between 50,000 and 60,000 emigrants moved west in a single day. In 1893, 100,000 people rushed land previously inhabited by Native Americans, homesteading and staking claims as quickly as they could.[3] Like the gold and silver rushes, land rushes created makeshift towns overnight, complete with informal systems of government and law. And while land runs did not turn as quick a profit for most emigrants as mining for gold did, there were plenty of speculators who staked claims only to sell them at a later date for significant financial gain. Indeed, the need to populate newly established towns in order to make money off the property was part of the land rush mind-set, and entire advertising campaigns were developed in order to lure people to settle on the western prairies. Whether for gold, silver, or land, the feverish pace of the westward movement created a belief system that placed value on easy access to riches and delight in the risk associated with acquiring them.

The Wild, Wild Web

Since the western rushes of the eighteen hundreds, the fever that defined the period has been used as a metaphor for other trend-driven developments in American life. For instance, the terminology of westward expansion was used to characterize the Internet boom of the 1990s. Like the gold mines and land of the West, the Internet promised investors quick and easy access to financial wealth. The "get in, get rich, get

The run for homes in Oklahoma. Courtesy of the Library of Congress.

out" mentality of many dot.com start-ups and initial public offerings (IPOs), resonated with the cultural attitudes found during westward expansion. Late-twentieth-century newspaper headlines made explicit the connection between everyday life in the 1990s and daily existence during westward expansion. "Internet Prescriptions Boom in the 'Wild West' of the Web," the *New York Times* proclaimed on the cover of its June 27, 1999, issue. "Net pioneers move on: Disenchantment sets in, and it's real," a *USA Today* headline lamented two years later. The parallels are clear even on a simplistic level. In the 1990s the challenge was to "rush" to cyberspace in order to stake a "claim" to a Web site, marketing idea, or product. In doing so, "settlers" believed that overnight transformation to millionaire status was highly likely. Symbolically, Monument Valley was replaced with Silicon Valley as the essence of the new frontier.

Western historian Patricia Nelson Limerick has described the similarities between the two eras in more detail:

Like the Internet boom, the California Gold Rush of 1849 was also a huge media event. It dominated national attention and it fixed certain expectations in the American mind-set: fortunes for the finding; riches waiting for men with the right pluck to come to seize them. . . . exaggerated investment claims, wild speculative swings, predatory investors taking advantage of the little guy's work, fights over claims (read "patent disputes"), constant tests of endurance and adaptability, and a custom of casual dress that makes it difficult to read status at a glance were the features of both booms.[4]

The similarities Limerick describes underscore the impact that westward expansion has had on the way Americans conceptualize their experiences. Newspaper articles printed in both periods further illuminate those connections. The *New York Times* "Internet Prescriptions" story opens as follows: "Dr. Leandro Pasos was 68 years old and struggling to make a living when, about a year ago, an unusual advertisement in a Seattle newspaper caught his eye. Doctors with active licenses, the ad said, could earn up to $10,000 a month doing 'fully automated on-line medical reviews'."[5] Without the words "Internet" and "automated on-line," the cover story and article could have been printed during the gold rush of 1849 rather than in the heyday of dot.com start-ups that captured the American public's attention at the end of the twentieth century.

Conversely, stories from the mid-1800s could just as well have been written during the 1990s, as the following lines, printed in the January 11, 1849, copy of the *New York Herald*, illustrate:

The spirit of emigration which is carrying off thousands to California ... increases and expands every day. All classes of our citizens seem to be under the influence of this extraordinary mania.... What will this general and overwhelming spirit of emigration lead to? Will it be the beginning of a new empire in the West, a revolution in the commercial highways of the world, a depopulation of the old States for the new republic on the shores of the Pacific?[6]

The report of people being carried off to California applied to the 1990s flurry of relocations to Silicon Valley as much as it did to the gold rush era of the eighteen hundreds. The questions the writer asks about the move west also resonate with questions surrounding the Internet frontier. What will the "new empire in the West" lead to, the writer asks, "a revolution in the commercial highways of the world?" The economic impact of the wild, Wild West parallels the financial impact of the wild, Wild Web, and the use of the word "highway" uncannily registers the contemporary preoccupation with the information highway at the heart of the technological frontier. The language of westward expansion, in other words, has helped Americans to conceptualize some of their most basic beliefs and social experiences, transposing the frontier of the nineteenth to the twentieth, and even twenty-first, century cultural phenomena.

MISSIONARIES AND MEDICINE

The idea that California during the gold rush was more promising than heaven was the type of suggestion that sent emigrants westward at a rapid pace. This association between religion and the West was further reflected in the fact that religious sects were popular influences during the westward movement. Disillusioned members of the Baptist religion, for example, repeatedly pushed the frontier west in what were commonly referred to as "traveling churches," groups who sought religious freedom in the expanding American frontier.

Circuit-riding Methodists were another strong influence. A Methodist minister traveled to an area of the frontier that had no established church. He gathered community members together, set up a Methodist place of worship, and then left the group to be led by a member of the new congregation, while he moved on to start the entire process in another area. As the West became more settled, circuit-riding was redefined as a system of itinerant ministers who served a number of congregations at once by rotating through them. The Mormon and Catholic religions also had a tremendous impact on westward expansion. The Mormon church fathers encouraged and enabled their congregations to travel to Salt Lake City where they could worship and live in accordance with Mormon doctrine. Catholic missionaries encouraged Native Americans to adopt Catholicism, recorded aspects of western history, and participated in early explorations of the region. The physical structure of the Catholic missionary makes a regular appearance in western films, drawing on the rich history of the Catholic Church in the American West. The frontier church also became a prominent symbol in western folklore, representing the tenets of Manifest Destiny and the basic Christian values believed to be crucial to every settler.[7]

In contrast to the pervasive presence of various religious sects in the West, medical care was limited at best. Common illnesses ranged from colds and rheumatism to pneumonia and malaria, popularly known as "the ager." Finding the appropriate treatments for those sicknesses was a challenge, especially if a town had no local doctor. Homeopathic and herbal remedies were one treatment method, and advice books like *Gunn's Domestic Medicine, or Poor Man's Friend* provided lay people with information about treating common illnesses. Frontier surgery was popularly referred to as "hunting knife surgery," because it was performed with a shot of whiskey and whatever sharp tools—including a hunting knife—could serve as surgical equipment.[8] Western doctors were readily recognized on their travels around the region by their distinctive horse-and-buggy form of transportation. The style was so commonly associated with frontier physicians that carriage manufacturers marketed buggies specifically for medical specialists, hailing them with slogans like "Doctors, Attention! Perfection At Last."[9]

Homemade remedies were another way pioneers tried to alleviate the diseases and discomforts inherent in western life, and such treatments were invested with curative powers, regardless of their true effectiveness. Flaxseed poultice, for instance, was applied as a cure for measles, turpentine and sugar were used to prevent worms, and skunk fat was deemed to cure sores. Native American treatments were adopted and incorporated into the remedies of emigrants, including sweat lodges, herbs, and reliance on the medicine man in place of a physician. The use of charms, medicine bundles, and other talismans were also borrowed from Native American culture as a way to ward off spirits that caused illness. Other westerners developed their own innovative remedies. As Nannie T. Alderson recounted, "All cowboys had a fixed belief that with coal oil they could cure anything."[10]

Another popular approach to treating illness was to purchase products sold in the traveling Medicine Shows and marketed in books like Dr. Richard Carter's *Valuable Vegetable Prescriptions for the Cure of All Nervous and Putrid Disorders*. Patent medicines, products that promised to improve all sorts of conditions, from nervous disorders to jaundice, were concocted by people without medical training and sold through persuasive sales pitches to pioneers in search of reliable cures. More often than not, patent medicines failed to effectively remedy the illness, but grand promises continued to persuade people to purchase them.[11] Where patent medicines offered pioneers manufactured treatments for their aches and pains, nature provided another curative source, and many emigrants moved west for the express purpose of improving their health, enjoying the reported benefits of hot springs, sulfur baths, and mineral water. Towns like Thermopolis, Wyoming, which claims to have the "World's Largest Mineral Hotspring," continue to draw tourists in search of natural cures and health treatments.[12]

FRONTIER JUSTICE

One of the most challenging aspects of western life was the maintenance of law and order in a land where population surged before formal systems of justice were fully in place. As gold seekers, land rushers, and other emigrants traveled quickly to the West, crime, theft, and other dangers to life and property traveled with them. Main-street shoot-outs, train robberies, Indian attacks, and bar brawls were among the most familiar western scenes, and they have provided popular culture with enduring images of the risks involved in western life.

While those individuals who arrived in the West ahead of established justice systems made an effort to transplant eastern practices of law enforcement to the western mining and prairie towns, many times those systems simply failed to take hold. As a result, communities created informal structures to regulate behavior and deal with criminal offenses on their own. In many mining towns miners developed their own rules about personal space and property. From general guidelines of behavior to strict definitions of punishment, early towns relied greatly on the rules by which they lived and kept the peace. Such makeshift laws varied from community to community, but as the West became more settled the systems of justice became more consistent and strict. Sheriffs and marshals were granted authority to form posses, collect taxes, and enforce laws. Courts and jails were built, trials became more just, and punishments were less arbitrary and spontaneous. The gradual progression of the region from a "wild" West to a law-abiding territory has been the subject of many western films and novels, which have the struggle for justice as the motivating force behind their plot. At the same time, the West has retained something of its original character, at least in the popular imagination, as a place where lawlessness still does, and even should, exist.

Duels, Vigilantes, and Private Eyes

Despite the growing success western communities had in making citizens and their property safe, many westerners chose to take the law into their own hands because they were dissatisfied with the effectiveness of the systems available to them. Duels were one way that people found to resolve individual differences, but groups of citizens also banded together for protection.

Many towns and communities, especially in California, had their own vigilance committees that swiftly acted to try and punish those individuals accused of breaking the law. Vigilante groups were not unique to the West. However, they played a particularly important role there as they straddled the line between protective service and capricious judgment. Punishment was often defined as public hanging, a symbolic way to warn potential criminals against transgressing the law as well as being a popular spectacle for western townspeople. The lynch law, meant to provide frontier communities with an expedient system of punishment, also increased the possibility that people could be hung for crimes they did not commit. At the same time, vigilante committees served a purpose in the relatively unregulated western communities, helping to monitor—or even incite—groups engaged in practices like cattle rustling, fence cutting, or other regional crimes.[13]

Another way that westerners dealt with the justice system was the use of private investigators. Allan Pinkerton, a Scottish native who arrived in the United States in 1819, was the country's pioneering private investigator. He made a name for himself early in his career after stopping a plot to assassinate Abraham Lincoln. In 1850 Pinkerton opened his own detective agency. The agency served individuals as well as the major railroads, which were under constant threat of being robbed. The Texas and Pacific railroads employed the Pinkerton agency to apprehend well-known outlaws like Sam Bass, Frank and Jesse James, and the Wild Bunch. The Pinkerton motto, "We never sleep," corresponded with the company's policy that no case was closed until it was solved.

Pinkerton's impact on popular culture was immediate and long-lasting. The familiar term "private eye" was probably the result of shortening the longer phrase "private investigator" to "private I," though Pinkerton himself was called "The Eye" and the Pinkerton logo featured a wide-open eye, thereby complicating the story of the term's origins. National interest in detective work was reflected in the era's voracious appetite for detective fiction, and Pinkerton capitalized on this trend by publishing best-selling dime novels, including *The Expressman and the Detective* (1875), based on his own experiences. Finally, in 1858, Pinkerton expanded his business when he opened Pinkerton's Protective Police Patrol, a uniformed-guard service that provided security to local businesses. The Police Patrol, predecessor to today's local security guards, and other Pinkerton innovations provided a measure of security to the frontier justice system while adding another element of intrigue and romance to the old West.[14]

Other examples of western trends in law and justice included the practice of fence cutting, a form of protest against the widespread use of barbed wire to delineate property lines and contain cattle. The familiar "Wanted" poster, which has appeared at least as often in western films as in real western towns, helped to round up criminals by publicizing their names and faces and offering rewards for their capture. The frontier sheriff, or marshal, with his gold, star-shaped badge is a standard character in tales of the Old West, as are the posses that allowed law enforcement officers to garner the resources needed to track outlaws through the seemingly endless open land and craggy mountains where bandits, desperadoes, and other criminals could hide.

WHITE HATS AND BLACK HATS

Popular culture has reduced the complex personalities faced by western lawmakers to the simple dichotomy of good guys and bad guys. As the saying goes, in westerns the good guys wear white hats and the bad guys wear black. The "bad guys" of the Old West, however, wore their outlaw status as something of a badge, and they have been remembered as often for being heroes as for their misdeeds. Similarly, the good guys of the West were not always the upstanding citizens they first appeared to be, and while they have borrowed from the Robin Hood philosophy of robbing the rich to pay the poor, their actions were often costly and dangerous ventures.

Wild Bill Hickok, Davy Crockett, and Wyatt Earp

The most notorious outlaws in the Wild West have become such integral parts of American popular culture that their names are almost household words. James Butler Hickok, better known as Wild Bill Hickok, was known as a lawman whose long hair and buckskin clothing seemed in keeping with his "wild" name. He built his reputation around a series of events that emphasized the fine line he walked between being a brave lawman and an outlaw gunman. Hickok was known for being mauled by a bear, for single-handedly killing three men in a single brawl, and for using his gun to break up drunken fights and to bring unruly citizens under control. His career reached its height in a gunfight in Abilene, Kansas, where he accidentally killed his friend and deputy, Mike Williams. Hickok was shot dead on August 2, 1876, and his image has been thoroughly incorporated into popular culture through portrayals in dime novels, Wild West Shows, films like *The Plainsman* (1936), and the television show *The Adventures of Wild Bill Hickok*. At his grave in Deadwood, South Dakota, a marker captures Hickok's frontier character: "Pard We Will meet Again in the happy hunting ground to part no more."[15]

Wild Bill Hickok's connection with other western figures is no more evident than in his rumored marriage to Calamity Jane. Born Martha Jane Canary, Calamity Jane made her name as a woman who wore men's clothing, worked as a scout for George Armstrong Custer, rode horses, and shot guns like the best of the Wild West's men. Mystery surrounding her personal life, including whom she married and whether she bore a child by Hickok, only added to her legend, as did her reputation for excessive drinking. During her life she capitalized on interest in the West by selling copies of her questionable autobiography, and appearing in the Buffalo Bill Wild West Shows and at the 1901 Buffalo Pan-American Exposition. Like other western women, such as Cattle Kate, Belle Starr, Annie Oakley, and Carrie Nation, Calamity Jane represented the lifestyle women could adopt in the West, a lifestyle that challenged gender roles, mixed fact and fiction, and created tough women who defined themselves in new ways.[16]

Whereas Hickok and Calamity Jane lived during the westward expansion period, Davy Crockett was a frontier hero before the gold rushes brought large numbers of settlers west. Known as a politician and a hunter, Crockett was famous in his own lifetime for representing "the common man," defined as a simple, uneducated person who symbolized a revolt against the cultivated East. His life was dramatized in *The Lion of the West* (1831) and popular biographies and autobiographies like *Sketches and Eccentricities of Colonel David Crockett of West Tennessee* (1833). Crockett's role in the Battle of the Alamo sealed his fate as a western hero. His name has been associated with tall tales and folklore of the Old West ever since, appearing, for instance, in *Davy Crockett's* Almanac from 1836 through the second half of the nineteenth century. In the twentieth century Crockett's name was revitalized courtesy of Walt Disney, and a Davy Crockett craze of the 1950s continued to perpetuate his role in shaping the West.[17]

Wyatt Earp and his brothers have been traditionally seen as law-abiding men who helped to keep peace on the frontier. Other tales, however, claimed that they were anything but honest citizens, stealing and killing as much and as often as the outlaws they apprehended. A friend of other western characters like Doc Holliday and Bat Masterson, Earp fashioned a career as a law enforcer, holding positions as constable, deputy, and assistant marshal in a number of western towns. In the early 1880s, Earp and his brothers settled in Tombstone, Arizona, where they held jobs and allegedly became solid citizens. In 1881, however, Earp's name became associated with the shoot-out at the O.K. Corral, an unfortunate event that involved Earp and his allies—Doc Holliday and the Earp brothers—against another local clan, the Clanton brothers. The event left some men dead and others injured. Despite the fact that his reputation in the town became shrouded in suspicion after the shoot-out, those few minutes at the O.K. Corral made Wyatt Earp a central figure in the mythology of the West. He has been the subject of countless books and movies, including *My Darling Clementine* (1946) and *Gunfight at the O.K. Corral*, released the same year.[18]

Other frontier good guys, for instance the Texas Rangers, Bat Masterson, and Judge Roy Bean, were known for their efforts to maintain law and order in a world that moved and changed as fast as they could keep up. While their solutions may not have always abided by the letter of the law, such men stand for the ideology of westward expansion more generally, namely the triumph of order over chaos and civilization over the wilderness.

Billy the Kid, Jesse James, and the Wild Bunch

One of the most legendary of frontier outlaws was Billy the Kid, a young man who made his name as a ruthless killer who was quick with a gun. Also known as simply "the Kid," Billy killed his first man in 1877, from which point his life consisted of a series of run-ins with the law, numerous arrests, and subsequent escapes from jail. He took part in a local skirmish known as the Lincoln County War that involved several murders. He was eventually convicted for one of them, the murder of Sheriff William Brady. Before the Kid could be hanged for the crime, however, he escaped from custody. Pat Garrett, the new sheriff, pursued, shot, and killed Billy the Kid on July 14, 1881. Within weeks, a biography of the Kid was published and eagerly read by a public who found his status as a dangerous frontier outlaw as intriguing as it was compelling. Dime novels featured the Kid as their main character, and even Garrett himself cashed in on the excitement by publishing a tell-all book entitled *The Authentic Life of Billy the Kid*. It was not until the early 1900s that more sympathetic representations of Billy the Kid were circulated in the popular media, most claiming that he fell into a life of crime by default and that he was more than the ruthless outlaw popular versions of his life had created. He has been portrayed in westerns from *Billy the Kid* (1930 and 1941) to *Young Guns II* (1990), and he remains a central character in the story of the Old West.[19]

Like Billy the Kid, Frank and Jesse James have been mythologized for their criminal behavior, though for the James brothers the crime of choice was robbery. In 1866, the brothers began a string of bank robberies and found themselves murdering innocent bystanders who got in the way of their success. Their exploits were daring as well as dangerous, taking place in the middle of the day and in busy locations. During their years of robbing trains, the James brothers were pursued by detectives from the Pinkerton Detective Agency who were hired to hunt and kill them. Instead, detectives accidentally fired on a house they thought was occupied by Frank and Jesse but which was actually inhabited by their mother and half-brother. The injuries sustained by the family from the incident won the James brothers sympathy in many corners of the West and the motive behind their robberies was recast, at least by some, as an effort to take from the rich and give to the poor. The Robin Hood interpretation of their lives was reflected in the sensationalism surrounding Jesse James's death. Newspaper headlines cried "Goodbye Jesse," and pictures of James lying in his coffin were sold as souvenirs.[20]

The Wild Bunch, popularized by Butch Cassidy and his partner, the Sundance Kid, was a relatively large gang known for the way its members spent money at local bars and brothels. Cassidy and Sundance became leaders of the Wild Bunch, and the gang gained recognition first for robbing banks and, when this proved an insufficient form of income, for robbing trains. The Wild Bunch boarded the trains as they slowed to make a stop and then used explosives to blast open the safes. The Pinkerton Detective Agency was hired to pursue Cassidy and Sundance, but they escaped, along with a female companion, Etta Place, to New York City. The three later went to South America, but their final days remain a mystery.

The story of Butch Cassidy and the Sundance Kid differs from other frontier characters. Unlike, for instance, Billy the Kid, the Wild Bunch gained little notoriety until the well-received 1969 film, *Butch Cassidy and the Sundance Kid*, hit the silver screen starring Paul Newman, Robert Redford, and Katharine Ross. The playful outwitting, outrunning, and all-around avoidance of the law has since become associated with these two figures, distinguishing them from other western robbers and adding a new element to the cast of characters who illustrate the West's struggle to maintain law and order. Other western legends, including Bonnie and Clyde, the Dalton Gang, John Wesley Hardin, and Wild Bill Longley,

Robbery of the express car (1877). Courtesy of the Library of Congress.

have played key roles in giving the frontier the danger and excitement that have fueled popular understanding of westward expansion.

THE INDIAN WARS

The opening of westward trails, such as the Sante Fe and Oregon routes, combined with the large number of people who hurried west with the gold rush and the Homestead Act, led to increased tensions between Indians and the American government. Conflicts between Indians and Whites resulted in bloodshed at the Sand Creek Massacre in 1864, and at the Fetterman Massacre in 1866. Infamous clashes—the Battle of Little Big Horn, and the Wounded Knee Massacre—have been memorialized in popular culture which has struggled with the realities of Native American displacement and the nationalism inherent in the ideals of Manifest Destiny. Films like *The Battle at Elderbush Gulch* (1913), *Broken Arrow* (1950), *Dances with Wolves* (1990), *Fort Apache* (1948), *Geronimo: An American Legend* (1993), and *Little Big Man* (1970) offer viewers different, even opposing, perspectives on the Indian Wars, responding, in part, to the social and political climates of the times in which they were produced. Similarly, books like *Black Elk Speaks* (1932), *Bury My*

Heart at Wounded Knee (1971), *The Plainsmen* series, first published in 1990, and the fiction of Charles King have also recorded the history and drama of the Indian Wars for an avid reading public. Songs like "Gary Owen," the paintings and drawings of Charles M. Russell and Frederic Remington, the television program *F-Troop*, and the in-progress Crazy Horse Monument, further reflect the unresolved issues at the heart of the Indian Wars.[21]

Participants in the Indian Wars have also been mythologized in popular culture. The Native American known as Crazy Horse refused to remain on a reservation and actively resisted Indian displacement. In 1876 he fought with Sitting Bull at the Battle of Little Big Horn against Lieutenant Colonel George Armstrong Custer, a military leader known for his victories in the Civil War and for his initiation of the Black Hills gold rush. Despite the defeat of Custer, Crazy Horse surrendered to the government in 1877. Rumors about his loyalty to the Native Americans spread, however, when it looked as though he was helping the military persuade the Lakota Indians to act as scouts against another Indian tribe, the Nez Percé. Crazy Horse's alliances were further questioned when it appeared that he was planning to take arms again. When he was arrested on September 5, he was killed by a soldier.[22] Depending on the political climate, Crazy Horse has been classified as a hero and a villain, and his role in the Indian Wars has been evoked in western memorabilia, including musician Neil Young's album by the same name.

Other icons of the Indian Wars include Sitting Bull and Geronimo. Like Crazy Horse, Sitting Bull also resisted the displacement of Native Americans from their lands. A Sioux Indian by birth, he was chosen by his tribe to be its leader against the American military, an honor especially noteworthy because the Sioux belief system did not include the need for leaders, but rather respected the individualism of all tribal members. At the Battle of Little Big Horn, Sitting Bull oversaw the defeat of the White army after experiencing a vision of dead soldiers in an Indian camp. He later fled to Canada in fear of retaliation, but he returned to the United States where he surrendered in 1881. Sitting Bull participated in the popularization of the frontier—and his own history—through his role in Buffalo Bill's Wild West Shows. He died in 1890 after returning to the Sioux people and continuing to encourage the maintenance of their Native culture.[23]

Finally, Geronimo was the last Native American to formally surrender to the United States, and his name has been incorporated into United States culture through the expression "Geronimooooo!" Although he has been known throughout history as Geronimo, his Indian name, Goyakla, bears little resemblance to that title. A respected and effective warrior, Geronimo was intermittently on the warpath and confined to reservations, from which he would inevitably escape. Like Sitting Bull, he par-

The Apache War—Indian Scouts on
Geronimo's Trail (1886). Courtesy of the
Library of Congress.

ticipated in his own development as an icon of popular culture when,
in Oklahoma during the 1890s, he "earned money by selling pictures of
himself and small bows and arrows with his name on them."[24] He became more familiar to Americans when his image was reproduced on
the cover of *Harper's Weekly* in a sketch by Frederic Remington. Geronimo's participation in the Trans-Mississippi and International Exposition
in Omaha (1898), the Pan-American Exposition in Buffalo (1901), and the
St. Louis World's Fair (1904) reflect his status as a well-known figure
who drew crowds and public attention, something Geronimo seemed to
encourage even as he fought the cultural loss such attention signified.[25]

Like the Indian Wars, the Spanish-American War also gave rise to
popular books, films, songs, and characters. Its connection to westward
expansion centers around the war's most popular heroes, the Rough Riders, and their leader, Theodore Roosevelt. Together, Roosevelt, also
known as Teddy or TR, and the Rough Riders captured the hearts of

Americans when they won the battle against Spain in the San Juan hills outside of Santiago. Other familiar westerners were also associated with the war, including illustrator and painter Frederic Remington and writer Stephen Crane.[26]

AMERICAN PRESIDENTS, POLITICAL CAMPAIGNS, AND THE WEST

As the West became a well-known, and beloved, aspect of the American imagination, presidential campaigns took advantage of any associations they could make between their candidates and the frontier. From Abraham Lincoln's log cabin origins to Ronald Reagan's role as western actor-turned-president, the West has provided fertile ground for fashioning political leaders into American icons.

Abraham Lincoln, Log Cabins, and Gold Bugs

The log cabin, long a symbol of the heart of American life, was deployed in a number of presidential campaigns during the nineteenth century. General William Henry Harrison's 1840 campaign, also known as the Log Cabin Campaign, emphasized the candidate's rural origins through the symbol of the log cabin and the slogan "The Ohio Farmer." The log cabin appeared on souvenirs in the form of household utensils, banners, badges, and posters. Miniature log cabins were attached to the ends of poles and carried in parades. Larger cabins were rolled on wheels. Songs were written to incorporate the symbol, as for instance in the "Log Cabin or Tippecanoe Waltz," and an inexpensive china pattern, known as "Columbian Star," featured a log cabin and plowman as its motif. A newspaper known as *The Log Cabin*, edited by Horace Greeley, reported on the Whig campaign trail and sported the familiar log cabin image in its masthead.[27]

Abraham Lincoln's 1860 presidential campaign also benefited from the candidate's humble origins in an Illinois log cabin, reviving the cabin as a symbol of political strength. In addition, the Republican Party developed Lincoln's identification with the image of the split rail that dramatized "at once Lincoln's heroic rise from humble origins, the mystique of the frontier, and the essential dignity of free labor."[28] Lincoln's identity was thereby closely associated with his roots in the West, which was considered to be

shrewd politics not only because of the critical importance of the western vote, but also because of the enduring fascination with the frontier and new mania over the Wild West among easterners. One of the most popular of all 1860 Republican campaign songs was "Honest Abe of the West." A token bore the plea

"The Great Rail Splitter of the West Must & Shall Be Our Next President." Others promoted Lincoln as "Honest Abe of the West," "The Rail Splitter of the West" . . .[29]

Through western symbolism, Lincoln captured the hearts of the American voters who elected him president and used him as a symbol of the fact that any American, no matter how humble in origin, could become the country's leader.

Finally, the 1896 race between populist William Jennings Bryan and Republican William McKinley centered around an issue of great interest to westerners, namely whether money should be minted in gold or silver. Bryan and the Free Silver party argued that silver should be coined at a ratio of sixteen ounces of silver for a single ounce of gold, thereby increasing the national money supply. In contrast, gold bugs, who opposed the minting of more silver coins, wanted to maintain the gold standard. The issue of gold versus silver led to slogans such as "Speech is Silver. Free Speech, Free Silver," "In Gold We Trust," and "16-to-1." Gold-colored lapel buttons shaped as bugs bore pictures of the candidates on their wings, and songs were written with titles like "Silver Sing" and "Honest Money." McKinley won the election, setting the history of the presidency down another course directly tied to westward expansion, that of Teddy Roosevelt and the Rough Riders.

Theodore Roosevelt, the Rough Riders, and Teddy Bears

Theodore Roosevelt forged an association between the West and the presidency that became a powerful campaign strategy pursued by candidates throughout the 1900s and into the twenty-first century. Roosevelt was involved in eastern politics throughout his early life, serving on the New York State Assembly from 1881–1884 when he cast an eye toward the presidency. The death of his wife and mother in 1884, however, caused Roosevelt to renounce his political ambitions—at least temporarily—and move west to Dakota Territory. There he was struck by the impact of the western land on its inhabitants, and he developed a belief that the ruggedness of the frontier was a positive influence on the character of those who lived there. The survival skills and physical exertion that the West demanded, Roosevelt believed, created a hardiness, and in particular a sense of manhood, that was lost in the comforts of nineteenth-century life. Roosevelt popularized his philosophy of the West in some of his many books, including *Hunting Trips of a Ranchman* (1885), *Ranch Life and the Hunting Trail* (1888), and *The Winning of the West* (1889–1896).

Teddy Roosevelt's arrival in the West was marked by his lack of experience "roughing it," and he was considered the classic dude or tenderfoot, a person who was used to the luxuries of eastern life. Roosevelt countered this image and proved himself worthy of the name "westerner" when he participated in a bar brawl, tracked and caught a group of thieves, and shot a mountain goat at far range.[30] Roosevelt's experience in the West set the tone for his return to politics, which he once again pursued when he returned to New York in 1886. He held several political offices in the 1880s and 1890s, including the role of assistant secretary to the navy during William McKinley's presidency. His resignation from that post during the Spanish-American War sealed his popularity and name recognition with American voters, for in doing so he joined the Rough Riders. A group of volunteer cavalrymen, the Rough Riders were composed of an assortment of frontiersmen, including cowboys and prospectors as well as educated easterners. The group congregated in San Antonio, Texas, for training and became so closely associated with Roosevelt that they were called, at different times, "Teddy's Terriers" and "Teddy's Terrors." The Rough Riders was the name that stuck, however, and it was in Cuba that they had their well-known victory. On July 1, 1898, the group, led by Roosevelt, charged and took Kettle Hill in the San Juan ridge of mountains around Santiago. The defeat helped put an end to the Spanish-American War on August 12, 1898, and from that point the story of Roosevelt and his Rough Riders became an integral part of the American imagination.[31]

The Rough Riders have been memorialized in many popular forms, including Roosevelt's own best-selling book *The Rough Riders* (1899), the successful 1927 film *The Rough Riders*, and the Turner Pictures 1997 movie *Rough Riders*.[32] The group adopted the tune "There'll Be a Hot Time in the Old Town Tonight" to mark their camaraderie, and at least one reporter claimed that they sang the song after their Cuban victory. The song was briefly used as a Roosevelt campaign song in 1904, but it had become so familiar that it was quickly dropped.[33] During his runs for election, pictures of Roosevelt on horseback in his Rough Riders uniform appeared "on several buttons, a multicolor tin serving tray, cloth broadsides, metal lapel pins, fobs, and a cast-iron figural bank."[34] In 1900, Roosevelt became McKinley's vice president and was unexpectedly catapulted to the presidency in 1901 when McKinley was assassinated. From the start, Roosevelt's role as president was closely associated with the West. "That damned cowboy is President of the United States!" one critic cried, and indeed Roosevelt brought a strong personality and energy to the White House. "Speak softly and carry a big stick," he would say, and the stick became one of the many symbols associated with TR, as he was known, throughout his political career.[35]

Roosevelt was also memorialized in popular culture through the familiar teddy bear which, some historians claim, was named after "Teddy" Roosevelt. During a hunting expedition Roosevelt was alleg-

Theodore Roosevelt as a cowboy rounding up steers labeled
as states (1904). Courtesy of the Library of Congress.

edly given the chance to shoot a cub bear that was tied to a tree. He
refused to kill the defenseless animal, preferring the challenge of a legitimate hunt to the ease of such a killing. The story of his decision was
captured in a cartoon that featured him walking away from the scene.
There were two consequences to this event. First, the cartoonist, Clifford
K. Berryman, created cartoons that depicted Roosevelt and the bear, cementing the association between the two in the popular media. Second,
an innovative toy company created the first teddy bear, naming the
stuffed animal after Theodore "Teddy" Roosevelt.[36] Other political car-
toonists have also used the West as a way to characterize—both posi-
tively and negatively—politicians and their decisions, drawing on the
rich symbolism the West provides to illustrate political beliefs and ideas.

Just about every aspect of Roosevelt's personality, experiences, and
looks were used in his campaigns for reelection in 1904, 1908, and 1912.
The toy bear was an important part of the paraphernalia used for reelection, in part because it countered Roosevelt's rough and tough mas-

culine image.[37] Other objects used in Roosevelt's campaigns included pipes that replaced the tobacco bowl with a carved image of Teddy's head. A whistle that was shaped like a grinning mouth and rows of teeth, marketed as "Teddy's Teeth," reflected his familiar grin and good humor. In addition to his teeth, Roosevelt's round spectacles and moustache became symbols of his personality, as did the Rough Rider's hat, usually accompanied by the "My Hat Is in the Ring" slogan and the infamous "big stick." Songs that marked Roosevelt's campaigns included "We Want Teddy For Four Years More," (1904), "You're All Right, Teddy" (1904), and "Teddy Come Back" (1910).[38]

J.F.K. and the New Frontier

On July 15, 1960, Senator John F. Kennedy accepted his party's nomination to run as the presidential candidate of the Democratic party. In doing so, Kennedy referred to the frontier in one of the most powerful speeches of all campaigns that have drawn on the West for imagery and meaning. The speech set the stage for how the West would be evoked during the second half of the twentieth century. Kennedy stated:

[W]e stand today on the edge of a New Frontier—the frontier of the 1960's—a frontier of unknown opportunities and perils—a frontier of unfulfilled hopes and threats. . . . I tell you the New Frontier is here, whether we seek it or not. Beyond that frontier are the uncharted areas of science and space, unsolved problems of peace and war, unconquered pockets of ignorance and prejudice, unanswered questions of poverty and surplus.[39]

Combining the frontier images of prosperity and violence, risk and reward, Kennedy used the West in his attempt to change the climate of American society. His reference to "uncharted areas of science and space" corresponded with what has become a familiar use of the word "frontier" to describe new advances in technology and medicine, fields in which the ideology of westward expansion continues to be frequently evoked.[40]

Texans and Cowboys: Lyndon B. Johnson, Ronald Reagan, and George W. Bush

Other candidates have used their associations with the West to augment their runs for the presidency. Harking back to Roosevelt's suggestion that men who live and thrive in the West are more masculine, and that the West makes individuals heartier and more self-reliant, politicians have drawn on those mythologies for their campaign strategies. Lyndon B. Johnson, for instance, emphasized his background as both a Texan and a westerner through campaign souvenirs that sported cowboy boots, Stetson hats, and other cowboy icons. Buttons read "My Brand's LBJ" and "Keep a Firm Hand on the Reins LBJ." Shot glasses featuring cowboy boots announced "You Bet Your Boots We're for Johnson!"[41]

Whereas Johnson used the symbols of the West to reinforce his personal image as a potential president, Ronald Reagan relied on his image as a cowboy—created by his role as an actor in many Hollywood westerns—to reach the same ends. Reagan's roles in westerns like *Sante Fe Trail* (1940), *Law and Order* (1953), and *Cattle Queen of Montana* (1954) had already established his connection with the virility inherent in being a westerner. His campaign capitalized on this association, featuring buttons and badges with the slogan "America, Reagan Country" and using patriotic symbols such as the Statue of Liberty and the Empire State Building as the backdrop to Reagan's Stetson-covered head.[42] Reagan the cowboy, in other words, was running for president, and Democrats countered the campaign with slogans calling Reagan "The Fascist Gun in the West."[43]

While Reagan explicitly used the West as the backdrop for his campaign, other presidential candidates have also borrowed from the frontier, though in more subtle ways. During the 2000 campaign, Al Gore was advised to remake his image by wearing more western-style clothing, including cowboy boots and jeans. Similarly, when Texan George W. Bush won that same election, the popularity of cowboy boots soared, especially when they were worn at the new president's inauguration which included the "Black Tie and Boots Inaugural Ball" put on by Texan supporters.[44]

Despite variations in the popular culture of the westward expansion era, trends and fads crossed the country quickly, making their way to prairie towns and mining villages alike. More notably, the spirit of the time captured the nation's imagination, creating a feverish desire to move west and a culture defined by the elements of a boom-and-bust economy. As the population increased, so did the country's recognition of, and interest in, westerners who had made a name for themselves by being on the right or the wrong side of the law. Those names—Billy the Kid, Wyatt Earp, Calamity Jane—became quickly integrated with the rapidly growing myths and folktales about the West, and the individuals themselves often added to the legend by writing and selling their stories, appearing in Wild West Shows, and acting in accordance with their reputations. Finally, national events like wars and political campaigns borrowed symbols from the West, further ensuring that the frontier would remain ingrained in the fabric of American popular culture.

2

World of Youth

To be a child during the period of westward expansion was to be defined by competing characteristics. On the one hand, children who "grew up with the country"[1] were introduced to the harsh realities of disease, death, natural disaster, and hard labor at an early age and were expected to take on tasks that they were sometimes physically ill-prepared to do. At the same time, memoirs and diaries of frontier childhoods are awash with descriptions of exploration, wonder, and play, all standard aspects of American youth. The mixed expectations western society placed on its children resulted in popular beliefs and behaviors that shaped the families and communities of the region. Western children became symbols of American individualism and adventure that have been repeatedly idealized in popular culture since the end of the nineteenth century. Throughout the twentieth century and into the twenty-first, American society has continued to popularize aspects of frontier childhood, capitalizing on the West's ability to represent what, by some standards, are viewed as vanishing aspects of American life, namely family values, the work ethic, moral truths, and tradition. Similarly, the West has been marketed to post-frontier children through the proliferation of western toys, television programs, and movies that create a nostalgia for the Old West that is more culturally convenient than historically accurate.[2]

YOUTH CULTURE IN THE AMERICAN WEST

In his fictionalized account of his western childhood, *Boy Life on the Prairie* (1926), Hamlin Garland comments several times that he and his young friends "looked exactly like diminutive men."[3] The phrase, made in reference to the clothing the youths wore, the work they did, and the attitudes they adopted, reflected a larger societal attitude toward frontier children. Rather than defining children as individuals who needed to develop the skills and acquire the knowledge necessary to become adults, westerners viewed the young as people capable of taking on the same type of work and responsibilities completed by grown men and women.

The demands placed on children registered larger cultural agendas about westward expansion, including the desire to find self-sufficiency, independence, and financial success in the new West. Pioneer children learned at an early age how to take care of animals, plow and harvest fields, cope with grasshopper plagues, and manage fires. For if families were to be successful on the frontier, they depended on contributions of every member of the family unit, regardless of age, size, or interest in doing so. In this way western children were very much like Garland described them to be—"little men" balancing precariously between their natural development and the social roles they were asked to fill.

Childbirth and the Westward Journey

The popular attitudes toward youths can be seen in the ways that childbirth, parenting, and the westward journey were recorded by early pioneers in journals and memoirs. Childbirth was a remarkably unsentimental experience during the trip west. Far away from doctors, midwives, and even other women, mothers-to-be endured labor and childbirth as they did the other difficult aspects of the trip. Diarists wrote only briefly about the experience, and while they did so with words of joy and happiness, just as frequently they commented about how the birth of a child had the unfortunate consequence of delaying the journey a day or two while the mother recovered enough strength to continue.[4] The no-nonsense records of childbirth on the trail underscored the fact that daily survival was foremost in the minds of pioneers, and that newborns, while loved and cared for, were also just another part of the experience. Other attitudes toward childbirth revealed the importance that books and self-education played in ensuring a healthy birth.

While the challenges inherent in childbirth on the trail or in early western towns are easy to imagine, once a child was delivered the threats to survival were far from over. One diarist described how children were in danger virtually all of the time.[5] Children tumbled off wagons and were run over by the heavy wheels, were trampled by animals, or drowned in river crossings. They got lost on the prairies while collecting food and were burned by the fires around which travelers cooked and warmed themselves. These events, while upsetting to parents, were so common that their occurrences were also viewed as inevitable parts of the trip.

Death was also viewed with contradictory emotions. On the one hand, the death of a child was seen as particularly tragic, especially since the West's future depended on the healthy development of new generations of westerners. The trend of photographing dead children reflected this sentiment. By providing a picture of the deceased child, peacefully posed in a comforting representation of death, a photographer helped family and friends remember the child through possession of a picture that could be prominently displayed in the home. At the same time, death was so common an occurrence that the loss of a child seemed to be just another hardship suffered in settling the frontier. Pioneers' matter-of-fact records of deaths and burials stood in contrast to the elaborate mechanisms for remembering children through photographs of their deceased bodies. Perhaps the two extremes offset each other. Where the need to keep moving west resulted in quick burials in unfamiliar land with little time for grief, the simultaneous desire to process such losses led to the photographic trend that made the loss visible and grief accessible.[6]

Idealized Children

While popular attitudes toward children seem to have mixed the practical facts of daily existence with the emotions surrounding birth and death, a unique frontier phenomenon appeared in the idealization of youth. Different from the sentimental culture that defined children in the nineteenth century, the idealization of youngsters originated in the fact that there were so few children present in the West, especially in the mining towns and other communities that had been settled primarily by men. Determined to head West, to get rich quickly, and to return home as soon as possible, men in mining towns and other locations found themselves in male company more often, and for longer periods of time, than they had ever anticipated. As the search for gold wore on, and as their time in the West extended beyond their original intentions, men became captivated by the rare sight of a child. By some counts there were eight, and in some locations even two hundred, men for every youth.[7] As a result, when children would appear in such a town attention would be lavished upon them. Songs were sung in their honor, gifts were given to them, and they were ogled in amazement. One reason for this idealization might be that, in contrast to the hardships of western life, children reminded emigrants of the lives they had left behind, of the paths they had abandoned in favor of hunting fortunes in the West. At the same time, children stood for the future, and therefore were symbols of westward expansion itself, which aimed at settling the land so that younger generations would be able to benefit.

Popular beliefs about the family also impacted children in terms of familial structure. Far from the social conventions of the East, the nuclear family took on a variety of less traditional forms. Single mothers were not uncommon, and the decision to raise children on their own reflected western women's sense of independence and social freedom. Such non-traditional families reflected a trend in western ideals that, out of necessity or choice, required a broader definition of family life than existed in the established communities of the East.

Work, Money, and Values

While some families were less traditional than others, all depended on the active participation of children in the daily life of settlement. Whether in towns or on farms, in the mountains or on the prairies, children were expected to help the family in whatever ways they could. Frequently this meant spending hours at repetitive tasks, or completing jobs that were physically demanding to even the strongest youths. Yet their contributions were invaluable because the amount of work to be completed was so immense. Hamlin Garland described the ambivalence children felt toward the work they were required to do as part of childhood. Being responsible for running the plow team through the field was a sign of adulthood, but the actual labor was intense. Tasks that were completely challenging for young children were part of a culture that depended on such efforts, regardless of the child's interest in, or even ability to, complete the task. The expectation that children help their parents, whose time needed to be spent on other chores, was sufficient to send boys and girls to the fields, intent on doing their best to help the family.

In addition to participating in the physical labor required to establish a life in the West, frontier youths also helped to provide their families with income. Local farm girls were frequently hired out as seamstresses or sent to work "in-town" at stores, while boys could earn money working on neighboring farms when they were not needed at home. A young person's wages were typically seen as belonging, at least in part, to the family as a whole. Some children obtained their own spending money by taking on odd jobs and other tasks for neighbors and local businesses.

As a side effect of the loose boundaries of western life, some frontier children became more familiar with drunken behavior, gambling, foul language, and sex than parents might have hoped. At the same time, a great emphasis was placed on children to adopt values of honesty, generosity, love, and respect. As Elise Dubach Isley recalled in her memoir *Sunbonnet Days*, "we were schooled in honesty. Today there are authors who scoff at the stories of Honest Abe Lincoln, but such persons were brought up in the cities in these later days when parents are too busy to teach honesty. I readily believed the story of Lincoln's long walk to return six cents to a poor widow whom he had unwittingly shortchanged. My father would have done the same thing."[8] The dual realities of fron-

tier childhood demanded that children be properly raised and well be-
haved, while it also introduced them to the more complex parts of
human existence.

The mixed experiences children had in the West—childhoods that
combined the joys of outdoor play with the drudgeries of hard manual
labor—resulted in what Liahna Babener has called "bitter nostalgia" for
the past. Close readings of childhood journals and diaries, as well as of
adult reflections about early frontier years, reveal a "deeply felt tension
between fondness for and resentment of their rustic life."[9] The ambivalence expressed by children who were raised in the West stands in contrast to the records of those people who left the eastern states, or other
countries, in order to settle on the frontier. Whereas these first-generation
settlers compared their new lives to the established towns and cities they
had left behind, their children had only the prairies and mountains to
define their youth. As Elliott West writes, frontier children "felt no tug
from another place. . . . [they] did not see themselves as a 'scattered people' since one must be scattered *from* someplace, and the West was the
only place they had ever known first-hand. They were not 'far from
home'; they *were* home."[10]

The One-Room Schoolhouse, Recess, and the Frontier Schoolteacher

Out of all the images depicting childhood on the frontier, there is none
more familiar than that of the children under instruction of a female
schoolteacher in a one-room schoolhouse. In this tableau, the teacher,
dressed in her best clothing to reflect the high social and educational expectations placed on her by the community in which she teaches, works
diligently with students ranging in age from early childhood to adolescence. The interior of the schoolhouse is simply decorated, a chalkboard
hangs on the front wall, and some pictures may be present on the other
three walls. The children write on slates and carry lunch pails, and at recess time they run outdoors to play games. The teacher calls them back to
class by ringing a bell and they pile into their seats, listen respectfully to
their stern but fair teacher, and learn the basics of reading, writing, and
arithmetic in the one-room schoolhouse on the isolated prairie.[11]

This image of frontier education has been popularized in books like
John Steinbeck's *East of Eden* (1952), television shows like *Dr. Quinn, Medicine Woman,* and countless other books, magazines, and films about the
American West. The reality of school in the West varied from location to
location, but the similarities were indeed significant. They began with the
teacher, usually female, who arrived in the West to educate the children
of pioneers. The trend in women becoming teachers began around 1840,
when Horace Mann claimed that the tendency to be kinder and

Miss Blanche Lamont at her school in Hecla, Montana (1893). Courtesy of the Library of Congress.

gentler than men made women more like children and, therefore, better cut out for teaching.[12] Catherine Beecher's *The Duty of American Women to Their Country*, which was widely read after its publication in 1845, further encouraged women to fill the country's need for educators, especially on the frontier where there was a shortage of teachers to meet the region's fast-paced growth. "It is WOMAN," Beecher wrote, "who is to come in at this emergency and meet the demand. Woman, whom experience and testing have shown to be the best, as well as the cheapest, guardian of childhood."[13]

Beecher's emphasis on women's aptitude for the field of education fueled a surge in the number of women who applied to be frontier teachers. Prior to the 1880s, such women were primarily from the East and willing to move to remote areas of the West where they taught in schools that varied from tiny dugouts barely able to house a handful of students, to large wooden structures with glass windows. Women did so for a variety of reasons, including a fascination with the frontier, a desire for independence, and a genuine love of teaching. As Beecher's comments underscore, female schoolteachers were a cheaper form of labor than men, and salaries reflected this fact. By some accounts, school boards hired and fired schoolteachers on a regular basis, not because they were poor teachers, but in order to keep salaries low by hiring the newest teachers who were also the lowest paid. When daughters of pioneers passed the required eighth-grade comprehensive exams, they too could become teachers. However, with the passing of teacher certification laws, they often had to take additional exams before entering the classroom. Once there, teachers were responsible not only for the education of students, but for the cleanliness of the school itself, the discipline of the classroom, and the rapid response to crises, including snake bites, injuries, and storms.

Given the range of responsibilities of frontier teachers, combined with their prominence in the community and their female gender, it is not surprising that the schoolmarm was—and continues to be—among the most idealized of western figures. An unmarried woman who arrived in an unpopulated town to hold a visible position that directly impacted the town's children inevitably became the object of much fascination, not only to those she taught, but to the men and women of the community. For single men, widowers, and other unattached males, the schoolteacher was viewed as an available female, a rarity in the early days of settlement. As Steinbeck writes in *East of Eden*, the "teacher was not only an intellectual paragon and a social leader, but also the matrimonial catch of the countryside. A family could indeed walk proudly if a son married the schoolteacher."[14] The fact that the teacher's contract might depend on her remaining unmarried only increased the romance around her. If she fell in love with, and chose to marry, a local farmer or cowboy, she would have to abandon her role as teacher, thereby giving up her financial independence and her profession. At the same time, the amount of attention a female teacher could receive in a town where women were scarce meant that romantic attachments were extremely common. Some couples kept their relationships a secret from the community in order for the woman to remain in her job.

The romance that built up around the schoolteacher has been reflected in popular novels about the West. Owen Wister's best-selling novel *The Virginian* (1902), for instance, introduces Miss Molly Wood, the schoolmarm, in a chapter titled "Enter the Woman." The title underscores the impact that a female schoolteacher could have on a small frontier town. In fact, without even meeting Miss Wood, the novel's main character, the Virginian, begins to fall in love with her. After reading her letter of application to teach in the town of Medicine Bow, the Virginian holds on to it "as if it were some token."[15] The narrator then asks, "Has any botanist set down what the seed of love is? Has it anywhere been set down in how many ways this seed may be sown? In what various vessels of gossamer it can float across wide spaces? Or upon what different soils it can fall, and live unknown, and bide its time for blooming?"[16] The schoolteacher charmed more men than the Virginian, however, and was the subject of playful conversations among the townsmen who were interested in courting her.

To the children who attended the one-room schoolhouse, the teacher represented a combination of cultured role model, firm disciplinarian, and comforting caregiver. Her position in the community, as well as her position in the classroom, made the teacher something of an idol and teachers reported that they tried to support this image by dressing as well as they could and upholding the values of the nation and the town. Part and parcel of this role was the fact that the teacher had to keep a wide range of children occupied and learning throughout the school day, a task that was especially challenging given the limited resources available to her and the sporadic attendance of her students. For instance, children in the first grade had to have work while the teacher instructed those in the fifth grade. Older boys had to be kept on task while younger children were the focus of attention, and the impulses of youths who spent much of the year working outdoors had to be contained. While the familiar image of the schoolhouse featured children writing diligently on their personal slates with pieces of chalk, many children did not have access to writing tools. As a result, teachers relied on oral forms of instruction and memory, including rhymes and sayings, as much as they depended on students writing information down and studying written material.

Schoolbooks were another rare commodity in the Old West, and just about every available text, from *McGuffey's Primer* to the Bible, almanacs, hymns, and songs were employed in the service of frontier education. A typical school library was composed, as one schoolteacher recalled, of

contribution[s] from the homes, kept on the shelf of the teacher's box desk. . . . There were a whole year's number of Youth's Companion, whose stories, informational articles, pictures and puzzles furnished recreation for all ages. Volumes of the Chatterbox, Harper's Young People and a few books of the right sort, including some of Louisa May Alcott's, made a sufficient variety of literature for our needs. The books were read aloud and the different characters were assumed by the pupils, who often "played them out" as they called it, at recess time.[17]

While learning occurred in the schoolhouse, the school yard was a site for physical activity, including games that began before the morning school bell and continued during recess. Hamlin Garland described how the "boys always went early [to school], in order to have an hour at 'dog and deer,' or 'dare-goal', or 'pom-pom pullaway.' It seemed they could

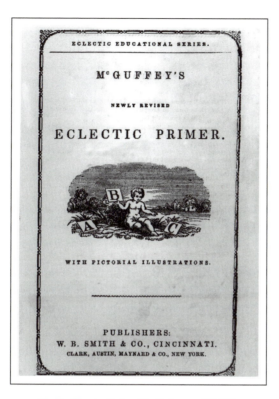

McGuffey's Eclectic Primer (1849).
Courtesy of the Library of Congress.

not get enough of play. Every moment of 'ree-cess' (as they called it) was made use of. With a mad dash they left the room, and returned to it only at the last tap of the bell."[18] Recess provided a needed outlet for all children, who played popular games like Anty Over, Red Rover, and Capture the Flag. Serving as a counterpart to exercising the mind in the classroom, recess was considered a time to exercise the body and teachers let children find their own methods of entertainment during the recess hour. Intervention was sometimes necessary, however, when boys engaged in fights or squabbles broke out. One pioneer remembered his female schoolteacher breaking up a fight as follows: "I had Charlie down with my knees on his arms, all prepared to start action on his nose, when Miss Thompson, on her way back from lunch, broke it up. She took us in and whipped us."[19] The teacher's dual role as educator and disciplinarian is clear here. Given the fact that some teachers were scarcely older than the students they taught, not to mention physically weaker than the bigger boys they taught, the demands on the teacher to keep order in the school are even more striking.

Teachers also found that their jobs included dealing with other aspects of their students' personal lives. Physical ailments were common and the teacher was often the first person to note illness and other problems. Some of these impacted the classroom itself, as in the example of chilblain, a painful itching that resulted from feet that were cold from the proverbial long walk to school in all kinds of weather. "Every one necessarily had chilblains," one student recalled, "and on warm days the boys pounded their heels and kicked their toes against the seats, to allay the intolerable burning and itching. . . . The banging, and scuffling of feet became so loud and so incessant at times that the recitations were interrupted, but the teacher, who had known the disease himself, made as little complaint as possible."[20] Bad weather could also create problems that the schoolteacher was expected to solve. The dangers of being caught in a storm either during the journey to or from school, or while in the school itself, was so common a part of the frontier experience that when a blizzard kept children snowbound in schools throughout the Midwest during the winter of 1888, the event was referred to as the Schoolchildren's Blizzard. The courage of a Nebraska schoolteacher named Minnie Freeman during the storm was further memorialized in a popular song called "Thirteen Were Saved, or, Nebraska's Fearless Maid."[21]

Finally, the frontier schoolteacher was not just an educator, but a social coordinator, helping to organize events for the town's children and adults. Spelling bees were a popular pastime that involved competitions between different age groups. As Andrew Gulliford record, "[s]pelling matches were keenly enjoyed on the frontier, and the colloquial phrase 'toeing the line' refers to barefoot children placing their toes on wooden floorboards in country schools while they lined up for spelling matches."[22] Gulliford goes on to describe the publishing success of Webster's *The Elementary Spelling Book*, familiarly called the Blue-Black Speller, that had a "printing of thirty-five million copies between 1855 and 1890. The 1866 edition alone sold 1.5 million copies, though ironically not a single definition was given for any of the words listed in its 174 pages. Americans learned to spell, but they did not really know the meaning of words they were studying."[23] Other events the teacher helped to coordinate included box lunch socials and dances, many of which took place on the school grounds or in the school if the structure was able to serve in that capacity.

Games and Circuses

The frontier school yard provided children with a site for physical, competitive games, but just outside the boundaries of the school appeared other forms of activity. Whether fun was created by the children themselves, or whether it appeared in town as part of a traveling show, the West was full of entertainment. Some of it took place within the home, centering around simple pastimes like playing the piano or reading, both silently to oneself and aloud to one another. In addition to reading, playing music, and coloring, frontier folk played "authors," a popular card game that asked players to identify well-known writers. In many cases the forms of leisure appealed to adults and children alike, creating a family-centered form of entertainment that helped build family unity.

There were other forms of fun that were especially appealing to frontier youths, that incorporated the play of games with the frontier itself. Hamlin Garland described how, at "night, during the full moon, nearly all boys and girls of the neighborhood met, to rove up and down the long swales, and to play 'gool' or 'pom-pom pullaway' upon the frozen ponds."[24] Other memoirs recalled that children were left to find their own entertainment. "We didn't have any organized athletics or physical education," Edwin Bennett wrote, "neither did we have any organized juvenile crime. The kids got their exercise walking to school and from our unorganized athletics such as One Hole Cat, Shinny, Duck-On-The-Rock and Barberoo, all games we could play without coaches, trainers, or supervision."[25]

Games were also a form of social connection in a world that was constantly changing and where children were frequently uprooted and moved while their parents searched for the right home. Children learned and played a variety of games that were known throughout the West, and that knowledge could gain them access to new school yards, and new friends, with greater ease. In the early years of expansion, such games were learned by word-of-mouth and by playing the actual games, bringing greater immediacy and meaning to the nature of frontier play. By the 1880s national publications such as *The American Boys Handy Book: What to Do and How to Do It* (1882) and *The Young Folks Cyclopaedia of Games and Sports* (1890) helped to record and standardize children's games across the country.[26]

Left to their own devices, western youths were inventive in their games, finding ways to create fun that led beyond the supervision of either schoolteacher or parent. One of the most anticipated of all childhood events was the circus.[27] Caged animals, panoramas, and other wonders made the traveling circus a highlight of western childhood. The circus brought the exotic "outside world" to the small towns that had sprung up across the frontier. In doing so, the circus gave younger generations a sense of awe about the land that existed beyond the farms and towns that surrounded them, thereby connecting young people to other parts of the country, and even the world, making frontier life a little less isolated from the urban centers of the nation.

Rag Dolls, Stick Horses, and Other Frontier Toys

Like children in other parts of the country, frontier youths played with toys that were both purchased and homemade. In general, toys were available in limited amounts, at least in the early years of settlement. Children who traveled west had only the toys that they brought with them, and while general stores stocked some playthings, their cost made them affordable only by the better-off families. As a result, children and parents were creative, inventing toys from the materials available to them in their surroundings and using them as part of children's developmental process, both in terms of understanding their surroundings and modeling the adult behavior they witnessed.[28]

Dolls were especially popular with young girls. Made from discarded fabric, the rag doll was a common plaything in the West. Easy-to-make rag dolls could be fashioned in a variety of sizes and even in a variety of stages, as Mary Foote recalled when she wrote that: "We hadn't accumulated many rags yet in our housekeeping, but enough were found to furnish the vascular tissues of a large rag baby which she placed in Georgie's arms with cooing words. Georgie looked at it with patronizing interest but was pleased."[29] The maternal imagery of the child, Georgie, holding the rag "baby" in her arms suggests that such dolls reminded girls of their expected future role as mothers. Other dolls were also familiar to frontier children, however, including paper dolls that could be dressed up, and simple corncob dolls made from the material at hand.[30]

Whatever the form, dolls were part and parcel of frontier girlhood, providing everything from creative expression to gender-role training. Other playthings were also common, again reflecting the significance of play in children's lives while also illustrating the creativity that frontier children resorted to in their efforts to have fun. Speaking of her girlhood in Arizona, for instance, an emigrant remembered that she created her own playthings, including horses made of grass and twigs, that reflected her childhood world.[31] Here again, children's toys were made from available materials, including flower stalks, sticks, and glass. At the same time, the content of the play reflected the children's understanding of the world around them and the process by which they acted out the adult roles they observed.

A final purpose for playthings in the lives of frontier children was to counteract the loneliness of lives lived in remote, sparsely populated regions. Using play to create companionship was also part of many pioneer childhoods, underlining the impact that growing up in small, isolated communities could have on western children. The creative response to such isolation suggests that while social attitudes might not have listed childhood friendships as the most important family goal, children themselves found such connections crucial to happiness and were willing to invent friends if they could not find real ones.

Finally, the gradual commercialization of childhood reached the West with the appearance of the mail-order catalog in the family home. Whereas goods were costly and hard to obtain during the early years of settlement, as the century wore on toys, clothes, and other goods became easier to purchase. Montgomery Ward and Sears Roebuck catalogs were especially popular, bringing to remote frontier homes pictures of products available to children. The arrival of such catalogs marked a shift in the world of frontier youth. With the availability of mass-produced toys and games came a decrease in the homespun, innovative playthings described with such care in pioneer memoirs. Of course the change was gradual, yet its occurrence—which paralleled the closing of the frontier—was significant, not only for its shift in attitudes toward western childhood, but for its quick incorporation of the West not as a lived experience, but as a commodified myth.

THE WEST IN AMERICAN YOUTH CULTURE

Since the beginning of the twentieth century, the West has continued to be closely tied to American youth culture. The myths of the West have been incorporated into the popular folklore of childhood stories, systematized into organizations like the Boy Scouts of America, and perpetuated and updated in television shows and Hollywood films. In almost every instance, the story of the frontier is simplified, reduced to its most basic elements, in order to instill the basic ideologies of American life into the culture of American childhood.

Teddy Bears and the Boy Scouts

One of the most beloved of American childhood toys has its origins firmly in the West. Named after Theodore, "Teddy," Roosevelt, the teddy bear appeared in several cartoons, including one that depicted Roosevelt in his trademark cowboy hat, with his arm around a small, stuffed bear. The cartoon was the brainstorm of Clifford K. Berryman, who created it in response to a story about Roosevelt's experiences during a November 1902 hunting trip. The story goes that the westerner, and future president, refused to shoot a captive bear, suggesting a humanity and compassion that contrasted with Roosevelt's Rough Rider image. The bear became a symbol for Roosevelt, and it appeared in other Berryman cartoons. Toy makers saw potential in the bear as a toy for children, and the teddy bear fad swept the nation.[32]

Whereas the teddy bear softened the western image of Rough Rider Teddy Roosevelt, other youth-centered forums sought to emphasize the

**Theodore Roosevelt as a Rough Rider
with Clifford Berryman's bear. Courtesy
of the Library of Congress.**

qualities of independence and self-reliance the West seemed to advocate. Toward this end, between 1911 and 1912 the Boy Scouts of America was established, thereby providing young boys with a program through which to safely experience aspects of frontier life while acquiring the skills that western existence had once required. "Earlier movements—the Sons of Daniel Boone and the Woodcraft Indians—had tried to inspire boys to spend more time camping and hiking and studying nature," Elliott West chronicles in a brief history of the Boy Scouts.

The first looked back to hardy pioneers as its model, the second to Native Americans. Boy Scouting, however, proved far more successful than either. Scouts emphasized an efficient organization, overseen by adults, that would continue indefinitely, bringing more young people in as others grew out of it. A "troop" was organized into smaller "patrols," while regional and national councils set policy and guidelines for the whole system. There would be common uniforms and equipment. Soon, the *Handbook for Boys* appeared, part of every scout's training, full of instructions, regulations, and lore. Its purpose, according to an early edition, was to make scouting "throughout America . . . uniform and intelligent." In 1912 the national organization began publication of a magazine, *Boy's Life*, sending it to each scout.[33]

While the earlier incarnations of the Boy Scouts drew their names more directly from popular frontier images, the Scouts effectively combined the adventurous spirit inherent in the project of westward expansion with the regimented hierarchy of the armed forces. As the terms "troops" and "patrols" suggest, scouting evokes the armed forces, while including an element of intrigue and adventure through the program's emphasis on acquired self-sufficiency. Interestingly, the title of the organization's magazine—*Boy's Life*—resonates with Hamlin Garland's classic tale of a pioneer childhood, *Boy Life on the Prairie*. The similarity further underscores the way the organization models itself on the Old West, and banks on boys' familiarity with the tales of westward expansion even as it instills an ethic of order and control that was lacking in the journeys of exploration and settlement undergone by the pioneers and miners themselves. The Girl Scouts, originally modeled after the Boy Scouts, sought similar opportunities for young girls, as did their counterparts, the Campfire Girls.

Davy Crockett, the Fifties, and Frontierland

The frontier made its strongest appearance in the youth culture of the 1950s, when a craze for all things western captured the nation. The newly popular Walt Disney launched a series of made-for-television westerns. Children's television programs were aired and became hits, including *The Adventures of Rin-Tin-Tin, Hopalong Cassidy, Annie Oakley, The Lone Ranger*, and *The Tom Mix Show*. The frontier saturated the popular youth culture of the fifties, a fad best illustrated by the love for Davy Crockett.[34]

On December 15, 1954, the television program, *Davey Crockett, Indian Fighter*, initiated a Davy Crockett fad that involved not just watching television shows and reading books, but singing "The Ballad of Davy Crockett" and purchasing Davy Crockett items in all shapes and styles. From The Davy Crockett Indian Scouting Game, to Crockett phonographs, cookies, and even ice cream, companies that sold children's toys had a marked proliferation of products with the familiar image of a buckskin-clad man wearing a coonskin hat. Davy Crockett clothing lines, school bags, records, and "ge-tars" were owned by American children, who found in Crockett a hero for their times. Crockett in particular, and the frontier in general, helped 1950s Americans make sense of their world. The West's emphasis on traditional values of self-reliance, and a clear distinction between the "good guys" and the "bad guys," resonated with a country recovering from World War II while simultaneously em-

Boys reenact the Battle of the Alamo (1956). Courtesy of the Library of Congress.

barking on a less military, but no less dramatic, Cold War ideology. The formulaic western, in which the good guys wear white hats and old-fashioned hard work wins the day, reinforced the country's desire to focus on families and values within its own borders, while keeping the perceived dangers from abroad at a safe distance, both geographically and psychologically.[35]

The 1950s fascination with the frontier was also captured in the establishment of Frontierland, part of the Disneyland theme park. During the park's 1955 inaugural year, Frontierland boasted a range of western-based attractions, including the Davy Crockett Arcade, Frontier Trading Post, Golden Horseshoe Revue, Mark Twain Riverboat, Mule Pack, and Stage Coaches.[36] Frontierland invited children "of all ages" to enjoy the Wild West within the safety of Disney's gates. By definition, Frontierland provided children with a fictional experience of the West, one aimed at entertainment rather than historical accuracy. Similarly, television and Hollywood westerns also depicted a West that was far from the experience of children who actually grew up there. Westerner Edwin Bennett described the contrast as follows:

At an age when two lines were a handful, all the . . . kids learned to drive four
horses properly, which gives me a laugh every time I see an outfit on TV and,
too often, when I see one in real life. Those amateur skinners would have a hell
of a time getting six lines or even four into one hand in a hurry and still have
control of the team. And the way they slap the horses with the lines is another
laugh.[37]

The contrast between the actual demands on frontier children and the
way those demands have been illustrated in popular culture brings into
relief the differences between the facts about the America West and the
roles television programs, movies, and toys have played in perpetuating
fictional myths of the era.

Little House on the Prairie

Whereas the western craze of the 1950s sought to instruct American
youths in the morals and behaviors that distinguished right from wrong,
the West appeared in the juvenile culture of the 1970s for a different
reason altogether. The popularity of Laura Ingalls Wilder's *Little House
on the Prairie* books spoke to American children of a national past rich
in family values, including the rewards of hard work and the joys of
simple pleasures. From the little house in the big woods, where the Ingalls family survived its first winter in the West, to Laura's job as a
frontier schoolteacher who falls in love with and marries a farmer, they
stand as a counterpart to the tales that have flourished in children's literature about boyhood during the westward expansion period.

While the best-selling *Little House* books were progressive in that they
provided young girls with their own stories of western life, the television
show became a hit in the 1970s because it projected conservative values.
The world in which its viewers lived was a world in flux. Social institutions like marriage were under attack and women challenged their
traditional roles as mothers and wives. In contrast, the hour-long television show, starring Michael Landon, opened with the comforting images of a nuclear family traveling along the sunny plains, mother and
father smiling with love as their three daughters tumbled down a grassy
hill. Calico dresses, cotton bonnets, and neat aprons adorned the girls
and each episode happily resolved itself with family members united in
their support and love of one another. That same love enabled the family
to survive even the toughest adversities, and the program's success
banked upon its neat endings. Offering viewers a nostalgic—though fictional—look at an American past free from the social confusion and
change of the 1970s, *Little House on the Prairie* drew viewers not only
from the target population of young girls, but from young and old alike.

Woody, Buzz Lightyear, and Kirsten, an American Girl

At the beginning of the twenty-first century, the relationship between the West and American children stood at an odd impasse. On the one hand, films like *Toy Story* and *Toy Story Two*—which take a cowboy for their hero and the Old West as a central theme—were blockbuster hits. At the same time, there was no pervasive cultural interest in the frontier, and in particular children expressed little deep fascination with the Old West, as fact or fiction. Classic western figures like Daniel Boone and Davy Crockett, along with the still-beloved *Little House* series, remained part of American youth culture, but they were outshone by the trend-setting Harry Potter and Pokémon characters. The shift is best represented by the *Toy Story* films, in which Woody the cowboy has to compete for the attention of his boy-owner with Buzz Lightyear, the astronaut. Woody's anxiety about losing his status with his owner, Andy, reflects the larger cultural trend away from interest in the West toward playthings that are more technologically driven.

One exception to the turn from the West as an inspiration for American toys can be found in the late-twentieth-century popularity of the American Girl dolls, a collection of expensive dolls that are based on different periods of American history. Kirsten Larson, as the company's Web site describes her, "is a pioneer girl of strength and spirit growing up on the edge of the American frontier in 1854—a world of wilderness and prairie, of log cabins and one-room schoolhouses."[38] Created to provide contemporary American girls with a representation of childhood in the old West, Kirsten comes with a book, *Meet Kirsten*, which describes her life as a pioneer child.[39]

Like every era in American childhood, the period of westward expansion held conflicting views toward, and expectations of, its children. On the one hand, frontier youths were expected to work as hard as the adults they lived with, actively participating in the process of settling the West and establishing a flourishing life there. On the other hand, western childhood was viewed as especially idyllic. Not only were children such a rare sight in some communities that they became idealized embodiments of the best life could offer, but childhood on the frontier was repeatedly described as a time of boundless exploration, adventure, and joy. The competing views, represented in diaries, magazines, and books of the time, have been reproduced for contemporary American children in order to emphasize the dichotomy of hard work and simple pleasure. The result has been a juvenile culture that borrows the best and worst from the American West in an effort to instruct today's youths in the basic values and lessons that frontier childhood can be found to symbolize.

PART TWO

POPULAR CULTURE OF WESTWARD EXPANSION

3

Advertising

The American West would probably not have been settled as quickly and thoroughly if it had not been for the rise of modern advertising. From promotional flyers aimed at luring easterners westward with the promise of large lots of land at low, affordable prices, to the ads for medicine, circuses, and other events that gave the old West an appearance of being established and civilized, the West was arguably won by the words and pictures that literally sold it to potential settlers. At the same time that the West is indebted to the field of advertising, the growth of advertising as a profession may not have caught hold in the United States as strongly as it did during the second half of the nineteenth century if it had not been for the project of westward expansion and the legends of the frontier that sprang from that period. The western United States and the world of modern advertising grew up in the same decades and have remained interconnected in significant ways ever since.

ADVERTISING THE WEST

From the first gold rush of 1849 through the beginning of the twentieth century, two agendas brought droves of travelers and emigrants to the American frontier. The first reason for increased interest in the West involved the cries of gold that echoed across the country, in newspapers, letters, and word-of-mouth stories that told of fantastic riches available to anyone willing to make the westward trip. At the same time, the availability of inexpensive land was a major impetus for western expansion. Speculators bought up large parcels of land with the goal of selling bits of it at a great profit. The transcontinental railroad systems that were completed during the second half of the nineteenth century made the journey easier and quicker to complete, giving distant western regions of the country the appearance of being closer than ever before, and drawing ranchers, farmers, and settlers westward in unprecedented numbers. Whatever the reason, the urgency with which emigrants traveled west intensified as the century wore on, making life on the frontier an experience of change, innovation, and entrepreneurship directly in keeping with the goals of advertising.[1]

Boosters, Railroads, and Promotional Flyers

The period of westward expansion would have been less successful without the advertisements that promoted the land and aided the rigorous journey. Newspapers publicized dates when departing groups of emigrants would start from one of several jumping-off, or starting, places. Promotional flyers sponsored by the government helped publicize land that had been made available through the Homestead Act of 1862. Advertisements created by the railroad companies ensured the development of towns along the transcontinental routes as they were in the process of being completed. Finally, real estate dealers, known as boosters, who had purchased land at low prices with the purpose of selling it for a profit, made every effort to convince settlers that their town was the best town, thereby ensuring the boosters' own financial gain and the settlement of previously unpopulated land.

As early travelers set off across the plains, they formed parties that consisted of families from a variety of locales. Groups and individuals wishing to make the journey did not have to set out alone, however, but could read the local newspapers and look for articles that recruited traveling companions. On February 27, 1846, for instance, the St. Louis *Gazette* published the following notice:

The Oregon emigrants from the Platte purchase will rendezvous opposite this place on the 15th of April next, preparatory to their departure for the land of promise. We give this notice in due time, in order that others from the adjoining counties, or other States, who have resolved upon going to Oregon may know at what point to assemble. Emigrants can be supplied in this place with all necessary outfits.[2]

Such notices helped travelers to join together for the trip across the country, which was made ostensibly easier by individuals traveling together in large groups. The language the statement used to describe the West— the "land of promise"—reflected the fundamental rhetoric behind westward expansion. The region west of the Mississippi was represented as a place of limitless potential and endless promise to those who chose to move there. The *Gazette*'s notice did more than announce travel plans, however. It also publicized the town of St. Louis as a place from which to head west and, concurrently, as a town so well stocked in supplies that it could provide emigrants with "all necessary outfits." The combination was important, for towns on the edge of the frontier depended on the money brought in by pioneers who would plan in advance to purchase their supplies at a particular spot along their route. Once in a town like St. Louis, from which they were to set off for unknown territory, travelers were at the mercy of shopkeepers who often charged exorbitant prices for basic goods that pioneers had no choice but to purchase before they left.

Citizens and owners of frontier towns were not the only groups invested in populating the West with emigrants. The U.S. government and the transcontinental railroad companies were also dependent on people being willing to move westward. The government needed people to populate the West to complete the process of dislocating the American Indians, to lay claim to the land itself, and to develop communities across the continent. Railroads, on the other hand, wanted towns to be located along their routes so that convenient stops could be made, supplies would be available, and repairs and other services would be relatively easy to access. In order to promote the journey, both the government and the railroads launched national advertising campaigns that reached easterners and Europeans alike. The challenge was to persuade potential emigrants to pack a wagon full of only essential possessions, and to travel to a region that they had never seen. People in established communities, with access to necessary products and goods and friends and family members, had little reason to uproot themselves. The question became, how could advertising convince them to do so?

Those who lured settlers west made every effort to answer this question. First, promoters made sure that the land was readily available to potential emigrants. More important, western land could be purchased at a price that was hard to refuse. The Homestead Act of 1862 met both criteria, offering 160 acres of free land to anyone who agreed to live on the land and farm it for five years. The response to the act's offer of land resulted in more than a million and a half applications for homesteads.[3] The railroads, too, made promises to prospective settlers, making it easy for them to purchase and finance large plots of land along the routes traveled by transcontinental trains.

What the government and the railroads had in common was an aptitude for persuasive advertising aimed at convincing individuals and families to give up the comforts of home and venture westward to live in an unfamiliar land. They did so through promotional flyers and other printed ads that made such a move seem hard to refuse. An ad for land

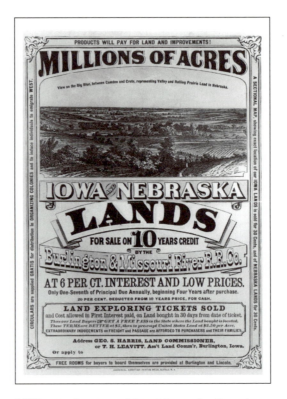

Millions of acres of land for sale. Courtesy
of the Library of Congress.

in Iowa and Nebraska, for instance, announced that "Millions of Acres"
were "for sale on 10 years credit" and available "at 6 per ct. interest and
low prices." The facts of the ad—the amount of land, the price it would
cost, and the way it could be financed—were all crucial pieces of information to potential emigrants. Land was not the only thing for sale,
however. A specific lifestyle and value system were also promised in ads
for the American Dream.

To promote such values, visual images and written captions were used
to project the characteristics by which the West was primarily being marketed. Many ads included attractive pictures of a "land of plenty" that
was supposed to be available to pioneers, lush with trees, water, and
grain. In addition, ads were typically annotated with captions like the
following: "To the West, to the West, to the Land of the Free . . . Emigration to Iowa and Nebraska, U.S. . . . HOMES FOR ALL! More Farms
than Farmers! More Landlords than Tenants! Work for all workers!"
Written in 1871 and targeting potential English emigrants, the ad offered

its readers several things. First, it promised life in the "Land of the Free." The type of freedom the ad invoked became clear in the last lines. Homes were available for everyone, employment opportunities were ample, and ownership was the rule, not the exception. For English farmers struggling to survive in a period of unemployment, oppression, and financial hardship, Iowa and Nebraska represented more than just land. The "millions of acres" also guaranteed the self-sufficiency and independence that were lacking in England. These themes would be expressed repeatedly throughout the period of westward expansion and they remain integral to the myth of the Old West in advertising today.

The tenets of real estate advertising on the frontier continue to manifest themselves in the commercial real estate magazines of the twentieth and twenty-first centuries. As Reuben J. Ellis argues, such magazines depend on the basic concepts of the Old West. The promotion of a new home, a new start, complete with a formal "closing" on the act of ownership, resonate with the goal of westward expansion, which was, ultimately, the "closing" of the frontier. As Ellis describes, real estate ad magazines are like dime novels because they rely

on indigenous materials, native authors ... Instead of the trappings and set pieces of the old frontier—Buffalo Bill, Kit Carson, evil Mexicans, bandits, mostly good/dead Indians, or even such fanciful inventions as the steam man of the prairie, the real estate ad magazine works from the lexicon of HUD, assumable contacts, starter homes, mature landscaping, insulated vinyl siding and the super owner financed deal of a lifetime.[4]

The idea that a plot of land and a home were synonymous with the American Dream continues to be the basis of popular advertising literature in the U.S. real estate market. Such ads assure today's "pioneer" homeowners that all the trappings of a new life will be theirs through the purchase of a contemporary "homestead" in the land of promise.

Ads Along the Trail and the Gold Rush Font

The plethora of advertisements aimed at drawing emigrants west were replaced, along the trails, with ads for services that could be found during the journey. In 1857, Helen Carpenter commented on the appearance of ads along the pioneer route, describing prominent ads for a Dr. J. Noble, physician.[5] Dr. Noble's ads were carefully placed so that as many people as possible could see them and they were brightly drawn in red. The idea that advertisements along a major travel route would help the advertiser to reap the benefits of a captive audience is similar to the purpose behind the modern billboard that informs drivers of services available along the highway.

The need to advertise in western towns was just as strong as it was along the trails or in the East. In order to mark the establishment of new businesses—which cropped up as quickly as there was a town to build them in—frontier towns adopted a style of sign that was distinctive in both its lettering and its simplicity. The lettering was almost universally done in what is now known as the gold rush font—a semi-elaborate style of straight letters with curled ends. Signs also tended to be simple. The name of the product or service being provided was often all that was printed on an otherwise plain background. Only occasionally was there a picture of the advertised item to accompany the words. The saloon, for instance, was simply advertised as "Saloon" while the butcher shop might be marked by a basic drawing of a cow. The style of advertising in frontier towns remains one of the most distinguishing marks of the old West, and the same lettering is used in popular culture to evoke the West. Whether in advertising for products or a tourist site, the familiar look of the gold rush font tells readers that there is an association between the frontier and either the product or the place being designated by the writing.[6]

Another form of frontier advertising was common in local newspapers. The newspaper was frequently the first service to arrive in a new town and the printed pages were used to advertise the town itself, as well as the services that were offered there. Such ads were noted for the range of subjects on which they focused. W. F. Rae commented on the ads he found in the *Elko Independent* newspaper. One, he wrote, was for "Ung Gen, Chinese Doctor," who claimed to be able to "attend professionally to all who may require his services . . . he is prepared to cure all diseases that may come to his notice."[7] Another ad, this one for druggists, said that the "firm intimated not only that it was ready to supply all drugs and to prepare all prescriptions, but also that it had on hand 'a large stock of paints, oils, window-glass, castor oil; also a large assortment of fishing lines and hooks of all kinds.' "[8] Other ads were for saloon drinks and local services. Whatever the product, there was an ad made to sell it. The range of ads printed in western newspapers, and the promises they made to emigrants and settlers, reflected the spirit of the gold rush and westward expansion in general. Here was a place where anyone could be anything, where personal histories could be eradicated and new personas quickly created.

Patent Medicine, P.T. Barnum, and Wild West Shows

Ads for medicines and entertainment—both meant to lift the spirits— were commonly plastered on the sides of barns, boats, rocks, and trees. As Christina Mierau quotes in *Accept No Substitutes*, during the 1880s a visitor to the United States commented that the land was "daubed from one end . . . to the other with huge white paint notices . . . an endless array of advertisements puffing off the medicines of pretentious quacks."[9] That the ads were for medicines underscores the widespread popularity of patent medicines in the old West—and in the country in general—as well as the elaborate advertising campaigns used to sell such products to customers across the region.[10] The ads were first based on the product's name, which followed one of several forms. Names could be alliterative—as in Dr. William's "Pink Pills for Pale People"—relying on the repetition of a particular sound or letter to help people remember the product. The name could also be boldly descriptive, as in "Wild Cherry Tonic! For the Cure of All Nervous Disorders, Dyspepsia, Jaundice, Bilious Complaints, Loss of Appetite & General Debility." These ads made grand claims that would catch a buyer's attention through their promises. Patent medicine names could also be more serious, meant to invoke the authority of the potion's inventor or to authenticate the formula by the claim of medical expertise as in "Dr. John Bull's Vegetable Worm Destroyer."[11]

Whatever the name, the ads themselves had to draw consumers' attention with bold lettering, engaging and detailed pictures, or brief descriptions of the ills the medicine was supposed to cure. Some patent medicine sellers resorted to a form of what today would be called an infomercial, printed ads in newspapers that looked like real stories but were actually fictional tales. These ads, which read like newspaper articles, complete with headlines, would describe an illness and then the subsequent cure through use of the specific product being marketed. The promises made through such advertisements were particularly intriguing to early westerners who found themselves far from doctors and dependent on their own homemade remedies to cure illness. Despite the fact that patent medicines were purchased in huge amounts throughout the frontier, consumers were often disappointed—and even endangered—by the treatments which were in fact ineffective and sometimes made of toxic substances.

A subgenre of patent medicine advertisements included products ostensibly made by Native Americans or by using Native American recipes and formulas. An ad for "Indian Compound of Honey Boneset and Squills," for instance, promised to treat illnesses of the lungs and throat. The ad featured a bare-breasted Native America woman in the act of picking leaves from a bush and putting them into a bottle of what is supposed to be the Indian Compound medicine. An entire line of products that was marketed as originating with the Kickapoo Indian tribe was also popular and included Kickapoo Indian Oil, Kickapoo Indian Worm Killer, and Kickapoo Indian Salve. In each case, the ads capitalized on the growing belief that American Indians possessed a knowledge of illnesses and cures that was outside of mainstream culture. Marking a

Indian remedies. Courtesy of the
Library of Congress.

shift from representations of Native Americans as dangerous and hostile,
to depictions of them as holistic and even magical healers, the advertisements of "Indian" remedies ironically reflect the simultaneous re-
pression of Native America culture in the West and the co-optation of
that culture in the service of westward expansion emigrants.[12]

While these early forms of advertising were relatively effective, the
field of advertising underwent a significant transformation with the appearance of P.T. Barnum, of the dynamic Barnum and Bailey circus. Barnum advertised his shows in such novel ways that he has been called
the father of advertising. First, he used every mode of print available in
order to promote his shows, including newspapers, flyers, and posters
that were plastered everywhere that they could possibly find and draw
an audience. The printed material was also unique. Not only was it full
of information, but it incorporated sensational headlines to entice people
to attend the show, making them look forward to the coming event and
to plan in advance to be there. This form of advance advertising was

extremely successful, and other people adopted Barnum's methods to create their own advertising sensations.

Buffalo Bill Cody was especially good at using Barnum's advertising style in order to draw audiences to his Wild West Shows. Long and narrow posters were used to inform people of the coming attraction, and each poster was divided into sections that illustrated and described a different feature of the show. "The Atrocious Mountain Meadow Massacre," for instance, was one segment of a Wild West Show ad, and the poster was illustrated with a drawing of covered wagons and their inhabitants being attacked by Native Americans. A smaller caption stated, "Realistic Attack on the Overland Mail! Sharp Shooting. Round Ups. Lassoing Real Buffalo by Genuine Cow-Boys." Each line described one of the many sights that would comprise that segment of the program. The combination of visual images with dramatic titles made such advertisements a success, ensuring the popularity of Wild West Shows across the country and packing show places with audiences who eagerly anticipated the programs.[13]

Catalogs, Trade Cards, and Magazines

In addition to posters, handbills, and other public forms of advertisement, products were marketed in additional means as well. The mail-order catalog was in essence one big advertisement aimed at developing consumer confidence and increasing consumer spending on products shipped through the mail. As a result of the improved mail service that allowed products to be sent at low prices, and the transcontinental railroads that could reach rural communities more quickly than ever before, the mail-order business boomed in the last decades of the nineteenth century. Montgomery Ward introduced its product line in 1872, offering people in isolated communities unprecedented access to goods that they needed or desired—so much so that the Montgomery Ward catalog became familiarly known as the "wish book."

The company's competitor, Sears, Roebuck & Co., was equally successful in capturing the attention of mail-order customers. Basing its empire on a customer-friendly approach to marketing, Sears, Roebuck assured its catalog readers that it was the "Cheapest Supply House on Earth," and, at least in its early days, the company claimed that customers did not need to send any money to receive their items. Instead, they would be charged on delivery. To reach the broadest market possible, the copy printed on the first page of the Sears, Roebuck catalog stated: "Don't think you live too far away. THERE IS NOT A TOWN IN THE UNITED STATES WHERE WE HAVE NOT SOLD GOODS."[14] Finally, compilers of the catalog reflected on its role as advertiser, stating: "We Deem that the Best Advertisement Any Firm Can Have is a well satisfied customer." The pictures in mail-order catalogs were drawn in keeping with the elaborate style of the Victorian period, which included ornate illustrations of the products being sold. The typeface, which was printed in various sizes, contained ample information and surrounded the picture.

Another venue for advertising products was the trade card. Small cards were included in brand-name packages and were collected and exchanged. Providing companies with an additional way to spread the word about a particular product, trade cards were not unlike the toys that are included in today's McDonald's Happy Meals, cereal boxes, and other products. Both reinforce the consumer's desire for the product because of the extra, "free," gift thrown in with the purchase, thereby further cementing the consumer's familiarity with—and, it was hoped, penchant for—the item.

Chromolithography also made its mark on nineteenth-century advertising by making it possible to produce brightly colored images that were easily reproduced. Posters with stock borders could be purchased and the particular event or product inserted into the sections that were left blank for that purpose. Boxes, wrappers, and other containers used to market products were colorfully decorated and sold as much for their artistic designs as for the objects they contained. Some chromolithographic advertisements were so attractive that they were hung on walls as decorations, erasing the line between the ad and the picture, between the marketplace and the home. Today, these brightly colored ads are collectibles, especially those that were originally used to sell western produce such as California fruits.

Finally, magazines were prime sites for advertisers to market their goods. Early magazines did not include ads, but rather focused on articles and stories, material that was entertaining to readers. With the appearance of magazines like *Ladies Home Journal*, however, which integrated ads into its pages, the market for advertising in magazines took hold. Not only did it make sense to publishers—who could make money on subscriptions as well as on the ads that companies placed in their magazines—but readers enjoyed the exposure that ads gave them to the latest and greatest in available products.

Travel Advertisements

As the West became increasingly settled, it also became a destination for travelers who sought the romance of adventure that the region continued to evoke. Travel advertisements helped to promote western excursions, making them among the most popular pastimes at the beginning of the twentieth century. In fact, the term "transcontinental" seems to have entered the vocabulary of tourism after the *Great Trans-*

Continental Railroad Guide used the term in its title. The tendency to see the West as a place of romantic beauty and pleasure, or, alternatively, as a place of entertainment and luxury, encouraged tourism in the region. At the same time, emphasizing the luxury of the transportation vehicle allowed travelers to overlook the realities that the region could be as dull as it could be dangerous. This dichotomy suggests a more general trend in American travel that chooses to see only the familiar, the pleasant, and the beautiful, and to ignore the less appealing parts of a trip.[15]

Twentieth-century advertising has borrowed from the old West, creating ads that either emphasize the adventure of western travel or use frontier images to sell products. An ad for Early Times Whiskey, for instance, focuses on the first transcontinental railroad trip. The ad pictures a group of men, dressed in late-nineteenth-century clothing, sitting in what appears to be an early Pullman car and drinking whiskey. Travel companies have also cashed in on the romance of western travel, building companies around names like Carlson Wagonlit Travel whose logo is a covered wagon. Airlines, such as Frontier, have also turned to the old West when choosing names. Finally, vacation spots in the West, including dude ranches, have relied heavily on advertising to draw customers.[16]

Brand Names

One of the most lasting trends in early western advertising came from the practice of branding horses and cattle, a practice that is related to the popularity of brand names throughout the late-twentieth-century United States. Originally, brands were placed on animals in order to identify ownership by a particular cowboy or ranch. As a result, the "letters, figures, or designs in a brand commonly bore some relation to the owner's name or to some event of either business or sentimental interest to him, and always were selected and placed in combination only after careful consideration as to the extent of their immunity from forging alteration."[17] Once a brand mark was settled on, the rancher registered with the local government office and gained exclusive rights to use it. The brands were recorded in a brand book that served as trademarking the symbol.

The practice of branding animals, while serving a utilitarian function in the Old West, also acted as a type of advertising by associating a recognizable symbol with a particular individual or group. As those symbols became familiar and ranchers could identify an animal's owner by the sign branded on its hide, the brand became a marker of the ranch in general. The more cattle there were with a particular brand, and the healthier those cattle were, the more positive was the reputation of that brand. Brands that were easy to alter were also subject to forgery. For instance, there existed "so-called 'brand artists,' 'brand blotters,' or 'brand blotchers,' these being gentlemen who, with ingenuity and a piece of hot metal, added marks to those already on the beast and made the final result identical with the 'artist's' registered brand."[18] Brand artists are not dissimilar to today's brand "knockoffs," companies that slightly adapt popular brands so they look enough like the original that consumers will buy the product, but are different enough that the company cannot be accused of trademark infringement.

The practice of branding appeared in related forms throughout the period of westward expansion. The rise in popularity of canned goods, for instance, created a new form of brand recognition that changed the experience of shopping at the general store forever. Whereas earlier in the nineteenth century goods were stored in large barrels or bins, with no names on them other than those of the products, the arrival of canned goods on market shelves created associations between the names on cans and particular companies. Advertising enhanced the connections by educating customers about why one product was better than another. The invention of the paper bag, combined with the marketing of canned goods, led to the creation of icons or symbols that were placed on the packaging of food, cosmetics, and other products to distinguish one from another.

The result of these changes in the local store meant that, during the last three decades of the nineteenth century, a new wave of brand-name products, complete with brand-name packaging, made an appearance on market shelves. Brands like Campbell's Soup (1869), Hires Root Beer (1876), and Quaker Oats (1877) were among the early brand names to gain and keep their brand recognition into the twenty-first century. Brands that were considered genuinely western included the Colt handgun, patented in 1835, Levi's jeans, patented in 1853, and the Stetson hat, created by John B. Stetson in 1865. Like the brands used by ranchers, these brand names had to be officially registered with the U.S. Patent Office as trademarks, formalizing the connections between a particular company, its product, and its symbol.[19]

As emigrants moved westward and the field of advertising grew, these two areas of American life depended on one another for success. Whether in the promotional literature for western land or the early development of brand-name products, advertising and the West went hand in hand. The result was a language of advertising that was easy to recognize and which tapped into several cultural ideals about the frontier. The American eagle, for instance, was a common feature of western advertisements, used to symbolize the nationalism inherent in settling the West. Indians also made regular appearances in early ads, usually in nonthreatening positions that reflected—and denied—ongoing subjugation and displacement. Manifest Destiny, in general, was part of the rhetoric used in ads to promote either the West itself or the products available to people who lived there. Masked by an emphasis on work, the message was clear that, as long as the West was won with effort and productivity, the win was legitimate.

THE WEST IN ADVERTISING

Not surprisingly, the values, ideals, and images of the West that drew emigrants to the frontier during westward expansion have become so deeply ingrained in the American consciousness that they have been primary features of U.S. advertising since the turn of the twentieth century. Whether western characters such as the cowboy; western clothing like the cowboy hat, boot, and bandana; or western scenery, such as the rugged terrain or the main street of a frontier town, familiar images of the West have formed the marketing basis for everything from food and clothing to cars and beer. Slogans that evoke the West's ideals of freedom and individualism have also thrived in the advertising industry, representing some of the most easily recognized products of contemporary American life. Whatever the product, if the ad depends on the West to sell it, basic ideals will be encapsulated in the advertisement and incorporated into the idea of what is being purchased.[20]

Almost as soon as the frontier was thoroughly settled, the myth of the West was incorporated into popular advertising. Western figures—Native Americans, buffalo, and cowboys, for instance—started to appear in ads for everything from alcohol to food. A 1913 campaign for Cream of Wheat, for instance, featured a western mail carrier, dressed in typical cowboy garb, depositing a letter into a roadside postbox inscribed with the words "Cream of Wheat." The caption on the ad read "Where the mail goes Cream of Wheat goes," suggesting that Cream of Wheat was so popular that it was eaten in even the remotest parts of the country. Like many ads that invoke the West, the Cream of Wheat ad was based on a familiar painting of the westward expansion period. Entitled "The Prairie Letterbox," the original painting by Rufus Zugbaum was reproduced as a sketch in *Harper's Weekly* on April 23, 1867.[21] The phrase also tapped into the contemporary popularity of mail-order catalogs that promised customers that they could receive products anywhere mail service was available.

Another early advertising icon, which appeared in 1919 as part of an advertisement for Argo's Karo syrup, was the Karo princess. Readily recognized as a Native American, the figure's body was a stalk of corn and her head was was adorned with a feathered headband. Whereas the Cream of Wheat ad glorified the development of the West, Argo's marketing strategy dehumanized the already displaced American Indians,

Wood engraving after a painting by Rufus
Zogbaum (1887). Courtesy of the Library
of Congress.

associating them with products—in this case, corn—and placing them
at the service of the people who had removed them from their land. The
Karo princess can still be found on boxes of Argo cornstarch, and the
husks of the corn, which look like her robes, open suggestively from
neck to waist.

   With the growth in production and popularity of automobiles, companies that made them adopted ads that borrowed from western images.
One of the most widely recognized of these early ads, produced in 1923
for the Jordan Car Company, helped to cement the association, in advertising, between cars and the West. The ad was created to market the
company's new Jordan Playboy convertible. The ad's target audience
was women. It included a loose sketch of a woman in a convertible, the
Jordan Playboy, moving rapidly past a cowboy who, depending on the
version of the ad, either lost or was losing his hat. The ad focused on
speed and action. The rather lengthy caption, which began "Somewhere

West of Laramie," reflected the ideals of the women's movement taking place in the political arena during the same time period that the ad was in circulation.

Somewhere west of Laramie there's a broncho-busting, steer-roping girl who knows what I'm talking about. She can tell what a sassy pony, that's a cross between greased lightning and the place where it hits, can do with eleven hundred pounds of steel and action when he's going high, wide and handsome. The truth is—the Jordan Playboy was built for her.[22]

Deliberately using the language of the cowboy—"broncho-busting," "steer-roping"—the ad challenged women to recognize themselves as the type of "new" woman who would be able to handle the Jordan Playboy. She is the "sassy pony" who can handle the power and speed of the car and is not worried about the impact her power might have on the men around her, here represented by the cowboy losing his hat as he charges along beside her, barely able to keep up. The mythical West of the cowboy is portrayed as outdated in contrast to the modern experience of the Jordan Playboy, an unusual turn for advertising which tends to romanticize the frontier and its legendary characteristics. The narrative style of the ad, which tells a story about the product, foreshadows a trend in 1990s advertising epitomized by the J. Peterman Catalog in which story-like copy replaced brief, descriptive captions.[23]

Car advertising has also drawn on the West as a symbol of the freedom and adventure that owning a car can offer consumers. Referring to the length of the pioneer journey, Mohawk Tires used the slogan "Westward Ho!" in order to underscore the durability of the company's product. Chevrolet adopted the popular slogan, "See the USA in your Chevrolet," thereby encouraging Americans to combine traveling throughout the West on family vacations with purchasing a Chevrolet in which to make the trip. Western scenery is often the setting of car and truck advertisements, especially if the scenery includes rugged terrain, steep mountain paths, and clear skies. Such ads turn to the western landscape as the symbol of open space through which driving can be exciting and fun, contrasting that land to the realities of most drivers' lives which involve busy highways and suburban streets, far from the rocky mountains of the West. Car manufacturers have also used western symbols to name their cars and trucks, as, for instance, the Cherokee, Navajo, or Bronco. Contemporary advertising incorporates the desire to live an adventuresome, mobile, independent life combined with the ownership of cars, trucks, and sport utility vehicles that companies want to sell. The result is a well-developed form of advertising that continually refers to the mythic existence of a West that once was unpopulated and open for exploration and adventure.

"Come to where the flavor is. Come to Marlboro Country."

There is no icon of modern advertising that incorporates the lore of the American West more effectively than the Marlboro Man. The epitome of the American cowboy, the Marlboro Man exudes independence and masculinity that are inextricably connected to the cigarettes he smokes. The Marlboro Man's image has evolved over time, responding to cultural changes in attitudes toward smoking, while meeting the demands of a public still drawn to the values the Marlboro ads put forth.[24]

To start with, the Marlboro Man was originally a woman. In the early days of production, during the 1920s, Marlboro cigarettes were marketed toward women through claims that the tobacco used in them was relatively mild. In addition, consumers could decide which tip to buy— Marlboros with a red or a white "beauty tip," a feature that symbolized luxury and femininity because lipstick marks would remain hidden from view. With the rise in awareness about links between smoking and cancer, however, Philip Morris, Marlboro's parent company, developed two innovations in the cigarette market during the 1950s. First, it created a filter that was supposed to decrease the amount of smoke inhaled into the smoker's lungs. Second, the company developed a flip-top box that prevented cigarettes from being easily crushed. Both the filter and the box were to be marketed under the Marlboro brand, but, in order to increase sales, the company decided to change the brand's image from one aimed at refined women to one targeting men who want to appear truly masculine.

As Leo Burnett, the head of the creative team that devised the original Marlboro Man campaign, recalls:

> We asked ourselves what was the most generally accepted symbol of masculinity in America, and this led quite naturally to the cowboy.
> The next natural question was: "If a cowboy were talking about flavor, what would he say?"
> This led to the phrase, *"Delivers the goods on flavor."*[25]

The first Marlboro Man was dressed as a cowboy who was conspicuously smoking a Marlboro cigarette. The campaign designers were afraid to keep the cowboy in every ad, however, and turned to "photographs of 'regular guys'. . . . who typified what has been referred to as 'masculine confidence.' "[26] In order to set Marlboro even further apart from other cigarettes, the advertisers decided to use a tattoo on the hands and wrists of each Marlboro figure. The tattooed hand that held the Marlboro cigarette kept viewers focused on the product and added to the romance of the men in the ads, who held typically masculine jobs as a pilot, a golfer, a rancher, or an officer.

As time went by, research determined that the cowboy was the most popular of the Marlboro Men and the advertising campaign returned to its original character, making him the only figure in a Marlboro ad. To reintroduce and reinforce the cowboy as the quintessential Marlboro Man, the campaign introduced a three-page advertisement in the January 1957 issue of *Life* magazine. Titled "The Marlboro Man, What's he like . . . ," the ad showed the cowboy/Marlboro Man at work in different settings, including on his ranch, where he discussed his life and his cigarettes. He told his audience that he owns his "own ranch . . . [and] ride[s] from one end of it to the other every day . . . I like the life a man leads out here . . . the good feeling of being your own boss."[27] His words recall those used in some of the early promotional literature aimed at drawing settlers to the West where they could be in charge of their own lives, live on their land, and be their own person. By smoking Marlboro cigarettes, in other words, people could still live the adventure of the frontier, could still indulge in the basic values that the West had always represented.

Other key aspects of the Marlboro campaign included the red-and-white box that stood out from its competitors in its simple, yet bold, design. Captions like "Come to Marlboro Country" resonated with the cry of "come west" heard throughout the period of westward expansion and Marlboro Country itself became a symbolic replacement for the American frontier. Other captions and jingles used throughout the course of the Marlboro Man's history included "Up before the sun, Travel all day long," and "the cigarette made for men that women like." While the former constructs the Marlboro Man as a modern westerner who, like the pioneers, cowhands, and emigrants before him, put in a long day of travel through the western land, the latter evokes the masculinity associated with life on the frontier. A more recent, and more pronounced, change in Marlboro advertising reflects yet another turn in the campaign's ongoing efforts to respond to the concerns of the American public while at the same time continuing to sell cigarettes. Although the Marlboro Man has always been pictured smoking a Marlboro cigarette, late-twentieth-century attacks on tobacco companies—a result of the research that documents the high risks associated with smoking—has left the Marlboro Man without his smoke. The word "Marlboro" is always somewhere on the current ads, and the Marlboro Man is readily identified by his cowboy fashion, his masculine good looks, and his rugged surroundings. Yet in several ads, the cigarette—the product being sold—is nowhere to be seen. The disappearance of the product, and the continued popularity of the brand, testifies to the strength of the association between the Marlboro cowboy and the cigarette he now seems to smoke only in private.[28]

Buffalo Bee, Marky Maypo, and Twinkie the Kid

That the Marlboro Man's cowboy image would have evolved during the 1950s is not surprising given the decade's preoccupation with everything western, reflected in television programs, movies, comic books, and toys. Other 1950s advertising campaigns that evoked the West focused on children's foods. Nabisco's Rice Honeys (1957) and Maypo's instant oat cereal (1958), for instance, featured frontier-like characters on their boxes. The front of the Rice Honeys' box included a picture of Buffalo Bee—a bee dressed in cowboy clothing, including a cowboy hat, two pistols, a bandana and cowboy boots. One of Buffalo Bee's two guns shoots honey at pieces of the cereal, thereby emphasizing how the rice puffs are "flavored with natural honey." Maypo's oat cereal centered on another cartoon character, Marky Maypo, who also dressed in western garb—a cowboy hat, bandana, and cowboy boots—and who eats his cereal with what appears to be great satisfaction. Both cereals exemplify how the West's image infiltrated all types of products during the 1950s— and beyond—drawing children to the table through the characters and images with which they were so familiar. The use of western characters to sell children food continued throughout the twentieth century, most recently through Hostess's introduction, in 1990, of Twinkie the Kid. The character, dressed in the standard "cowboy" garb of boots with spurs, a bandana, and a cowboy hat with his name on it, is a play on the western outlaw, Billy the Kid.

A more controversial western image can be found in an advertisement for Kellogg's Nut N' Honey cereal. Meant to play on the cereal's name, the television ads for Nut N' Honey were built around people in situations where, when they said the cereal's name—Nut N' Honey—others thought they were saying "nothing honey." One such ad featured cowboys around a chuck wagon at which the cook, ambiguously named Cookie, prepares the meal. When the cowboys ask what's to eat, Cookie says "nut n' honey"—meaning the cereal—but the cowboys hear "nothing honey" and are offended—or threatened—by what they perceive to be an intimate response. Challenging the masculine image of the cowboy perpetuated by ads such as those for Marlboro cigarettes, the Nut N' Honey ad is ambiguous and even subversive in its depiction of male relationships.[29]

Fast-food chains like Arby's and Roy Rogers have also used western icons to evoke the legend of frontier food—hearty, satisfying meat that is available in ample portions. The Roy Rogers chain has adopted not only the name of the famous singing cowboy, but the figure of the buck-

"You need only one soap—Ivory Soap"
(1898). Courtesy of the Library of
Congress.

ing bronco, the cowboy hat, and mountain sunset in its ads. Wells Fargo
bank has drawn on its history as a stagecoach operator by depicting the
stagecoach in most of its late-twentieth-century marketing campaigns.
Finally, even Ivory Soap has drawn on the West to emphasize its product's effectiveness in an ad that featured a cowboy who, at the end of
his day, sets up camp only to pause in the midst of his activities to wash
his hands in the river with Ivory Soap.[30]

Chaps, Lady Stetson, Schweppes

Sometimes the use of western imagery to create advertising icons and
to sell food products has depended on the juvenile humor and cartoon-
like cuteness of the characters. Yet the West has also been used to sell a
more sophisticated style of living, a spirit that can be acquired through
the purchase of certain items. Perfumes and colognes are given western

Wells Fargo Bank advertisement. Courtesy of Wells Fargo.

names and symbols in order to promote a series of personal characteristics that can ostensibly be adopted or enhanced by wearing the advertised scent. Lady Stetson, for instance, was marketed with the figure of a woman in a Stetson hat—an article of clothing typically associated with cowboys—in its campaign. The ad's caption read "A Declaration of Independence," suggesting that a woman who wore Lady Stetson would have access to all of the benefits that were previously only available to men, specifically personal and sexual freedom. If a woman wore Lady Stetson perfume she declared her right to run her own life, a belief at the heart of American culture as suggested in the country's founding document—and the perfume's founding statement—the Declaration of Independence.[31]

What might be considered the male version of Lady Stetson, Ralph Lauren's Chaps, a cologne that is made for men, has also been marketed on the idea of freedom and independence. The difference lies in the origins of those characteristics. Whereas women who wear Lady Stetson declared their independence—which suggests that such freedom was previously unavailable to them—men who choose to wear Ralph Lauren's fragrance are reclaiming something that they always had access to but which has been lost in modern life. The ad copy states that the West is "not just stagecoaches and sagebrush. It's an image of men who are real and proud. Of the freedom and independence we all would like to feel." The use of the words "would like" implies that while men long to experience the "real and proud" manhood inherent in the western myth, they are not always able to do so. Chaps is the solution to the problem. The cologne can be "put on as naturally as a worn leather jacket or a pair of jeans"—cowboy garb that stands in stark contrast to the business attire most men are required to wear in their daily work lives. More important, Chaps is the "West you would like to feel inside of yourself," a statement reinforcing the notion that men want to be the "real" men of the Old West but that they need to adorn a scent in order to do so.[32]

Other companies have drawn on the popular images of the American West in order to advertise their products, including alcoholic and non-alcoholic beverages. Coors, originally brewed in 1873, claimed to have been made with "pure Rocky Mountain springwater," drawing on the idea of the West as a place that remains untainted by modern industry and, by association, civilization. In the 1950s, Schweppes took a different tactic in order to sell its tonic water. Over the caption "Piutes greet Big Chief Tonic Water from over the seas," Schweppes pictured a group of Indians, in their traditional dress, surrounding what appears to be a traveling salesman who is taking bottles of tonic water from his case. The Indians look on with interest as the man, who on second look seems more like a patent-medicine seller, demonstrates the benefits and good taste of the drink. The play on "Big Chief," which makes the "chief" the seller rather than the Indian, is a prime example of the advertising fads of the 1950s which represented Native Americans as gullible, backward members of U.S. culture. This ad stands in direct contrast to a television ad that ran in the 1970s and used a Native American to illustrate the impact pollution was having on the country.[33]

The American West was developed, to a large extent, through the work of early advertisers whose ads offered settlers a new life in the promised land of the frontier. At the same time, the field of advertising sharpened its skills during the period of westward expansion, when advertisers found innovative ways to persuade people to make the westward journey and buy particular products. Since the early 1900s, advertisers have used the old West as the basis for some of the field's most memorable ads, tapping into the deeply held beliefs and myths surrounding the frontier. In doing so, advertising has helped to reinforce the notion that the American West is a central aspect of American life.

4

Architecture

The popular architecture of the American frontier—from pioneer times to the present—reflects the ambition and imagination inherent in the undertaking of westward expansion. Whether temporary canvas tents or primitive, earthbound dugouts, the buildings erected by the earliest emigrants proved efficient and innovative, if not always clean and dry. The false-front structures typical of boom towns marked the widespread belief in expansion despite the short-term challenges of the undertaking. In the twentieth century, the deeply felt connection to the land, which played such a critical role in so many aspects of western life, appeared in fashionable architectural styles such as the bungalow, the ranch, and the structures produced by the Prairie School. The imagination at the core of frontier architecture lives on in popular western sites such as Disneyland and Las Vegas.[1]

THE HOMESTEAD ACT AND EARLY FRONTIER HOUSES

Prior to 1862, pioneers who wanted to establish themselves on the frontier, and to erect homes and farms there, were required to purchase plots of land directly from the government and to pay taxes on them. The financial burden of such purchases, combined with the cost of constructing buildings, plowing and farming the land, not to mention setting up community schools and governments, proved prohibitive to many potential emigrants. As a result, the free land movement, championed by Horace Greeley, was signed into law by President Abraham Lincoln on May 27, 1862. Commonly known as the Homestead Act, the measure allowed any U.S. citizen to choose a surveyed but unclaimed plot of land up to 160 acres in size. After five years of living on and cultivating the land, settlers could, for a small fee, acquire titles to their tracts. If homesteaders wanted to purchase their land after six months, they could do so for the standard price of $1.25 per acre. Alterations to the Homestead Act were passed as the nineteenth century wore on and larger areas of land were settled. While many homesteaders failed to successfully develop their land, the Homestead Act helped to propel pioneers westward, where they built structures on land previously unclaimed by White Americans, thereby changing the face of the West forever.[2]

Twelve-by-twelve Houses and Rolling Cabins

Despite what appeared to be its generous nature, the Homestead Act proved too restrictive for some settlers who were eager to make their land claims. In fact, many homesteaders found innovative ways around the restrictions and requirements of the government acts, including the erection of miniature cabins that measured twelve inches by twelve inches, instead of the mandated twelve feet by twelve feet, or houses on wheels that could be moved from one claim to another.[3] These creative departures from the norm helped settlers take advantage of the opportunities afforded them by the Homestead Act and, while essentially illegal, added to the popular lore about the American West.

Tar-Paper Shacks, Tents, Wagons, Cloth Houses

In contrast to the playful efforts of emigrants determined to claim large tracts of land, the majority of early westerners were focused on erecting structures that would provide them with the most basic forms of shelter. As one settler described it, the most rudimentary buildings were also the most common. "There were more tents and cloth houses within sight than any other kinds of dwellings," she wrote, "and it was nothing strange to see a company living in a wagon."[4] Simple shacks covered in tar paper, the same wagons that carried people west, or canvas-covered frames were among the most familiar buildings found in early western communities. Simple tents and shacks were practical given the fact that emigrants—especially during the gold rush—quickly and frequently moved from one site to another depending on the availability of gold and other minerals. Wagons and canvas houses also allowed pioneers to set up housekeeping on newly established claims while they built more permanent, if still primitive structures, such as the dugout, the sod house, and the log cabin.

"Our First Home": The Dugout and the Soddy

When western emigrants decided to end their journey, the first order of business involved building a house. Pioneers who were accustomed to homes built from wood were faced with a new challenge: to build a house on a vast plain with few, if any, trees in sight. Emigrants were resourceful, however, and the earliest frontier homes relied on the available resources of the western land. The sod house and dugout were small, one-room buildings in which all of the family's activities took place. The room could be divided by a piece of fabric or a quilt to create a semblance of privacy, but even then every square inch of these early houses was needed to serve multiple purposes, including cooking, entertaining, sleeping, and working. While pioneers were protected from the elements in their frontier homes, they were nonetheless surprised, and even dismayed, by their first experiences of living in one.

The dugout was the most rudimentary architectural design, consisting of a house that was literally dug out of the earth. Pioneers would find a hill or any embankment that they would then carve out into a living space of anywhere from ten to fourteen square feet in size. A small window and a door tended to be the only openings, and these were framed by limited amounts of available lumber. The interior of the dugout could be supported by a pole or rafters, while a single chimney or stovepipe jutted from the roof. The walls and roof were patched with grass, sod, or even manure to keep out the rain and cold. The thick insulating sod with which these homes were built, however, and the low-lying nature of the buildings, made them surprisingly adept at managing the extreme temperatures of the plains, which could range from burning hot to frigidly cold. Despite its benefits, the dugout was extremely difficult to keep clean, since all four walls, the ceiling, and the floor were made from dirt. Not only did soil and dust regularly fall onto the furniture, food, and beds within the dugout, but bugs and snakes fell from the roof as well. Many pioneers tried to keep their dugouts as clean as possible by tacking fabric to the walls and ceilings, but the fact that the house was built into the soil made the wetness and dirt an inevitable part of daily life. Moreover, because the dugout was constructed in the natural swells of the landscape, it could be difficult to locate if a traveler was unfamiliar with the surrounding landmarks or if rain or snow hampered vision.[5]

The sod house—commonly called the soddy—was a slight improvement over the dugout. Whether the soddy evolved from the dugout as a way to add space, or whether the house stood alone as a separate structure, the soddy looked slightly more like a traditional building. Built from slabs of sod that were carefully cut from the ground into brick-like pieces, the house was formed by placing sod blocks around a simple frame of door and windows. The walls were thick—typically about two

Oklahoma dugout. Courtesy of the Library of Congress.

feet in width—and the roof was made of the same strips of sod as the rest of the structure. Like the dugout, the soddy leaked when it rained and became infested by various bugs, snakes, and even rats. Bedbugs were a particular problem, as were fleas and other biting insects. Yet the sod house was a functional structure that protected its inhabitants from the ravages of winter and the heat of summer, allowing early westerners to exist in basic, though efficient, comfort during their first years in the West.

The underground dugout and early sod house were such familiar architectural styles to early westerners that songs like "Dugout Lament" and "The Little Old Sod Shanty" appeared in the popular music of the nineteenth century. The lyrics of the songs reflected the rugged conditions of these early homes, yet there was a simultaneous pride expressed in living under those conditions. For these most rudimentary of American homes symbolized the hardships pioneers endured, the resourcefulness they relied on, and the determination with which they established themselves on the frontier. In fact, despite its primitive nature, the dugout was esteemed by its owners. Many families had their pictures taken in front of their first frontier homes, and the photographs are similar. The families stand in front of houses, careful to expose to the camera windows, doors, or other objects of particular pride. Prized possessions— a piano, for instance—are moved outside and included it in the picture. Some families took pride in decorating the exteriors of their soddies, lining potted plants along windows or even hanging bird-cages—birds included—to front walls.

Throughout the twentieth century and into the twenty-first, the sod house and dugout have continued to represent pride, endurance, and independence. The fascination with underground houses underwent a brief revival in the twentieth century, when environmentalists in search of nontraditional homes promoted them as alternatives to suburban or urban living quarters. While some members of this movement claimed that "by 1985 approximately thirty percent of all housing will be underground," the demand for underground living seems to have disappeared from most Americans' definition of the dream home.[6] Although the dugout will probably never return as a widely favored style of building, it remains a symbol not only in the popular lore of the West, but in the figurative "home" of players in America's national sport of baseball.

Log Cabins and Mail-Order Houses

Log cabins were distinguished from the more polished log houses, which included hewn logs, plaster or stones to fill in the walls, and shingled roofs.[7] Cabin designs were usually imported by western immigrants, the styles originating in European countries. One of the most common frontier styles was the Finnish-influenced, single-pen cabin, commonly known as the "Anglo-Western cabin" or the "Rocky Mountain cabin." Characterized by a single gabled entrance, over which a roof projected to protect the entrance from snow or rain, the Rocky Mountain cabin closely matched the popular image of the frontier cabin and appeared in widely seen contemporary prints published by, for instance, Currier and Ives.[8] Like soddies and dugouts, cabins were constructed from available materials. In Leadville, Colorado, the sometimes haphazard completion of cabins was described by one observer as follows: "cabins wedged in between stumps; cabins with chimneys made of flowerpots or bits of stovepipe,—I am not sure but out of old hats; cabins half-roofed; cabins with sail cloth-roofs; cabins with no roof at all,—this represented the architecture of Leadville homes."[9]

While log cabins have come to stand for the rustic but homey existence of frontier families, in reality wooden houses were not as snug as they are imagined to have been. Like inhabitants of other frontier structures, however, owners of log cabins found ways to adapt to their new homes, using rag carpets, newspapers, and other fabrics to plug leaks and add comfort. The familiar story of President Abraham Lincoln's humble beginnings in a log cabin underscores the way America has adopted the log cabin as a symbol of industriousness and equal opportunity in a land where, the saying goes, anyone can be president. The idealization of the log cabin, and its association with the romantic tales of the Old West, influenced American architecture outside the frontier as well. As early as the 1880s and 1890s, summer homes across the country were charac-

William and Cora Warren ranch, North Piney, Wyoming. Sashes from
Sears, Roebuck & Co. (1900). Courtesy of the Museum of the Mountain
Man, Pinedale, Wyoming.

terized by an unfinished, log cabin style, including rustic furniture, exposed beams, and animal-skin rugs.[10]

By the 1870s, another option for pioneers was the mail-order house,
as exemplified by the portable iron house. In shape, the iron house
looked much like a log cabin, but the advertisement for the structure
emphasized the differences. Iron homes could be put together quickly
and inexpensively and they did not catch fire. They were also easy to
move, matching the desire for mobility in western life. As westward
expansion progressed, emigrants could also order by mail specific structures—for instance, window sashes and doors—to update and improve
their homes.

Furniture, Wallpaper, and Frontier Interior Decoration

Although early buildings were rustic in appearance, settlers worked
diligently to make them comfortable and welcoming inside. Since fine
furniture was not readily available, settlers made use of a range of materials to construct makeshift tables, chairs, and even walls. Moss was
used for mattresses, featherbeds were sewn to increase comfort, and tat-
tered clothing was transformed into rag rugs and bed quilts. Rush-
bottomed chairs were common, as were simple dishes and cooking
utensils. Pictures were hung on walls. Any piece of furniture or other

C. L. bunkhouse with newspapers used as wallpaper (1903). Courtesy of the Museum of the Mountain Man, Pinedale, Wyoming.

object that succeeded in making the trip west—a piano, tea set, birdcage, or set of china dishes—was carefully and proudly displayed in even the most primitive dugout. A Bible was also a prized item and was not only read, but exhibited on a designated shelf.

Settlers were especially interested in covering the walls of their houses, both to help keep the interior dry and warm and to brighten up the drab coloring of the wood or sod. Some women made their own versions of wallpaper from old clothes or blankets. Other emigrants recycled paper used for other purposes. On their journey west a couple stopped at a ranch and found the walls covered in pages of the *Police Gazette*, which boasted pictures of scantily clad women.[11] Magazines of any kind—mail-order catalogs, newspapers, journals—served the same purpose as the *Police Gazette*, covering the sod or unfinished wood with a wallpaper like no other. As communities became more established, however, printed wallpaper was also used, as were other prefabricated materials.

As time went by, Victorian trends in interior decorating made their way west, resulting in homes that displayed the popular styles of the period. A heavily decorated room was the primary result, as the following description of an ideal Victorian dining room indicated. "Rich colors, deeply tufted sofas, machine-carved furniture in Turkish or Queen Anne styles, large pictures with ornate gold moldings, fancy wallpaper with complex borders at the top, and elegant patterned rugs" were the basis for the traditional middle-class home.[12] Velvet drapes, whatnot shelves, and ornate stoves were also common, as were Japanese prints and objects. Elaborate chandeliers and candlesticks were typical. Far into the frontier, contemporary decorating trends were evident.

Western interior design drew national attention in the early 1900s when designers like Thomas Canada Molesworth created distinct, rustic furniture. Molesworth began the Shoshone Furniture Company in Cody, Wyoming, in 1931, and his furniture was quickly recognized for incorporating the western dude ranch style sought by vacationers. The designer was commissioned to furnish hotels in Montana and Wyoming, as well Buffalo Bill's former ranch, the TE Ranch, the Rockefeller ranch, and Dwight D. Eisenhower's den.[13]

Open Ranges, Barbed-Wire Fences, and the Corral

The extension of most frontier houses was the land around them, from what could be considered the front yard to the areas used to pen livestock. As a result of the Homestead Act, pioneers were able to claim relatively large pieces of land. The challenge involved how to enclose that land without having access to the timber needed to build lengthy wooden fences. Hedges were one of the most popular solutions, and emigrants planted hedges in strategic places so that livestock could be contained and land plots demarcated. Hedges became obsolete, however, when Joseph Farwell Glidden, a De Kalb, Illinois, farmer, came across a county fair exhibit of barbed wire created by Henry M. Rose. Seeing the wire's potential, Glidden improved upon its design by adding short pieces of twisted wire that were wrapped at intervals around the double strands of wire fencing. The result was an effective, inexpensive fence that seemed to solve the problems of how to enclose the wide-open spaces of the West. The invention was patented by Glidden in 1873 and barbed wire became, almost overnight, a marketplace success. Competitors tried to develop alternative styles and the wire was eagerly purchased by homesteaders across the frontier.[14]

Widespread use of barbed wire significantly changed the face of the West. No longer could livestock escape or grazing herds ruin farmlands. The wide-open spaces of the plains became well-defined pastures, much to the benefit of farmers. Yet not everyone was happy with the use of wire fencing. Cattle drives could no longer take place, animals were often seriously cut by the sharp fences, and previously accessible land was no longer available. Some people rebelled and, in keeping with the frontier phrase "Don't Fence Me In," sought to maintain the open range of the Old West by cutting fences. In the end, the invention of barbed wire marked a major turning point in the development of the West, enabling farmers to cultivate their lands in efficient ways that would have been impossible without it.

The cousin of the barbed-wire fence, the corral, was a wooden pen used to hold horses and other livestock. The term also referred to the circle made by pioneers who, while traveling west, rounded up as many wagons as possible in the shape of a circle. They did so to protect themselves from attacks by animals and Indians, and to keep cattle and horses from escaping. The corral is mythologized in one of the most notorious of all western tales: Wyatt Earp's shoot-out at the O.K. Corral.

Tepees and Wigwams

Like many other aspects of Native American culture, the tepee, also know as the wigwam, became a stereotypical shape in the world of frontier architectural styles. Used only by some Native American peoples, primarily those living on the Great Plains, the basic tepee consisted of poles arranged in a conical shape and covered with animal skins or bark. The popular assumption that all Native Americans lived in tepees disregarded the variety of cultures within the Native American population and the resulting differences in architectural styles among their homes. The stereotype was powerful, however, and toward the end of the 1800s actually resulted in a decorating trend that reflected various American Indian motifs. Like the log cabin, the tepee seemed to mark a uniquely American, though curiously exotic, style of dwelling and it has been thoroughly absorbed into popular culture.[15] By the early twentieth century, for example, a brochure for the first dude ranch, the Eaton Ranch located in Wolf, Wyoming, stated: "The tents of the ladies and the gentlemen are carefully segregated for mutual comfort . . . and a special row of tepees is arranged for married couples."[16] Visual images of Native American life—from dime novels to early westerns—have further reinforced this simplistic understanding of common American Indian structures. To advertise both their history and authenticity, museums and other tourist attractions in western states commonly erect a tepee on their lawns.[17]

FRAME, STONE, AND BRICK BUILDINGS

As communities became established, and settlers had a chance to spend time on construction, permanent and durable structures were erected. From ranches to bungalows, the impact of western architecture on the rest of the United States has been remarkably strong, incorporating a regional flare with a respect for the land that has made such structures truly original.

Victorian Influences, Mormon Architecture, and the Beehive

The architectural trends of Victorian America found their way west in many forms, often through widely published architectural plan books, and the popular magazines that were circulated in the second half of the nineteenth century. As a result, buildings based on Italianate, Greek Revival, and Gothic architecture appeared throughout the West, especially in the last decades of the nineteenth century. Rich and poor alike adopted designs promoted in magazines and plan books, creating larger and smaller versions of the same house depending on the owner's income. Grand, central staircases, welcoming front halls, decorative wooden moldings, and patterned veneer flooring (known as "wood rugs") were features of this trend and, though clearly eastern imports, they played a role in the design of many western towns.[18]

The Mormon communities that sprung up around Salt Lake City embraced much of the Victorian philosophy of housing and followed designs promoted in the popular pattern books of the time. With an expressed "antipathy to nature," early Mormon settlers created homes from raw materials finished in ways that emphasized decorative, handcrafting principles. Logs, for instance, "were usually sawed or hewn square and were thus deprived of their identity as round trees," while "organic irregularities of stone were chiseled into a smooth regularity of pattern pleasing to the settler's eye."[19] Mormon builders adapted several specific styles for their homes—central-hall, double-pen, temple form, and hall and parlor—but owners personalized the structures with individually designed dormer windows.

On both the interior and exterior of many Mormon buildings could be found the shape of a beehive or the image of an eye, two key symbols in Mormon life. The beehive represented the "industry, harmony, order and frugality of the people, and the sweet results of their toil, union and intelligent cooperation."[20] Newel posts and doorknobs were carved like beehives and the symbol could be found on many local buildings, including leader Brigham Young's house. The beehive has remained a cultural motif for the Mormons. In Utah it is represented on the official state seal as well as being the logo of institutions like Brigham Young University and the Utah State Highway Patrol.[21] The beehive is also featured on road signs around the state. The all-seeing eye has not fared as well as a popular symbol. In the early decades of the Mormon settlement the eye, "which exhibited God's interest in all of man's endeavors, was often used on buildings, periodicals, and certificates" in order to signify Christ's second coming.[22] The eye was adopted by groups like the Masons, but it also appeared over Mormon-owned businesses as a way to encourage Mormons to support their own economic development rather than shop at stores owned by people from other religious backgrounds.

The Prairie School and the Bungalow

While trends in Victorian architecture traveled from the eastern states to the frontier, some of the strongest reactions against their ornate nature originated, and flourished, in the West. More specifically, a philosophy of functionality and simplicity developed in the 1890s, and its leading proponents had western roots. The use of, and emphasis on, natural materials like stone and wood provided a fresh form of decoration—one that countered the artificial decorations of Victorian times. Similarly, cleaner, simpler lines replaced the ornate carvings and patterns of Victorian moldings and frames. Plain white plaster, as opposed to dark, patterned paper, covered the walls. Finally, the new designs emphasized the importance of buildings that fit in with the environment. Rather than underscoring the fact that they were manufactured, such structures, it was argued, should be part of the landscape, should blend, for example, with the rolling prairies rather than stand out against them.[23] The Prairie School, promoted by Louis Sullivan and Frank Lloyd Wright, was a prime example of this new architectural philosophy. As its name suggests, the Prairie School sought ways to create connections between a building and the land around it. While most architects consider the Prairie School a serious—as opposed to a "popular"—movement, Wright in particular has become something of a popular icon and his designs can be found on anything from umbrellas to men's ties.[24]

The early 1900s saw a popularization of these reforms in architecture, especially in California's widespread adoption of the bungalow-style house.[25] A practical and affordable example of the ideals promoted by prominent designers, the bungalow had simple lines, could be constructed from materials native to the state in which it was built, and used space efficiently in a relatively small interior. The bungalow became so popular in the first half of the twentieth century that most magazines—including *Women's Home Companion* and *Ladies Home Journal*—included drawings of the new design in their pages. In addition to meeting the new desire for simplicity and function, the bungalow also captured the growing fascination Americans had with the West as reflected in the popularity of western radio programs and movies, as well as the growing national interest in western tourism.

The bungalow craze caught on so well—especially in suburban Chi-

A Western ranch house (between 1887 and 1893). Courtesy of the Library of Congress.

cago, Boise, and Salt Lake City—that manufacturers began producing prefabricated versions. The "Take Down House," for instance, was a three-room bungalow that could be transported from one location to the next, providing its owners with a portable house that was as much a vacation home as a permanent residence. The connection between the bungalow and nature, especially in the West, was so strong that Sears, Roebuck even offered a prefabricated model of the house that was called the "Yellowstone."[26]

Ranch Houses

Another popular style of house that originated in the West was the ranch. The ranch had its roots in the simple adobe structures, topped by a flat roof, that were commonly found in southern California and parts of the Southwest. In California the roof was altered from a flat to a pitched angle in order to protect the home from water left after heavy rains. Over the course of the nineteenth century, the ranch gained a front veranda, a finished floor, and a black tarred roof. Yet the basic struc-ture—a rectangular-shaped, single-story building—remained essentially the same. A slight variation, the Texas ranch, was built from wood and consisted of what amounted to two separate log cabins set some distance apart, with the space between them covered by a single roof that ran the entire length of the building. The ranch was the style adopted by many western ranchers, and it has appeared on the set of multiple westerns as "typical."[27]

In the 1950s the ranch experienced a renaissance, matching the cultural interest in western life with the desire to adopt a western-style home. The fifties-style ranch was characterized by its single-story structure topped by a low-pitched roof. Like the bungalow, the ranch was popular in California and reflected the simple, out-door stereotype of California life. Unlike the bungalow, however, which remained one of the most popular architectural styles until the 1930s, the ranch was promoted on the basis of its interior floor plan and its modern ability to bring outside and inside into closer contact. Sliding glass doors, plate-glass windows, and patios enabled homeowners to feel more in touch with the outdoors. In addition, the interior space was more open, allowing rooms to serve multiple uses, and built-in closets and cabinets provided for efficient use of space.[28]

Ranches and Recluses

With the rise of tourism, ranches also came to stand for rustic resort facilities, places to which busy families could escape the pressures of modern life and return to a more basic existence. Dude ranches gained popularity in the 1930s as Americans embarked on the new national pastime of touring their own country. Early dude ranches provided only basic amenities and promised visitors the authentic experience of living in western-style structures and participating in the daily life of a working ranch. Later such facilities became more luxurious, though they retained their "back-to-the-wilderness" feel through rustic buildings and furnishings.[29] In the 1990s, the popular definition of the ranch shifted again when Hollywood personalities such as Michael Keaton, Meg Ryan, Glenn Close, and Jane Fonda built large, ranch-style homes in the western states of Montana and Wyoming.[30] Ironically, the reason the stars gave for moving was the desire to escape from the urban life offered them in southern California, the home of the original ranch-style architecture.

BOOMTOWNS, CHINATOWNS, AND GHOST TOWNS

The architecture of the frontier cannot be discussed without mentioning the boomtown and the ghost town. Boomtowns, communities that sprung up overnight across the West, appeared at sites purported to be rich in gold, silver, and other minerals. As gold seeker Franklin Buck wrote:

Downieville is one of the richest mining towns in the State. Upwards of $2,000,000 has been dug there this season by some three or four thousand men. The last 50 miles of the way to Downieville is only a mule trail, no wagons are

The opening of Oklahoma. Guthrie, 1889. Courtesy of the Library of Congress.

seen in the streets, everything is packed and yet in this "hole in the ground" as it is called, you will find two hundred buildings, two saw mills, a theatre and all the necessaries of life and cheap, too, for this country.[31]

The contrast between the solitary mule trail and the bustling town typified the rise of boomtowns throughout the West. Makeshift buildings would appear within hours in previously uninhabited locations, and in no time a small town would be bustling with people eager to make their fortunes. Marked by buildings hastily thrown together in close proximity and with little deliberate town planning, boomtowns generally grew up around a central street. Merchants occupied many of these makeshift structures, providing townspeople with all forms of goods and services, including gambling saloons, taverns, brothels, newspaper offices, and the all-American general store. Temporary governments also developed in boomtowns, where outlaws made their names and gambling, drinking, and prostitution thrived. The typical boomtown appears as the setting of many films, stories, and folklore about the Wild West, from the opening scenes of *Stagecoach* to the successful *Tombstone*, named after just such a town. In their time, Deadwood, Dodge City, Carson City, and Tombstone were recognized across the country as the most notorious boomtowns and, therefore, some of the most symbolic places in the Old West.[32]

Among the boomtowns settled by White, western European, and Mexican peoples were also communities known as Chinatowns. Predecessors of the urban Chinatowns that mark cities like San Francisco, Los Angeles,

Chicago, New York, and Boston, early western Chinatowns provided Chinese immigrants with a place in which to celebrate traditional holidays and ceremonies. The exploitation of Chinese laborers in the West, and the prejudice expressed against them by non-Chinese westerners, led Chinatowns to have unsavory and immoral reputations. Today, urban Chinatowns are home to many people of Asian background, but they also function as tourist attractions, especially in cities with large Chinese populations like San Francisco.

While most boomtowns ambitiously sought to establish themselves as permanent communities in the American West, the majority of them were abandoned as quickly as they were founded. A mining town that was no longer profitable for miners, for instance, could disappear overnight, as one westerner described: "The next morning there appeared in monstrous, white, chalked letters, on the side of the big flume, the words, 'Dried Up.' . . . Soon, tents were struck, houses taken down, stores broken up, and the once busy mining 'Bar' was almost deserted."[33] Once the mines dried up, or the railroad drew settlers to new locations, many boomtowns became ghost towns, left to deteriorate with few, if any, inhabitants.

If boomtowns became ghost towns by virtue of being abandoned, they were not forgotten by either American culture or American tourism. Some towns, like Grafton, Utah, became the locations for films like *Butch Cassidy and the Sundance Kid*. Other ghost towns, capitalizing on the romantic history of the West—and in particular the towns that formed the center of early Western life—have been reinvigorated. Cripple Creek, Colorado, for instance, has kept and restored much of its original frontier architecture, making it an attraction for travelers in search of a taste of the Old West. Central City, Colorado, has also restored its original buildings, as well as its original form of entertainment, gambling. Similarly, Telluride, Colorado, has used its frontier-like main street to become a trendy ski resort in which vacationers dine and shop in western-style structures. From boomtown to ghost town and sometimes back again, the buildings of frontier towns have retained their prominence in American culture as physical reminders of the early days of westward expansion when anything was thought to be possible.[34]

False-Front Buildings

One of the most easily recognized architectural styles of the boomtown was the false-front building. From original photographs to Hollywood films, the false-front structures of Main Street were hallmarks of frontier towns. Constructed to look like an established building, with windows and cornices included, the false front was exactly that: a flat front wall that was attached to a simpler structure behind it. Other elements of the

Abandoned buildings on the main street of a ghost town. Eureka, Colorado (1940). Courtesy of the Library of Congress.

false-front building included a portico, or low roof, hung over the wooden sidewalk, protecting it—and people on it—from sun, rain, and snow. The raised sidewalk kept pedestrians from getting their shoes too muddy or dusty. If the building had more than one floor, an outside stairway provided access from the ground to the second story, permitting tenants or customers to come and go without passing through the first floor. False-front structures were built of whatever materials were available and housed the essential institutions of the frontier town, especially the saloon, general store, and livery, as well as the offices of the town newspaper and the local attorneys. False fronts were frequently built in different architectural styles and hung with signs in order to help passersby distinguish one building from the next.

False-front buildings stood for the hopeful spirit in which early western towns were established, but they were also extremely practical, especially given the unpredictable nature of western communities. As one woman described, "most of the buildings were of flimsy construction and were taken down and put up again wherever the railroad made its next stop."[35] The plain faces of the structures were hung with signs that not only informed people what service or good could be obtained inside, but which also added a unique look to the frontier's version of Main Street.

Boardinghouses, Hotels, and Saloons

Other key buildings are worth noting for their contributions to popular conceptions of the frontier. As an alternative to sleeping in a wagon, dugout, or cabin, travelers used to pay to lodge overnight in one of the numerous boardinghouses or hotels that grew up around western towns and trails. Early boardinghouses were essentially pioneer cabins whose owners were willing to take in travelers overnight, sometimes for a small fee but often in exchange for little more than the traveler's stories and company. A step up from staying in someone's home was to pay to sleep in a rustic tavern, usually a small log cabin, which might contain a loft in which to house passersby. Basic in every way, including dirt floors that were only slightly improved upon by planking, the earliest taverns served the simplest of needs. As increasing numbers of emigrants crossed the continent, however, taverns located in strategic places along the trails were expanded to include a bar or a dining area. Sleeping space was often limited to a few rooms and even fewer beds, so travelers found themselves in close quarters with strangers and with little, if any, privacy. Bed linens were not typically available and travelers who wanted such luxuries had to bring their own bedrolls with them. Bedbugs and other insects were a common problem that was only aggravated by the fact that most people chose to sleep fully clothed, thereby leaving behind them any foreign materials they were carrying and taking with them anything they picked up.

Generally, accomodations in public lodgings met only the simplest needs of weary travelers, as the following description by a woman who was traveling west illustrates. As you reached the top of the stairs, she wrote:

you found yourself in a hall extending the whole length of the building, and of just sufficient width to allow a passage by the side of the stairway to the front end. The partitions on each side were wholly cloth, and, at distances of about four feet apart along the whole length of the hall, on both sides, were narrow doorways. Looking into one of these doorways, you saw before you a space about two and a half feet wide and six feet long, at the farther end of which was a shelf or stand, on which you could place a candlestick. . . . At the side of this space were two berths, one above the other; and these berths, so situated, were the only sleeping accommodations afforded by this hotel.[36]

Another basic form of housing was available in the unusual form of the "prairie monitor, or dugout, built underground and connected to stables by a subterranean passage. Dugway, 100 miles west of Salt Lake City, was the most famous."[37]

Related to the tavern was the saloon, a structure embedded in myths of the Old West. A general description of a frontier saloon follows:

The saloon may be a single-roomed plank cabin, neatly papered. On the wall may hang pictures of Abraham Lincoln and General Garfield, with a few comic sporting prints. A bar runs part of the way up the room, and is spotlessly clean; behind this counter against the wall are a few shelves decorated with specimen-bottles of wine, spirits, etc.; underneath, sugar, lemons, and ice, if these luxuries are attainable; a stove, three or four chairs, a bucket of water with a dipper, complete the furniture.[38]

Other common features included a gilt mirror hung behind the bar, a billiards table, a gambling table, a piano, and a place to dance. During the Spanish-American War, red, white, and blue decorations were hung from the walls as were sporting prints and other pictures. The "most widely distributed of all saloon pictures, F. Otto Becker's *Custer's Last Fight*" ended up in virtually every saloon when, "in 1896 the Anheuser-Busch Brewing Company . . . [gave away] more than 150,000 copies" of the print.[39]

In wealthier communities the interior of the saloon was even more decorative. Walls were wainscoted on the bottom while "the upper portion [was] covered with paper displaying abstract designs, gilt flowers, or such classical scenes as an allegorical treatment of the four seasons. A frieze, a stile, and corner pieces contributed to an ornate, neoclassical appearance. Paintings and French plate mirrors adorned the walls, while chandeliers lighted the tables and bar."[40] The bar itself was central to saloon design. In communities not yet fully established, where the saloon might be housed under nothing more than a tent, the bar was one of the most noteworthy features in town, even if it was makeshift. In more established communities, with sturdier, more permanent buildings, the bar could be elaborately carved and polished while the mirror and shelves standing behind it became the centerpiece of the saloon's social life.

Unlike taverns, the saloon did not provide overnight housing for travelers. Those who sought an alternative to the rustic accommodations of boardinghouses and taverns, and who were lucky enough to have some money to spend, could stay the night in some of the West's landmark hotels. As early as 1859, the Menger Hotel in San Antonio, Texas, opened its doors. The Menger is known not only for its proximity to another famous western structure, the Alamo, but for its association with Theodore Roosevelt, who is said to have sat at the hotel's bar along with some of his Rough Riders. With its Spanish-influenced architecture, including an open lobby, two-story verandah, and private rooms, the Menger was a place of comfort for weary travelers. The architectural style of hotels differed from place to place. Some were simple structures that fit in with the false-front buildings of the main street. Others, like the La Fonda in Santa Fe, New Mexico, were built in the Spanish colonial tradition while still others, like Cliff House in San Francisco, Hotel Del Coronado in San Diego, and Hotel Laramie in Laramie, Wyoming, were large, majestic buildings meant to house many people in the best of style.[41]

Forts, Theaters, and Other Frontier Buildings

The range of architectural styles from the Mississippi, through the Great Plains, to the Pacific ocean, is vast. However, several additional types of buildings were commonly seen throughout the westward expansion period. Early on, forts were the outposts of the American government and provided some of the only refuges from weather, animals, and threatening Indians. Forts took many architectural forms, depending on the materials available to build them. In the Southwest, forts tended to be adobe-style buildings like the Alamo, while in northern regions they were more likely to be made of timber. The structure of a fort was aimed at defense. Some forts were shaped as four simple blockhouses connected by four log walls to create an enclosed square. Other forts were simply rows of barrack-like garrisons or houses meant to provide shelter to troops and other travelers.

As boomtowns and other communities sprung up, additional structures also made an appearance. Theaters, for instance, were either built into saloons or stood on their own in the popular false-front style of western towns. Known as opera houses, many of these buildings still exist today. The Bird Cage Theater in Tombstone, Arizona, for instance, is a tourist attraction, boasting 140 holes made from bullets during Tombstone's heyday. The Bird Cage is a one-story adobe building built with a low, flat, false front and three arched doorways. The popular site provided entertainment in the form of honky-tonk and cancan dancing. Boxes known as "bird cages" hung above the floor, each housing a woman. In contrast to the Bird Cage, other western theaters were modeled on those found in the East, and included domed ceilings, multilevel seating, and walls painted in vibrant colors edged in gold.[42]

ADOBE AND TERRITORIAL STYLES

The American Southwest, with its warm, dry climate, developed its own popular styles of architecture during westward expansion. Prior to the influx of emigrants, southwestern buildings tended to be made of adobe, with arches forming simple doors and windows. Influenced by Spanish architecture, these early structures were made of adobe brick with flat, earth-packed roofs.

As pioneers moved across the Southwest, a new type of architecture, known as the Territorial style, became predominant in the region. A variation of the Greek Revivalism favored by builders in the East in the early decades of the 1900s, early Territorialism (1848–1865) was characterized by the use of sawn lumber and windows paned with glass. These materials had not been available prior to westward expansion and their appearance in the Southwest changed the structures that existed in that region. The use of square beams and simple window frames also marked this first stage. The Middle Territorial Era (1865–1880) continued to reflect newly available materials but in more dramatic ways. Numerous new forts were built during these years, consisting of the traditional adobe walls but including more complex wooden trim around the glass windows and doors. Two-story homes, fronted by wide, covered, two-level verandahs were also commonly seen with numerous windows flanking a central door. The door and the windows were outlined in relatively wide wooden frames that were sometimes carved in symmetrical designs.[43] A variation on the popular architecture of the period included the Gothic Revival forms, also known as Folk Gothic or Gothick which included design aspects of the Middle Ages, such as sharply pointed church spires and roof trim.

Finally, designs of the Late Territorial period (1880–1920) differed from earlier trends because they included classical details and decorative carvings, especially on doors. With the appearance of the railroad, the Southwest was infiltrated by multiple architectural forms, such as Italianate, Queen Anne, Colonial Revival, and World's Fair Classic.[44] Other southwestern designs included the mission church, low buildings constructed around open-air patios and distinguished by covered arcades and heavy, tiled roofs.

"Remember the Alamo!" . . . "Yo Quiero Taco Bell"

Popular culture has embraced the architecture of the Southwest, offering simplified versions of adobe structures to American tourists, viewers, and consumers alike. The fall of the Alamo has been commemorated by turning the adobe building where the event took place into a national landmark and popular tourist attraction. While the entire fort draws visitors to San Antonio, Texas, it is the main structure itself—which tourists walk through to reach the rest of the site—that people come to see. Featured in numerous films, from Hitchcock's *Vertigo* to Steve Martin's *Three Amigos*, the mission church, the adobe pueblo, and the Territorial-style fort form some of the most familiar styles in southwestern buildings. Finally, the popular fast-food chain Taco Bell models its restaurants on the traditional adobe structure.

FROM FRONTIER TO FRONTIERLAND: POPULAR WESTERN SPACES

Whether from necessity, innovation, or desire, the architecture of the American West has resulted in building styles that can be easily recognized as originating on the frontier. The same impulses that drove emigrants west—ambition, adventure, freedom—seem to have had a lasting impact on the region, an impact evident in twentieth-century monuments of popular architecture. Symbolized by the World's Columbian Exposition of 1893, which itself exhibited a range of architectural styles, the West is marked by the presence of institutions that are unique in design and purpose, many of which arise directly from the cultural heritage of the Old West.

Las Vegas

Las Vegas is among the most unique of American cities, a never-closed town where visitors can gamble everywhere, in major casinos like Caesar's Palace as well as in small laundromats and convenience stores. The architecture of Las Vegas is striking in its flamboyance and its lack of unity. A hodgepodge of architectural styles, the only common characteristic of Las Vegas architecture is the fact that the structures, in particular the casinos, blend multiple forms into a single building. "The complex program of Caesars Palace," for instance,

includes gambling, dining and banqueting rooms, nightclubs and auditoria, stores, and a complete hotel. It is also a combination of styles. The front colonnade is San Pietro-Bernini in plan but Yamasaki in vocabulary and scale . . . the blue and gold mosaic work is Early Christian tomb of Galla Placidia. . . . Beyond and above is a slab of Gio Ponti Pirelli-Baroque, and beyond that, in turn, a low wing in Neoclassical Motel Moderne.[45]

Not only do the styles differ within a single building, but they also differ between buildings. Among the designs that can be seen on the Las Vegas Strip alone are Miami Moroccan, Moorish Tudor, Bauhaus Hawaiian, and Art Moderne, to name just a few.[46]

Despite its contemporary existence and its relatively young history as the gambling capital of the United States, Las Vegas contains many specific references to its frontier history. The confusion of styles, for instance, recalls the false-front buildings of early western towns, where different forms stood side by side in the ready-made appearance of an established community.[47] The large fluorescent signs, clustered down the Las Vegas Strip, can be imagined without their electric bulbs as related to the simpler, but no less conspicuous, signs of early boomtowns. Such signs are not dissimilar to those hung on the fronts of early western buildings. They "are bigger in scale and higher outside than inside in order to dominate" their setting and draw people to the interior of the building.[48] The names of casinos such as The Golden Nugget and the Frontier even more explicitly remind visitors of Las Vegas's place in American western history. Indeed, the thematic nature of most casinos and nightspots encourages the illusion of entering a different place or time. Becoming part of the Wild West upon entrance to the Frontier casino makes visiting Las Vegas an experience not just about gambling but of transforming oneself, temporarily, from everyday existence to fantasyland.

Disneyland

Las Vegas is not the only western institution designed to provide fantasy-like experiences for its visitors. Disneyland, established in the 1950s in Anaheim, California, was the brainchild of Walter Elias Disney. Born in Chicago in 1901, Disney began his life just as the frontier was said to be officially "closed." He was raised in the town of Marceline, Missouri, and elements of his small-town, western upbringing can be easily found in features of the Magic Kingdom. Main Street, the fantastically cheery entrance to Disneyland, mirrors main street architecture found throughout America. Even more dramatically, the inclusion of Frontierland as one of several "lands" that visitors can experience at the park underscores the place the West holds in American culture. Frontierland's attractions include predictable icons of the Wild West: Cottonwood Creek Ranch, Fort Comstock and Legends of the Wild West, Pueblo Trading Post, The Lucky Nugget Saloon, and Thunder Mesa Mercantile underscore how integrated western architecture is in American popular culture.[49]

The West is home to other architectural sites that reflect a similar ambition that seems to prevail throughout the region.[50] Even during westward expansion, Salt Lake City's Mormon Tabernacle proved a structural wonder. The center of religious life for the Mormon church, the Tabernacle took forty years to complete and holds enough seating for 10,000 people. Built of massive blocks of granite that had to be imported from miles away, the building was completed in 1892. Towering above the rest of Salt Lake City, the building is capped by a tremendous dome that, rumor has it, was inspired by Mormon leader Brigham Young's reflection that "the best sounding board in the world [is] ... the roof of my mouth."[51]

5

Fashion

There is no easier way to evoke the era of westward expansion than through the clothing that has come to symbolize the pioneers, cowboys, and Native Americans who lived during that time period. Whether sunbonnets, calico dresses, war bonnets, chaps, cowboy hats, or bandanas, the clothing of westward expansion was originally designed to allow for maximum durability and protection in a harsh, unpredictable environment. When pioneers set out on the westward journey, they often brought popular eastern fashions with them, only to find that such clothing served no purpose on the trip or in their new home. Nonetheless, frontier life devised its own fashion trends and fads. Throughout the period, an interest in style tied emigrants to eastern civilization and their fashion resourcefulness helped them to adapt to a demanding land. Western clothes began to symbolize a romanticized version of the West when actors in Wild West Shows and early Hollywood films donned them for their performances. Other frontier garments have been repackaged, if only in name, into popular American products. Throughout the twentieth century, western clothes went in and out of mainstream fashion, yet they have continually symbolized the individualism, industry, and perseverance at the heart of the westward enterprise.

FROM FASHION TO FUNCTION

While emigrants left the East aware of the prevailing fashion trends that marked the period, the rigorous journey west soon replaced interest in fashion with interest in survival. Early guidebooks discussed the typical clothing that emigrants packed for the trip, but such styles were soon swapped for makeshift clothing sewn from whatever fabric was available and based on functional, as opposed to fashionable, patterns. Nevertheless, popular clothing and fabrics did appear throughout the frontier, as did interesting efforts to adapt the trends of the East to rugged western life.[1] The diaries and personal accounts of the Old West reveal an ongoing interest in fashion, especially by women, and western townspeople were relatively quick to bring the most recent clothing styles to the frontier. Yet the reality of frontier life made keeping up with trends challenging at best, and emigrants frequently created unique clothing styles that were more appropriate to their surroundings.

Travel Clothes, Calico, and the Realities of Western Life

The popularity of guidebooks written for emigrants setting out on the westward journey led to a common list of clothing packed by many travelers. Guidebooks gave advice on what clothes to pack and how much to bring given the trip's duration and demands. As one guidebook author suggested:

I would advise you also if you want to take any dry good with to get a large lot of cotton Hdkfs Some Blue calico and lots of small beeds and all Shuch little Trinkets but for you own use get Shoes & Boots enought to last you at least two years & lots of Sattenetts or Home made Jeanes but all these artikles if you have the money you can get them here cheapter than you can in Springfield for the reason the merchants keep all Shuch things expresly for the emegrants and they do not sell well to any body else.[2]

As the author states, simple fabrics and articles were needed for the trip and multiple copies of some items, such as shoes, were necessary given the wear and tear that emigrants would face. Despite these suggestions, however, travelers typically brought their fine eastern clothes with them, only to discover how inappropriate they were for both the journey and the process of settling in the West. In general, the more fashionable the finery, the less durable it was and the more quickly it had to be replaced.

Many pioneer diaries describe how eastern fashions were discarded through a practical recognition that style was less important than usefulness. As a result, travelers invented forms of clothes that proved more durable and effective in their new environment. The trend toward darker colors and fabrics, like calico and muslin, that were more durable and easy to care for, marked the popular fashion of the westward journey and settlement. A pioneer woman explained the rationale behind such trends when she wrote that "the ideal morning dress for women who do their own work is of calico, not so dark as to be gloomy in its suggestions, nor so light as to show every spot that may happen to soil it.

It is simply but tastefully made, so that laundering it will not be too difficult or tedious, and so that it will not be too nice to wear every day."[3] Whereas life in the East allowed the luxury of following fashion fads from season to season, early settlers defined style in keeping with their existence.

Although women were more outspoken about their new definitions of style, men too were struck by the change they underwent as they moved across the country. One man wrote in a letter home: "You speak of looking at my picture . . . It will give you a faint idea of me now. I have not put a razor to my face since leaving N.Y. It is not the fashion here, for it would cost a dollar. Dirty shirts are all the fashion as it would cost $12 per dozen to have them washed."[4] He comments in a later letter that he washes his own clothes, has traded white shirts for calico patterns and red flannel, and has recognized the frontier fashion trend of wearing buckskin.[5]

While the dependence on fashion trends was impractical, the fact that so many emigrants commented on their clothing suggests that there was continued interest in what was being worn in the East. More specifically, there was curiosity about how newly devised western tastes differed from those "back in the States." Women sent letters eastward inquiring about what was in vogue and detailed descriptions of dress patterns were exchanged through the mail. When easterners visited their western friends and relatives, eastern clothing styles were scrutinized, discussed, and copied. Clothing was also used as a kind of keepsake or reminder of loved ones from whom pioneers were separated, and women sent bits of fabric back and forth across the country as a form of maintaining connections. Whether discussion of fashion trends, details about clothing being sewn and worn, or pieces of fabric, clothing was a topic that women in particular used to keep them emotionally connected to the homes they had left behind.

Makeshift Materials

The transition from eastern to western life required novel definitions of style, and a different understanding of material resources. In order to survive the westward journey, not to mention the process of settling in territory with limited access to provisions such as clothes, frontier men and women created their own trends by being resourceful and creative. Using what one had—whether that meant turning the remnants of an old dress into curtains or a burlap sack into pants—was a mark of pioneer innovation and is documented in many descriptions of life in the West. For the earliest pioneers in particular, the recycling of clothing had surprising, but also life-saving, results as it allowed settlers to stay warm and dry under some of the most difficult conditions.

Hand-Me-Downs and Burlap Sacks

Unlike the habits of easterners, which allowed individuals to replace clothing from one season to the next, westerners needed to get as much use as they could out of the clothes they brought with them across the country. Such necessity resulted in the common practice of wearing hand-me-downs, which meant that clothing outgrown by one person—whether a child or an adult—was passed along to someone else who could use it. If there was no one to give an item to, or, as was more often the case, no one from whom to receive a needed piece of clothing, existing clothes were relentlessly recycled in creative ways. Dresses were taken apart and recut in the same style to fit another wearer. Pieces of shirts, shawls, and blankets were cut down to make clothing for children. Lace was used for curtains. Petticoats were torn apart to line cabin walls. Even the smallest scraps of fabric were saved to make quilts that would keep families warm during cold winters. Existing clothes were also patched and reinforced so that they lasted as long as possible. "Foxing" was a method commonly used by cowboys to reinforce store-bought trousers.[6] If there was any way to keep fabric in circulation, it was done.

Like the used clothing that was recycled and recut to make new clothes, unusual materials were resorted to in an effort to keep settlers clothed. One of the few sources of new fabric came in the form of burlap sacks used to store food goods such as flour. For pioneer women in desperate need of fabric from which to make new clothes, those sacks were used to construct everything from pants and undergarments to baby clothes. One emigrant wrote that "Someone had said that the real pioneer in Kansas didn't wear any underwear, but this was not true of the Ellis County pioneer, and the clothes lines with undergarments advertising I.M. Yost's High Patent Flour were the best evidence."[7] In the face of limited material resources, pioneers were especially creative, forming, in the process, their own popular methods of making, and remaking, clothing.

Sunbonnets, Bare Feet, and Moccasins

In addition to recycling existing clothing, westerners developed their own forms of popular fashion, unique to their environment and based on the realities of frontier existence. One of the most familiar pieces of frontier apparel was the sunbonnet, which was "the badge of the American farm woman."[8] The widespread adoption of sunbonnets rose not simply from the desire women had to protect themselves from the pain of sunburn, but from the general trend toward keeping skin as pale in color as possible. Because being tan was negatively associated with the color of Native American skin, pioneer women were especially fearful of being browned by the sun. In addition to the sunbonnet that provided protection for the face, women covered other exposed parts of their bodies, such as their arms, with creative fashions like stockings with the feet cut out.[9]

If the use of stockings underwent dramatic change, the use of shoes was also altered. Many pioneers recorded that going barefoot was a widespread practice during the warm months. An alternative to bare feet was a pair of moccasins, and travelers recorded buying or trading for pairs of these durable, comfortable shoes to replace their own which wore out on the journey. More than just useful, however, moccasins became a fashion item in their own right. Helen Carpenter wrote in detail about how she acquired her own pair:

Reel went down the hill and took supper with the French men and their squaws. He traded a pair of shoes that he did not want for a pair of nice moccasins for me. They were made by the Utes and are much nicer then the Sioux Indians make as they put on soles of buffalo hide with stitches half an inch long. The buckskin was smoked in tanning and is a beautiful tan color. A piece of scarlet broadcloth edged with several rows of white beads decorates the top of the moccasin and from either side of this extends around the top of the quarters . . . a little drop curtain effect fringed by making fine cuts an inch deep around the edges. To fasten securely on the feet they are tied with a string that is run through little slashes cut in the top. I feel quite proud of them.[10]

Women seemed particularly taken with this element of Native American culture, a precursor to the interest contemporary tourists have in buying articles unique to the countries they visit.

WOMEN'S DRESS

Women were especially challenged by western life, in part because the clothes they brought with them from the East were so unsuitable for the frontier. Long skirts that collected dirt and dust, took a long time to dry, and were difficult to clean were exceptionally incompatible with the harsh conditions under which pioneer women lived. In an effort to make the most of their existing clothes, which did, after all, retain the hallmark of fashion left behind in the East, women tried to adapt their eastern apparel to western life through unusual inventions. One solution was known as an "instant dress elevator." An advertisement that ran in the Leavenworth *Daily Times* during December 1874 made this claim: "You can raise your skirt while passing a muddy place and then let it fall, or you can keep it raised with the elevator. It keeps the skirt from filth. It can be changed from one dress to another in less than two minutes."[11] The price of this marvelous item was only seventy-five cents. While the

Mrs. O.C. Bundy (right), corner, Cutler and Water Street, looking West.
Courtesy of the Montana Historical Society, Helena.

instant dress elevator was particularly inventive, many women simply shortened their dresses, thereby creating a trend in skirt length. Skirt width was another problem, however, as the wind would easily blow more voluminous skirts in all directions. Women reported tackling this problem by sowing bars of lead and rocks into their skirt hems to keep the fabric weighted down.[12]

Mother Hubbards, Bloomers, and Gymnasium Costumes

Small alterations sometimes did the trick, but whole new outfits were also created to solve the problem of frontier women's wear. The Mother Hubbard, also called the "wrapper" or the "prairie dress," was a loose dress that had no structured waist but was gathered by a belt or tie. The Mother Hubbard caused quite a bit of controversy, despite its obvious benefits. The garment was comfortable, could be worn over layers of undergarments in the cold months, was loose-fitting and cool in warmer weather, and was suitable for wear throughout a woman's pregnancy. Yet the dress was considered especially unattractive and even hazardous by some pioneers. The shapeless style stood in stark contrast to the fitted clothes common in eastern fashion, and women did not have to wear corsets underneath the Mother Hubbard outfit. More alarmingly, in Pendleton, Oregon, it was reported that "the voluminous swishing skirts were frightening horses on the streets and causing serious accidents. In

1885, they [the city fathers] met and solemnly passed an ordinance out-lawing Mother Hubbards unless worn tightly belted."[13] Women were warned that they would be fined if they violated the ordinance. The adoption of the Mother Hubbard was a subject of so much discussion that the local *Kansas Farmer* newspaper held debates on the matter in its pages, including poems that parodied the style.[14]

Other popular inventions in female dress included the very functional bloomer and gymnasium costumes. Bloomers, which were made of a short, tunic-length dress and a pair of loose-fitting pants, were perhaps the best-known nineteenth-century dress reform creations, receiving at-tention in the popular press in part because of their association with the early women's rights movement. For women traveling across the conti-nent, the bloomer costume, named after its inventor, Amelia Bloomer, was particular useful. Not only did the outfit do away with the problem of long skirts that collected dirt and remained wet for uncomfortable periods of time, but the use of pants permitted women more physical movement.[15] Like other costumes aimed at improving the function of women's clothing, the bloomer was a passing fad that met with mixed reaction. Some emigrants, like Jane Kellogg, remarked that "we wore bloomers all the way, the better to enable us to walk through the sage-brush. They were made with short skirts and pants reaching to the shoe tops. Everyone wore them."[16] In contrast, others found bloomers unfem-inine and refused to adopt them. Whatever the position, bloomers made an impact on the popular fashion of westward expansion, providing many women with a model of practical dress that made their journey easier, if not more conventionally stylish.

Like bloomers, gymnasium costumes were functional outfits that re-placed long skirts with short ones and covered a woman's legs with full pants. More specifically, gymnasium outfits consisted of bloomer pants, skirts, white stockings, and laced boots. Used for physical education clas-ses by women's colleges in the East, the gymnasium outfit was shaped to allow women to move more freely than traditional dresses. As one woman traveler wrote, "When compared with the long, slovenly, soiled calico gowns worn by the other women of the train, these simple cos-tumes elicited many commendatory remarks."[17]

The Mormon community created its own version of practical women's dress in what was known as the Deseret Costume. Based on the bloomer, which Mormon women often wore in their own westward travel, the Deseret was designed by Brigham Young. The outfit consisted of bloomer-style pants over which a loose tunic was worn. An eight-inch-high hat covered the woman's head, which was partially shaded by the hat's rigid brim.[18] Meant to be functional, as well as to symbolize Mor-mon society, the Deseret Costume, like other reform outfits, existed only as a passing trend in frontier fashion. The more conventional calico dress,

later replaced with eastern fashions that arrived as western towns became more established, remained the most common apparel for pioneer
women. However, the impact of these alternative women's clothing
styles paved the way for women who wore pants, donned cowgirl outfits, and experimented with practical, durable clothing that defied stereotypes of female dress.

Special Occasions and Going to Town

There were times when men and women would do their best to dress
up, especially for holidays like the Fourth of July, events like balls, and,
for those living on remote properties, the trip to town. For these and
similar occasions, attention to dress was taken seriously, although that
often meant donning a shirt or dress that was only slightly less worn
than any other. The Fourth of July, Christmas, dances, and church services were particular favorites, and westerners celebrated in as much
style as they could muster. The simplicity of dress during these occasions
reflected the interest westerners had in popular fashion, yet the limited
means they had to adopt every passing fad. Women's best outfits would
be worn on trips from homesteads into town, another event that received
special attention. As the West became more prosperous, however, and
as ready-made clothing became more easily available, demand for luxurious goods increased.

Fashion Trends in the West

While many pioneers were less concerned with fashion than with daily
survival, others felt that clothing marked a symbolic connection to the
eastern lives they had left behind. In particular, fashionable clothes reminded them of the more refined aspects of eastern culture and the personal connections that had been disrupted by the sheer distance of
westward emigration. Many pioneer women remained keenly interested
in the styles popularized in magazines like Godey's *Lady's Book* and recorded their desires to stay abreast of current fashion in letters to eastern
friends.[19] When easterners visited their western friends, the clothing they
brought with them and wore became the source of much discussion.
Local newspapers imported eastern ideas about fashion to the frontier.
Mail-order catalogs and magazines devoted exclusively to fashion also
brought images of stylish apparel to the West, and as towns became
more established, and families became settled and more prosperous, the
emphasis on fashion increased. The result was a steady, though somewhat delayed, appearance of fashion trends in frontier towns and villages.[20]

Hoop Skirts

One of the most popular fashions to make its way across the continent was the hoop skirt. It was prominently displayed in fashion magazines and eventually in western shops. The skirt's impractical nature was commented on by many pioneers who found the trend impossible to adopt. Despite the challenges inherent in adopting hoop skirts on the westward journey or in frontier life, the style was in much demand among western women. In fact, the hoop skirt made such a splash with these women that those who could not purchase the garment found ways to adapt their own skirts to the trendy style. In one town women managed to "improvise their own [hoops] by stitching wire clothes lines and grape vine into their petticoats."[21] The simultaneous attraction toward, and rejection of, the hoop skirt points toward a trend in popular western fashion. While emigrants, for the most part, desired to keep up with the cultured trends of the East, they also were all too aware that to survive in the West fashion had to be functional in ways that did not concern easterners.

While definitions of popular fashion inevitably shifted from one region of the frontier to another, and from one year to the next, throughout the entire period of westward expansion men and women recorded the trends unique to their particular time and place. For instance, one fashion fad was the widespread use of nightcaps, presumably worn to protect the pillow covers from the hair oil that virtually everyone wore. Men in particular wore hair oil. It made westerners' hair look more like the smooth, straight styles of the Native Americans, than anything else.[22]

Trends in men's clothing included pants—frequently made of broadcloth—that were loose and unpressed; creases were unacceptable. Suspenders typically held the pants up. Long coats and matching vests, also made of broadcloth, were worn over high-necked linen, cotton, or broadcloth shirts and a bow-tie was wrapped around the neck. Paper collars, as well as paper cuffs, were widely substituted for cloth ones because they could be thrown away, were readily available through mail-order catalogs, and saved the wearer from having to do excessive amounts of laundry. A similar invention, known as the dickie, was a shirtfront that could be tucked into a vest. A pocket watch, made by the Massachusetts-based American Horologe Company, was a common accessory. Watches were hung from chains made of gold links, including the "Dickens" chain which was named after Charles Dickens, the English novelist who was widely read in the East and the West. Low-heeled boots and a black wool bowler or slouch hat completed a typical men's outfit, as can be seen in the photographs of westerners and in numerous western films and television programs.[23]

The Look of the Law

While pioneer men and women used knives and shotguns to hunt, cook, and protect themselves, in western towns weapons took on other uses. Knives and revolvers were standard possessions, whether owned by lawmakers, lawbreakers, or ordinary citizens. Some shirt cuffs were made wide enough to hide a knife or gun that was strapped to the wearer's arm, but holsters were the more typical holding place for revolvers. Both waist and shoulder holsters were regular parts of men's attire and continue to be a standard aspect of the western outfit in popular culture venues. It was the guns themselves, however, that took on the element of a fashion fad in the Old West, appearing in multiple styles and colors with names like "Buntline Special," "Lightning," and "Frontier." A proliferation of brands—Colt, Smith & Wesson, and Remington, for instance—resulted in a variety of guns that could serve different purposes. Manufacturers distinguished their brands by details such as engraving the barrel and muzzle or making the handle out of ivory. Guns could be purchased at the general store or through the mail. Along with the emblematic sheriff's badge, they mark the good guys and the bad guys of Hollywood westerns. Gun names have been used to market other products, for instance Colt 45 Malt Liquor, underscoring the deep association that guns in the American West have had with other aspects of popular culture.[24]

Ribbon, Makeup, and Saloon Girls

Much of western fashion was simple and functional, but there were exceptions to this rule. Owning a piece of ribbon was a small, but popular, luxury. As one woman wrote, "no matter how ordinary her clothes or how rough her task, nearly every woman wore her bit of ribbon."[25] Whether worn around the neck or in the hair, the integration of ribbon into an otherwise plain outfit was a common sight. The use of makeup, too, was not unheard of and rouge in particular was applied to women's skin. Homemade versions of store-bought cosmetics, some made from beet juice, were common, since most women had little money to spend on such extras. The use of rouge was often associated with saloon girls and prostitutes, however, who could be recognized by their "chalk white faces, scarlet painted lips and cheeks, sometimes with a red feather or red bow in their hats, and leading a little dog on a leash."[26] In communities where prostitution existed, women shied away from any look that resembled rosy cheeks for fear that they would be mistaken for a "loose" woman.

Clothing worn by prostitutes has become a form of popular culture in its own right. From early films like *Stagecoach* (1939), prostitutes can be recognized by their showy dresses that stand in contrast to the stark, unadorned clothing of their female counterparts. Feathers, ruffles, short hemlines, visible stocking seams, all signify, in the media, a western woman with loose morals, and that image has been remade throughout the twentieth century. Showy clothing is so closely associated with prostitutes that portrayals of them in twentieth-century television and film—for instance Julia Roberts in *Pretty Woman* (1990)—always incorporate it. Conversely, viewers always know that a prostitute has been redeemed when she gives up not just the practice of selling sex, but her loud clothing as well.

Mail-Order Clothing, Dress Patterns, and the General Store

Several developments in the fashion industry greatly impacted westerners' ability to keep up with eastern fashion. The availability of mail-order catalogs, like those of Montgomery Ward or Sears Roebuck, brought fashion trends to even the remotest pioneer homes. Filled with pages of available goods, including entire sections devoted to ready-made clothing, mail-order catalogs allowed frontier families to view and purchase mainstream fashions. Indeed, such catalogs helped to standardize what was considered "in style" by illustrating, and making available, the same clothing from coast to coast. For westerners in particular, whose access to ready-made goods was limited, the arrivals of mail-order catalogs were greatly anticipated. The proliferation of mail-order catalogs in the late twentieth and early twenty-first centuries only further demonstrates how deeply embedded the culture of shopping by mail is in American life.

If Montgomery Ward and Sears, Roebuck brought ready-made clothing to westerners, dress patterns helped to further standardize American clothing. Early dress patterns were available in popular magazines like Godey's *Lady's Book* or *Leslie's*, appearing either as small diagrams that could be scaled up to life-sized sketches, or printed as tissue inserts that could be traced directly onto fabric. While availability and use varied throughout the West, patterns did enable pioneers to keep up with contemporary fashions. The Singer sewing machine, which made sewing clothes quicker and easier, added another dimension to the homemade apparel that marked western life. Both inventions helped to popularize standard fashion styles, thereby increasing the desire among westerners to keep up with the latest trends.[27]

A final contribution to frontier fashion was the general store which, for the majority of westerners, was the primary source of material goods. As a result, the store, which stocked everything from flour and candy to dishes and guns, played a central role in determining what pioneer families wore and what goods they had access to. As the clearinghouse for fabrics, shoes, ready-made clothes, and other dry goods, the general store was the center of many frontier towns, providing items essential to survival as well as luxury goods that kept up with fashion trends and styles.[28]

Whatever the origins of western clothing designs, popular culture has reproduced a common, predictable pioneer outfit that is typically used by actors and actresses who are playing nineteenth-century emigrants. The sunbonnet, calico dress, and apron are the standard clothes seen on actresses in television programs and western movies. Men wear cotton shirts, pants held up with suspenders, sturdy boots and, frequently, a hat. These easily recognized markers of the West have shaped widespread notions of what clothing styles looked like during westward expansion. While they capture some truths about frontier fashion sense, such outfits also simplify the range of clothing that was actually worn during the period.

COWBOY CLOTHES/COWBOY CHIC

Beliefs about the clothing worn by cowboys during the second half of the nineteenth century have been reduced, over the past century, to a collection of familiar items that quickly identify the wearer as a "cowboy." The broad-brimmed cowboy hat, bandana, holster, chaps, vest, and cowboy boots comprise the basic uniform needed to identify an authentic cowboy figure. These items have much in common with what Old West cowboys actual wore to work the range and herd the cattle by which they earned their wages. At the same time, however, Hollywood films advertisements, books, and products bearing the cowboy image have shaped popular notions of cowboy fashion. Perhaps the best-known representation of the cowboy uniform is the Marlboro Man, whose simple, rugged clothing makes him the epitome of the modern cowboy figure. Indeed, cowboy clothing projects a hardworking, self-reliant, earthy image that, in the early twenty-first century, is consciously adopted by politicians and musicians alike.[29]

Frontier Clothing

The clothing of frontier men, and in particular cowboys, developed from the demands of men who made their living on ranches, herding cattle, riding horses, and living outdoors. The cowboy hat, which evolved out of the sombrero worn by *vaqueros*, Mexican cow-herders, was a staple garment that protected the wearer from the sun, rain, wind, and snow. Typically broad-brimmed, brown or beige in color, and extremely durable, the most popular cowboy hat was the Stetson, a name associated with the West ever since the brand's inception and nick-named, at various points in its history, "The Hat of the West" and "Boss of the Plains."[30] Other products have capitalized on the Stetson name, including Stetson cologne for men, adding to the hat's role in lore about the Old West. The bandana, another cowboy essential, was usually made out of blue or red cotton, and it served multiple purposes on the range. Worn about the neck in order to protect the skin and absorb perspiration, the bandana became a popular souvenir of western life in the 1920s and 1930s when it was sold at rodeos and other western exhibitions, printed with slogans and images of cowboy life. Popular cowboy clothing that has remained constant over time include chaps, seat-less pants made of suede, wool, or sheepskin. Chaps were available in a range of styles, including those known as batwing, Texas leg, woolies, Cheyenne leg, or Chaparrejos.[31] Other cowboy apparel included vests, fringed gloves, slickers, spurs, and belts. The essential elements of cowboy garb were quickly integrated into popular culture from the early 1900s as the Old West became more of a myth than a reality. Brand names like Stetson, Levi's, and Colt are well known today and have become so associated with the West that other products have adopted their names in the hope of making sales based on their image.

Singing Cowboys

The cowboy outfit, as represented in Wild West Shows, dime novels, and early Hollywood films, was fortified in the twentieth century by the rise of the singing cowboy and the national tourism industry that brought Americans west. From dude ranches to pageants to rodeos, the West became one of the most popular images in American consumerism and all things western, especially clothing, began to sell. Catalogs like *Stockman-Farmer, Miller Stockman*, and *Rodeo Ben* offered shoppers west-ern wear through the mail, making what was considered "authentic" western clothing available throughout the United States. Country-western musicians also adopted cowboy clothing as their costumes, for-going the hillbilly look for the style of embroidered shirts, Stetson hats, and ornately decorated boots.

Although styles changed from year to year, or decade to decade, as when the square-toe boot was replaced with the pointed-toe model, sev-eral articles have comprised the standard cowboy uniform in popular culture. In addition to the embroidered, yoked shirt with whipcord pip-ing and snaps up the front, the singing cowboy wore cowboy boots, a belt with a buckle (preferably one with a name emblazoned on it and won at a rodeo), and a bandana around the neck. Pants took many shapes, from suede chaps to denim jeans, and shirt collars, like boots, were typically pointed. Stetson hats were the most popular, but other

Blue jeans and cowboy boots. Courtesy of
the Library of Congress.

brands, such as the Miller and the Bill Cody, competed for recognition.
Cowboy outfits were available for women and also for children, whose
desire for such clothing stemmed from the popularity of television shows
like *The Lone Ranger* and *Hopalong Cassidy*.[32]

Nudie and the Rhinestone Cowboy

Designers of western clothes, including N. Turk and Rodeo Ben, made
their names in the 1930s, 1940s, and 1950s when they created lavish outfits for singers and performers. One of the most noteworthy of these
designers, Nudie Cohn, changed the face of western clothing when he
created his "Nudie" costumes for Hollywood stars like Tex Williams,
Roy Rogers, Gene Autry, and Dale Evans. Nudie, a Russian immigrant
who arrived in the United States in the 1920s, made his living in a variety
of ways, but most successfully as a tailor. In 1947, Nudies of Hollywood
opened its doors and vibrantly colored, rhinestone-studded western cos-

tumes became the most sought-after style of movie stars and singers alike. Lavishly embroidered with western images—for instance, a Native American face in full headdress or a coyote in the desert—Nudie apparel was extremely expensive. Made from leather, gold lamé, and other exotic fabrics, the clothes were luxury items affordable only by the few. Not only did Nudie make clothes, but his white Cadillac, known as a "nudiemobile," was recognized everywhere by its "pistol door handles, silver-dollar-embedded leather upholstery, topped off by longhorns mounted on the front."[33]

Nudies have remained popular clothing items among television, movie, and music stars, who collect and wear them as part of their fashion statement. At the beginning of the twenty-first century, they even made something of a fashion comeback, as the wildly successful designer Tommy Hilfiger claimed. "A few years ago," he stated, "I was researching clothes and rock-star costumes for my book, 'Rockstyle,' and Nudie just kept coming up. I started finding them in stores. They were so over the top, borderline obnoxious; the colors were outrageous. I used that inspiration in my spring 2000 collection. It's funny, but it's very appropriate stuff right now, slim, high-cut armholes, lots of handwork."[34]

Ralph Lauren and Western Revival

In the late 1970s through the 1980s cowboy/cowgirl couture reached new levels of fashion chic when designers like Ralph Lauren began to incorporate western elements into their clothing lines. In the fall of 1978, *Vogue* reported, in an article titled "Why Not the West? Range-style dressing takes over," that:

If you missed the message: Western gear is the going item—tooled belts, ten-gallons, sky-high boots, fringes, leather. . . . There's tacky Western—rhinestoned pink velvet pants, shirt and matching hat, boots, and belt . . . Then there's kicky Western, custom-made Western, marginal Western, and Western by Ralph Lauren, which is none of the above.[35]

Not only was western-style clothing the rage with everyone from French actress Catherine Deneuve and singer John Denver to artist Andy Warhol, but other western products also found a market niche in the 1970s and 1980s. Indeed, Ralph Lauren created something of an empire from the country's obsession with the West. His cologne, Chaps, the clothing line by the same name, not to mention his home furnishings based on the colors and fabrics of the American West, made Lauren one of the most popular designers of the decade. In contrast to the loud colors and showy styles of designers like Nudie, Lauren's understated, sophisticated, yet simple products appealed to many American customers in search of a new style that could be incorporated into everyday life. The look showed up in all aspects of popular culture, including the nighttime hit television show *Dallas*, which featured J.R. Ewing adorned in his signature cowboy hat and his brother, Bobby, who wore western-style cowboy garb to work on the family ranch.

Cowboy Chic at the Turn of the Century

If the 1970s and 1980s marked a widespread revival of interest in western clothing, the beginning of the twenty-first century saw an increased interest in what might be called the "cool factor" that western clothing, especially for men, can be used to evoke. In the world of country-western music, which has relied heavily on western clothing as the trademark of its stars, a new interpretation of cowboy chic appeared in the acts of musicians like Garth Brooks, Randy Travis, and Clint Black. Often referred to as "hat acts," these singers replaced the brightly colored, busy cowboy outfit of earlier decades with simple cowboy hats, boots, and shirts that reflected the austere, monochromatic fashion of the 1990s. This new version of cowboy fashion, in other words, made country-western music stars suddenly chic, drawing positive attention from the media and the fashion critics alike. The result, especially in the case of Brooks and Black, was a country-western stardom that successfully crossed into the pop music charts, gaining mainstream music fans in the process.

In a parallel effort to use cowboy clothing to reach a greater audience, in the year 2000 presidential candidate Al Gore worked to redesign his image with the American public. Developed in consultation with feminist author Naomi Wolf, Gore's new apparel was supposed to include cowboy boots, which, it was hoped, would make him seem more down-to-earth, more hip, and more in touch with everyday Americans. The presidency of George W. Bush has been marked by its own western fashion trend in the form of cowboy boots, illustrating yet another way that the West continues to symbolize the fundamental values at the heart of the American imagination.[36]

At the beginning of the twenty-first century, western clothing made something of a comeback as a fashion statement, as is evident not only in presidential campaigns, but in the publication of books like Debby Bull's *Hillbilly Hollywood* (2000) and Lisa Eisner's *Rodeo Girls* (2000). The exhibit, *How the West Was Worn*, compiled by the Los Angeles-based Gene Autry Museum, and the appearance, within three months, of two articles on cowboy clothing in the style section of *The New York Times Magazine*, further illustrate the recurrent impact cowboy style has had on American fashion.[37]

BLUE JEANS: A FRONTIER ORIGINAL

Blue jeans, the popular fashion of the American West, became a clothing staple that has come to represent American values and been transformed over time in response to shifting social and economic trends. Jeans, so sought after abroad that young people smuggled them into former Soviet countries, are among the most enduring icons to emerge from the period of westward expansion.

Levi Strauss and the History of Levi's

Despite the fact that Levi Strauss's name is indelibly associated with the brand of jeans manufactured by Levi Straus & Co., the origins of Levi's jeans involved not just Strauss, but his partner Jacob Davis. In fact, Strauss, who arrived in San Francisco in 1853, sold clothing and other dry goods for nearly two decades before his name became associated with blue jeans. In 1872, a tailor named Jacob Davis invited Strauss to be his partner in making clothes constructed with rivets for durability. A year later, in 1873, Davis and Strauss received a patent for an "Improvement in Fastening Pocket-Openings" and the pair began manufacturing what were called "waist overalls" with copper rivets. Waist overalls, now called jeans, were made out of blue denim and brown cotton duck, but the denim, which was manufactured in Manchester, New Hampshire, and was a sturdier, more durable fabric, became the material of choice. The resulting blue jeans have remained popular around the world a century after their first appearance in the American West. They have also come to symbolize basic American values, some enduring over time, others developing through an association between jeans and a particular historical period.[38]

Blue Jeans and American Values

The first jeans sold well, not necessarily because they looked good but because, like many popular western fashions, they were extremely functional. Diary entries of early pioneers often referred to homemade versions of the pants. Indeed, jeans were first worn by laboring men—miners, cowboys, railroad workers—who found jeans to be reliably resistant to hard work and rough conditions. It was not until the early 1900s that denim became a stylish item in other parts of the country, which had previously viewed the pants as functional rather than fashionable. The new interest in blue jeans developed in response to the growth of tourism as a pastime, a trend that created the need for casual clothes, as well as the widespread, appealing image of the Old West in

An early ad for Levi's. Courtesy of Levi
Strauss & Co.

early movies, books, and advertising. During the Depression denim jeans
were popular because of their durability and, simultaneously, they became associated with working-class values and the spirit of American
endurance. In the 1940s, denim became part of mainstream fashion when
a designer named Claire McCardell used the fabric to make chic, yet
practical, clothing for women.[39]

By the 1950s and 1960s blue jeans had become a symbol of youthful
rebellion when Hollywood stars like Marlon Brando and James Dean,
not to mention Elvis Presley, wore them. Country-western music stars
also adopted denim pants as a staple in their costumes, and new brands
were created to compete with Levi's for name recognition and consumer
allegiance, especially Wrangler whose name explicitly evoked the West.
The Hollywood love affair with blue jeans, combined with the growing
adornment of denim by rock-and-roll stars, brought the pants squarely
into mainstream youth culture, in both the United States and abroad.
The pants were popular with the 1960s counterculture and with hippies,

who wore them styled as bell bottoms and hip huggers. As Frances Fitz-Gerald writes, "Sometime in the mid-sixties large numbers of white, middle-class young people suddenly and quite spontaneously took off their middle-class clothes and put on the dress of working men—blue jeans—and took up the erotic music of the black working class."[40] Jeans became a sign of rebellion against the ostensibly uptight conventions of the previous generation. They reflected a popular clothing style that signified stepping outside the boundaries of mainstream culture.

Calvin Klein and the Decade of Brand-Name Jeans

In the 1980s, a new trend in fashion reversed the counterculture chic of blue jeans, setting off an obsession with brand names that continued into the twenty-first century. Fashion icons such as Gloria Vanderbilt, Vidal Sassoon, and Calvin Klein appeared on the scene with a new type of pants known as designer jeans. Unlike the traditional Levi's that signified equality and hard work, designer jeans stood for status, money, and good taste. The hallmark of designer jeans was the conspicuous appearance of the designer's name on the pants, usually on a back pocket. Consumers did not set out to buy a pair of jeans, but rather bought a pair of Calvin Kleins or Sassoons. Along with the rise in popularity of brand-name jeans came a proliferation of new jeans styles. From baggy jeans to acid-washed jeans to jeans dyed in different colors, the 1980s marked a revolution in an old-time American favorite. The shift was indelibly marked on the American fashion scene by the infamous, genre-changing Calvin Klein commercials which featured a half-clothed Brooke Shields provocatively claiming: "Nothing comes between me and my Calvins."

While brand-name jeans continued to have appeal throughout the 1990s, shopping for jeans at boutique stores like The Gap, J. Crew, Banana Republic, and Abercrombie and Fitch enjoyed increased popularity during the late twentieth and early twenty-first centuries. The cut of jeans remained important to trend-driven consumers, yet the brand or designer became associated not with jeans alone, but with entire clothing lines. Designer labels became less conspicuous and, in some demographic groups, the grunge look made a brief appearance, emphasizing not high style, but pre-worn, pre-torn fabric.

At the beginning of the twenty-first century, blue jeans remained best-selling items in American fashion. As the enduring symbol of American self-reliance, innovation, and hard work, jeans are worn, as they were in their early years of existence, as functional pants that are well worth their price. As the attire of choice for musicians like Bruce Springsteen, jeans also evoke the ideals Springsteen's lyrics revere. They can be worn to deliberately evoke a casual look that suggests the American ideal of equality for all, regardless of race, creed, or socioeconomic background. Jeans are, perhaps, the most democratic of all American fashions. They are available to everyone and reflect the spirit of the gold rush period, when they were invented.

POPULAR FASHION AND NATIVE AMERICANS

American Indians also adopted aspects of western fashion. In some instances they did so out of sheer necessity, for example when they accepted, and wore, government-issue blankets to keep warm. But as Indian and emigrant culture became increasingly intertwined, Native Americans also participated in some of the West's fashion trends. Hoops, for instance, which were so popular with settlers, were also of interest to local Indians who wore them on top of, rather than beneath, their clothing.[41] While Native Americans may have embraced some aspects of western clothing, their own clothing style became inextricably linked to popular culture. The familiar image of Native Americans garb includes feathered warbonnets, buckskin pants, beaded jewelry, and fringed moccasins. Different Native American tribes may in fact have worn some or all of these garments, yet the popular picture of their dress is more the product of the Wild West Shows, dime novels, paintings, and movies that represented Native Americans throughout the nineteenth and twentieth centuries.[42] Such venues paid little attention to the distinctions between different tribes and the fashions that marked those distinctions. In fact, popular culture has reduced numerous complex societies with unique clothing styles and traditions to a single stereotype that we now recognize as the standard "Indian" outfit. This shift was under way by the beginning of the twentieth century and was heightened in the 1920s when the combination of affordable automobiles and new highways led tourists to the West. There Americans visited the sights of the frontier and, as part of their experience, wanted to see Native Americans. Wild West Shows and other forms of western entertainment were concerned that Native Americans did not look "Indian" enough, an anxiety that led to the creation of a false, though popular, stereotype. As Craig Bates describes it,

In the late 1920s, the National Park Service and the Yosemite Park and Curry Company erected pseudo-Indian "wigwams" of pine poles and canvas, while encouraging local native Californians to "dress up" for the event [Indian Field Days]. New clothing styles flourished, some women created unique dresses, others obtained Sioux beadwork, and some integrated articles of Miwok ceremonial regalia with these. This blending resulted in an unmistakable "Indian" atmosphere."[43]

During the last decades of the twentieth century an effort was made to counteract this simplistic view of Native American dress by restoring authenticity to the media-based images of Native American culture. More accurate pictures of Native American dress have been included in children's books, television shows, and movies in an effort to distinguish native cultures and traditions from one another. Yet the enduring view of Native Americans—regardless of their tribal roots or historic period— remains that of the feathered headdress and buckskin chaps with bow and arrow clasped firmly in hand.

The fashion icons of westward expansion—including the sunbonnet, cowboy hat, calico dress, moccasins, and gun holster—are immediate cues that their wearer belongs in the American West. That such icons are so deeply imbedded in the popular imagination is further evidence of the lasting impact the frontier has had on American culture. Such apparel has come to stand for the courageous, industrious, and diligent individuals who traveled and lived in the West under rugged, demanding circumstances. At the same time, the convenient reduction of a historical period which spanned several decades, and which involved people from different national and ethnic backgrounds, overshadows the diversity of clothing styles that enriched frontier culture. While popular images of westerners dressed in predictable garb are remade in everything from designer clothing lines to Halloween costumes, the fashion of the American frontier remains one of the most easily recognized of any period in American history.

6

Food

Food provides an overlooked but ever-present backdrop to familiar images of frontier life. Whether a picture of emigrants eating around a brightly flaming campfire under the vast sky of a western night, the first sight and smell of food prepared by the chuck wagon cook, or the lone Clint Eastwood-style cowboy drinking coffee in the early morning, the presence of food brings the West to life in crucial ways. Emphasizing the need for nourishment after a long day of travel, the legendary abundance of produce available on the frontier, or the satisfaction provided by a hearty meal cooked over a fire, images of western food are also threaded throughout popular culture. Best-selling cookbooks, chain restaurants, and brand-name products have capitalized on the positive associations that exist between the frontier and the food thought to have been eaten there. Yet the reality of western cuisine was somewhat different. Food was often difficult to come by and extremely expensive. Natural resources were quickly depleted as the numbers of emigrants crossing the country swelled. Storage and cooking facilities were so basic that many ingredients spoiled and familiar recipes had to be adjusted in unexpected—and sometimes unappetizing—ways. The popular trends in food varied depending on time and place, yet some fundamental themes dominated the period of westward expansion, laying the groundwork for contemporary representations of food on the American frontier.

ON THE TRAIL

The food that was taken, prepared, and consumed along the trails of the West was both familiar and inventive, combining the best of tried-

and-true recipes with the need for creativity based on available ingredients. Whether the meal was meant to feed a family of pioneers who had stopped along their journey or a cowboy getting ready to move his cattle northward, food along the trail consisted of available ingredients cooked with the most rudimentary utensils. Still, the romanticism that has been attributed to the campfires, chuck wagons, and the experience of eating in the great outdoors overshadows the hardships inherent in creating nourishing meals from supplies packed days, weeks, or months before they were actually consumed.

Stocking the Covered Wagon

When emigrants set out for the West, they carried with them supplies that would ostensibly last for the duration of the journey. Guidebooks like Joseph E. Ware's *The Emigrant's Guide to California* (1849) stated that for each traveler the following food should be packed: "a barrel of flour, or 180 lbs ship biscuit that is kiln dried, 150 to 180 lbs bacon, 25 lbs coffee, 40 lbs sugar, 25 lbs rice, 60 lbs beans or peas, a keg of clear cooked beef . . . a keg of lard, 30 to 40 lbs of dried peaches or apples, also some molasses and vinegar."[1] Food for the journey was stored carefully in the wagons, and pioneers prudently planned to store enough food to last for several months of the arduous trip. Midway through her journey, Sallie Hester recorded that "we live on bacon, ham, rice, dried fruits, molasses, packed butter, bread, coffee, tea and milk as we have our own cows. Occasionally some of the men kill an antelope and then we have a feast; and sometimes we have fish on Sunday."[2] During the journey, emigrants were forced to adopt new ways of cooking and eating. "Although there is not much to cooke," one diarist wrote, "the difficulty & inconvenience in doing it, amounts to a good deal."[3] The problem, it seemed, was that "by the time one has squatted around the fire & cooked bread & bacon, & made several trips to & from the wagon, washed the dishes (with no place to drain them) & gotten things ready for an early breakfast, some of the others already have their night caps on—at any rate it is time to go to bed."[4]

Nooning, Buffalo Chips, and Independence Rock

Cooking and eating outdoors was a challenge, but as emigrants became accustomed to living within the confines of their wagons, and to eating only what they had brought with them or what they could find along the way, they found effective ways to make the most of what was available. During the daily lunchtime stop, called "nooning," animals were given a break from walking, men were given the chance to hunt for fresh meat or fish, and women and children quickly learned the value

Emigrants to the West (1881). Courtesy of the Library of Congress.

of collecting buffalo chips. Euphemistically called "chips," buffalo dung was commonly used along the trail as fuel. Collecting buffalo chips became a daily activity that helped pioneers cope with the lack of wood necessary to create a fire over which to cook and around which to keep warm. Emigrants found other creative ways to combine the experience of traveling with the necessity of eating. In an effort to have fresh butter throughout the trip, for instance, many emigrants took advantage of the rocking motion of the wagon to create a natural type of butter churn. "The milk is carried in a can swung to the wagon bows overhead," one traveler wrote. "By noon (if the churn works well and it seldom fails), there is a ball of butter the size of a hickory nut and innumerable little ones like shot. If the day is hot, we have hot milk; if cold, we have cold milk, but unlike the 'bean porrage' of school days, it is never 'nine days old' "[5]

While much of the trip westward was long and tiring, food became part of the celebrations that broke up the journey, bringing relief to the monotony of the crossing. Many travelers aimed to arrive at Independence Rock on the Fourth of July, thereby being able to celebrate the holiday at one of the landmark sites of the voyage. Special foods were saved for this day, part and parcel of the trend among westerners to observe Independence Day with enthusiasm and joy. Toward this end, pioneers prepared special meals and desserts, using what they had to turn an ordinary day and meal into a extraordinary marker of their pursuit of a new life in the West.

Land of Plenty

Natural resources, including wild fruits and vegetables, provided another form of easy-to-come-by fare for hungry travelers. At least in the early years of emigration, before the land had been depleted, fruits, berries, and herbs could be picked from the trees or pulled from the ground along the way. Indeed, the move to western settlements was promoted in part by the promise that unsettled regions of the continent contained an abundance of natural resources that could be used as food. Meat was also available in the course of the journey. Antelope, prairie dogs, and buffalo could be killed and served for the evening meal. In places like Death Valley, salt could be "picked up in great lumps in the sand,"[6] while in other regions freshly caught fish could be incorporated into the pioneer diet. Minnie Miller recounted that "Prairie chickens and sage hens were plentiful. Our first experience in shooting these dark meated game birds brought us a pot pie occasionally, but this required extra time and we scarcely like to loiter."[7]

As Miller implies, efficiency was a concern of most travelers, for food supplies tended to dwindle long before the trip was over and fatigue made the daily effort of cooking difficult. Time-saving strategies were common. Beans, for instance, "were a mainstay of most [emigrant] parties, as they could be cooked all night, mixed with meat scraps, and eaten at lunch and dinner the following day. Equally popular were 'portable foods,' such as pemmican (a mixture of beef and fruits) and jerked meat. ... Pocket soup, equally portable, was stock made from veal or pig's trotters dried to the consistency of solid glue that could be stored for years, then easily dissolved in hot water."[8] Canned goods, once they became available, were also common, as was anything that could help nourish emigrants who were far from places where basic foods could be quickly and easily replenished.

The need to keep food on hand throughout the lengthy journey was aided by trading posts that were located sporadically along the major travel routes and which provided travelers with the opportunity to restock essential supplies. Settlers who were already established in cabins, dugouts, and adobe buildings along the way shared what they could with passersby. Along the trail, pioneers also described how sharing cooking supplies and ideas helped them form new connections and relationships during the long journey, relieving some of the anxiety and isolation that accompanied the departure from family members, towns, and homes in the East.

Chuck Wagons, Cowboy Cooks, and Coffee

Some of the best food of the westward expansion period was prepared by cowboys and chuck wagon cooks who created meals on the open prairie. Cowboy cooks were especially popular at the height of trail drives during which herds of cattle were moved from Texas to northern destinations where they could be sold at market. While the setting was simple, and the ingredients basic, the cowboy meal was known for its flavor and heartiness. Consisting of coffee, meat in the form of beef, salt pork, or bacon (also called "overland trout"), bread, and possibly a sweet dessert, cowboy cuisine was a cultural phenomenon in its own right, complete with dialect, customs, and characters.

The cook, whose skill determined the success of the daily menu and the satisfaction of the cowhands who depended on for him their meals, was a central figure and distinct personality in the life of a cowboy camp. The cowboy cook has been figured in popular culture as a leather-skinned man whose ability to create delicious meals is matched only by his cantankerous nature. Wishbone, in the television show *Rawhide*, is just such a character, as is Curly in the movie *City Slickers* (1991).[9] Among the rugged cowboys of the Old West, the cook provided an interesting combination of manly camaraderie and domestic ability, further complicating his relationship to the men for whom he worked. Indeed, in a type of role reversal that appeared across the frontier in various forms, the male cook was known for a culinary expertise that overshadowed the domestic skills of many frontier women.

Part and parcel of the cook's stereotypical image was the process by which he completed his tasks. While early cooks prepared meals over open fires, in the 1860s the well-known chuck wagon came into existence. The chuck wagon began as a sort of cupboard on wheels and evolved into a more elaborate system that included fold-down tables and enough cubbies and hangers to hold the equipment—pots, spices, utensils, and other materials—that the cook needed to feed the cowhands.[10] Chuck wagons could be personalized with pictures and other decorations, but the vehicles were primarily functional. As B. Byron Price reported, the "market demand in the mid-1880s led the Studebaker Brothers Manufacturing Company of South Bend, Indiana, to produce the 'Round-up Wagon,' especially designed for feeding hungry cowboys in the field. Priced at two hundred dollars, the sturdy 1888 model was equipped with zinc-lined mess boxes front and rear."[11]

The culture of the chuck wagon, with its cook and its food, was unique and in keeping with the overall rugged existence of the cowboy. Meals tended to be held three times a day, beginning early in the morning when the herds had long distances to travel. The call to mealtime, or grub, took the form of ditties, loud sounds, and no-nonsense words. Whether he clanged lids together or shouted out calls of "Grub!" and "Roll out and bite the biscuit," the cook was a crucial figure in the life of the cowhand, and he earned his right to chants as unappetizing as "Piss ants in the butter, / Flies in the meat, / If you bastards are hungry / Get up here and eat."[12]

Meals were cooked using Dutch ovens and cast-iron skillets that, by the 1890s, could be ordered by mail from catalogs like that of Sears, Roebuck. Every meal was prepared using the same set of utensils, and the recipes, as one cook recalls, were

simple, some were so darn basic you couldn't hardly understand 'em. For example, a biscuit recipe might have been written like this;
  Flr, wt, bk sd, s, mix well, cook over a fair fire till done.
They were also big on measurements involving a handful, a scoop. A dipper of some sort. Maybe even a smidgen, a bit, and a pinch.

If recipes were simple, so were the meals they created. Typical fare included meat that, if not fresh, was salted or dried as jerky, a cousin of the popular beef jerky available in convenience stores even today. Beans, usually the red pinto bean known as frijoles, were boiled or fried in the tradition of Mexican cuisine. Finally, bread could take the form of biscuits, corn bread, or sourdough bread. As with other examples of the frontier fondness for expressive names, popular meals were given colorful titles such as "son-of-a-gun stew," "spotted pup rice pudding," "six-shooter coffee," and "pigeons in disguise."[13]

If there was one crucial part of the cowboy meal, it was the coffee that was consumed in large quantities at virtually all cowboy spreads. Large pots of coffee were kept hot on the fire throughout the day, and cowboys refilled their cups as often as they desired. The coffee was known for being strong and black, and a handful of ground coffee per cup was not an unusual recipe to ensure the drink's strength. Some cooks roasted their own coffee beans, but as factory-roasted beans became more available, the purchase of ready-to-use coffee became a common practice. Manufacturers, recognizing a strong market for coffee products in the West, took advantage of the demand by creating brands especially geared for those consumers who lived on the trail. As B. Byron Price describes, Arbuckle Brother Company, located in Pittsburgh, Pennsylvania, became the leading coffee provider to the West by creating fresh, easy-to-use coffee products with strong brand recognition. The 1873 trademark for the brand that Arbuckle targeted in the West, Ariosa, featured a flying angel. Toward the end of the century, according to Price,

Arbuckles included a stick of peppermint candy in each package and, beginning in 1893, collector's trading cards featuring animals, countries of the world, U.S. states, and recipes. Two years later they began to offer coupons redeemable for any of dozens of premiums, ranging from lace curtains and wedding rings to Torrey razors and small-caliber revolvers. During the 1890s the company exchanged 108 million coupons annually for some 4 million premiums, including 100,000 wedding rings, 819,000 handkerchiefs, and 186,000 razors.[14]

The W. W. Terrett cow outfit on roundup (with Arbuckles coffee).
Courtesy of the Library of Congress.

Coffee was such an important staple in the cowboy diet, and Arbuckles did such a good job of promoting their product, that the coupons became widely recognized by westerners, and were even used, on occasion, as a form of currency at local stores.[15]

Cannibalism

In contrast to the comforting image of pioneers and cowboys eating around a campfire, cannibalism is also intricately tied to the popular story of westward expansion. As a result of the attention paid to the Donner party, who, in order to survive, ate the remains of deceased members of their emigrant group, the idea of cannibalism in order to survive quickly became a part of western lore. The Donner experience in the Sierra Nevada Mountains was printed and reprinted in the popular press, and the story was told and retold across the continent for months after it took place. The practice of cannibalism, as well as the need to eat domestic animals when supplies ran out, was a factual part of the westward journey. Such experiences gave the topic of food during the period of westward expansion a morbid, sensationalistic tone. In some ways, however, the fascination with cannibalism reflected an important truth about the cross-country journey: It could be a physically rigorous and unpredictable trip that forced emigrants to survive on limited resources in a hostile environment. That more cases of cannibalism were not reported might be the surprising fact, especially since the amount of food settlers began with rarely lasted for the entire journey.

LOCAL SALOONS, PULLMAN CARS, AND HARVEY RESTAURANTS

While life on the trail demanded creativity and patience in the planning, preparation, and consumption of meals, eating establishments known for providing westerners with excellent food and drink were an important part of frontier life. Even the most makeshift town had at least one local saloon in which miners and townspeople gathered to drink and eat. With the completion of the transcontinental railroad, new opportunities arose to feed westerners and to develop uniquely western cuisine. Such trends made their mark on the western landscape and set the stage for continuing patterns in the popular culture of frontier foods.

Saloons, Whiskey, and the Free Lunch

The local saloon was the central meeting place for most western towns, especially in the early years of expansion surrounding the gold rush. As a site of socializing, eating, and, most important, drinking, the saloon has been memorialized in countless pictures, museums, films, and books about the Old West. Whiskey, the drink of choice, was called by many names, including Taos lightning and tarantula juice. Made of a wide range of ingredients, sometimes whatever was easy to come by, "a shot of whiskey" has become synonymous with the lonesome cowboy at the local bar, the moment leading up to a classic frontier showdown, or an assertion of masculinity. The shot glass itself has its origins in the frontier saloon, where it was used as a vehicle for quickly consuming the alcoholic beverage of one's choice. The cowboy, the sheriff, the shot glass, and the bottle of whiskey made the saloon a marker of the Wild West, a place where outlaws communed, the law attempted to find justice, and women were notably absent.

While saloon owners were not at a loss for customers, they did find ways to entice passersby into one bar rather than another. The concept of a "free lunch," in fact, has its origins in the West, as one chronicler described:

The custom of the country is to drink as often as possible. The bar-keepers ingeniously speculate on this predilection of their fellow citizens. It is common to find a "free lunch" and a free supper provided in the more important Californian

Across the Continent (1870). Courtesy of the Library of Congress.

barrooms. Any one may walk in and take luncheon or supper gratis. He has several courses from which to choose, or he may take a portion of each. Soup, fish, made-dishes, joints, and vegetables, are on the bill of fare of a "free lunch." At the free supper the variety is equally great. In both cases the viands are good in quality, are well cooked, and are served by attentive waiters. Although no charge is made, yet it is understood that every one who partakes of either meal must take a drink afterwards.[16]

The free lunch gave way to the related notion of the freeloader—someone who took the meal but did not purchase a drink, thereby getting, literally, something for nothing. By competing for customers through the offer of free food, saloons became some of the earliest restaurants in the West, paving the way for other eating establishments that would appear as towns became formally established.

The Dining Car and the Harvey Restaurants

Early western travel was known for the paucity of good food available during the trip. One traveler wrote that "From Red River to El Paso there are few accommodations for eating, beyond what are afforded by the company stations to their own employers. In time, arrangements will be made to supply good meals at these points. The first travelers will find

Fred Harvey Eating House and Sante Fe Station, Chanute, Kansas
(between 1890–1910). Courtesy of the Library of Congress.

it convenient to carry with them as much durable food as possible."[17] As
train travel became increasingly popular, the problem of good food became one that entrepreneurial westerners sought to solve. Prior to the
invention of the Pullman car, travelers would stop at predetermined
places along the railroad line and eat their meals at restaurants that
served the area. While some of these services provided fine food with
equally fine service, they were inconsistent, unpredictable, and cost travelers time from their journey. Two developments met different aspects
of these problems, namely the Pullman dining car and the Harvey restaurant chain.

The dining car was revolutionary in several ways. First, it allowed
passengers to take their meals while the train continued to move, thereby
saving them from having to stop several times a day on the lengthy
journey across the country. Second, the opportunity to eat on the train
in a car specially designed for the purpose, provided travelers with a
pleasant diversion from the monotony of the cross-continental trip. Travelers found much to celebrate in the ritual of having three prepared
meals a day, served in style in the dining car as the scenery rushed by
outside the window.

In 1876, forty-one-year-old Fred Harvey changed the face of western
restaurants and travel fare when he opened the first of his popular Harvey lunchrooms along the Sante Fe Railroad line. Harvey's mission was
to provide travelers with good food served at modest prices in pleasant

environments. Train conductors wired ahead to let the cooks know how many meals to prepare, and the food was hot and waiting when passengers disembarked. The lunchrooms were well designed, and the meat was first-rate, acquired from the best western stockyards and cooked by the best chefs available.

The setting and food helped to seal the success of Harvey's restaurant, as did the well-run service that featured the popular Harvey Girls as waitresses. Harvey Girls were well-paid employees, easily recognized by the crisp black uniforms that distinguished them from the customers. Harvey asked the waitresses to sign a contract stating that they would uphold the rules of the establishment, not get married for at least a year, and live in the housing provided by the business. Not only were the waitresses held to high standards, but customers were as well. For instance, Harvey required men to wear coats before being served in the restaurant. He expected his customers to act in appropriate fashion for a public eating place. As Harvey's restaurants gained name recognition and critical approval, new franchises were opened on different parts of the railroad's cross-country route, making Fred Harvey's name nearly synonymous with frontier train travel. By promoting the enjoyment of eating, Harvey restaurants became destinations in and of themselves and provided a model for other chain restaurants that would develop across the United States over the course of the twentieth century.

The association between travel and food is an American phenomenon that has continued to make its mark in the popular culture of the West. From roadside restaurants featuring the frontier's mythic characters—Paul Bunyan and his ox Babe, for instance—to franchise chains with western origins like White Castle hamburgers and Roy Rogers restaurants, Americans long to have convenient, efficiently prepared, and appetizing food when they are "on the road." Late-twentieth-century changes in the structure of airports, which now provide travelers with an abundance of dining choices, can similarly be viewed as the inevitable development—over the course of a century—of the idea behind Fred Harvey's restaurants, which made travel in the United States at once efficient, convenient, and gastronomically satisfying.

IN THE TOWNS: SETTLERS, MINERS, AND FOOD

The process by which towns developed during westward expansion depended to a great extent on where emigrants settled and whether or not they remained there. During the gold rush, these factors were determined by where gold was discovered and how long it could be successfully mined. In these cases food would be brought to the town and sold in boomtown establishments that could disappear overnight. For pioneer families, the homestead might be miles from the nearest store and, as a result, trips "to town" in order to shop became focal points of the family outing. In either case, food was not as easy to come by as it had been in the East, and patterns of purchasing, storing, cooking, and consuming developed in response to the new challenges presented by frontier life.

The General Store and the Mail-Order Catalog

Western settlers depended on their own resources—farm-raised crops and animals—for much of their food. Whether supplies were brought to the farm, or whether the family went to town and brought items back to the home, the general store was the center of food shopping in the Old West. If the general store did not have the desired products, the mail-order catalog served as a useful alternative. Providing consumers with access to food that was not always easy to find at the local market, catalogs allowed pioneers to have products delivered by mail to even remote locations. One pioneer woman described the significance of mail-order goods to her husband, Shy:

One of Shy's other demands was to get some gun-powder tea. I finally got hold of some from Sears Roebuck. When you live ninety miles from town, a Montgomery Ward or Sears Roebuck catalogue gets read more than the Bible or Shakespeare. When I saw gun-powder tea listed, I ordered a pound and made some tea. I suppose I did not brew it the right way or his taste might have changed. Anyway, he did not like it and said it was because the mail order houses were using a substitute for the real stuff.[18]

By comparing the Montgomery Ward and Sears, Roebuck catalogs to some of the most cherished of all western reading materials—the Bible and Shakespeare—the woman illustrates the revered place that mail-order services held on the frontier. Her husband's reaction points to another problem inherent in the production and purchase of western food, however. What pioneers bought, and what they thought they bought, were not always one and the same.

Inflation

If westerners could find, in the local store or in the mail-order catalog, the ingredients they needed to make appetizing meals, they could not always afford to buy them. Inflation was a rampant problem in the West, leading to wildly different prices from one town—and even one day— to the next. Because of the effort it took to bring food to remote locations, the difficulty involved in keeping it fresh, and the desire to make a profit from a captive audience, the high price of food was a regular topic of conversation among early westerners. Reflecting the gold rush mentality of feast or famine, emigrants paid the exorbitant prices when they could, often spending all of their daily earnings and more on basic necessities of food and drink.

Fresh Food, Canned Goods, and Recipes

While most vegetables, meats, and grains were purchased or picked fresh from western farms, the tin can became a convenient way to serve food that would be impossible to keep fresh in other forms. Prior to the Civil War, tin cans were in circulation but their numbers were relatively limited. With the onset of the war, however, and the need to feed soldiers more than basic goods that were prone to spoiling, canned food became a popular way to keep food fresh. Cans were easy to transport and allowed soldiers to vary their diet, providing them with vegetables like tomatoes, and fruits like peaches, even when they were out of season and difficult to get.[19] Oysters were a particularly popular delicacy that were available in a can. Emigrants, miners, cowboys, and other participants in the process of westward expansion found tin cans useful and canned products became so common that "[e]veryone in the country lived out of cans, and you would see a great heap of them outside of every little shack."[20]

Once the food was purchased, harvested, or stored, recipes became the focal point of western cooks. Pioneers shared recipes with one another, borrowing ideas and culinary tips that helped them produce the best food they could in a setting that lacked the resources easterners were used to having at their disposal. Recipes were handed down from generation to generation, and cookbooks from "the States" were the source of many a successful—if slightly adapted—meal. Newspapers, too, provided information about the most popular recipes, the newest ingredients, and the best cooking methods. Measurements in recipes were not the exact science that are considered part and parcel of today's cooking. Amounts were estimates. For instance, two heaping tablespoons might be called "the size of an egg" or a pound of butter could be described as equivalent to "2 teacups well packed."[21] Similarly, for those settlers fortunate enough to have a stove to cook on, as opposed to simply an open hearth, temperatures were determined by the feel of a hand. A 350-degree oven was considered ready when the cook's hand could "be held in oven 45 seconds," while the same hand could be held on the oven for only 35 seconds when the temperature was between 400–450 degrees.[22]

Just as the recipes were adapted to meet the new lifestyle of emigrants in the West, so too were the names given to those concoctions, names which reflected a western spirit of cooking and eating. Cathy Luchetti describes some instances of creatively named foods in her cultural history of western cooking, *Home on the Range*. Some pioneers, she writes, affixed interesting names to their dishes, hoping to add a dash of glamour. San Jose, California, settler Bertie Bray dubbed her fried bread palillies "Baptist Cake," a meditative dish matched only by her second invention, the wild-blackberry "slump." This froth of berries and flour would make a light-headed start from the pan but always collapsed back on itself in a puddle of dank mushiness. Best-known to westerners was a "bread and meat" mainstay called "gosh," made up of day-old-biscuits, picked to pieces and seasoned with black pepper along with wild, dry sage leaves sprinkled with water. "Gosh" was the familiar short term for a food that caused much protest, such as "Gosh, will we have to eat that again?"[23]

The humor with which westerners dealt with so many aspects of their new lives repeatedly created forms of popular expression that were unique to the American West. In cooking, as in other areas of pioneer life, names literally described some aspect of the thing to which they were attached. The resulting dialect captured in a curious way the self-effacing, reality-based nature of the period, which asked individuals to make the most of circumstances that could be as trying as they were exciting.

HOLIDAYS AND POPULAR TREATS

In addition to filling the basic nutritional needs of emigrants, food was a central part of holidays and other special occasions, especially those that brought people together socially. While pioneers found themselves longing, in such instances, for the familiar meals and items available to them in the East or in their home countries, they were quick to devise their own festive feasts to mark celebrations and important events.

Christmas Dinner, Penny Candy, and Dr Pepper

One of the key holidays celebrated by westerners was Christmas, and the Christmas dinner was a crucial part of the day. Regardless of their circumstances—how little or much they had in the way of resources and ingredients—westerners found a way to create a hearty meal on Christmas Day. Keturah Belknap captured the robustness of pioneer cooking when she wrote in her journal:

Time passes on and now it is time for the Holidays. What will we have for Christmas dinner? . . . Firstly; for bread, nice light rolls; cake, doughnuts; for pie, pumpkin; preserves, crab apples and wild plums; sauce, dried apples; meat first round: roast spare ribs with sausage and mashed potatoes and plain gravy; Second round: chicken stewed with the best of gravy; chicken stuffed and roasted in the dutch oven by the fire, for then I had never cooked a meal on a stove.[24]

Oranges were popular Christmas stocking stuffers and fresh snowfalls were prime opportunities to make molasses-on-snow candy by pouring a warm molasses and brown sugar mix into pans filled with snow. When the liquid hardened, the resulting candy was eaten or saved for special occasions.[25]

Homemade candy was easy to make, but candy such as peppermint sticks, which was available for purchase in general stores across the West, was a favorite treat for young and old alike. Other mass-produced favorites that could be purchased in the West included birch beer and soda waters infused with flavor. One of the most enduring carbonated beverages, Dr Pepper, has its roots in the West. The true story of how Dr Pepper got its name is unclear, but one version claims that it all began when a young drugstore attendant fell in love with the daughter of the store's owner. The girl's father, the owner, was a doctor whose name was Pepper, and he disapproved of his daughter's relationship with the young man. To keep them apart, Dr. Pepper fired his young employee, but the man had learned something during his work there: how to combine a mixture of syrups into a tasty soda fountain drink. These skills came in handy when the man took a job at a pharmacy called the Old Corner Drug Store in Waco, Texas. There he delighted his customers by serving them his popular drinks. One of those drinks was especially well received and the customers, who knew about the young man's love affair, facetiously called the concoction Dr Pepper.

Whether or not this story is true, there is evidence that a young Waco, Texas, drugstore employee, Charles Alderton, served his fountain customers a soda that they thought was extremely tasty. In the late 1880s and early 1890s the syrup that made the drink was packaged and marketed by R.S. Lazenby, who owned the local Artesian Bottling Works. The syrup was so popular that, "by 1910, Dr Pepper syrup had become one of the principal freight items hauled from Waco by the Wells Fargo Express."[26] Dr Pepper was first introduced to the American public at the 1904 World's Fair in St. Louis, and it was quickly embraced by soda drinkers across the country. Dr Pepper was also an early pioneer of catchy advertising, periodically changing its slogans from "King of Beverages" and "Old Doc" to "Drink a bite to eat at 10, 2, and 4" and "the friendly Pepper-Upper."[27]

Picnics, Box Lunches, and Restaurants

Food was an important focus of western communities, becoming an excuse for social gatherings and a reason for public events. Barn raising, quilting, and other work-related activities, known commonly as bees, were designed to combine work with socializing, where townspeople would gather to collectively finish a task and then join together for a celebratory meal. Picnics were another event centered upon food. In fact, perhaps the only part of a frontier picnic more important than the meal was the location. Western picnics, while sometimes held on the open prairies or at local sites, were just as often held at a specific destination of interest, for instance among the great redwood trees of California. Other social events that focused around food included the candy pull and the box lunch, both of which involved eating to encourage romance. The candy pull required men and women to work as partners, pulling the stretchy candy until it was smooth. They could also each put an end of the candy string into their mouths, eating their way toward one another along the length of the candy. Similarly, the box lunch was a form of fund-raising that allowed men to bid on lunches made by the townswomen.

THE MELTING POT: INTERNATIONAL INFLUENCES AND LASTING LEGACIES

The presence of pioneers and travelers from a multitude of countries—Germany, Sweden, Ireland, and Italy, to name a few—resulted in an eclectic mix of ingredients, recipes, and foods across the American West. The legacy of the multicultural characteristics of the frontier remain at the forefront of popular twenty-first-century foods, many of which can be traced back to the period of westward expansion, when cultural connections developed in the western parts of the country.[28]

Restaurants and "American" Cuisine

Local eating establishments sprang up quickly in the West, partially as a result of the melting pot of ethnic groups that had emigrated there. One westerner described the diversity of available foods in the following terms: "There are houses of refreshment at every turn—the American Tavern, the French Restaurant, the Spanish Fonday, and the Chinese Chow-Chow."[29] Emigrants from Spain, France, China, and Germany sought to find familiar cuisine in the new territory. Yet western restaurants met the needs of more than just people seeking food from their countries of origin. They also introduced westerners to a wide range of cuisines. The experience of new foods—whether enjoyed or tolerated—was an important part of both survival in, and assimilation into, a territory that took shape based not upon a single group but on multiple nationalities.

Chilies, Barbecue, and Chiclets

The impact of Mexican cuisine on frontier diets cannot be underestimated. Not only did the cowboys, pioneers, and miners who traveled through the Southwest inevitably come into contact with Mexican cooking, but they borrowed from the ingredients and recipes of the Mexicans with whom they interacted. Life in the Southwest meant an introduction to the taste and use of common Mexican ingredients like chilies and tortillas, as well as to dishes like colache, made from vegetables. Whatever the original influence, the late twentieth century saw a rise in the widespread popularity of Mexican food, with an influx of restaurants opening up and serving customers chips, salsa, burritos, and tacos. Such food, while connected to genuine Mexican cooking, has been considered to be less Mexican than "Tex-Mex," adapted to fit the dietary needs and desires of southwesterners and Texans. Chain restaurants like Chili's, Chi Chi's, and the Border Café have cashed in on the Tex-Mex phenomenon by offering customers large portions of food at reasonable prices. The fast-food chain Taco Bell has perfected the process of preparing Mexican-style food to fit mainstream American taste with its menu of burritos and tacos aimed at those in search of a cheap, quick, and flavorful meal.

The barbecue, another American pastime with Mexican roots, comes from the word *barbacoa*, a Spanish word use to describe the process of cooking meat slowly in a pit. Barbacoa was a cooking method common in colonial Mexico and adopted by westerners who lived in what is now Texas. The barbecue is so much a part of American cuisine that the word can be broadly used to refer to any time a meal is cooked on a grill. Barbecues are the focus of summer holidays like Memorial, Independence, or Labor Days, and typically include grilled hamburgers and hot dogs. Barbecue and steak sauces are an industry in and of themselves, offering consumers easy ways to flavor their meat, in contrast to the slow cooking and flavoring that defined the original barbecue process. Some steak sauces, like A-1, developed under western influence, carry frontier-style labels.[30] Drinks with a Mexican origin—like the Margarita—have also found their way into the popular dining of the United States.

One of the least-known connections between Mexico and popular American foods concerns the origin of chewing gum. The main ingredient in gum is a product of the sapodilla, a tree from the Mexican jungle, whose sap is known as chicle when it is dried. According to one account, chicle came to the United States and became the popular chewing gum when, during the war of 1836, General Sam Houston took Mexican General Antonio López de Santa Anna prisoner. After the war General Anna lived in New York for some time, and he brought with him, for whatever reason, a piece of chicle. The nature of chicle made it a possible substitute for rubber and General Anna worked for a brief time with an inventor, Thomas Adams, to find ways to use the material most effectively. Before any results were found, however, the general suddenly returned to Mexico. His habit of chewing chicle, however, a habit which other people had adopted, led to Adams' production of the first gum made from the

Mexican sap. Chiclets, a specific brand of gum, was a later invention, but the roots of chewing gum remain tied to the country of Mexico and the events of westward expansion.[31]

Corona, Colt 45, and the Silver Bullet

Perhaps because of the long-standing association between the West and the saloon, between the frontier and drinking alcoholic beverages, American beers have drawn on the Wild West in their marketing strategies. Colt 45 Malt Liquor, for instance, takes its name from the gun by the same name, a gun that was commonly used on the frontier and which has its own Old West lore. Similarly, Coors Light has dubbed itself "The Silver Bullet," perhaps capitalizing on the Lone Ranger legend in which the hero used only silver bullets. In the year 2000 Miller Brewing Company featured the West in ads marketing its Henry Weinhard's brand. The campaign presented a cowboy duel and the caption "Henry's. The West's Premium Beer."[32] Taking on the West from another angle, in the 1980s Mexican beer experienced a surge of recognition when Corona became a regularly requested drink at bars across the United States. The Corona fad was marked by the ritual of serving beer with a slice of lime wedged in the top of the bottle, the juice of which was squeezed into the drink before it was consumed. Perhaps a derivative of the Mexican *michelina*, a drink created by pouring beer onto an inch or two of lemon juice, ordering a Corona with a slice of lime remains the most authentic way to drink the beverage.

Chow, Chop Suey, and Chinese Food

Other groups significantly influenced American food, especially the Chinese. In fact, the Chinese brought one of the words most commonly used in the United States to describe food itself: chow. Through their presence as workers on the transcontinental railroad, and in their cohesive communities—known as Chinatowns—in major cities throughout the land, the Chinese have made their cuisine a permanent part of the American landscape. Chinese restaurants are popular in almost every region of the country, and take-out Chinese is almost as American as apple pie. The depth to which the local Chinese restaurant is ingrained in popular culture can be seen in television shows like *Seinfeld*, which spent an entire episode on the subject. Chinese take-out is almost a narrative cliché in many movie and television plots where Chinese food is shown being ordered, delivered, and eaten as an indication of how to satisfy the late-night hunger of tired lovers. Ironically, while Chinese food is easily recognized by its names—chow mein, fried rice, or Kung Pao chicken—one of the most familiar of all, chop suey, is not Chinese at all but an American invention noted by the prefix sometimes added, as in American chop suey.

Cowboy Cookbooks, Buffalo Burgers, and Beef Jerky

The romantic image of campfires, chuck wagons, and eating along the trail has created an industry in its own right. Cookbooks claiming to offer recipes from the Old West abound and are distinguished by claims of authenticity. *The All-American Cowboy Cookbook* (1995), for instance, claims to include "Over 300 Recipes from the World's Greatest Cowboys." The book features not only recipes from men and women who are cowhands—in real life or as actors—but photographs of them on bucking broncos or in stills from western films. *Buffalo Bill's Wild West Cowboy Cuisine* (1996), on the other hand, focuses on recipes but also includes pictures and drawings of Buffalo Bill's Wild West Shows. Splatterware, dishes designed with a solid base flecked with another color on top, is standard equipment sold in camping supply stores and pictured in western cookbooks to further validate the fact that the meal is genuine. Whatever the gimmick, cowboy cookbooks promise true cowboy cuisine and authenticate their promises by featuring pictures and descriptions of cowboy life, either real or imagined. Other contemporary western foods include buffalo burgers, beef jerky, and the generic food brand, "Western Family."

Starbucks, Rice-a-Roni, and Log Cabin Syrup

By association or simply location, the West has remained a strong force in the food trends of the United States. Tapping into the legend of midwestern President Abraham Lincoln, who started his life in a humble Illinois log cabin, P.J. Towle, a Minnesota grocer, named his original maple syrup "Log Cabin Syrup." The syrup was sold in a metal container shaped like a small log cabin and was a leading seller in the competitive syrup market for much of the twentieth century.[33] In contrast, popular products like Rice-a-Roni had no connection with the frontier but were marketed through a fabricated association with the San Francisco cable cars, creating the catchy jingle "Rice-a-Roni, the San Francisco Treat." Finally, the coffee industry king—Starbucks—located in Seattle, Washington, has brought widespread attention to the northwestern region of the United States simply as a result of the company's strong name recognition and its reinvention of the sociable coffee shop as a contemporary version of the old-time saloon.

The food of the West was marked by scarcity, innovation, and diversity. The enduring images of eating around a campfire, of cooking over an open flame, of shopping at the general store, and of joining neighbors in a well-prepared meal are countered only by the realities of spoiled food, dwindling supplies, and necessary sacrifices. The participants in the expansion of the West were more likely to experience many of these conditions rather than only a few, yet, in the end, they brought new-found appreciation for basic, freshly cooked meals, an appreciation that has led to an enduring legacy of western—or western-influenced—foods in the world of twenty-first century popular cuisine.

7

Leisure Activities

The hardships of daily existence in the Old West were offset by the pastimes that settlers, miners, cowboys, and travelers turned to as they sought relaxation, social connection, and good old-fashioned competition. The most popular of such diversions rose from the spirit of westward expansion itself. The fads of the era—devices used to detect gold, superstitions focused on tommy knockers, and tall tales told about oversized vegetables—reflected the sense of boundless opportunity and unpredictable good luck that characterized the gold rush. Similarly, the proliferation of competitive games—from shooting contests to sack races—resonated with the struggle for law and order in the newly established boomtowns and the land outside their limits. Finally, the isolation and hardship that defined the experience of settling and farming the American prairies produced sewing bees, surprise parties, and town picnics that helped to enhance community spirit and establish social relationships. Whatever the means, entertainment on the frontier consisted of more than the familiar images of gambling, drinking, and prostitution. Yet these forms of recreation served specific functions as well, making life in the West more enjoyable and adding to the unique culture and customs of the region that still exist—in folklore if not in real life—even today.

FADS

Like any time period, the era of westward expansion produced fads in keeping with the social, political, and economic concerns of the times. From practical inventions to slang language, the fads of the period were aimed at solving common problems, making sense of new experiences and places, and creating a spirit of humor in the face of hardship and frustration.

Inventions: Mining Devices, Water Witches, and Grasshopper Pans

Among the many inventions that appeared in the West during the second half of the nineteenth century, some of the most relevant were developed in order to meet the immediate needs of prospectors and settlers who faced obstacles to their respective goals of finding gold and establishing homesteads. The men who went west during the gold rush of 1849, known as placers, searched for gold using a shallow, flat-bottomed pan that separated pieces of gold from sand, silt, and other materials. The prospector at work with his pan by the riverbed has been depicted in popular representations of the gold rush, as has the moment when gold is discovered in the sifted remains. Another frequently represented picture of the gold rush is of miners who sought gold in quarries or in underground mines. While images of gold mining suggest hard work, the hunt for gold was extremely intense and a prospector could search for long periods of time without discovering a site rich in the mineral.

Time was money in these cases, and the desire to find gold as quickly as possible led to the invention of numerous gold-detecting machines, which promised to find gold with greater ease than prospectors could expect to do on their own. Peep stones, prophetic dreams, forked sticks, and doodlebugs were among the many mechanisms relied on to speed up the process of mining, leading men to riches at the quickest pace possible. Expectations were often thwarted, however, as machines failed to live up to their promised claims and miners found themselves resorting to the laborious process of searching for evidence of gold with little help from inventions that had promised quick miracles.

While miners turned to faddish inventions to find buried treasure, other emigrants scoured the ground for drinkable water, which was not always easy to find. Just as the mining devices that promised to uncover gold quickly and easily, the water witch claimed to detect water hidden underground. Journals and diaries recorded the use of water witches, and even instances of their success.[1] The fascination with water witches reflected not only the inherent belief that those who participated in the project of westward expansion were bound to succeed, but that this success would come through a combination of hard work, imagination, and faith in the process.[2]

In contrast to mining devices that aimed to make miners rich, and water witches whose purpose was to help westerners with their basic

Mining devices. Courtesy of the Library of Congress.

survival, grasshopper pans illustrated the creativity necessary to respond to the inevitable natural disasters that plagued the settlers. The periodic attacks by hoards of grasshoppers led to the destruction of crops, clothing, furnishings, and any other items the grasshoppers could devour. Grasshopper plagues could be unexpected and devastating, and settlers conceived of all kinds of tools by which to protect their property and stop the insects. The attacks were so serious that in some states legal measures were adopted to try to limit the damage. As the following example depicts, the adoption of the promising, but ineffective, grasshopper pan was one measure taken:

The legislature also permitted itself to be taken in by an inventor with sheet iron pans for sale. The pans were eighteen feet long, four feet wide and three or four inches deep. The inventor explained to the legislature that if the pans were filled with coal oil, and then were dragged broadside across the fields, the grasshoppers would hop into the oil, and after the pan was full they could be burned. After listening to this likely story, the legislature passed a law empowering townships to buy grasshopper pans. Our township bought a large number of the pans and lent them to the farmers. We were among those who dragged the pans across our fields, but as the pan was dragged, as many insects hopped to safety as hopped into the pans.[3]

The inventions of westward expansion, like much of the era's popular culture, were quickly created devices that tended to promise more than they delivered. The willingness of emigrants to believe in the claims made for such fads reflects a greater American belief that there is always an easier way to complete tasks and meet goals. Further evidence of the role that inventions—and the process of invention—have continued to play in American life can be seen in the proliferation of new gimmicks and products advertised on television and in magazines for remarkably low prices and promising amazing results.

Mining Superstitions, Fool's Gold, and Tommy Knockers

In addition to the use of inventions to discover gold or ease the hardships of western existence, numerous superstitions developed in the small towns and daily activities of emigrants, especially miners. Some miners believed that "striking it rich" happened only when the prospector had literally thrown down his pick and given up his search, at which point the pick would make a strike, uncovering gold.[4] A related superstition was expressed in the saying, "one more round for luck," which illustrated the idea that a mine will become fruitful after a miner has walked away from it. In response to this belief, miners would continue to mine a vein without success for fear of losing out on the bonanza it might one day yield. Events considered to be signs of bad luck in a mine included wearing a tie, changing clothes, falling timber, and the presence of a woman.

If miners failed to be bothered by superstitions as they sought a gold strike, they were often misled by the appearance of the aptly named "fool's gold," or pyrite, a gold look-alike reflected in the statement, "All that glitters is not gold." While mica could easily trick a miner—especially a newly arrived one—into believing he had struck gold, the term "fool's gold" suggested the pride miners felt at being able to recognize the object of their efforts, as well as the intensity with which they sought to acquire gold of true value.

Perhaps the best known of all mining superstitions was the belief in the presence of tommy knockers. A tradition brought to the American West by miners of English and Cornish descent, tommy knockers were described as small men who worked in the mines and helped miners find mineral-rich areas by creating tapping noises that miners could follow. They also saved miners from potential harm and, on occasion, were known to play pranks in the mines, such as taking tools or knocking things over. Tommy knockers have continued to capture the imagination of Americans. They have been the subject of a best-selling book by Steven King, *The Tommyknockers* (1988), and the moderately successful film by the same name.[5]

Names, Naming, and Western Words

Western inventiveness was not limited to mechanical devices but expanded readily and playfully into the very language spoken by the people. Be it the naming of a town, a creek, a person, or an experience, emigrants took pride in ascribing to what they considered an uncharted wilderness the words that helped them to define it. In doing so, they symbolically claimed the land as their own, implicitly disregarding the names given to the West by Native Americans. The process of naming also helped to construct those aspects of western culture that distinguished the land west of the Mississippi from the states to the east.

Places were named in several different ways. Some sites were named for the people who discovered or settled them, like Pitman Valley in Arizona, which was named for Elias E. Pitman who started a cattle ranch there in 1862.[6] Other geographical areas were named for their appearance, including Red Lake, an Arizona site that was named for its red appearance after it rains.[7] Similarly, the natural elements at a particular location could evoke a particular name, as in Gobbler Point—a place where turkeys were known to gather—or Buzzard Roost Mesa named after the buzzards who lived there.[8] Still other sites were named for events that occurred there. Sarah Royce wrote about the origins of a town named Hang-Town: "I had heard the sad story (which, while it shocked, reassured us) of the summary punishment inflicted in a neighboring town upon three thieves, who had been tried by a committee of citizens and, upon conviction, all hung. The circumstances had given the place the name of Hang-Town."[9] Whatever their origins names of sites like Cripple Creek Canyon, Grizzly Peak, Rattlesnake Tanks, and Skull Valley are distinctly western in their use of image-provoking words, and their appearance in popular culture predictably evokes the old West.[10]

In contrast to terms that described places, other utterances communicated aspects of western culture that required recognition or were significant to the region. For instance, as emigrants gradually made their way west and became experienced in the customs of the region, a tradition of pride arose among those who had survived there and who understood the culture. Terms like "greenhorn," "dude," and "Johnny-come-lately" were developed in reference to newcomers, individuals who, as "Johnny-come-lately" suggests, had just arrived in the West. These newly arrived emigrants were easy to spot, as the following description illustrates: "Those who are accustomed to buffalo hunting are almost instantly upon their fleet horses, and in chase, while those unaccustomed to such scenes, 'green horns,' as they are called, are in the greatest confusion, adjusting saddles and martingales, tightening girths and spurs . . . and giving their friends, wives and children, all manner of assurances of their unparalleled success . . ."[11] The term "dude," which described a person who dressed fashionably, was directed at those travelers who arrived in their best clothing despite the rugged lifestyle that the West demanded. An offshoot of "dude," found in the words "dude ranch," developed to designate those individuals who paid for vacations at ranches in order to get a "real" western experience.[12]

While some western dialect was specific to the experience of settlement, other words and phrases have influenced American language by injecting new words into everyday speech. The mining industry itself built an entire language system which has remained in use in contemporary dialect. Terms like "lucky strike," "strike it rich," and "pay dirt," to name just a few, evolved from the experiences of miners who eagerly sought their fortunes in the gold rush. Other expressions, like "you bet"

derived from the gambling table as a shortened form of the commonly heard dealer's question, "How do you bet?" or "Do you bet?" By the 1860s a New York correspondent would report that "You bet" was the most popular and most used expression heard in San Francisco. A new gold camp that sprang up eight miles east of Nevada City in 1860 was named You Bet.[13]

"Seeing the elephant" was another common phrase that was used "to symbolize the dream to dig great riches in the new land. It originated from the experience of going to the circus and not being favorably impressed with the much-touted elephant."[14] To see the elephant meant "facing up to difficulties, of enduring the worst possible ordeals, and someone surviving."[15] Still other common phrases, including variations on "circle up the wagons," "rollin,' " and "smoking the peace pipe,"[16] have remained alive in American dialect, registering yet another way in which westward expansion permanently altered the face of American life.

Other Old West words that have remained in American speech reflect some of the less appealing aspects of western life. The word "stinker," for example, was used to refer to the men who skinned buffalo carcasses which had remained frozen on the prairies. "Stinkers" were men who took the hides, reaping the hard-won benefits of the original hunters. The word continued to be used to express "contempt and hatred," and today it denotes someone who has frustrated the speaker.[17] "Stiff" was another term used to deride or express contempt for someone, and at least one author has argued that the word originated in Dodge City. There the respectful attitude towards death—expressed in the word "corpse"—was replaced with a more "stinted" attitude which referred "to the dead in which they had no special interest, and, from this, the word received an appropriate application to such people as suggest death or worthlessness . . ."[18]

Finally, people were given—or gave themselves—lively titles which seemed ready-made for celebrity or star status. The most familiar of these were Calamity Jane, Buffalo Bill, and Wild Bill Hickok, each of which was eventually used to market the individual's performances in Wild West Shows and other popular culture phenomena of the period. Yet average people also adopted names that described some characteristic which, for better or worse, defined them, for instance Arizona Pete and Woodchopper Mike. The use of proper social titles—Mr. or Mrs.—were less frequent than these made-up names by which individuals became known. Ironically, just as naming the places of the West further disenfranchised the Native Americans, the names westerners invented for themselves were a playful rendition of the ways in which Native Americans gained their proper names: through an association with their personal characteristics or actions.

Medicine Men, Sulfur Baths, Promising Remedies

Traveling medicine men, who peddled cures for every ailment, represented just one of several different fads in the world of frontier health. Many emigrants claimed that the West itself was therapeutic for a range of physical illnesses, and they encouraged their friends and relatives in the East to make the journey for this reason alone. Others found that the natural elements of the West, such as the hot springs around the Great Salt Lake, were restorative. Whether the manufactured remedies marketed by medicine men, or the natural remedies discovered by travelers, cures for every ailment were readily available in the West. Emigrants bought or tested those cures with little evidence of their effectiveness, foreshadowing the willingness of Americans today to believe in—and buy—the latest medical miracle despite questionable evidence of its ability to actually cure anything.

SOCIAL EVENTS

The range of social activities available to westerners was limited only by the imagination. While some events were imported from the East, these were frequently altered to meet the resources available in the place and time they were enjoyed. New types of gatherings were also developed in response to the needs of community members whose lives demanded hard work and attention to daily survival. The result was a collection of social activities that were at once playful and productive, reflecting the general sentiment of life in the Old West.[19]

Surprise Parties, Bees, and Rendezvous

Social gatherings were typically planned in advance and celebrated specific events, including birthdays, Christmas, Independence Day, house warmings, and weddings. Other events were more spontaneous and took place any day of the year. The surprise party, for instance, was a popular fad defined by the unexpected arrival of a group of well-wishers at someone's home. The individual would be "surprised" by the well-wishers, who would bring food and entertainment for all to share throughout the evening.[20]

Other types of gatherings were organized around an activity or a theme. The most common of these was the "bee" during which neighbors would gather to build a house, sew a quilt, or complete other tasks that were easier done by a group than by an individual. House raising, barn raising, and haying bees were typically attended by both men and women, while quilting, sewing, and crocheting bees were popular among women only. Whatever the objective, a bee was an occasion during which pioneer men and women combined work with friendship, thereby strengthening community connections in the process.

Annual community events were also central to the frontier experience, even from the earliest days of the trappers. The rendezvous, known as a trappers' holiday, was an annual event during which trappers met at a predetermined site at the end of trapping season. The initial purpose of the rendezvous was to provide trappers with an opportunity to turn in the furs they had successfully collected during the winter and to gather supplies that they would need for another year of trapping. The event developed into a grander affair, however, as individual trappers were enlivened by the company of others after their long months alone. The combination of whiskey, food, and music made the rendezvous a festive event. Towns like Pinedale, Wyoming, continue to reenact the rendezvous in annual celebrations of the historic events that took place in their environs.[21]

The Fourth of July and Christmas were also celebrated in the old West with great gusto. "The glorious 'Fourth' has passed," one emigrant wrote. "The little brothers tried to make it seem like 'Fourth of July back home' by marching to the tune of 'Yankee Doodle,' with tin pans as drum accompaniment, with flags and banners of red flannel."[22] Festivities ranged from picnics and outings to bands and fireworks, which were viewed as especially exciting by holiday participants. Like the Fourth of July, Christmas was marked by family dinners, gifts, and gatherings that were as celebratory as any Christmas in the East. Although the gifts might have been smaller in size or fewer in number, the spirit was not lost on those who had ventured west in search of a new life.

Hug Socials, Games, and Contests

In contrast to the work-oriented nature of bees, events like hug socials, candy pulls, box suppers, and picnics were arranged to provide westerners with the opportunity to socialize with others, primarily the opposite sex, and sometimes at a price. Hug socials, like twentieth-century teenage kissing parties, allowed participants to hug one another after paying a set fee. Similarly, candy pulls required men and women to act as partners pull a stringy, sugary candy until it broke. Alternatively, two persons could take ends of the stretched strip of candy in their mouths and eat their way along the piece until their mouths met in a kiss. Other games included blindman's bluff, charades, and Old Mother Wobble Gobble, each of which required players to physically participate in the activity. Box suppers were prepared by women whose male partners were expected to pay—or even bid—for the dinners that had been put together, anticipating the practices of contemporary auctions.[23]

In addition to party games, the West provided men with a place for masculine competition that was expressed and channeled through a range of rugged contests. From logging rivalries in which success was measured by the speed and accuracy of wood chopping, to team-pulling competitions that, like today's "monster truck" competitions and tractor pulls, focused on the weight and distance a team of animals could haul a load in a designated time, contests were popular activities. In addition to providing pleasure to spectators, such games transformed the hard work of the frontier into a measurable expression of expertise. Similar types of contests included challenges centered around mining, drilling, and plowing. Organizations such as the Masons and the Grangers were also present on the frontier and provided another social outlet for men in the Old West.

Finally, board or card games were also widely enjoyed. Dominoes and cribbage, for instance, were typical games played in the West, as was the popular card game Authors, in which players were asked to identify well-known writers. Imported from the States, the games were familiar to easterners and westerners alike. By the 1890s, board games were being created about life in the West. In 1895, Milton Bradley marketed the *Game of Mail Express or Accommodation* which included a map of the United States as it existed in 1894. That same year Parker Brothers Inc. sold *The Little Cowboy Game*, which featured a steer and a cowboy in the center of the board's track. The company also created *Buffalo Hunt* (ca. 1890s) and *Game of Buffalo Bill* (1898) which included a board with pictures of Native Americans, buffalo, and Buffalo Bill. By the beginning of the twentieth century, board games had reflected the change in western transportation, as in Milton Bradley's *The Tourist, A Railroad Game* (ca. 1900) and by 1938, in conjunction with the popular radio shows about

Playing cards (1936). Courtesy of the Library of Congress.

the West, Parker Brothers Inc. offered *The Lone Ranger Game* to American players. Playing cards also included images of the West, with frontier icons such as the buffalo or Native Americans on face cards.[24]

Train Watching, Sightseeing, and Photography

Other social activities were more individualistic or less socialized, providing alternatives to bees and contests. As the transcontinental railroad made its way across the country, it became a focal point for the towns that built up around its stations. Citizens interested in the new form of transportation would head down to the station to watch the arrivals and departures of the trains and travelers. Sightseeing also grew in popularity as travelers began exploring the West for fun, stopping at well-publicized sites like Yosemite or Yellowstone National Parks. From the earliest days of expansion, local towns boasted a photographer whose shop was a favorite stopping place and whose camera provided pictures of emigrants that could be sent to relatives and friends "back East."[25]

Practical Jokes, Humor, and Hoaxes

The serious business of settlement and survival on the frontier was countered by the westerner's propensity for laughter, tomfoolery, and tall tales. The Old West was known for its unusual humor, its riddles, and the hoaxes played by townsmen and newspapermen alike. Local parties tended to be incomplete without the practice of baby switching, a prank depicted in Owen Wister's *The Virginian*. Before the time of babysitters, parents brought their infants to dances and other social gatherings where the children were placed together apart from the activities. During the course of the evening, tricksters would move the babies around so that an unobservant parent collected and took home the wrong child.[26]

An unusual form of entertainment was the "hokey pokey," a joke that "[w]as the means of great sport among the gang in early days. If the stuff [a liquid concoction] was applied to any animal with hair, it had a wonderful effect. For the time being, the animal just went crazy, and it seemed the more sleepy and good for nothing the horse was, the better he would perform under the effects of the medicine."[27] Newspaper reporters were also known for playing practical jokes in the form of hoaxes, telling stories of fabricated people, places, and events to the vast entertainment of their readers. Exaggerated tales of heroic deeds, oversized crops, and unusual animals were also promoted in the best tradition of believe-it-or-not stories, while riddles and jokes were recorded in newspaper columns and passed by word of mouth and from town to town. For instance, although there were reports that one-hundred-and-sixty-pound catfish had been caught in Kansas during the summer of 1859, there were also exaggerated claims of huge ears of corn and other produce that were pure fiction. Newspaper reporters like Dan de Quille made up stories about entire towns that did not exist, informing readers about events that never happened.[28]

Some of the most popular and enduring of these tales focused on the pioneer man. Whether early stories of anonymous trappers, the legends of Davy Crockett, a real man whose name became attached to a more or less fictionalized character, or Paul Bunyan, a giant whose primary companion was an ox named Babe, tales of frontier adventurers caught listeners' attention. Crockett's image in particular, and the tales told about him, were reproduced in newspapers, magazines, and almanacs across the country.[29] Heroes in some ways, pranksters in others, these characters symbolized the frontier spirit of ambition combined with a humor that protected them against arrogance. Americans responded enthusiastically to the stories of such western myths, incorporating them into popular culture.

CALIFORNIA PRAYERBOOKS, MONTE, AND SOILED DOVES

The most common image of the westerner at play is that of the card-playing, whiskey-drinking, prostitute-seeking cowboy or outlaw whose definition of fun seemed synonymous with risk and danger. More than any other forms of entertainment, playing cards, gambling, and drinking at the local saloon reflected the lottery-like spirit of westward expansion, especially of the gold rush periods. Prevalent prostitution on the frontier further reflected the "anything goes" attitude of the region, an attitude that has been reinforced—accurately or not—in the popular culture of and about the period.

Card games were one of the most common forms of entertainment on the frontier. Easily transported from place to place, and open to endless creative adaptations of one game or another, cards were the westerner's best friend. One emigrant stated that

Cigars were employed by some, others were engaged at rifle-practice at empty bottles thrown into the water, but by far the greater number were engaged in the study of the "California prayerbook"—as a pack of cards are profanely designated—a weapon which a native or an acclimatised settler rarely ever stirs abroad without, such is their all-absorbing passion for the game; and most careful, too, are they of their missal, which they carry in a nicely fitting case . . . [30]

From poker and monte to seven-up and euchre, card games were known and played across the West. They provided entertainment as well as a common bond between strangers. In a land where familiar faces were few and far between, two people could engage in a game that they both were familiar with though they had never met one another before they sat down to play. Card games were not always played to a fair end, however, and cheating was a common practice. Players were torn between the impulse to follow the rules of the game with the desire to break them. Such ambivalence reflected the greater cultural tendency to institute laws only to find exceptions to them.

Gambling

While gambling did not originate in the American West, it became inextricably linked with the era of westward expansion and the experience of the frontier. Gambling on the frontier was widespread, and even the most basic mining towns were known to operate gambling tables in some primitive form.

Westerners had mixed feelings about the impact that gambling had on the people who indulged in it and on the towns that supported it as a pastime. Some emigrants saw gambling as a positive influence. As one of them wrote, "Our city has improved very much since last month. Two new gambling saloons have been opened. One of them 'See's Exchange' will rival anything in New York."[31] Other westerners were more skeptical, however, and viewed gaming as a problem that went right to the heart of the West. "[T]he open gambling halls," another diarist wrote, "[had] gold piled conspicuously upon tables in open doorways, to tempt the weak ones, who had earned their money through hard labor."[32] Indeed, the gambling tables could take every penny a person had in no time at all and fortunes were won and lost overnight. Participation in such ventures was encouraged not only by friends and acquaintances, but by newspapers and publications on the subject. One westerner wrote:

I might, to be sure, take up a newspaper and find a mild deprecation timidly shrinking into the corners of one page, while staring out on the opposite one, in the most flaunting and attractive type, would be a *true story*," calculated to sow the black seed even in virgin soil, uncontaminated by a germ of indigenous vice. . . . There can be little doubt that the tendency of the article, or its intent to entrap some other miner, who has made "a respectable rise," to yield to the promptings of his "good genius," which, pointing to one of those "fashionable haunts," bids him enter, and win "100,000 dollars, if only he can refrain from attempting the *impossible achievement* of breaking the bank."[33]

The moralistic tone of this description underscores the level to which the debate over gambling was taken. Yet the popularity of gambling was undeniable. From games of chance like poker, roulette, and faro, to confidence games like monte, the audience for gambling continued to increase as the West became more settled. So prevalent were some of the games—for instance, seven-up—that they became icons used to brand cattle. Throwing dice was another common game of chance that was easy to transport and quick to play.

The ready interest in gambling may have sprung from the experience of the gold rush, which was itself a sort of gamble. Men and women who left their homes and moved west in search of gold were willing to speculate on their chances of success. Giving up their homes, taking any money they possessed with them, and investing it in search of a fortune to be made in an elusive gold strike, miners easily compared their work to winning the lottery. In this light, it is not surprising that lotteries were another popular form of gambling by which westerners could wage a small amount of money on the chance of winning a great deal.

Whereas mining offered an easy comparison to gambling, the early pioneer who tried to establish a homestead and farm the land also engaged in a form of betting. As one pioneer described, many times large tracts of land were purchased with the intention of making them cattle ranges or of cutting hay; but the purchase being chiefly on credit, or with borrowed money, and the returns being long in coming, interest ate up the purchaser, and often involved him hopelessly. In the mines, it soon became an admitted adage that "mining was a lottery"; but it was not more so, than such business enterprises as these.[34]

Whatever the form, the basic tenets of gambling were at the heart of the western enterprise. Risking big to win big was the name of the game for the pioneer, the miner, the explorer, and every other individual who traveled across the American continent. The pastime has continued to be a cornerstone of western culture through the existence of Las Vegas, where gambling and prostitution are established as two of the region's primary industries.

Drinking

Gambling was readily found in most western saloons, where drinking alcohol was the popular pastime. Another form of western entertainment that has been memorialized in popular culture, the old western saloon and the alcohol it served were a centerpiece of the frontier town. Whether the beverage was known as tarantula juice, bug juice, or Taos lightning, whiskey was the drink of choice and the shot glass was the most familiar container from which to drink it. Saloon customs existed in even the remotest frontier watering holes, and newcomers could be easily recognized by their failure to adhere to them. Drinking in the town saloon has been captured in nearly every western film. One familiar sequence involves the cowboy or outlaw who enters the room and makes his way to the bar under the watchful eyes of the people already drinking there. The bartender, who stands behind a large wooden bar, pours the newcomer a shot and pushes it toward him. After the man has taken his drink, a confrontation of one sort or another takes place, depending on whether the character is the film's hero or villain. Drinking at the town saloon has been, and remains, a central component of western popular culture.

Prostitution

Prostitutes, commonly referred to as "soiled doves," were easily found in western towns from the earliest days of expansion. While the women who worked as prostitutes tended to be uneducated and poor, and while their existence was fraught with social, physical, and economic risks, they have been glorified in popular culture as honest and moral despite their occupation. In truth, prostitution increased as male miners and explorers demanded female companionship, and though some women were able to support themselves financially, most were less fortunate and spent their lives on the margins of frontier society.

Prostitutes could be found in several locations, depending on the town. The local saloon included women known as hurdy-gurdy girls, who first danced with men, then took them, for a price, to rooms upstairs. Some prostitutes worked from separate buildings known as brothels, which looked like regular houses from the outside. The existence of a red-light district, an area of town in which prostitution was allowed to exist, was also common and easily recognizable so that a man in search of companionship could find it. In some places prostitution was a controversial practice that was relegated to the town's outskirts, where cribs, or small rows of shacks, were built and used by prostitutes for their activities. During the building of the transcontinental railroad, prostitution sprung up in what was known as "Hell on Wheels," towns that moved as the railroad progressed, continually providing workmen with the food, drink, cards, and women to satisfy their needs.[35]

Whatever the locale, prostitutes were readily available throughout the frontier and in some areas their presence led to unique cultures. In Albuquerque, New Mexico, for instance, brothels were distinguishable from other buildings by the names of resident prostitutes printed above the doorways. Prostitutes also adopted names to use for their work, including Diamond Lil, French Erma, Pegleg Annie, and Timberlane Jane.[36] Other unique aspects of brothel life included the use of brass tokens to pay for a prostitute's services, the common practice of advertising, and the publication of directories that served as guidebooks to "pleasure resorts" of the West. Known as "Red Books" and "Blue Books," these directories gave addresses and descriptions of the buildings in red-light districts, dance halls, and other places prostitutes serviced in towns from Denver to Los Angeles.[37]

The image of the frontier prostitute in popular culture is of a woman scantily dressed, heavily made-up, and ready to meet a man's needs. As a primary female presence in western films, the prostitute has typically represented the woman outside the bounds of society who yearns for nothing more than acceptance, in spite of her "fallen" status. She is often martyred, and sometimes even saved, making her a controversial yet surprisingly sympathetic figure in western literature, films, and television programs.

HOBBIES AND SPORTS

If gambling, drinking, and prostitution were some of the more familiar, and less savory, of western diversions, there were many other western activities that were social, intellectual, and wholesome in nature.

Lady's Chain. Courtesy of the Library of Congress.

Music, for instance, was a central form of entertainment in the Old West, and most towns had a band comprised of whatever instruments were available. Town bands played at local community events as well as for holidays such as Independence Day. The military also had bands, and soldiers who traveled west with their regiments were certain either to participate in, or listen to, the military band perform. Cowboys also developed their own form of music as entertainment, singing to pass the time but also to calm or direct their herds. In homes as well, musical instruments were played for the enjoyment of the entire family, and visitors would also gather around to hear the family musician play.

Like music, the performance of plays was a social activity in which many westerners at a single location could engage. The military was especially adept at producing first-rate performances.[38] In contrast to the community-oriented nature of dramatic performance, other hobbies were solitary, including reading, crocheting, or sewing. Westerners read a wide range of materials, not only popular novels but everything from almanacs and mail-order catalogs to local newspapers and national magazines.

One of the most enjoyable western pastimes was dancing. From dances in private homes to balls in public buildings, dancing provided social interaction and required some innovation when the male-female ratio was out of proportion. One early westerner wrote that "The dances were

Making a Tenderfoot Dance (1907). Courtesy of the Library of Congress.

held in our living room, and there were always so many extra boys that
some of them would have to tie handkerchiefs around their arms and
take the girls' part in the square dances."[39] The simplicity of private
dances in individual homes stood in contrast to the public dances and
balls that drew large crowds from a wide geographical area. Formal balls
were greatly anticipated events that could last all night. As western
towns grew in population, and as greater numbers of women settled in
them, dances and balls became more common and were well attended.
Similarly, less formal dances, such as the square dance, were also popular.

Whether simply learning to waltz, or to do the cancan, the fandango,
or the square dance, dancers prided themselves on being able to keep
up with the popular moves of the time. Toward this end dancing schools
were established to instruct westerners in proper dance style and eti-
quette, thereby improving their skills at balls and other social functions.
Often dances served as rites of passage for newcomers to the West, as
in the practice of making the "tenderfoot" newcomer "dance" by shooting at their feet.

The Ghost Dance (1898). Courtesy of the Library of Congress.

The Ghost Dance

One western dance that did not originate in the desire for entertainment or socializing was the Ghost Dance. It was first performed around 1870 by a Northern Paiute Indian, Tavibo, who spread the belief that deceased Native Americans would return to earth while Whites and others would fall into holes and disappear. By performing a traditional dance, Tavibo claimed, he could interact with the dead. While this initial appearance of the Ghost Dance caught the interest of some Native Americans, it was the reappearance of the dance—and its beliefs—in 1890 that led to a popular trend among numerous Indian tribes, including the Sioux, Arapaho, Shoshone, and Cheyenne. Corresponding with the intense effort to remove Indian tribes to reservations, and the resulting damage to Native Americans culture and history, the Ghost Dance has been viewed as a reaction to the profound loss Native Americans experienced during the period of westward expansion.[40]

Traveling Entertainment

Entertainment often came to the West in the form of traveling groups or individuals who made their way from one remote town to another, playing to captive audiences and making names for themselves in the growing cities. In a letter to relatives, Franklin A. Buck described "a 'Medium' in town. Last night we made up a private party to test his spiritual arts. We sat around a table for some time and he called on the spirits to manifest themselves by tipping the table. This was done. The table was moved to all sorts of ways; tipped over entirely and finally tipped toward a man by the name of Jones."[41] Not everyone believed in the ability mediums claimed they had to speak with spirits, but their presence brought a healthy dose of both skepticism and wonder to audiences in search of distraction from everyday life.

Other traveling performers included musicians, dancers, singers, and even lecturers, who spoke on the controversial topics of the day and drew surprisingly large groups of listeners. Minstrel shows were also popular, performances in which African American songs and jokes were performed by impersonators, usually Whites, who darkened their skin with coal or makeup. As one female pioneer described, the "most exciting [entertainment] of all . . . [was] an occasional 'nigger' minstrel show. The performers were always white men blacked up."[42]

Competitive Sports, Community Games, and Animal Fights

Traditional forms of competitive sports made their way quickly across the frontier and emigrants reported engaging in, watching, and betting on such athletic events as wrestling, boxing, horse racing, and rifle shooting. As sports activities that centered on the success of one person and the defeat of another, competitions emphasized the ruggedness of western life and the self-reliance that was the basis of survival there. Such events also provided spectators with action-filled rivalry that allowed them to root for one participant over another.

Other frontier games were socially oriented, being played at picnics, holidays, and other social events. Leapfrog games, wheelbarrow competitions, and sack races, for instance, were played regularly by people of all ages. Warm-weather sports included baseball games, croquet, and tennis, while in the winter ice skating and sleigh riding were common activities. Horseback riding, a primary form of transportation for many westerners, was also enjoyed as a form of entertainment. Such activities fostered a sense of community and built relationships while also entertaining westerners in important ways.

A final form of frontier sport involved the practice of getting animals to fight one another, or in capturing or hunting animals who were otherwise known to roam free. Buffalo hunting, for instance, was an early pastime that was done as much, if not more, for sport than for food. The result of widespread buffalo hunting was the near extinction of the animal. Bull baiting, on the other hand, was an early predecessor of the modern rodeo. Men on horseback roped the bulls and pulled them to the ground. Dog fights and cockfights were also popular, allowing men to bet on the winners and thereby join one great pastime to another. The bear and bull fight, an event in which a bear was brought to a bull pen and the animals were provoked by onlookers into fighting, was also common.[43]

From activities meant to provide social contact to games that illustrated the western reverence for quick riches and winner-take-all attitudes, the pastimes of the frontier were as diverse as the people who lived there. Meant to bring people together as much as to encourage competition between neighbors, the activities westerners engaged in added to the unique culture which defined the period of westward expansion and which continues to shape the West today.

8

Literature

In many ways American literature has always focused on the topic of westward expansion. From the earliest pioneer days, the line against which the unexplored wilderness tenuously stood was, quite literally, to the west of populated communities, making the idea of "the West" inherent in the American experience. As a result, the image of the frontier is deeply embedded in even the earliest sermons, novels, newspapers, and poems. In fact, the essential tenets of the traditional western genre—civilization versus the wilderness, the individual versus society, and change versus stasis—are embedded in U.S. literature from 1620 to the present. For while the period of westward expansion was marked by the popularity of particular literary works—from authors like William Shakespeare, James Fenimore Cooper, and Bret Harte, to genres such as dime novels and cowboy poetry—in a larger context, the West as a symbol and as a topic has permeated a wide range of American literary texts.[1]

EARLY AMERICAN LITERATURE

From the start, colonists thought about themselves as existing on the border between the wilderness of the land they inhabited and the civilization they brought to the land, seeing their life's work as an "errand into the wilderness."[2] More specifically, their existence in the New World was based on their belief that, as a people, it was their destiny to civilize the untamed land, bringing the Christian life to its inhabitants. Toward this end, sermons directed congregations of men and women to spread the word of God from the shores of the Atlantic Ocean to the West, and warned listeners about the perceived failure of this pursuit. The messages delivered by ministers throughout the New World incorporated versions of the same directive: Westward movement was essential to the successful existence of White settlers.[3] As settlers moved across the frontier this concept continued to motivate them, and it was reinforced in the popular literature of the pre-gold rush period.

Travel and Captivity Narratives

Whereas popular writing promoted mythical images of the New World, eighteenth-century travel and captivity narratives told of the rewards and dangers of exploration. Early travel literature, such as J. Hector St. John de Crèvecoeur's *Letters from an American Farmer* (1781–1782) was widely read by audiences at home and abroad as a way to gain firsthand information about the New World. Such narratives provided readers with "real-life" tales—though often in a fictionalized form—about the land outside of the established colonies. These texts acted as a form of propaganda and advertisement for westward expansion as they typically touted the opportunity to live and farm on idyllic and fruitful lands. Early travel narratives were transformed during the period of westward expansion into personal travelogues such as Francis Parkman's *The Oregon Trail* (1849), as well as the infamous guidebooks that pioneers consulted for their journeys away from the eastern states.

At the same time that travel writings encouraged people to move west, captivity narratives caught the reading public's imagination with reports of the terrors involved in being captured by savage Indians. Captivity narratives tended to follow the same story line, first describing the author's initial capture, her time in captivity, and her ultimate escape. Authors were primarily White settlers—usually women—whose Christian virtues were threatened during their time among Native Americans. While frequently based on fact, captivity narratives tended to be sensationalistic, emphasizing the barbaric nature of the Indians and the challenges faced by "civilized" Whites who were forced to live with them for varying amounts of time. Mary Rowlandson's *Sovereignty and Goodness of God* (1682), one of the best known early captivity narratives, describes the author's reliance on God during the trials of her years as a captive. Perhaps the most popular captivity narrative of all time, however, which also incorporated the basic elements of the genre, was John Smith's story of being seized by Native Americans only to be saved by the princess, Pocahontas. The legend of Smith's salvation begins with Smith, who, in the hands of the uncivilized natives who seized him, is about to have his head crushed between two stones. At the last minute, Pocahontas intervenes and saves his life. The story of being taken hostage by barbaric Indians is reversed when, years later, Pocahontas is held against her will by an Englishman, Samuel Argall. Unlike Smith, however, who is eager to escape his Indian captors, Pocahontas is treated graciously during her captivity, eventually converts to Christianity, and marries a White by the name of John Rolfe.[4] Whether Whites or Native Americans are held captive, the distinction between civilized and savage peoples is typically made clear in such narratives in which native life is depicted as inferior to that of Whites and so is to be feared and avoided.

The popularity of captivity stories waned as westward expansion continued and the Native Americans became further removed from the land they had once freely roamed. The fears and prejudices inherent in the genre, however, appeared in other written forms throughout the eighteen hundreds. Diaries of nineteenth-century pioneers continued to express residual anxiety about the possibility of being captured by Native Americans during the westward journey, and the widely read dime novels depended heavily on the captivity plot. In the twentieth century, the captivity theme appears in its essential form in numerous western films, including the Disney version of the Pocahontas story. The genre has been turned on its head, however, in blockbusters like *Dances with Wolves* (1990), which represents Indian captivity as preferable to life among environmentally destructive Whites.[5]

Cooper's Leatherstocking Series and Bird's *Nick of the Woods*

Sermons, travel journals, and captivity narratives were all preludes to the founding tenets of the western novel created by James Fenimore Cooper in his Leatherstocking series. Beginning with *The Pioneers* published in 1823, the series of five books was a tremendous commercial success. Each successive volume moved further back in time, to the days of the earliest settlers described in *The Deerslayer* (1841). The intervening novels, in order of publication, included *The Last of the Mohicans* (1826), *The Prairie* (1827), and *The Pathfinder* (1840). Centered on the White hero of the series, Natty Bumppo, the Leatherstocking novels established the western genre as male-dominated, existing on the border between civilization and wilderness, and focused on the self-reliance of its hero. The books quickly became best-sellers and ushered in the official era of the literary western.

The Leatherstocking tales and their hero, Natty Bumppo, concentrate on a world populated by male characters and experiences. Bumppo, a Daniel Boone type of figure, is noteworthy for the fact that his closest companion is a male Native American named Chingachgook. Not only do Chingachgook and Bumppo epitomize an early form of male bonding, but their relationship supercedes any romantic attachment Bumppo might feel for female characters whom he repeatedly meets. Moreover,

**The Seaside Library Edition of James
Fenimore Cooper's *The Deerslayer*.
Courtesy of the Library of Congress.**

female characters in Cooper's novels tend to be one-dimensional versions
of good or bad women whose destinies are often directly correlated with
their virtues. In *The Deerslayer*, for instance, the haughty, suggestively
sexual sister, Judith, is referred to, at the end of the novel, as the mistress
of a British soldier; while the kinder, moral sister, Hettie, is rewarded in
heaven through an early death. The majority of the action in the novel
is completed by men, while the female characters further the kidnapping-
and-rescue plots by being captured by Native Americans. This male-
centered universe is crucial to the literary western, which is focused on
frontiersmen who find meaningful and lasting companionship, not to
mention rivalry, among themselves rather than with women.[6]

In addition to being predominantly masculine in focus, the Leatherstocking tales also examine the tenuous line between civilization and the
wilderness. The majority of Cooper's novels take place in wilderness
settings, and while they illustrate the ostensibly inevitable march of civ-

ilization across the eastern part of the country, there is nonetheless a mixed message in the books about the relationship between what is tamed and untamed. Natty Bumppo and the characters he meets do not see the wilderness only as a place to be domesticated, nor do they view the Native Americans only as savages to be civilized. Cooper makes Bumppo's closest companion an Indian, thereby representing the Native Americans in a positive way. The author challenges the Indian/White dichotomy in other ways as well. Throughout the series, Natty acquires numerous Indian-given names that signify his development from a young to an old man. He is first called Deerslayer, then Hawk-eye, Path-finder, and, finally, Leatherstocking. Cooper's use of names is significant, for in giving the White scout Indian names, the author blurs the distinction between Whites and Native Americans. Moreover, while Leather-stocking is constantly in contact with civilization in the forms of families, towns, and settlements, he also constantly leaves those realms in favor of the unsettled land to the west. In other words, Natty Bumppo/Leath-erstocking bridges the world of the Whites—who are moving west-ward—and the Native Americans—consequently being displaced. In doing so, Cooper's hero anticipates the issues at the heart of the western genre.

Finally, the Leatherstocking series emphasizes the individualism and self-reliance of its hero, thereby establishing the role model for future western heroes. Leatherstocking depends almost entirely on his own abilities and judgment and stands outside of the traditional forums through which decisions tend to be made. He is, in many ways, a pre-cursor to the stock figure of the cowboy, who lives a lonesome life, mov-ing in and out of society, never in need of other people, and always able to fend for himself. Moreover, Leatherstocking forgoes interpersonal re-lationships, preferring a solitary life to a married one and finding his best companions in other loners who populate the fictional West.

Cooper has been criticized for his inaccurate descriptions of locations, his writing style, and his depiction of Native Americans that were deemed too sympathetic by his contemporaries. In 1837, author Robert Montgomery Bird responded to Cooper's representations of Native Americans in his best-selling novel *Nick of the Woods*. The main character, Nick, also known as the Jibbenainosay, is a supernatural figure who vi-olently murders Native Americans. The novel is notably different from Cooper's in its creation of savage Indians and a wilderness filled with frightening spirits and gruesome experiences. The contrast between the two authors marks a division in cultural attitudes toward Native Amer-icans, yet Cooper's vision superceded Bird's as the foundation for future works of western fiction. Cooper's representations of the complex rela-tionship between Native Americans and Whites, the cultivation and ex-ploitation of American land, and the anxiety surrounding domestic life have continued to make the books relevant to today's readers. When they were first published, Cooper's works were also avidly read by European readers, fueling a foreign interest in frontier adventure novels. And although a 1996 film adaptation of *The Last of the Mohicans*, starring Daniel Day-Lewis, was a commercial failure, Cooper has remained a staple of American literary classics and the grandfather of frontier fiction.

LITERATURE ON THE FRONTIER

While there were several forms of American literature upon which later western fiction was based, there was also reading material made popular by those who journeyed west and settled the land during and after the gold rush. These books, papers, and magazines both encouraged migration and brought eastern ideals into the mining communities, boomtowns, and isolated prairie homes that marked the period of expansion.

Guide Books

Some of the most widely read—and deeply deceptive—literary materials were the guidebooks pioneers used to direct them across the country. Emigrants' guidebooks, as they were commonly called, provided potential pioneers with an array of information about what to expect during the lengthy trip to the Pacific Ocean. Bearing names such as *A Journey to California* (1841), *The Emigrants' Guide to Oregon and California* (1845) and *The Gold Regions of California* (1845), guidebooks described what supplies to take—including clothing, furniture, animals, and food—what routes were most direct, and where to stop along the way. Typically authored by a single individual—who may or may not have actually traveled the routes being described—hundreds of the guidebooks were published, some only a few pages in length. Readers were tantalized by the sights they would see along the trails and the gold they would find upon their arrival. By some accounts the emigrants' guidebooks were the best advertisements available for westward expansion, and they can be credited with inducing pioneers to travel west.

Despite their popularity, the guidebooks were notoriously inaccurate in their information. Not only did they misinform readers about the types and amounts of supplies necessary to make the journey, but they misrepresented the length of time it would take and provided incorrect maps. Such inaccuracies had grave results for emigrant families who had taken the books at their word. Some emigrants found themselves out of food and supplies while still hundreds of miles from their destination. Others found themselves weighted down by the sheer number of things they had put aboard their wagons, which became too heavy for the

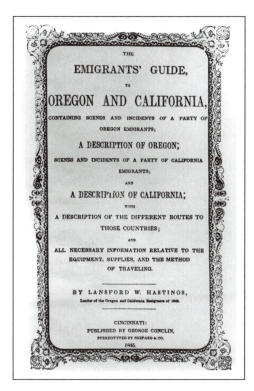

Cover of The Emigrants' Guide, to
Oregon and California, 1845. Courtesy
of the Library of Congress.

weary animals to haul. Some things were therefore discarded mid-trip. One reason the guidebooks were so faulty was because they were not necessarily written by individuals who had made the journey themselves. Rather, they were simply descriptions of a single individual's exploratory wanderings of the West as opposed to a guide for making the journey quickly and efficiently with family members in tow. Most significant, however, the books were inaccurate because they were speedily published in order to capitalize on the gold rush periods in which vast numbers of emigrants were on the trails. Some guidebooks directed travelers through certain towns, where they became captive audiences for the goods being sold in the local trading post. All in all, the books, while clearly inspiring emigration and providing some basic parameters for the journey, were often more a hindrance than a help. Still, the sheer volume with which they were printed and purchased makes them some of the most popular reading materials of the time. Contemporary computer games like *The Oregon Trail* incorporate guidebooks into their materials, asking players to imagine themselves following the original texts used by emigrants to cross the country.

Popular Authors, the Bible, and Weekly Story Papers

In contrast to the guidebooks which were read primarily to gain knowledge of the West, other reading materials were chosen purely for entertainment. The Bible was a mainstay in western homes. Westerners could quote entire passages by heart, the book was that essential to their lives. Foreign authors were especially popular, in particular William Shakespeare, whose plays were read and performed throughout the West. Novels such as *David Copperfield* and *Great Expectations* by Charles Dickens, and the poetry of Alfred, Lord Tennyson were also standard reading fare from abroad. American writers whose works were widely read included Harriet Beecher Stowe (*Uncle Tom's Cabin*, 1852), Nathaniel Hawthorne, and Herman Melville. James Fenimore Cooper and Washington Irving, who both wrote about the West, were read for their accounts of frontier experiences.

Many of these novels were originally published in serial form, in the popular weekly magazines that brought fiction to large numbers of readers. *Harper's* magazine and Frank Leslie's newspaper were two of the most popular "weeklies." They were read throughout the country, providing short stories and serial novels which kept people buying the publications from week to week. Story papers were illustrated with woodcut prints and were inexpensive to purchase. They typically included works by foreign authors who, because there was no international copyright law, did not have to be paid. Conversely, foreign authors also took up the subject of the American West in their fictional writings, further reinforcing an international image of the wilderness and frontier.[7]

Given their access to magazines and journals, westerners were surprisingly up-to-date with contemporary news, and they read avidly. In 1857, Franklin A. Buck wrote that he read the *Boston Weekly Journal, Harpers Weekly*, and the *New York Tribune*. He stated that he received "the Alta, Golden Era, and Trinity Journal by the year. The 'Alta Cal' is the leading paper on the Pacific Coast and always contains all the news from South America, the Islands, China, Australia and the East Indies."[8] Journals were a sound alternative to books that were a rare commodity for many emigrants, who read them over and over again and shared them with their neighbors.

Newspapers

Newspapers, with names like the Tombstone, Arizona, *Epitaph*, were established in the West even before the mass migrations inspired by the hunt for gold brought large readerships to frontier towns. A town with only a saloon and a jail to its name typically included a newspaper among its fundamental services. Newspapers served a range of functions in the Old West, from providing local news about births, deaths, and marriages, to keeping townspeople up-to-date on national events. Yet newspapers were also a form of entertainment. They could be counted on to report tall tales about bizarre beasts or incidents of shoot-outs and other violence. Newspapers were known for their popular hoaxes, a type of story partially invented by frontier journalist Dan de Quille, a long-time writer for Nevada's *Territorial Enterprise*. De Quille's friend, Mark Twain, developed and perpetuated the hoax as a standard form of western literary humor.

Western editors helped to draw people to their town by using the newspaper to promote its virtues. Because newspaper offices had equipment to print documents, they became the unofficial repositories for records in many towns. Newspapers were also political mouthpieces for western statehood and other pressing issues of westward expansion. Papers were widely and thoroughly read, and they helped to create the enduring myths of the West by publishing stories about George Armstrong Custer, the assassination of Wild Bill Hickok, Calamity Jane, Billy the Kid, and the shoot-out at the O.K. Corral. In fact, it was the newspaper of Harrisburg, Texas, that first printed the words "Remember the Alamo," thereby recording, in 1836, one of the longest-lasting slogans in American history.[9]

LITERATURE ABOUT THE FRONTIER

While frontier audiences provided fertile ground for guidebook authors, newspaper reporters, magazine publishers, and fiction writers, the West itself became the subject of literary penmanship. From sensational dime novels to short stories with regional flavor, the literature about the frontier created a new aspect of U.S. society that continues to influence popular culture in the twenty-first century.

Dime and Nickel Novels

The most popular literature between 1860 and 1900 was the dime novel. Recognized by its distinctive salmon-colored cover, the dime novel sold—for ten cents apiece—to mass reading audiences during the second half of the nineteenth century. While authors of such fiction focused on subjects ranging from detectives to Native Americans, the dime novel that had the West as its setting was by far the most successful.[10] A hybrid literary form, the dime novel borrowed heavily from captivity narratives and from Cooper's Leatherstocking tales, creating a new, sensationalistic version of the frontier for readers to purchase, first at news-stands but later through the mail. Dime novels were originally published by Erastus Beadle who, after finding a market for inexpensive song-books, created a sort of literary gold rush with his new books. Formulaic in plot and short in length—about 30,000 words per volume—the dime novel was cheaply produced and inexpensively sold, thereby allowing new volumes to be printed on a weekly basis. Legend has it that dime novel authors could write a complete work in record time, even as quickly as a single day.[11]

Dime novels were initially marketed as a uniquely American form of literature, thereby differentiating themselves from the weekly story papers and other publications that contained fiction by foreign writers. As Bill Brown writes,

> By repeatedly emphasizing that theirs was a series of "National and American Romances," of "Purely American Novels" written by Americans about America, the Beadles both differentiated their work from the republication of European fiction and coded their enterprise as a patriotic project, responding to the ongoing call for a national literature (expressed by the same journals . . . that continued to serialize fiction by English writers—William Thackeray, Charles Dickens and Wilkie Collins).[12]

The uniquely American subject matter on which dime novels were mar-keted, however, was surprisingly unoriginal in relationship to early forms of American literature. The first dime novel published, *Malaeska; The Indian Wife of the White Hunter*, reads remarkably like a combined captivity narrative and domestic novel. Its focus on the heroine, Ma-laeska, a Native American woman who is separated from her White hus-band and son, is atypical of later popular dime novels that were primarily about White males. However, the story is especially interesting for that very reason, providing readers with a counter-narrative to the myth of White explorers conquering the West with no cost or conse-quences. *Malaeska*'s immediate popularity was only outdone by the suc-cess of dime novels that told an opposite tale of the West, in which heroic men saved Whites and killed Native Americans with increasing violence and one-sidedness as the genre progressed.

The first truly "western" dime novel, *Seth Jones; or, The Captives of the Frontier*, shifted focus by centering around a White male character and by drawing its fundamental plot from Cooper's novels, in particular *The Deerslayer*. Based on a White hunter whose main task is to save other White settlers from Native American threats, *Seth Jones* promoted the more enduring image of the West as a dangerous land in need of culti-vation. The novel quickly sold over 500,000 copies, at least in part as a result of its original advertising scheme, which featured a series of advertisements asking "Who is Seth Jones?" followed by another cluster of images depicting the character and the caption, "I am Seth Jones."[13] This emphasis on the hero dime novel set the stage for the most successful of the dime novel series that changed over time in accordance with shifting demands and interests of mass audiences. As Christine Bold writes, "The imperative to produce a hero transcending class and region remained paramount, but as the figure was inserted into different cultural environments, his specific lineaments changed: the hunter gave way to the scout, the cowboy, the outlaw, the frontier detective, and the freelance law-enforcer."[14]

The development of the western hero can be traced in other popular dime novels. Like Seth Jones, who was more of a hunter and scout, Buffalo Bill, at the center of Ned Buntline's *Buffalo Bill, the King of the Border Men*, also assumes this role. In contrast, Deadwood Dick, star of novels like *Deadwood Dick, The Prince of the Road; or, The Black Rider of the Black Hills*, is something of an outlaw who takes justice into his own hands as he deems fit. The violence contained in publications like dime novels became such an issue of moral concern that the U.S. Post Office "censored inflammatory outlaw stories from 1883 through the turn of the century by refusing mailing privileges. In response dime publishers turned to moralistic adventure stories, fastening particularly on the heroic cowboy."[15] Another incarnation of the frontier hero, the cowboy appeared as the most enduring figure of western popular culture, later starring in radio shows, television programs, and films about the Old West.

The dime novel built on the literature that came before it, reinforcing and also developing the literary western's essential framework. Other key elements included the use of ungrammatical language that reinforced the image of the West as a less cultivated place with less refined individuals. For instance, in *Deadwood Dick, The Prince of the Road*, the author provides the following dialogue:

"Go to blazes!" shouts back Jehu, giving an extra crack to his whip. "Who'n the name o' John Rodgers ar' drivin' this omnybust, pilgrim?—you or I?"[16]

Not only is this exchange difficult to understand, but its dialect underscores the lack of education and refinement that became a stereotype of the West. The settings of dime novels also fortified the fundamental images of the West still held today by including saloons, stagecoaches, and campfires. And while the dime novel included female characters, some of whom, like Calamity Jane, became western legends in their own right, the male-dominated West remained the focus of the popular books. In the end, the dime novel paved the way for literary forms like the romance and the detective novel as well as popular television programs like soap operas and made-for-television movies which are formulaic in plot and engage the reader's emotions in an effort to gain an audience.

Pulp Magazines and Comics

Western stories were also published in pulp magazines like the popular *Western Story Magazine*. Christine Bold succinctly describes their form and history:

These magazines were miscellanies of short and long fiction with various features like quizzes, letters pages, and factual articles. They contained more material than dime novels, they appeared weekly or monthly and cost 10¢ or 15¢. Pulps had been invented in 1896, when Frank Munsey . . . [declared] that people would pay for sensational stories, printed closely together on cheap pulpwood paper without illustrations. At the beginning of the twentieth century, many publishers . . . followed his profitable examples; but it was only after 1919, when pulps began to specialize, that they reached the height of their popularity. Street and Smith [publishers] were first with that innovation, turning their New Buffalo Bill Weekly (itself a reprint series out of Buffalo Bill Stories) into the all-Western *Western Story Magazine*.[17]

Pulp magazines, including publications such as *Wild West Weekly*, contained western stories similar in form and content to the dime novels of the nineteenth century, thereby providing mass audiences with more sensationalistic stories of adventure in the Wild West. These magazines were widely read until the mid-twentieth century when the decrease in sales corresponded with the introduction of western television shows and films into American homes.[18]

Another outlet for western stories was the comic strip, as well as the comic book, both popular with children and adults. Reducing the elements of the literary western to their most basic form, comics have represented the West in both original features like *Tumbleweeds* and *The Far Side*, and in offshoots of other popular western figures like the Lone Ranger and Buffalo Bill. Comics support the conventional images of the West, yet also provide a humorous venue through which to challenge those images or to show their inherent contradictions and blind spots. Like other forms of western literature, such as the tall tale or the hoax, comics question, or at least poke fun at, the characteristics at the heart of the genre.[19]

Cowboy Poetry

Making its first appearance soon after the Civil War, cowboy poetry became a staple of western ranch life, providing a creative outlet for ranchers and other land and livestock workers. Composed and recited primarily by cowboys, cowboy poetry focused on the cowboy way of life, including the unique western environment. Such verse was originally published in local newspapers beginning around 1870, and it could be found in magazines and even collected in books. Despite the use of print to circulate cowboy poetry it was most frequently spoken, in the tradition of oral poets. As a result, numerous variations of a single poem have been known to exist, the words changing from one recitation to the next. While some of those changes may have been the natural result of faulty memorization, others are deliberate attempts to adapt a poem to a new situation. The flexibility of such verse is key, for cowboy poems by nature draw as often on writers like Shakespeare as on parodies of the way cowboy life is mythologized in folklore, stories, and films.[20]

Despite their various origins, cowboy poems can usually be recognized by catchy rhythm, traditional rhyme scheme, and job-specific subject matter. Cowboy poems like "The Creak of Leather," by Bruce Kiskaddon, are marked by a rhythm which tends to be that of the ballad, in which the last word rhymes in every two lines or every other line.[21] The result is a song-like verse that strengthens the alliance between cowboy poems and cowboy songs.[22] The language of the stanza is also significant because it includes informal words like "mornin'," "jest," and "hoss" to convey the image of the cowboy. This refusal to adhere to the tenets of standard English gives cowboy poetry a local and personal flavor which creates powerful images for the reader and listener alike.

In addition to structure and language, the subject matter of cowboy poetry is predictable. The celebration of life on the land, including its challenges and changing culture, are common topics, as are the hardships of the trail; important events such as death, marriage, and birth; as well as nature, the seasons, bravery, and love. These subjects arose from the fact that cowboy poems were often composed during the day's work. As the cowboy performed his duties he was able to create poems in his mind which could then be recited when he was in the company of other men, around the campfire or at the chuck wagon. Using the world around him as his muse, the cowboy poet captured and recorded some of the most descriptive images of frontier life that are available to contemporary readers.

The widespread popularity of cowboy poets and poetry has waxed and waned since the early 1900s. Some of the early cowboy poems have made their way into the campfire repertoire, including such Yukon tales as "The Cremation of Sam McGee" and "The Shooting of Dan McGrew." The better-known versions of the conventional cowboy poem stand on the verge of being ghost stories or warnings to listeners about the "strange things done in the midnight sun/By the men who moil for gold." Indeed, this tradition of telling stories lives on in the campfire traditions of the Boy Scouts and Girl Scouts of America, as well as at countless summer camps around the United States. In the late 1980s, cowboy poets made something of a comeback, appearing on The Johnny Carson Show and gaining renewed recognition by the American public. Gatherings of cowboy poets also saw a revival in the last decades of the twentieth century, and National Public Radio continues to feature its own cowboy poet, Baxter Black, in regular programming. In many ways, however, the strongest strain of cowboy literature lives on in a slightly altered form through the increasingly popular field of country-western music, where many of the basic tenets of cowboy poems are frequently brought to life in musical form.

Regional Fiction and Frontier Writers

Not only did the western landscape become the focus of individuals who worked the land, but the West itself produced well-known literary movements and writers. The literary roots for writers like Bret Harte, Mark Twain, and Stephen Crane were their western experiences. Harte's poems and short stories made him well known in the western literary culture of San Francisco and, when he became the editor of *The Overland Monthly*, his reputation flourished with stories like "The Luck of Roaring Camp." Harte spent close to twenty years living and working in California. His sketches, "A Night at Wingdam (1860)." "The Legend of Devil's Point" (1864), "A Legend of the Cliff House" (1865), and "Early California Superstitions" (1865) capture the local color of the era. Known for his vivid depictions of frontier gamblers, prospectors, ranchers, and women, Harte has significantly impacted both the West, and western literature, through his ability to capture the frontier with language.

Samuel Clemens, better known as Mark Twain, also made his literary name by writing about—and in—the West. During his time as a reporter for the *Territorial Enterprise*, the local newspaper for the Nevada Territory town of Virginia City, Clemens first adopted his Twain pen name. In 1862, while working for the newspaper, he published a hoax about finding a petrified man on the plains, which was reprinted by newspapers in San Francisco. Other frontier articles included "My Bloody Massacre," "Information for the Millions," and "Buck Fanshaw's Funeral." "Jim Smiley and His Jumping Frog," printed in 1865, was a humorous parody of the traditional tall tale that earned Twain recognition by eastern and western audiences alike. Twain used his western experiences as a newspaperman and a prospector in the satiric fictional work *Roughing It* (1872), a comic autobiography. His most popular fiction, *Tom Sawyer* (1876) and *The Adventures of Huckleberry Finn* (1885), developed from Twain's expertise at capturing the richness of western life.

Hamlin Garland also drew on the West, developing a specialty of representing farm life in the prairie states. *Main-Travelled Roads* (1891) and the story "Up the Coule" try to counter the romantic image of farming life that was popular in the American press. Garland's autobiographical works, including *Boy Life on the Prairie* (1926), offer a more idealistic image of childhood in the West while other works engage political and social events of the time. *The Captain of the Gray-Horse* (1902) and *Cavanagh: Forest Ranger* (1910), for instance, examine the tensions between westerners and the newly created Forest Service, while *Hamlin Garland's Observations on the American Indian* (1895) and *The Book of the American Indian* (1923) explore the issues surrounding the experiences of Native Americans.

Like Garland, Stephen Crane depicted the West in many of his short stories, including "The Bride Comes to Yellow Sky" (1898) and "The Blue Hotel" (1898). Crane borrowed images of the West—and the stereotypes of that land—from the popular dime novel. He even poked fun at the dime novel's readers in stories like "The Blue Hotel." The story includes a character named the Swede, an ambiguous representation of immigrants who played a key role in the frontier experience. Ole E. Rölvaag, a Norwegian who moved to the Dakota prairies, gave voice to the immigrant frontier experience in *Giants in the Earth: A Saga of the Prairie* (1927) and its sequel *Peder Victorious: A Tale of the Pioneers Twenty Years Later* (1929). Willa Cather's fiction, especially *My Ántonia* (1918) and *O Pioneers!* (1913), offered a female perspective on immigrant life. Her novels present the challenges pioneers faced in farming the land as well as their love of the land. They do so with a clear eye toward the female immigrants who farmed the land and lived there.

Other late-nineteenth and early-twentieth-century writers who drew on the West for their subject matter, or whose literary origins were on the West coast, included Frank Norris, Jack London, John Steinbeck, Joaquin Miller, and Sinclair Lewis, to name but a few. Poetry was also popular, especially lyric poems and heroic ballads which were readily published in many western newspapers. The role San Francisco played in the western literary scene became central in the mid-twentieth century when, during the 1950s and 1960s, authors like Jack Kerouac and Alan Ginsberg appeared on the literary scene. Kerouac, in particular, made images of the West relevant to the social atmosphere of the 1960s through his best-selling book, *On the Road* (1957).[23]

The Literary Western

At the turn of the century, Owen Wister gave the tenets of western literature a modern twist in his novel *The Virginian* published in 1902. Based on the story of a western cowboy with roots in Virginia, the novel's hero clearly combines the tension between civilization and the wilderness, which stands at the center of the literary western. Wister's novel builds on the conventional images of the West, adding the elements of romance and violence that so captivated early readers. *The Virginian* went "through six printings in six weeks and sixteen printings in its first year. It was the top seller in fiction from 1902 and fifth for 1903."[24] The novel set off a new wave of western novels during the first half of the twentieth century and became a staple in the genre of westerns, being adapted as a television show in the 1960s and as a film several different times.

Other novelists who followed in Wister's footsteps include B.M. Bower, Clarence Mulford, and Max Brand, all popular western novelists in their own right. Bower, a woman who wrote under an androgynous pen name, brought strong female characters to the frontier, especially in her popular novel *Chip of the Flying U* (1999). Mulford created the figure of Hopalong Cassidy, who later became the subject of radio programs and television shows. Brand was one of the most prolific western writers, publishing novels but also short stories in magazines. While each of these writers created a unique version of the West in terms of characters and plot, the fundamental formula of the western was firmly in place.

Two of the greatest benefactors of that formula were Zane Grey and Louis L'Amour. Grey, who lived from 1875–1939, incorporated two important elements into the western: the hero's love of a woman, and a relationship with the land that can lead to a spiritual regeneration of the characters. For Grey, the western landscape produced heroes and villains. His stories are erotically charged with forbidden or resisted love relationships between the heroes and the female characters. The admittedly clichéd descriptions of romance nonetheless significantly contributed to the development of the western. For unlike Cooper's frontiersman who chooses a solitary life, Grey's men are at least drawn to, and sometimes even capitulate to, the charms of women.

At the same time, the relationships that develop between Grey's men and women are rather one-dimensional. In *The Last Trail* (1979), for instance, the female character, Helen, reflects upon meeting the "borderman," Jonathan. Grey writes,

She could not carry on the usual conventional conversation with this borderman, but remained silent for a time. She realized more keenly than ever before how different he was from other men, and watched closely as he stood gazing out over the river. Perhaps something she had said caused him to think of the many pleasures and joys he missed. But she could not be certain what was in his mind. She was not accustomed to impassive faces and cold eyes with unlit fires in their dark depths. More likely he was thinking of matters nearer to his wild, free life . . . [25]

The scene reveals a new depth in fictional frontier women who reflect on the world around them, yet its romantic overtones suggest the dark, mysterious stranger of popular romance novels and the male character is still clearly drawn to the freedom of the land. Novels like *Riders of the Purple Sage* (1913), *The Light of Western Stars* (1914), and *The Lone Star Ranger* (1914) mark the early stages of Grey's popularity, which rapidly expanded from 1910 to the 1930s. With the rise of the motion picture industry, Grey's novels were turned into popular Hollywood films, further perpetuating his recognition as one of the best-known western writers of all time.

Louis L'Amour has been the most widely read of all western authors, surpassing even Zane Grey in the number of readers he reached and the amount of money he made from his writing. L'Amour's career began with publication of *Hondo* in 1953, which was quickly turned into a film starring John Wayne. L'Amour published over one hundred books and short stories focused primarily on the American frontier, most memorably on the Sackett, Chantry, and Talon families, pioneers whose experiences covered a range of decades and witnessed drastic changes in the West. Like Grey, L'Amour incorporated romance into his fiction, developing female characters who had a genuine role in the story lines. His novels are action-oriented and focused on strong male characters, including their home and family life. L'Amour's contribution to American history and culture was marked by his award from Congress of a National Gold Medal in 1983. That L'Amour's recognition occurred during the presidency of Ronald Reagan, a westerner known as the "cowboy president," reflected a larger national obsession with the West as a central symbol in American life.[26]

CHILDREN'S LITERATURE

While adults have clearly been the target of literature written in and about the West, children have also been a primary audience for such material. Popular forms of children's literature, for instance the Little Big Books Series, Golden Books, and a variety of comic books, have brought the stories and myths of the Wild West to children in easy-to-read and simplified forms. The result has been that generation after generation of children have read about the American frontier, perpetuating both the myths and the realities of westward expansion.

In many ways, the field of children's frontier literature is gender-specific. Certain types of books have been traditionally popular with boys, while others have been mostly read by girls. For instance, from Mark Twain's fictional *Tom Sawyer* to the historical-turned-mythic figure of Daniel Boone, boys have been the primary audience for children's literature about the frontier. Even the occasionally violent cowboy figure was transformed into a more acceptable role model for boys in the form of the clean-cut scout featured in nickel westerns, as well as in magazines like the *Wild West Weekly* and *Young Rough Riders Weekly*.

In contrast to the adventure-oriented theme books about cowboys, Native Americans, and Daniel Boone, other books about the West focus on domestic and traditionally female topics. The Little House on the Prairie series, written by Laura Ingalls Wilder, centers, as the title suggests, around the maintenance of the home, the family, and personal values. In general, each of Wilder's books is based on a period in her own life and follows her family's struggle to survive on the relatively empty frontier lands of the western states. The first book, *Little House in the Big Woods* (1932), describes the Ingalls family's early years in the West, while the other books, including *Little House on the Prairie* (1935) and *Little Town on the Prairie* (1941), follow the family's moves through Missouri, Minnesota, and the Dakota Territory. Each publication in the eight-volume series corresponds with a new phase in Wilder's own childhood, adolescence, and adulthood, thereby providing young, primarily female, readers with parallels to their own development. The importance of family, hard work, and moral action are also at the core of Wilder's books, which instruct their readers as much as they entertain them. While the Little House series—and its 1970s television adaptation—emphasizes stereotypically female issues, the stories explore many of the themes central to the more conventional western, including civilization versus the wilderness, the individual versus society, and change versus stasis. The heroine of the books is also something of a liberated woman herself, suggesting that even in stories about women, the frontier promotes self-reliance and conventional role-defying behavior.[27]

A more recent version of the frontier myth for girls is found in the popular American Girl books, specifically in the story of Kirsten, the American pioneer girl. Each character in the series represents a particular period in American history, and the books which accompany the dolls illustrate and describe the details of that era. Kirsten's representation of westward expansion is especially interesting in its narrative about the pioneer girl's challenges and experiences, as well as in its depiction of her daily life. In the American Girl company's description of "Meet Kirsten," the character is introduced as Kirsten Larson, "a pioneer girl of strength and spirit growing up on the edge of the American frontier in 1854—a world of wilderness and prairie, of log cabins and one-room schoolhouses."[28] Not only is Kirsten a pioneer girl, but she and her family are Swedish immigrants and the book that goes along with the Kirsten doll discusses what it was like to speak very little English, to live in a lonely Minnesota town, and to adapt to a new culture. More progressive in its representation of women in the West, not to mention of nonnative speakers of English, the American Girl series offers, through Kirsten, a more liberated version of frontier girls, marking, perhaps, some of the ongoing changes made to the conventional frontier myths.

NEW LITERARY WESTERNS

As the American Girl series illustrates, the static representations of the West in literature were challenged throughout the second half of the twentieth century in an effort to represent a less biased and more complex picture of the frontier. In 1961, Larry McMurtry published his popular novel, *Horseman, Pass By*. It was followed by *The Last Picture Show* (1966), *Lonesome Dove* (1985), and *Buffalo Girls* (1990). McMurtry's fiction tends to focus on changes in the West, in particular in Texas where many of his novels are set. While each of these novels looks at the passing of the frontier, *Lonesome Dove*, centered around a western cattle drive, won the Pulitzer Prize and initiated a resurgence of popular interest in the western as a literary form and also as a subject appropriate for television and Hollywood movies. McMurtry's representation of the West is not as positive as other popular writers, and his characters search more frequently for meaning in the western landscape. In fact, *Buffalo Girls* and *Anything for Billy* (1989) challenge the myths of Billy the Kid and Calamity Jane, underscoring McMurtry's attitude toward the West, past and future.[29]

Other popular western writers include authors like Aaron Latham, author of *Code of the West* (2001), a book that combines the King Arthur legend with the cowboy myth. Cormac McCarthy's Border Trilogy explores, as the title suggests, the border between Mexico and Texas in novels like *All the Pretty Horses* (1993), *The Crossing* (1995), and *Cities of the Plains* (1999). Peter Bowen's novels, *Coyote Wind* (2000) and *Specimen Song* (2000), center on the experiences of Montana cattle brand inspector Gabriel Du Pre. Bowen is also known for his Yellowstone Kelly books, historical westerns about Yellowstone Kelly, "Gentleman and Scout." Humorous interpretations of the western novel, for instance *The Terrible Teague Bunch* (1978) by Gary Jennings, take up where comic strips and comic books left off, undermining the seriousness of the West through humor and ridicule. Other contemporary authors who have made their names through the western genre include Max Crawford, Terry C. Johnston, and Edwin B. Shrake.[30]

Several women have also tackled the subject of the West by challenging ethnic and gender stereotypes and by authoring fiction that looks at the omissions in texts produced by White, male writers. Leslie Marmon Silko, a writer of Indian descent, grew up on a Laguna Puebla reservation and has written extensively about her very different vision of the American West. Silko focuses in particular on the tension between contemporary life and the traditional culture of American Indians. In *Cere-*

mony (1977), for instance, the main character struggles to recover from his experience in World War II by returning to life on a reservation. The redeeming characteristics of Indian culture are apparent throughout Silko's writing, and her representation of the complex relationship between the two worlds is honest and realistic. Silko's fiction gives voice to an overlooked, and extremely rich, part of the American West and the popularity of her work, especially in the 1980s and 1990s, reflects the changing views of the West held by readers.

Like Silko, Louise Erdrich has offered readers a revisionary understanding of the West. Whereas Silko set her fiction in the Southwest, Erdrich chose the plains of North Dakota as the region for her novels. In *Love Medicine* (1984), *The Beet Queen* (1986), and *The Bingo Palace* (1993), Erdrich explores the interplay of tradition and change. One contribution she makes to the conventional writing about the West lies in her emphasis on the spiritual aspect of Native American culture. She includes visions and spirits in her stories. In contrast to more traditional western plots, which glorify the hero's individualism and self-reliance, Erdrich's use of the spiritual not only returns Indian belief systems to the foreground of western writing, but also offers an alternative understanding of how life is experienced and interpreted.

Numerous authors have contributed further to the genre of Native American writings. Barbara Kingsolver's *The Bean Trees* (1988), *Pigs in Heaven* (1993), and *Animal Dreams* (1990) focus primarily on female characters, celebrating their strengths and resources as opposed to making them stock romantic figures in relation to cowboys and other heroic men. Sherman Alexie's *The Lone Ranger and Tonto Fist Fight in Heaven* (1994), *Indian Killer* (1998), and *Reservation Blues* (1996) marked the last decade of the twentieth century with stories about contemporary Native American life. Other widely read Native American fiction includes James Welch's *The Heartsong of Charging Elk* (2000), Thomas Kin's *Truth and Bright Water* (2000), Joy Harjo's *The Woman Who Fell From the Sky: Poems* (1996), and the works of N. Scott Momaday and John Trudell.

The literature of and about the American West begins with the settlement of the earliest New England colonies. It takes shape in the early nineteen hundreds, and reaches its peak in the second half of the century in the form of dime novels and popular literary forms of the western. The common threads throughout the changing forms include the emphasis on a male-dominated world, the tension between civilization and the wilderness, and the struggle between the individual and society. Even recent variations on, and revisions to, the conventional western adopt these issues in an inverted form, further reinforcing how central they are to popular images of the American West.

9

Music

The music of westward expansion is among the most unique music the United States has produced. Rich in images of land, work, struggle, love, and loss, the music of the frontier, from the gold miners of the 1850s through the MTV stars of the twenty-first century, captures the fact and fiction of the American West. From its inception, the music was as often used to promote the promise of the West as to express the challenge inherent in living and working there. Both as advertisement and coping mechanism, the lyrics and melodies of frontier ballads, cowboy and mining tunes, campfire ditties, and barroom songs played a central role in the expression of the western experience. During the twentieth century frontier minstrelsy was repeatedly transformed through the popularity of singing cowboys, the rise of rock and roll, the appearance of heavy metal music, and in the old standby of the love ballad. Building and borrowing from the myth of the West, country-western music in particular has embraced the legacy of early frontier song through its reliance on the cowboy as the subject of lyrics and as the model of its musicians. Primarily classified as a subgenre of the popular, Top 40 culture until the last decades of the twentieth century, country-western was revitalized with the rise of MTV. The result has become an increasingly popular, and increasingly mainstream, genre in terms of sound, audience, and production.[1]

MUSIC AND EVERYDAY LIFE

Music played an important part in the daily life of pioneers as they braved the strenuous journey and began to establish new lives in western settlements. Many emigrants brought instruments with them on their journey, though these were frequently abandoned, along with other extraneous items, when lighter loads were necessary to complete the trip. Whenever possible, instruments such as fiddles, guitars, mouth organs, harmonicas, brass instruments, drums, and pianos were used to accompany individual and group singers who performed around campfires, in dance halls, at parades, and in private homes. The Sears, Roebuck and Montgomery Ward catalogs offered settlers mail-order access to new instruments, as well as to sheet music, metronomes, and books on how to play anything from the piano and banjo to the mandolin or fife. Also available by mail-order were Ball Room Guides and Call Books, which brought dancers and musicians together in one of the most popular activities of western towns, the local dance. From songs sung during the actual journey to music played at events and for entertainment, emigrants imported familiar eastern music to the West and used it to comfort, inspire, and reassure themselves and each other during the trip and in their new homes.

The Journey Westward

The westward journey, whether completed by boat, by wagon, or by foot, was at once physically rigorous, emotionally draining, and intellectually boring. Music helped emigrants to cope with these different experiences by providing a distraction that was community-oriented, words that reflected internal feelings, and an activity that was enjoyable. During her journey by sea, for instance, Mrs. Jane McDougal wrote that she "[w]ent on deck after tea, walked awhile with Mrs. Bowdin. Capt. Thomas sung us 'The Bride' & the 'Rose of Allandale.' Afterward Capt. Forbes got out his accordion & played while he and Capt. Thomas accompanied with their voices."[2] Here familiar songs were used to pass the time of the voyage and to bring small clusters of travelers together.

For Catherine Haun, another pioneer, songs met an additional need. Describing a fellow traveler with a gift for music, Haun wrote: "The familiar tunes that he played upon his harmonica seemed to soften the groaning and creaking of the wagons and to shorten the long miles of the mountain road. 'Home Sweet Home,' 'Old Kentucky Home,' 'Maryland, My Maryland,' 'The Girl I left Behind Me,' 'One More Ribber to Cross,' seemed particularly appropriate and touched many a pensive heart."[3] For Haun, music not only helped to relieve the boredom of the trip but also was an outlet for the emotions that were part and parcel of making such tremendous life changes. The fact that the songs she lists refer to either home or what was being left behind illustrates the mixed emotions experienced by many westbound pioneers. Singing helped to express despondent feelings upon arrival in the West, as one mother, in a letter to her son, illustrated when she wrote: "I felt badly to think that I was detined [*sic*] to be in such a place. I wept for a while and then I commenced singing and made up a song as I went along. My song was this: to California I did come and thought I under the bed I shall have to run to shelter me from the piercing storm."[4] By putting experiences into song, westerners expressed their feelings and comforted themselves.

Music was not just used to lighten heavy hearts, however. In the evenings when camps had been set up and dinner had been eaten, music was used for other reasons as well. Singing around campfires during the journey was, when possible to do, a social way to end a long day of travel. It often helped to offset the melancholy described above. The image of singing around a campfire is deeply embedded in American popular culture, through national groups like the Boy and Girl Scouts of America as well as in western films and folklore about the frontier. That one of the original reasons for the ritual was to bring travelers together and to rejuvenate them at the end of the day marks the communal nature of both the campfire and campfire songs as they have been passed down through the generations.

Entertainment and Events

While music played a role in the journey west, it was also an important part of creating social systems in frontier towns. There were numerous means through which music provided entertainment in western communities, from formal gatherings in which local musicians met to sing and play instruments, to informal, spontaneous performances. Music brought people together and provided entertainment in private homes. Many families had pianos by which people congregated, especially in the evening, to sing songs like "Shall We Gather at The River?" and "Pass Under the Rod."

In addition to music played in private homes, other musical gatherings entertained the entire town. Local bands were a common facet of western communities, providing music in parades as well as at local establishments like saloons and dance halls. The Dodge City "Cowboy Band" was an especially well-known group that traveled as far as Washington, DC, to perform. Looking much like an early version of what would become the standard country-western band, each member of the eighteen-man Cowboy Band

wore the uniform of the cowboy. A large sombrero took the place of the ordinary hat, while a blue flannel shirt was substituted for the white-blossomed shirt, and a silk scarf took the place of a neck tie. Leather leggings, supported by a cartridge belt and scabbard, a navy six-shooter, and spurs on boots completed the dress of this famous band of musicians.[5]

Bands were popular among the townspeople. If there were no instruments to play, singing and clapping took their place:

Some "play-party" games were actually dances without orchestras, the participants furnishing their own music by singing rhythmic verses as they moved through intricate dance forms. Spectators added their bit of gaiety by clapping hands and stamping feet to the beat of "Skip to My Lou," "Weevily Wheat," "The Girl I Left Behind Me," or "Old Dan Tucker."[6]

Other musical entertainment was available in the form of "frontier musicales, especially popular around Army posts where groups of musicians were more likely to be available than anywhere else on the frontier. Favorite numbers were such tunes as 'Tenting Tonight,' 'Old Hundred,' 'Nearer My God to Thee,' 'Annie Laurie,' and 'When the Swallows Homeward Fly'."[7] Concert performances by singers like Kate Hays, Lola Montez, and Caroline Chapman were also well-attended forms of musical entertainment. Traveling from the stages of cities like San Francisco and Sacramento, California, to the remote locations of boom-and-bust mining towns, these performers captured the attention of many westerners with their singing and dancing routines. While musical performances were welcomed and attendance was high, some westerners complained about the trend to play music while actors were speaking their lines.

Music was also used to mark private and public events. The Fourth of July was always well celebrated in the West, with music in the form of bands or other performances. The Christmas Ball was another annual town event at which music played a key role. On a private level, the tradition of the shivaree, a wedding-night celebration, made its way west, resulting in raucous but no less enjoyable music. Music was used to mourn deaths as well, usually with hymns. Deaths during the westward journey, not to mention in the early years of settlement, were extremely common occurrences, but they were no less acknowledged for their frequency. A traveler described the combination of making do with available resources, while adhering to familiar rituals. Hymns in general were a familiar and popular form of music, sung in and out of formal church services. The image of pioneers in rustic churches singing hymns like "Bringing in the Sheaves" has regularly appeared in popular television programs about the West, for instance, *Little House on the Prairie* and *Dr. Quinn, Medicine Woman*.

MUSIC OF THE WESTERN EXPERIENCE

Music accompanied westward expansion in part because pioneers brought songs, instruments, and lyrics with them on the journey. However, as the West began to take shape and, as experiences unique to the West began to unfold, music which reflected the land, labor, and love of the frontier gradually evolved.

Borrowed Tunes/Original Words

The music that has recorded the experience of the Old West can be recognized by several key characteristics found in the majority of songs sung in the early years of westward expansion. First, the tunes were borrowed from familiar pieces of music from the East, as well as from English ballads and Irish folk tunes. Whatever the source, western music depended for tunes on well-known songs like "Pop Goes the Weasel" and "Comin' Through the Rye," the familiarity of the tune making the songs easy to learn and simple to communicate. The words that accompanied those tunes, however, were unique, either because they humorously parodied the song's original lyrics or because they cleverly represented the new experience of life in the West. The words and stories that comprised the songs of the frontier were taken from newspaper stories or from pamphlets, broadsides, or books. Others were simply made up, their origins deriving from an event or story. Songs, by nature, were orally communicated and, as a result, the records of early western music are somewhat inconsistent, especially in terms of the exact words that were sung, as these could be altered from one singer to the next. The lyrics tended to rhyme in a structured pattern. The simple rhymes helped people to memorize the songs more easily, encouraging the circulation of such tunes among miners, cowboys, and other westerners. Such dissemination resulted in numerous versions of the same song. For instance, the popular song "The Little Adobe Casa," is "only one of several offspring of "The Little Old Sod Shanty" . . . [including] "The Little Vine-clad Cottage on the Claim," the popular woman's "Reply to the Little Old Sod Shanty," "The Little New Log Cabin in the Hills" . . . and even "The Little Red Caboose Behind the Train."[8]

Collections such as *Put's Original California Songster* (1854) were among the earliest and best-known publications of old western songs and helped both to standardize the multiple versions and to further familiarize westerners with the music of the gold rush. When the songs were performed there were some basic guidelines to which musicians adhered. The fiddle typically accompanied old frontier songs, and the banjo became increasingly popular over time.

A five-stringed banjo (picked, not strummed) [was] the natural accompaniment . . . the singing . . . was an exceedingly serious business, no matter how humorous the words. Enunciation had to be distinct, so that the story would be clear to every hearer; but an emphatic rhythm, usually audibly tapped out by one toe, was an integral part of the folk singer's performance, even when the idea expressed in the text would not seem to require this monotonous accent. The style was never emotionally interpretative, for convention required understatement. Delivery was deadpan rather than dramatic. Moreover, when a folk-singer came to the end of his song he stopped without warning.[9]

Western music had a distinct sound and sense. Whether the subject was mining life, the open range, or the cowboy existence, there were themes and expressions commonly used to communicate to listeners.

Songs of the Forty-niners

Perhaps the earliest western music can be found in the songs of the forty-niners, the miners who first rushed across the country to make their fortunes in gold. Performed in makeshift theaters and saloons, published in the popular press, and collected in cheaply printed volumes, the songs were constantly changing as new miners in different settings adapted the words to fit their own experiences. While the tunes typically came from eastern songs like "Oh, Susanna!" (which became, for instance, "Oh, California"), the words were recycled over and over again as new waves of emigrants traveled west. Songs like "Seeing the Elephant," one of the first to be written in the West, were hugely popular, as were those by John A. Stone, also known as Old Put, who published small collections of tunes in *Put's Original California Songster* and *Put's Golden Songster* (1858). Other popular collections included *Gold Digger's Song Book* (1856). Frequently written by minstrel troupes and aimed at capturing in music the essence of placer mining life, the songs of the forty-niners offer a unique perspective on the first rush of westward expansion.

The songs that remain from this era trace the voyage west, by boat and by wagon, and express the longings, expectations, and realities of the gold rush experience. Indeed, they capture with concrete, often humorous images, the details of mining life. The songs are at times sentimental, as in "I Often Think of Writing Home," which tells the tale of a miner who considers writing home but who rarely does.[10] They also describe the reasons emigrants headed west or make fun of the impact that the journey had on relationships. The very popular song "Joe Bowers" chronicles a young man's journey to California to establish a homestead for his sweetheart who turns out to be fickle and marries another man.[11] Another version of the love-gone-astray story, "Sweet Betsy from Pike," describes Betsy and Ike, a young couple who endured endless obstacles during their travels west, only to have their relationship end when they arrived there.[12] Other songs either express a darkly humorous version of the journey or a parodic description of life in the mines. For instance, songs with titles like "California Stage Company," "Humbug

Steamship Companies," and "When I Went Off to Prospect" challenge the popular belief that the trip west was an easy one and that life upon arrival in California was immediately prosperous. The parody present in many mining songs may have developed in response to the arduous, continuous, and often futile nature of mining itself. The daily existence of the forty-niners was far from comfortable or easy, and the humor so evident in their songs may have provided a way to endure the challenges of life. Whatever the reason, satire marks these early western songs with a unique flavor that is easy to recognize.

While the forty-niners' songs were often humorous, they also were surprisingly informative. For instance, in "Crossing the Plains," the lyrics tell about the number of days, amount of food, and impact on cattle that occurs during the westward journey.[13] More factual than many of the guidebooks upon which emigrants depended to make the journey safely from the East, early mining songs provided westerners with an alternative form of communicating about the rigorous trip to the land of gold.

Cowboy and Frontier Songs

Whereas mining songs were primarily sung for entertainment, cowboy music served an additional purpose. Cowboy work songs marked the time during cattle drives, calmed cattle during long cattle marches, lulled cattle to sleep at night, provided comraderie during evenings on the plains, and captured the experience of the cowhand. While songs were commonly passed around among cowboys, specific ranches also tended to have their own popular music:

Nearly every well established ranch had for its own individual song a set of verses of its own making. Some "smart" cowboy would lead off composing these verses, which the outfit would take up, chorusing in whenever the song was sung. When a puncher from another outfit drifted into camp, he was expected to sing any new song he might know or new stanzas to an old song, and to teach them to the camp he was visiting. In exchange, he took the novelties his hosts knew. Thus songs like "The Old Chisolm Trail" became of interminable length.[14]

Cowboys used music as a social tool, as a way of recording their experiences, as a form of entertainment, and as a companion to their work. The result was a wide range of music that, when drawn together, recorded a unique aspect of American life.

Collecting Cowboy Music

Historians owe a debt to "Jack" Thorp who spent decades riding among cowboys to collect and record their songs, which were rarely written down and only learned by word of mouth. Published in his *Songs of the Cowboys*, the ballads and lyrics Thorp recorded reveal unique aspects of the cowboy life. The challenge Thorp faced was not only to track down as many of the cowboy songs as he could, but to trace individual verses as well. In his autobiographical essay about this search, entitled "Banjo in the Cow Camps," Thorp wrote that when he asked a young cowhand to repeat a song he had been singing,

he knew only two verses—that's all. And none of the other hands in camp knew more. That was one of the difficulties encountered in the earliest effort to assemble the unprinted verse on the range. None of the cowboys who could sing ever remembered an entire song. I would pick up a verse or two here, another verse or two there.[15]

Songs like "The Old Chisolm Trail," Thorp claimed, "were sung from the California Line to Mexico, and there were thousands of verses; nobody ever collected all of them."[16] In addition to the challenge of capturing every verse of every song, there was also the difficulty of determining which verses, and even which words, were original since the lyrics varied from one singer to the next, resulting in multiple versions of a single tune.

Themes

The themes of frontier music were so predictable that early song collections were organized by topic.[17] Songs like "Whoopee Ty Yi Yo, Git Along, Little Dogies," "Good-by, Old Paint," "The Lone Star Trail," and "The Cowboy's Dream" chronicle the experience of life on the trail. While the work they describe is mostly driving a herd, these songs also lament the cowboy life which takes the singer away from his home, sweetheart, and family. Many lines express the emotional isolation of cowboy life. In contrast, songs like "The Old Chisolm Trail" and "The Crooked Trail to Holbrook" illustrate the manner in which such songs were meant to entertain and pass the time on long journeys.

While many cowboy songs consisted of sentimental phrases or inoffensive language, cowboy lyrics also tended to be so bawdy that collectors like Thorp edited them for content. "Bucking Bronco" is one example of the role editing played in taming the language of popular frontier music. When Thorp recorded the lyrics he deliberately altered the innuendoes implicit in the song's description of a woman who warns other women about the dangers of a cowboy and his "rawhide."[18]

The suggestiveness of such songs corresponded with the more lively aspects of the cowboy's life, namely when he rode into town after months on the trail. With money in his pocket, a saloon and women at hand, the cowboy of the plains sang drinking songs that celebrated the wild characters of the West and the lawlessness that ostensibly existed there. Songs such as "Billy the Kid," "Sam Bass," "Jesse James," "Rye Whiskey," "The Bad Boy," and "The Durant Jail" reflect a different side of life on the plains. "Sam Bass," one of the most popular of these tunes, tells the tale of a man who falls in with the wrong crowd, and goes on a spree only to end up riddled with bullets after robbing a train.[19]

Finally, cowboy songs were the context for sayings that are recognized today in slightly altered form. Echoes of the cowboy toast, "Up to my lips, and over my gums; / Look out, guts, here she comes," for instance, can be heard in parodies of dieting such as "Up to my lips, over my gums; / Look out, hips, here it comes." The term "dogies" occurs repeatedly in such tunes and refers to the calves that were herded along with the mature cattle. The term, by some accounts, first was used in "The Last Round-Up," and the phrase "git along little dogies"—or variations of it—is a staple in western lore. It turns up in "Rawhide," the theme song of the television program by the same name, not to mention the hit film *The Blues Brothers*, and, in the late twentieth-century, the music for a Wal-Mart commercial.[20]

Other favorite topics of frontier songs included horses, cowgirls, rangers, and home. Songs like "The Texas Rangers," "When You and I Were Young, Maggie," "The Rambling Cowboy," "The Sante Fe Trail," "Red River Valley," and "Lone Driftin' Riders" have added to the myth of the West and the wealth of popular culture around it. But as the frontier life of the cowboy was replaced with barbed wire, railroads, and established towns, songs like "The Old Time Cowboy" came into vogue, marking the cowboy's longing not for home or for love but for the Old West.

Sheet Music, RCA Victor, and Radio

Western music's transition from a regional, primarily oral form of communication to mainstream public recordings was directly linked to three factors. The development of sheet music and the publication of song books standardized frontier songs and increased their visibility by making them available in stores and through mail-order catalogs. Around the same time, RCA Victor began recording the best-known music of the Old West, especially cowboy songs, including Carl T. Sprague's "When the Work's Done This Fall," as well as "The Old Chisolm Trail" and "The Zebra Dun." Now audiences across the country could hear, as well as sing and play, the old western tunes. Finally, the popularity of radio stations like 5XT, KFRU, and KVOO, all out of Oklahoma, which featured western bands like Otto Gray and his Oklahoma Cowboys, brought the sound of western music to greater numbers of Americans. The rise of Hollywood films further cemented the image, as well as the sound, of the West in the American consciousness. The national popularity of country radio also brought the early, local country stations into contemporary life.

SINGING COWBOYS, COWGIRLS, AND THE GREAT DEPRESSION

The rise of radio and film brought with it a new development in the popularity of cowboys, music, and the West. The singing cowboy brought the traditional country music of the rural, southeastern United States into contact with the mythic heroism of the western cowboy. The result was the genre of country-western music that, by helping country or "hillbilly" music to shed its image as the music of impoverished, rural people, initiated a form that has remained popular into the twenty-first century.[21]

Gene Autry and the Mail-Order Guitar

The premier singing cowboy was Gene Autry, whose popular success revolutionized the look and reception of country-western music. Autry himself had western roots and spent his early life in Texas and Oklahoma. He also worked with a medicine show, performing music with the traveling group. In the late 1920s, Autry performed his music on radio stations. He later traveled to the National Barn Dance in Chicago, a performance hall that primarily featured country music. In 1934 he appeared as a singing cowboy in the film "In Old Sante Fe," and a new period in western music took off with lightning speed.

The singing cowboy was a heroic figure who paused in the midst of events large and small to sing songs like "I'm a Cowpoke Pokin' Along" and "Fetch Me Down My Trusty .45." While the songs incorporated western images, the clothes that filled the singing cowboy's wardrobe were especially noteworthy. The cowboy hat, bandana, cowboy boots, and western-style shirts adopted by Autry and other performers changed the physical appearance of the typical country-western music star who until that time had primarily worn overalls and other rural clothing. The impact of this shift can be seen throughout the twentieth century, from the gimmicks of the "rhinestone cowboys" to the understated yet nonetheless western dress of 1990s stars like Garth Brooks and Chad Brock.[22] Autry's impact on popular culture is evident in the proliferation of products and entertainment that bore the Autry name. His use of the guitar also helped to make the instrument the primary choice among country singers. In the 1930s, Sears, Roebuck offered a Gene Autry Guitar, a mail-order item that could be purchased by those enamored of the singing

An ad for the film *Springtime in the Rockies* (1937). Courtesy of the Library of Congress.

cowboy. Autry was featured in films like *Springtime in the Rockies* (1937), and his name appeared on cowboy spurs, cowboy boots, billfolds, lunch boxes, cap pistols, watches, bikes, board games, and clothing. In the 1940s and 1950s Autry's image could be found on the cover of coloring books, comic books, and the popular "Little Golden Books" for young readers.[23]

Autry's success was followed by a proliferation of similar singing cowboys, including Tex Ritter, Ray Whitley (whose song "Back In the Saddle Again" was a phenomenon in its own right), Eddie Dean, Slick Montana, and Roy Rogers. These singers were more popular on screen than they were on records, making the singing cowboy and his offshoots more closely identified with Hollywood than the recording industry. Other musicians also reaped the benefits of the singing cowboy phenomenon. Bands and duet groups, including Jimmy Wakely and Margaret Whiting, Foy Williams and the Riders of the Purple Sage, Chuck Wagon Gang and The Prairie Ramblers, performed at the National Barn Dance and as backup groups for the Hollywood cowboys. Roy Rogers' group, Sons of the Pioneers, enjoyed significant success with songs like "Tumbling Tumbleweeds" and "Way Out There." The result was a wave of singers whose dress, band names, and music brought western influence to country music throughout the 1930s and into the 1940s. By the 1950s, Rex Allen marked the last of the popular singing cowboys as post–World War II America became disenchanted with the optimistic, heroic image the figure represented.[24]

Woody Guthrie

One of the most recognized of Depression era musicians to contribute to the music of the West was Woodrow Wilson Guthrie. Guthrie's contributions to western music arose primarily from his own experience of the West, from a childhood in Oklahoma to his years in the dust bowl of Texas and his travels to California during the Great Depression. Guthrie wrote about the latter time period in *Dust Bowl Ballads* which brought him national attention in the 1940s.[25] His songs, focused on the years of the Great Depression and the lives of migrant workers, spoke to a generation who traveled West in search of work and a new life. Songs like "Pastures of Plenty" represented and even legitimated the plight of migrant laborers and connected them to the land. His best-known song of all, "This Land Is Your Land," further celebrated the connection between the American people and their geographical heritage. And while the lyrics refer to cities like New York, the majority of images are of the West: California, redwood forests, endless skies, golden valleys, wheat fields, and dust clouds.[26]

Patsy Montana and the Singing Cowgirl

During the Great Depression female country singers adopted the West as a major theme in both their music and their appearance. Patsy Montana initiated the first wave of cowgirl singers with songs that reflected the new, independent image of the country-western music star. Titles like her most popular song, "I Want to be a Cowboy's Sweetheart," as well as "I Wanna Be a Western Cowgirl," "The She Buckaroo," and "I Only Want a Buddy Not a Sweetheart," not only helped to define the cowgirl as a central figure in country music, but directly evoked the mythic western hero, the cowboy, as her partner. Dressed in clothing that was easily recognized as "western," including a cowboy hat and boots, fringed leather skirt, and a bandana around her neck, Montana completed her image with a gun slung in a hip-style holster.[27]

The effect was to make the clothes of the Old West a key component of many female singers' repertoire. Other cowgirl musicians followed Montana's lead, including Louise Massey, Rosalie Allen, Texas Ruby, Patsy Cline, Loretta Lynn, and Laura Lee McBride. Patsy Cline and Loretta Lynn also borrowed from the cowgirl image, though their music has been classified more as country than country-western. Current female vocalists such as Reba McIntire, LeAnn Rimes, and Shania Twain have updated Montana's pioneering form by creating stylish, hip renditions of the cowgirl figure. Montana's impact on country-western music was more significant than providing a role model for future female vocalists, however. In addition to her looks, Montana conveyed a distinct message: Women, too, have "cowboy" characteristics. They can be independent, free, self-reliant, and still be with their man. An unexpected feminist ring, in other words, is present in Montana's songs, again setting the stage for future female musicians in the field.[28]

Western Swing and Honky-Tonk

Two other forms of popular music that developed during the first half of the twentieth century and directly or indirectly evoked the frontier were western swing and honky-tonk. Western swing originated with the music of a fiddler named Bob Wills, who had learned to play the guitar by purchasing a lesson book through the mail-order Sears, Roebuck catalog. Wills had traveled with a Medicine Show, thereby experiencing the West firsthand, and he played in a variety of bands early in his career. It was "Bob Wills and His Texas Playboys," however, that made a difference in western music. Not only did Wills and his group introduce drums, steel guitar, and elements of swing-jazz bands, but they popularized songs like "San Antonio Rose" and brought fine dance music to American entertainment. Wills and his Texas Playboys did not fully adopt the cowboy-style clothing of musicians like Autry, but they did wear cowboy-style hats, thereby maintaining a visual connection to the western roots of their music. With the help of musicians like Tex Williams and Spade Cooley, western swing remained popular through World War II and into the 1950s, when it began to draw fewer crowds.[29] Trend-driven western dances and dance music continued throughout the century, however, including the Electric Slide, danced to songs like Texas Little's "God Blessed Texas," Bobby Brown's "My Perogative," and GrandMaster Slice's "Electric Slide."[30]

Honky-tonk music, which was performed in, and named after, the cheap, noisy saloons of the same name, differed from western swing in two ways. First, honky-tonk music was less about the West than other music related to the frontier, in part because it focused more on what some have called "hillbilly" images of rural or working-class American life, and drew on the old standby themes of drinking, loving, and cheating.[31] Second, whereas the Texas Playboys tended to downplay the cowboy image in their dress, honky-tonk musicians like Hank Williams' Drifting Cowboys readily adopted the cowboy apparel. Indeed, honky-tonk's popularity perpetuated the cowboy myth through the music's reliance on increasingly elaborate cowboy costumes, a trend that marked country-western music through the late sixties when a renewed interest in more conservative subjects changed the content of country-western lyrics.[32]

Home on the Range, State Songs, and Musical Showtunes

While types of music can be directly associated with the American West, individual songs about the frontier were also popular during the 1930s and 1940s. One of the most beloved frontier songs, "Home on the Range," experienced hit status in the early 1930s after the election of Franklin D. Roosevelt as president. Legend has it that upon his election, Roosevelt was serenaded outside of his New York City residence by reporters singing the song. Allegedly, Roosevelt claimed that the song was his favorite and, from that point on, "Home on the Range" was adored by the American public. As Kirke Mechem writes, "Everybody sang it, from Lawrence Tibbett to the smallest entertainer. Radio chains, motion picture companies, phonograph record concerns and music publishers had a field day. . . . At its peak the song was literally sung around the world."[33]

As with other western folk songs, the author of "Home on the Range" was difficult to trace and different versions of the lyrics were documented at different times in the song's history. Unlike other western songs, however, the popularity of "Home on the Range" led to false authorship claims, lawsuits, and such public controversy that historians sought to track down the earliest printed version of the song, which was finally pinpointed to February 26, 1876. Originally written by Dr. B. Higley, the song's lyrics have changed in an interesting way. The line, "I would not exchange my home on the range," as recorded by John A. Lomax in his collection of frontier songs, takes on a different meaning in Higley's version, which reads, "I would not exchange my home *here to* range" (italics added). The difference between the two lines illustrates how the transformation of frontier lyrics over time actually helped to popularize them by making their meaning relevant to more people. Whereas in Higley's version the singer says he would not leave his personal home in order to range—or move about—on the plains, the Lomax version appeals to a broader audience. In the place of a specific home as distinguished from the rest of the prairie, a home "on" that prairie or range, embraces the entire land of the West, indicating that the singer would not leave the range itself, for *it* is home. In 1947 the tune became the state song of Kansas.[34]

Like "Home on the Range," the well-known show tune "Oklahoma!"

An ad for the film *Calamity Jane* (1953). Courtesy of the Library of Congress.

was also adopted as a state song. The title song from Rodgers and Hammerstein's musical by the same name, the lyrics to "Oklahoma!" include the celebratory lines about life on the plains.[35] *Oklahoma!* also introduced and popularized songs like "The Farmer and the Cowman," "Kansas City," and "Little Surrey with the Fringe on Top." *Paint Your Wagon, Annie Get Your Gun,* and *Calamity Jane* also took the West and its legends as their subject matter, further emphasizing the way that music has contributed to widespread ideas about westward expansion.[36]

Pop, Rock, and the West

The American West—including the land, its inhabitants, specific states, and specific states of mind—has been the subject of popular music outside of the country-western genre as well. Indeed, the tremendous number of musical titles, lyrics, and phrases that in one way or another refer to, or evoke, the American West demonstrates the depths to which the frontier has been embedded in the American psyche, including in the genres of pop and rock music. The West as a place of freedom and beauty is evident in John Denver's "Rocky Mountain High," while the West as a dynamic environment is clear in Escape Club's "Wild Wild West." Western icons appear in the Rolling Stones' "Wild Horses," America's "Horse with No Name," Neil Young's "After the Gold Rush," Bon Jovi's "Blaze of Glory," and 10,000 Maniacs' "Painted Desert," "Campfire Song," and "Gold Rush Brides." Upbeat celebrations of western states are epitomized by the Beach Boys' "California Girls" and "Surfin' U.S.A.," as well as The Mamas and the Papas' song "California Dreamin'." Less positive views of the West can be seen in The Eagles' "Hotel California" and "Desperado," as well as Eric Clapton's "I Shot the Sheriff." Songs that elicit the Old West include Pet Shop Boys' "Go West," Electric Light Orchestra's "Wild West Hero," Bon Jovi's "Wanted Dead or Alive," Adam and the Ants' "5 Guns West," and Big Star's "Way Out West." Finally, the West appears in lyrics, as well as titles, such as in the Barenaked Ladies' "It's All Been Done."[37] Where mainstream musicians have incorporated the West into their best-selling songs, musical groups like Black Lodge Singers have combined traditional Native American rhythm with lyrics directly drawn from popular culture. *The Kids Tape*, for instance, includes "The Mighty Mouse Song," "Looney Tunes," and "Micky Mouse Minnie Mouse & Pluto Too."[38]

Outlaw Musicians and Urban Cowboys

Despite the variety of western icons that have been incorporated into music about the West, throughout musical forms, singers, and lyrics, the cowboy has been the most prominent and resilient.[39] In contrast to the singing cowboy, however, whose appearance was wholesome and optimistic, in the 1970s and 1980s two different cowboy types appeared in the music world. Growing out of the conflicted decade of the 1960s, during which the United States questioned its long-standing values and challenged the essential goodness of its beliefs, the outlaw musician brought more aggressive lyrics and new presence to country-western music. The outlaw cowboy, on the other hand, was perhaps the antithesis of the good, clean, all-American image put forth by Gene Autry. Singers like Waylon Jennings, David Allen Coe, Willie Nelson, and Kris Kristofferson were noteworthy for their rebel attitudes, songs, and styles. Far from the white-studded cowboy suits of previous decades, these singers donned worn clothes and hats, and sported long hair. In many ways the outlaw cowboy figure fit more closely with earlier versions of the rough and rugged American cowboy who had undergone multiple image transitions throughout the first half of the twentieth century. The music played by these musicians, in albums like Willie Nelson's "Red Headed Stranger," "The Outlaws," and "Highwayman," dealt with traditional country-western topics but also emphasized the experience of being an outsider, a loner, an alien in American culture. Songs like "Mammas Don't Let Your Babies Grow Up to Be Cowboys" and "Ladies Love Outlaws" reflect the rebellious nature of the outlaw musician and his relationship to the cowboy image.[40]

In contrast to the cowboy figure represented by the outlaws, another version of the cowboy singer appeared on the music scene in the 1970s and early 1980s. As Kenneth J. Bindas describes, this modern cowboy "was no longer self-assured and happy about his life of wandering and flight."[41] More specifically, Bindas claims:

"The Lonesome LA Cowboy" (1973), by the New Riders of the Purple Sage, depicts an urban cowboy at odds with his own image and living a life that seems devoid of any mythic quest or heroic deeds. Later this theme would help to rejuvenate the cowboy image in popular music as a result of the John Travolta movie *Urban Cowboy* (1980). Nevertheless, the New Riders' and Travolta's cowboy was a far cry from the earlier ones and seemed desperate to retain his image of the mythic West in the face of life's realities.[42]

Marked by flamboyant cowboy suits, hats, and boots, and invoked in the title of Glen Campbell's song "Rhinestone Cowboy," the urban cowboy seemed closer to the image projected by Autry and Rogers. Although the late-twentieth-century interpretation was less confident and optimistic than its predecessor, the outlaw and urban cowboys were not the final transformation of the cowhand in American popular music. A hybrid figure would end the century on a new note, one that met with new heights of popular success.

MTV AND NEW COUNTRY-WESTERN SINGERS

While the image of country-western music was identified mainly as a subcategory of popular music throughout much of the twentieth century, the rise of MTV and music videos changed the genre. A new generation of singers began to appear on the country-western video scene and to be played regularly on country-western music stations. Attractive, provocative, and fashionably dressed, these new singers have helped to bring country-western into the mainstream of American popular music. The result has been an updated interpretation of the cowboy/cowgirl singer, including crossover hits and controversy.

Hat Acts

In the 1980s and early 1990s, country-western images changed yet again, both on stage and on video. Performers like Randy Travis, Garth

Brooks, George Strait, and Clint Black were in many ways updated singing cowboys more clean-cut and conservative than the outlaws of the
previous decade but also more hip than the Gene Autry figures of the
early twentieth century. In understated cowboy hats, jeans, and shirts,
this new wave of singers offered audiences a sleeker, minimalist rendition of the cowboy figure. Often dressed in black, Travis, Brooks, and
others sang songs that drew parallels between the Old and New West,
offering contemporary listeners an updated cowboy hero. Songs like
Brooks' "Rodeo," Black's "Nobody's Home" and Strait's "The Cowboy
Rides Away" evoke western icons in their titles and lyrics. The attitudes
expressed in the songs of these male singers range from encouraging
individualism, as in Brooks' "Against the Grain," to the losing-at-love
ballad of Clint Black's "Killin' Time."

Brooks and Black were among the most notable crossover musicians,
finding their way into mainstream music and popular culture. While
Brooks may have arguably "crossed" from country-western to pop music
more readily than Black, Black has found his own connections to the pop
culture world. Not only did he sponsor QVC's campaign for online shopping, initiated in conjunction with Microsoft in 1995, but his picture appeared on boxes of Kellogg's cereals as part of a campaign with the
American Heart Association. Cereal buyers could order "an exclusive
poster" of Black, as well as his most recent CD by calling a number on
the box.[43] A humorous offshoot of the mid-1990s popularity of country-
western music can be seen in the presence of Riders in the Sky, a spin-
off of the cowboy musician. The group was so popular that they starred
in their own TNN television show starting in 1996.[44]

The New Cowgirl Singer

When Shania Twain first broke into the country-western music world,
what most people commented on was her navel. Dressed in body-
conscious, fashionable, and revealing clothes, Twain, along with young
female singers like LeAnn Rimes, Trisha Yearwood, Terri Clark, Patty
Loveless, Mary-Chapin Carpenter, and Faith Hill, shifted the definition
of the female country-western singer. Through their hip songs about female identity, independence, and real-life experience, these performers
captured the attention not only of female listeners in the country-western
genre, but in the Top 40 forum as well. In doing so, they began to blur
the line between pop and country-western music, even producing different versions of their songs for each audience.[45] Other groups followed
suit, including the Cowboy Junkies, Ranch Romance, and the Dixie
Chicks, all-girl bands who identifed themselves as country-western musicians but whose songs crossed over to the mainstream market.

A crucial aspect of the new cowgirl singers' success was the availability of MTV and music videos.[46] While Shania Twain and her contemporaries identified themselves with the genre through clothing easily recognized as "western"—denim, suede, cowboy boots—their fashion choices were more sleek and sophisticated than the flashier clothing worn by their country predecessors, for instance Dolly Parton, Barbara Mandrell, or Tammy Wynette. The resulting images were provocative, sexy, and alluring, and female country-western musicians found their new image featured and debated in a variety of forums, including *People Magazine*, *Entertainment Weekly*, *Seventeen*, and the *New York Times*.

While the music video drew listeners through the visual appeal of singers like Twain, the songs they were singing proved just as engaging. On the one hand, Twain's "Whose Bed Have Your Boots Been Under?" the Dixie Chicks' "Cowboy Take Me Away," and "Wide Open Spaces," as well as Faith Hill's "This Kiss," tap into the traditional subjects covered by country-western lyrics—western icons, western land, romantic love, and heartbreaking loss. On the other hand, there is an interesting openness about women's lives in these and other new country-western songs. "Cowboy Take Me Away," for instance, associates a girl's coming-of-age with the freedom evoked by western space. The chorus suggests that girls are not always perfect and that they too need space to explore who they are. Other songs, like Twain's "Honey, I'm Home" and "Man! I Feel Like a Woman," as well as Mary-Chapin Carpenter's "He Thinks He'll Keep Her," play with, and even challenge, male and female stereotypes. Panty lines, PMS, midlife crises, and politically correct approaches to intimacy (Twain's "If You Wanna Touch Her, Ask") are sung with a combined humor and honesty that is refreshing, and clearly appealing, to a wide range of listeners.[47]

"Murder on Music Row"

The popularity of singers like Shania Twain and Garth Brooks challenged the boundaries between country-western and Top 40 music. This new cohort also created a rift in the country-western music world, as was evident at the 2000 Academy of Country Music Awards program, when a number of musicians who appeared on stage to accept awards proclaimed their pride in only being played on country-western music stations. That sentiment stood in direct contrast to other winners like Faith Hill. The ideal image of the twenty-first century country-western female star, Hill's award-winning video (Breathe) and popular song climbed both the country-western and Top 40 music charts, a crossover between the country-western and pop music realms that is viewed by some country-western musicians as a betrayal of country-western authenticity. The tension was most evident when country-western traditionalists Alan Jackson and George Strait sang "Murder on Music Row" together, while the audience cheered at the lyrics' sentiments about the negative impact that rock and roll has had on traditional country-western music.

While musicians who have defined themselves as country singers continue to cross over into the pop charts, the future of country-western music seems uncertain. If stars like Shania Twain and Garth Brooks can draw audiences from the country and Top 40 worlds, will they lose their identity as country-western musicians? While the image of the American West has typically been reinforced by its relationship to popular culture, country music, which has borrowed so extensively from the myths of the cowboy and the frontier, seems curiously threatened by its connection to the pop world. The significance of cowboy hats and the love of "wide-open spaces" seems at stake as opposing forces within the field of country-western music battle to keep tradition alive in the twenty-first century.[48]

10

Performing Arts

The close-knit relationship between popular culture and western history is nowhere more evident than in the field of the performing arts, from westward expansion to the present. What made a live performance, motion picture, or television broadcast popular can be viewed as directly tied to the cultural and social concerns of the moment in which it was produced. The fact that the material of early western theater performances fluctuated from conventionally moral social norms to risqué vaudeville performances reflects the fact that such shows were held in towns struggling to establish social order. That the most popular period of western television programs occurred during the 1950s, and that these shows emphasized patriotism, nationalism, and the clear-cut difference between good and evil, mirrors the concerns of post–World War II society and the international anxieties of the burgeoning Cold War. Finally, that the twentieth century would end with a flourish of western-based films, of which only a limited number would be successful, records what may be the inability of a culture preoccupied with technology and financial success to find resonance in one of the most American of all genres, the western.[1]

PERFORMANCE IN THE OLD WEST

The gold rush drew vast numbers of settlers to towns in the West, and the existence of those towns drew a wide range of entertainment. Popular forms of entertainment on the frontier can be generally categorized as serving two functions: to civilize the West and to provide an escape from the severe hardships of daily life there. Theater, music, and dance arrived in the West either as performances that had been popular in the East—for instance productions of *Uncle Tom's Cabin* and plays by Shakespeare—or as entertainment which focused on the social norms that were imported from the East.[2]

Theater

From the earliest days of settlement, theaters were integral to the social fabric of western towns.[3] Traveling minstrel shows were run by soldiers in the years prior to the gold rush, and provided entertainment at forts and other outposts. As pioneers ventured west, and as mining towns sprung up in previously unpopulated areas, theaters became central to the towns. Early performances were held on stages that were part of the local saloon, general store, or hotel. Whatever the facility, the proprietor either made floor space for a makeshift stage or designated a room in the building as the "theater."[4] Given the close association between the bar and the stage, performances were attended by rowdy, drunken audiences whose like or dislike of the entertainment was revealed in what they threw onto the stage: coins and bags of gold dust if they were happy; rotten vegetables and other offensive items if they were not.

Saloon theaters were also home to other forms of entertainment, including "hurdy-gurdy girls," named after instruments like the barrel organ that used a crank to produce music. Such performers entertained saloon-goers with dancing and singing, local and inexpensive versions of more professional dance shows. "Honky-tonk" was another predominantly western form of entertainment. Honky-tonk traditionally took place in "a saloon theatre, usually with a dance-hall attached to it, which featured girls and drinks in equal proportions. The typical Honky Tonk had a number of curtained boxes, where male patrons were visited by the show-girls, and it was the duty of the girls to solicit drinks (as many as possible) from the occupants."[5] The image of the saloon as the western town's center of entertainment has been perpetuated in western films and television shows—The Long Branch Saloon in *Gunsmoke*, for example—further embedding the theater in the national lore about frontier life.

Despite the hold that saloons had on the realm of the performing arts, as early as 1849 professional theaters such as The Eagle Theater in Sacramento opened to the public. The first performance held at The Eagle was *The Bandit Chief; or, the Forest Spectre*, on October 18, 1849. Other theaters were quickly built, providing entertainment to the miners who flocked west in response to the promise of quick riches.[6] One of the most reputable of all western theaters was in Salt Lake City, Utah, which attracted the most popular acts and record numbers of attendees. Built in 1862, the Salt Lake Theater was not a place where religious tenets were reinforced through onstage performances, but rather a forum for professional actors who were able to bring first-rate drama to the Mormon community. As Brigham Young, the Mormon leader, stated: "If I were placed on a cannibal island and given the task of civilizing its people, I should straightway build a theatre for that purpose."[7] The Salt Lake Theater was one of the most popular and successful of the early western performance halls, attracting the most accomplished actors and actresses and rewarding them well for their work.

Eastern Imports, Shakespeare, and Name Recognition

Shows that met with success in the East were often imported to the West and produced in the Salt Lake Theater as well as at other, smaller halls. For instance, the popular stage rendition of Harriet Beecher Stowe's novel *Uncle Tom's Cabin* (1852) was performed throughout the West and heralded by parades that included "18 Real Georgia Plantation Shouters, Mlle. Minerva's New Orleans Creole Girls' Fife and Drum Corps, the 'Original Whangdoodle Pickaninny Band,' Eva's $1500 gold chariot, a log cabin" and numerous other spectacles.[8] This tendency to supplement the actual performance with parades and other events was not uncommon and helped to promote the show through a form of entertaining advertisement. At the same time, such events extended the single night at the theater into a longer period, providing westerners with multiple forms of entertainment whether or not they attended the actual performance.

Among the most popular performances to be produced in the West were Shakespeare's plays. Whether they reminded their audiences of eastern society and the social norms and human issues evoked by Shakespeare's work, or whether the bawdy humor of the plays provided westerners with diverting entertainment, is hard to determine. What is certain is that westerners flocked to view performances of *Othello, King Lear*, and *Hamlet*. Building on the fact that books containing Shakespeare's works were among some of the most popular reading materials of the nineteenth century, actors performed the plays in traditional and nontraditional ways. Plays were parodied, for instance, in what were known as Ethiopian Dramas, performances by African Americans. They were also re-titled and changed to incorporate issues of the day, as when the "San Francisco Shakespeare Club in 1876 presented *Hamlet, The Dainty: A Travesty*, incorporating jokes on Chinese coolies and Sitting Bull, and political puns on the Hayes-Tilden election."[9] Whatever the form, Shakespeare's plays were among the most regularly performed and most beloved of shows produced in the developing West.[10]

Performances were usually done by traveling actors, who journeyed together and performed as groups. Actors traveled throughout the West, to remote mining towns as well as to established cities such as Chicago, Sacramento, Denver, Virginia City, and San Francisco. Many actors longed for the time when they had enough name recognition to strike out on their own, as was the case of Edwin Booth who successfully played at theaters throughout the frontier. Other easily recognized names included Dr. Robinson, a Maine native also known as "the Yankee Robinson," who was an actor, manager, and playwright. Robinson performed his own creations for the miners after his arrival in San Francisco in 1849 and, in collaboration with James Evrad, opened the Dramatic Museum in San Francisco. Robinson gained popularity by satirizing other performers through off-color rhymes and burlesque reproductions of other actors' stage work.[11]

Women were especially popular in western theaters, most likely in direct ratio to their absence from daily life. As a result, performers like Kate Hays, a concert singer also referred to as the "Nightingale of Erin" and the "Swan," drew "very good houses" full of men eager to come into contact with females.[12] Indeed, female performers were so popular that when they were on stage, male members of the audience, hungry for female attention, threw them gifts. Lola Montez (1818–1861) was an especially popular actress who drew such attention from her audiences. Early in her career she had met with only limited success until she began performing in San Francisco in 1853 where, it is claimed, she attracted some of the most enthusiastic audiences in the city's history. She was especially known for her controversial dance *la tarantella*, or tarantula. Considered by some to be inappropriate for a public performance, the tarantula dance was characterized by the dancer's provocative movements. That suggestiveness undoubtedly contributed to Lola's popularity, which was so great that a local mountain, Mount Lola, was named after her. It was not until another female performer, Caroline Chapman, appeared on the scene that Montez's popularity began to wane.

Chapman came from a family known for its acting ability. In fact, the Chapmans had traveled west on what may have been the country's first showboat—a riverboat marked by a sign stating simply, "Theater." Caroline Chapman quickly succeeded in undermining Montez's position as an actress by parodying her in burlesque performances, including the famous spider dance. In doing so, Chapman drew audiences to her own performances and Montez began to lose some of her popular appeal. Rather quickly, Montez retired from the stage, but in her new life she met, and in many ways mentored, California's next performing sweetheart, Lotta (born Charlotte) Crabtree. Lotta began her career as a child performer and made her name by appearing in variety shows, programs including a number of different acts that were humorous in nature.[13] Other offshoots of traditional theater included genres such as melo-

Lola has come! (1852?). Courtesy of the Library of Congress.

drama, sentimental morality plays in which heroes won and villains lost, and minstrel shows, also popular on the western stage.

Local Theater, Lectures, and Oscar Wilde

While westerners were clearly drawn to professional entertainment, they also found ways to enjoy themselves through less formal and more local versions of the performing arts. Townspeople formed their own bands to perform on stage and in parades. Groups organized dances, balls, and even dancing schools that provided events for audiences as well as activities in which townspeople could participate. Bear, dog, and cockfights were popular, as was boxing. Opera and other musical performances drew large audiences and provided westerners with songs they learned by heart. As the West became more established, other local versions of performing arts became popular. For instance, in Carmel, California, outdoor theaters were created where artists attempted to write and perform plays that were drawn from uniquely western material. Similarly, during the late nineteenth and early twentieth centuries, dancers like Loie Fuller and Isadora Duncan created new forms of dance that reflected the West's vast, rolling landscape.

Whereas the theater offered westerners amusing distractions from daily life, the Lyceum, which ushered authors and poets to western towns, provided an intellectual form of entertainment. Focused on topics ranging from religion to philosophy to women's rights, lectures drew crowds as much for their subject matter as for the personalities—including popular writers like Mark Twain and Charles Dickens—who lectured. The playwright and poet Oscar Wilde had a tremendous impact on western popular culture. A proponent of the aesthetics movement, Wilde had a philosophy, already a fad in England, based on the belief in "art for art's sake." Aesthetes ridiculed and denounced the tastes of Victorian culture, promoting instead the external reflection of internal beauty, the reading of poetry, the renunciation of machinery, and a return to nature and handcrafted objects. In England, the aesthetic movement had been ridiculed in the local papers and magazines, and Wilde had been pinpointed as the leader of the group. The popular press associated Wilde with flowers—in particular the lily and the sunflower—and with phrases such as "too, too" and "too, utterly, too" which reflected an affected and exaggerated form of speaking. Wilde gained further attention through his physical appearance, which included long, unbound hair, pants of either knee or floor length, and pointed shoes tied with ribbons. The author was known for wearing colors such as pink or rose, and he encouraged others to do the same, to liven up typically drab wardrobes.

P. T. Barnum and the Traveling Circus

While speakers like Wilde provided westerners with a form of intellectual entertainment, early circuses provided escape from ordinary life. The circus brought high-wire acts, live and exotic animals, trick ponies, clowns, tightrope walkers, and other daring amusements to remote towns. Surviving treacherous journeys across the region—especially given the transportation of live animals—the circus drew large numbers of westerners to its tents. The competition between traveling circuses was intense—each billed itself as the best—and the precursors of today's most recognized shows were part of the Old West tours. Most significant, the origins of today's Barnum & Bailey circus emerged in 1881, permanently adopting the slogan "The Greatest Show on Earth." In 1882, P.T. Barnum's acquisition of Jumbo the Elephant from the Royal Zoological Gardens in London caused a stir in both England and America. Jumbo has remained a symbol of circuses, appearing on most advertisements for such events. The elephant also became the mascot of Tufts University after Barnum dedicated Jumbo's remains to the school when the elephant died. Barnum was also closely associated with another western icon,

Grizzly Adams, known in dime novels for his daring feats with live grizzly bears.

Medicine Shows

In many ways a close relation of the circus, the traveling Medicine Show provided audiences with a combination of theatrical performance, informative lecture, and sales pitch. The goal of the Medicine Show was to attract crowds in order to sell medicinal products—with names such as "Dr. Morse's Root Pills" and "Kickapoo Indian Oil"—to individuals who had little access to such products. The medicine show began with a ballyhoo, or advertisement, in the form of handbills, newspaper ads, and contemporary billboards. Once the audience was in place, the entertainment began, including performances as diverse as *Uncle Tom's Cabin*, fortune-tellers, magicians, minstrel shows, ventriloquists, and hypnotists. Free songbooks were passed out to audience members to encourage sing-alongs as well as to visually advertise the products that were about to be pitched. Following the entertainment was "the spiel," during which the medicine man would describe the possible ills that members of his audience might be feeling. The aim was to make the audience feel sick with the illnesses being described. Once the symptoms were suggested, the Medicine Show concluded by introducing the audience to products ranging from stomach bitters to painkillers and salves.[14] The shows were immensely popular and "remedies" sold swiftly, perhaps because of the high alcohol levels they typically contained. As government restrictions on false advertising and alcohol content tightened, and as other sales mediums such as radio and television came into existence, Medicine Shows slowly disappeared from the popular landscape. Before they did, however, the shows established a connection between performance and sales in a way that can still be seen in television commercials for skin and health care products.

THE WEST AS AMERICAN MYTH: FROM REALITY TO ROMANCE

As the West became settled, images of the disappearing frontier began to appear in popular forms of entertainment. The geographical frontier, in other words, had barely closed before it began to be memorialized as myth through the performing arts. From the 1870s on, American drama started to depict the frontier as its subject. A great number of these plays were cast in the genre of melodrama, in which good was rewarded and evil punished, all through the interactions of a hero, heroine, and villain.[15] The West was a frequent topic of musicals and operas as well.

Puccini's opera, *The Girl of the Golden West* (1910) based on the play by David Belasco, was set in a western mining town and included common western motifs such as gambling, the saloon, and the highwayman. In 1943, Rodgers and Hammerstein's production of *Oklahoma!* established the genre of musical theater with a showstopping combination of music, dancing, and story line. Based on the lives of southwestern farmers, *Oklahoma!* show tunes include some of the most easily recognized American lyrics. Other musicals, such as *Annie Get Your Gun* (1946) and *Paint Your Wagon* (1951), remained musical hits late in the twentieth century, marking the continuing resonance of western themes in American performance art. Moreover, many of the most popular stage performers were known not in a single genre but in several, moving easily from roles in Wild West Shows to radio program personalities to motion picture stars.

Wild West Shows, Buffalo Bill, and Annie Oakley

Perhaps the best representative of the shift from reality to myth was the Wild West Show, popularized by Buffalo Bill. The Wild West Show gained in popularity as the actual West became increasingly integrated into American life. As living conditions improved, as law and order became consistent, as the herds of buffalo dwindled in number, and as the Native Americans were removed to reservations, Americans flocked to Wild West Shows which depicted the West as it once was, or perhaps more accurately as it was imagined to have been. The rise of the Wild West Show corresponded almost exactly with the closing of the frontier, allowing Americans to see the legend of the frontier through the world of entertainment. Buffalo Bill embodied this shift, this moment when historical fact became romantic fiction.[16]

Born William Frederick Cody, Buffalo Bill spent his first years in Iowa and grew up in the Old West. He worked as a messenger and rode the Pony Express, fought in the Civil War, and took part in numerous fights with Native Americans as he traveled the still unsettled frontier. According to his autobiography, Cody received the name "Buffalo Bill" when he served as a buffalo meat supplier to railroad workers between 1867 and 1868. The name became useful when, in the course of his relationship with Ned Buntline, author of popular dime novels, Buffalo Bill became the hero of Buntline's stories and plays. Cody made the transition to the stage when, during a trip to New York, he made an unplanned guest appearance at Buntline's play "Buffalo Bill, the King of Border Men," which depicted his adventures on the frontier. Finding that the audience not only enjoyed the play but the appearance of the "real-life" hero, Cody began to make regular stage appearances in a number of plays based upon similar themes of his adventures in the West. He gained enough popularity to publish his first autobiography in 1879 and to become the subject of approximately seventeen hundred dime novels over the course of his life. His flair for writing also led to his authorship of his own dime novels and ultimately to a new genre of entertainment known as the Wild West Show.[17]

The Wild West Show, which had its heyday between approximately 1883 and 1938, was a live performance which grew out of Cody's plays and focused on typical scenes and events from the period of westward expansion. For instance, the Wild West Show "included a demonstration of the Pony Express, an attack on the Deadwood stagecoach, bucking broncos, roping and riding of wild steers, horse racing, shooting by Doc Carver, Buffalo Bill himself, and Captain A. H. Bogardus . . . and a spectacle introducing buffalo, elk, deer, bighorn sheep, mustangs, and longhorns."[18] The show also included Native Americans who played themselves, reenacting the scenes that allegedly composed their role in western history. Sitting Bull, for instance, toured with the show in the mid-1880s, becoming a star himself. Other Wild West Show stars became the subjects of dime novels with names like "King of the Cowboys" and "The Cow-Boy Kid." Cody's original show was copied by other entrepreneurial entertainers around the turn of the century who, eager to cash in on the lucrative nostalgia for the Old West, toured not only throughout the United States but abroad as well. The 101 Ranch Wild West Show, for instance, made efforts to capture the audience as well as Buffalo Bill did, but it never quite succeeded in doing so. Cody's show remained the most beloved, as was evident at the 1893 World's Columbian Exposition in Chicago which marked the show's most successful year. Advertisements, souvenirs, programs, and other memorabilia—including key fobs, commemorative coins, plates, and bandanas—were eagerly collected by Wild West Show audiences as mementos of their attendance at these popular events.

One of the most memorable members of Buffalo Bill's Wild West Show was Phoebe Ann Moses (1860–1926), better known by her stage name Annie Oakley, or, as she was dubbed by Sitting Bull, "Little Sure Shot." Oakley and her husband, Frank Butler, joined Buffalo Bill's Wild West Show in 1885 after Sitting Bull "discovered" them and their shooting act. While part of Oakley's popularity arose from her appealing good looks and engaging interactions with her audiences, she was in fact a "sure shot" who was able to shoot coins out of her husband's fingers and cigarettes out of his mouth. She became an entertainment sensation and one of the first western heroines through her role in Cody's shows. Her image appeared—both during and after her lifetime—in comic books, movies, and dime novels, not to mention becoming the subject of Irving Berlin's musical *Annie Get Your Gun* (1946). It seems more than coincidental that Oakley's popularity coincided with the women's suffrage

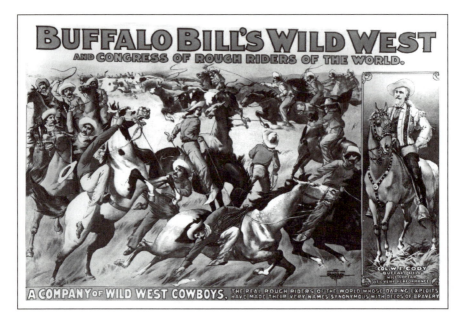

Buffalo Bill's Wild West and Congress of Rough Riders of the World (1899). Courtesy of the Library of Congress.

movements in both the East and the West. As women became more influential in the West, and as they called for inclusive rights as citizens, the presence of women in popular culture also grew. That Annie Oakley aimed to be "seen as a lady" while simultaneously demonstrating her bravery and precision with a weapon traditionally used by men, underscored the desire both to promote women's rights and to retain characteristics of femininity. As Glenda Riley describes, Oakley's image in popular culture has shifted as American culture has changed its attitude toward women, reminding us again that the representation of Annie Oakley and other western icons is tied to the historical moment in which that representation is produced.[19]

The Wild West Show remained popular until the 1930s, though its form changed along with the times. In the 1920s the Wild West Show became identified with its offshoot, the rodeo, and by the 1930s such performances were generally connected with circus acts. By this time, radio programs had started to take over the role of perpetuating the myth of the Old West and Wild West performances started to feature radio personalities like the Lone Ranger and Tom Mix.[20] In many ways, the Wild West Show was the precursor to all twentieth-century performances based on western themes. Indeed, the Universal Studios Stunt Show—connected at its roots to the Wild West Show's reenactment of the Wild West—is one of the theme park's most popular sites. In it, visitors can watch two "westerners" perform an old-fashioned frontier shoot-out, reinforcing the images of the West popularized by Buffalo Bill and his traveling show.[21]

Rodeo

As the Wild West Show began to wane in popularity, it branched off into two distinct forms of entertainment. As a mainstream type of performance, the Wild West Show was replaced by western movies. As a means by which cowboys could exhibit their skills in the ring, the Wild West Show segued into the professional sport of American rodeo. In fact, during its height, the Wild West Shows had incorporated the term "rodeo" to designate exhibitions of cowboy skills and rivalry. In other words, the rodeo was once part of the Wild West Show; yet by the mid-1920s the rodeo had surpassed those shows in popularity. Originating in the actual range-cattle industry, the rodeo focused on the skills of cowboys to ride, rope, and wrestle horses and cattle. In the twentieth century, rodeo became associated with particular regions of the United States, remaining popular in specific pockets of the country as opposed to nationwide. In many ways, the fact that rodeo has not become part of mainstream American popular culture makes it one of the remaining true forms of western entertainment. Other western traditions, such as country and western music, have crossed into the realm of conventional popular songs, eroding the characteristics that clearly separate it from other genres of music. Rodeo, in contrast, has remained popular within a subculture of American life, thereby retaining many of its original characteristics and connections to the Old West. Viewed primarily on cable television stations, the rodeo has yet to draw the mass audiences of other subculture performances, like wrestling. As a result, the rodeo appears more authentic than its faddish counterparts.[22]

Radio

Whereas rodeo has remained popular within particular regions of the United States, western radio programs quickly became a mainstream phenomenon. In particular, the radio show became a central part of American popular culture, drawing listeners from almost every walk of life. The West provided much of the fuel for this revolution, as is evident in Gene Autry's 1929 appearance as "Oklahoma's Yodeling Cowboy," which inaugurated some of the most popular programs of early radio. *Death Valley Days* followed in 1932, providing listeners with both fabricated and real stories of western life. But it was 1933 that proved the banner year in western radio shows. *The Tom Mix Show*, featuring the

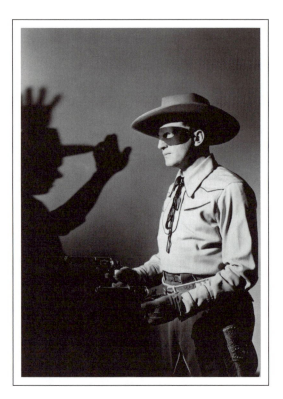

". . . and keep them up!" The Lone Ranger
(1943). Courtesy of the Library of
Congress.

real Tom Mix who had actually experienced life on the frontier, brought western drama to listeners everywhere. Mix's show was especially aimed at drawing children and, not coincidentally, was sponsored by cereal maker Ralston. A commercial success, the program promoted listener participation by asking children to solve some of Tom's problems and by sending objects mentioned in the program—badges, rings, and other devices—to children in exchange for a box top from Ralston products. Similarly, Tom Mix comic books could be traded for box tops, thereby reinforcing the relationship between the radio program, its listeners, and the show's sponsor.[23]

The same year that *The Tom Mix Show* went on the air saw the introduction of another well-received program, *The Lone Ranger*. Set in the Old West, *The Lone Ranger* featured three of the most beloved icons of the American frontier: the Lone Ranger, "that masked man"; Tonto, his faithful friend and sidekick; and Silver, his trusty horse. The program struck a chord with American children and introduced lasting phrases such as "Hi-ho, Silver! Away!" into American language. While *The Lone Ranger* may be viewed by today's standards as guilty of stereotyping Native Americans in the figure of Tonto, whose speech is marked by phrases such as "Me Tonto" and "You Lone Ranger now," it also endeared his characteristics to American listeners. Moreover, the "William Tell Overture" is easily recognized as the program's theme song, along with the familiar opening lines by announcer Fred Foy, "Return with us now to those thrilling days of yesteryear."

The Lone Ranger and Tonto became the subject of television shows, comic books, and children's stories throughout the twentieth century, incorporating the question "Who was that masked man?" into everyday American speech. Like many early radio programs about the West, *The Lone Ranger* made the leap to television and gained in popularity and commercial success. As late as 1982, Lone Ranger dolls were produced by Gabriel toys. The company also marketed a Lone Ranger series that included plastic figures of Tonto's horse, Scout, a western town, and other figures from western lore. Clayton Moore, the most recognized actor who played the Lone Ranger, continued to make appearances in his mask until his death in 1999. So popular has the figure of the Lone Ranger been in American culture that Jim Lichtman, the author of *The Lone Ranger's Code of the West* (1996), has been paid "to give his corporate training and character talk, 'Values, Ethics and the Lone Ranger,' to executives and school children. Given a fictional vignette in which participants find themselves in a difficult situation, the seminar teaches them to contemplate a resolution with the provocative question: What would the Lone Ranger do?"[24]

The Western

While radio programs and stage performances captured attention for their depictions of the West, it was the advent of television and motion pictures that crystallized the popular image of the American frontier. From the earliest days, the West, just beginning to disappear as a place of open and unsettled territory as Hollywood evolved, became a favorite subject of motion pictures.[25] Westerns can be studied by their subject matter, which focuses on the most familiar icons of the West: the railroad, outlaws, the cavalry, Native Americans, pioneers, cowboys, and sheriffs. They can also be looked at through the lenses of the actors and directors who became synonymous with the genre: Gene Autry, Tex Ritter, William Boyd, Roy Rogers, John Wayne, Clint Eastwood, John Ford, Howard Hawks, and John Sturges. Yet in terms of understanding their relationship to popular culture, westerns—frequently referred to as "oa-

Movie set for a western. Courtesy of the Library of Congress.

ters"—can best be studied by examining the historical moment in which they were produced.[26]

The Silent and Early Film Era

Early Hollywood movies successfully focused on western themes, bringing the frontier to life in theaters across the country. The subject matter was well suited to films that lacked sound and relied on familiar images and actions to tell their story. Moreover, actors in early films were often already familiar to audiences through their appearances in other western performances, for instance radio programs or Wild West Shows. This crossover from one form of entertainment to another helped the fledgling motion picture industry to draw audiences with such films as *The Great Train Robbery* (1903), *Custer's Last Fight* (1911), *The Virginian* (1914), and *Covered Wagon* (1923).

B Westerns and Nationalism

With the addition of sound and new, more sophisticated technology in the late 1920s, the western underwent some significant changes. As Phil Hardy writes, the 1930s "opened decidedly inauspiciously for the Western. The last years of the silent cinema had brought a significant drop in the popularity of the Western, whose sexless and saintly characters were clearly out of step with the liberated twenties."[27] The B Western revived the genre's popularity with such films as *Billy the Kid* (1930), *Cimarron* (1931), and *Stagecoach* (1939). Produced and viewed during the Great Depression, the B Western was inexpensive to make and appealed to audiences with its simplistic distinctions between good and evil, as well as with its characteristic singing cowboy. By the 1940s, in the shadow of World War II, the B Western took on new characteristics that reflected the cultural concerns of the time. The success of films like Henry King's 1939 *Jesse James* "inspired a number of glamorized biographies of outlaws from the major studios . . . [and] these films, many of them in colour, reintroduced 'big themes', such as the Winning of the West, to the genre. Above all, they celebrated Americanness."[28] Reflecting the nationalism of Americans during World War II, Hollywood films reinforced American values while reflecting the violence of the period.

Juvenile Westerns

Although westerns of the 1940s may have been marked by an increase in violence, made-for-television westerns and serial television programs cemented the success of the western with commercial appeal. Borrowing from the popularity of big-screen stars like Tom Mix, television westerns helped to draw audiences to the small screens in their own living rooms through programs popularly known as "horse operas." Targeted at children, and aired at times that would draw young audiences, the juvenile western, in particular programs like *Hopalong Cassidy, The Lone Ranger, The Cisco Kid, The Adventures of Wild Bill Hickok,* and *The Adventures of Rin Tin Tin,* combined western drama with commercial sales in an optimistic, if somewhat prescriptive, formula.[29] The result was a television and marketing phenomenon that stands today as the model of television shows that similarly increased network ratings and promoted sales of sponsors' products. Other programs, including the *Howdy Doody Show,* added not only to the popular culture of the era, but to the language of American children who knew that the answer to "What time is it, kids?" was "It's Howdy Doody time!"

Hopalong Cassidy, starring William Boyd, was a particular success in both film and television, initiating a marketing craze with children in the late 1940s and early 1950s. As J. Fred MacDonald describes, products with the "Hoppy" image on them included "Hoppy roller skates, wastebaskets, lamps, soap, and wristwatches . . . One million Hopalong Cassidy jacknives were sold in the first ten days of their availability."[30] While the Hoppy products fueled the program's commercial success, *Hopalong Cassidy* was popular in part because he represented the family-oriented, patriotic ideals of the 1950s. Hoppy reinforced those ideals through his model behavior and paternal influence. Not only did Hoppy never drink, smoke, or use crude language, but his Troopers Club, which gave members "a membership card, secret code, and the *Trooper News*,"[31] asked its new members to pledge by the eight-point creed as follows:

To be kind to birds and animals
To always be truthful and fair
To keep yourself neat and clean
To always be courteous
To be careful when crossing streets
To avoid bad habits
To study and learn your lessons
To obey your parents[32]

Other western heroes also had creeds. For instance, Gene Autry's "Ten Commandments of the Cowboy" included, "A cowboy is kind to small children, old folks, and to animals," while Roy Rogers' Riders Club Rules emphasized "Be Brave But Never Take Chances." In each case, the cowboy took on a paternal role that tried to shape the viewer's behavior. The impact this type of western had on an entire generation of television audiences is evident in the singer Don McLean's nostalgic song about his boyhood hero, Hopalong Cassidy. Written in 1970, McLean's song looks back at a period in American culture when the cowboy stood for what was good and moral in the country. This vision was soon to shift, however, as the western began to blur the lines between black and white.[33]

Adult Westerns

In contrast to the optimistic outlook of the juvenile western, the adult western represented a more complicated moral and social landscape to its audiences. In Hollywood, Phil Hardy notes, two films marked this shift: *Broken Arrow* (1950) and *High Noon* (1952). "The former," he claims,

inaugurated a cycle of Indian Westerns which treated Indians and their culture sympathetically (if, for the most part, patronizingly), while the latter was the first of an informal series in which social issues such as civic responsibility were raised in a rather self-conscious fashion. Both films reflected a growing, and general, unease with their times that formed the backdrop to many of the decade's finest films.[34]

Among those successes were *The Tall Men* (1955), *The Searchers* (1956), *Rio Bravo* (1959), *Shane* (1953), and *High Noon* (1952). At the same time, television westerns were changing their look as well. *Gunsmoke* (1955)

Rawhide (1958), and *Bonanza* (1959) were among the most popular of adult television westerns. Such programs broke the code of earlier westerns by casting attractive men in complex roles that emphasized rugged masculinity. Whereas Hopalong Cassidy drank sarsaparilla (otherwise known as root beer) and was always on the right side of the law, the new western hero depicted more realistic figures that drank, smoked, and even cavorted with saloon girls. They were emotional, and even angry, as opposed to sentimental and paternal. The commercials that were broadcast alongside adult westerns advertised adult products. The Marlboro Man, the epitome of the new cowboy, appeared in one.

The popular appeal of the adult western, beginning in the 1950s and lasting into the early 1970s, was staggering. As J. Fred MacDonald writes,

What began as four series in late 1955 became 28 by the fall of 1959. That year, too, the networks aired as many as 17.5 hours of adult Westerns weekly. This figure represented almost one-quarter of all evening programming. . . . One observer reported that in terms of film footage, TV Westerns by 1959 represented the equivalent of 400 feature films per year—more product than was produced during the so-called Golden Age of the B Western.[35]

Adult programs and films, like *Maverick* and *The Gambler* series, offered viewers a different perspective on the frontier by featuring characters like Maverick and Brady Hawkes, respectively, gentlemen gamblers who tried to uphold the law and their values in the face of corruption and seduction.

Spaghetti, Domestic, and Mock Westerns

While the adult western marked a time of vast popularity for western programs, in the 1960s the western had again changed its look. The results were numerous and mixed. Some of the most popular westerns of the late 1960s and early 1970s were marked by their resonance with the cultural and social agendas of the time period. *Bonnie and Clyde* (1967), *Butch Cassidy and the Sundance Kid* (1969), and *The Wild Bunch* (1969), for instance, were hits at the box office. The films reflected the cultural tension around new definitions of romance and authority. *Bonnie and Clyde* and *The Wild Bunch* were noted for their bloody death scenes. Other films elegized the passing of the Old West or took place in the western landscape, but at a more recent period in American history. At the same time, the 1960s saw a resurgence of comic and parodic westerns marked by *Cat Ballou* (1964), a trend that continued throughout the second half of the century with *Blazing Saddles* (1974). Popular for its tasteless humor and parody of westerns in general, *Blazing Saddles* is one of the top grossing westerns of all times.

In contrast to humorous renditions of the western, the "spaghetti western" is noted for its violence, its reliance on formula, and its new version of the cowboy. The phrase "spaghetti western" was coined in reference to a number of western films produced in Italy, where the term was translated "macaroni western." As Christopher Frayling writes, the spaghetti western "started a craze among film journalists for applying culinary labels to 'inauthentic' or 'alien' Westerns: 'Sauerkraut Westerns' (produced in West Germany), 'Paella Westerns' (international co-productions shot in Spain), 'Camembert Westerns' (made in Fontainebleau [France]), 'Chop Suey Westerns' (made in Hong Kong), and, most recently, 'Curry Westerns' (financed and made in India)."[36] Nearly synonymous with the spaghetti western, Clint Eastwood brought the form to life through his depiction of The Man With No Name in Sergio Leone's *A Fistful of Dollars* (1964). The dollar trilogy—including *For a Few Dollars More* (1965) and *The Good, the Bad and the Ugly* (1966)—changed the western permanently by adding cynicism and darkness to the genre. The form's popularity with American audiences may have resulted, at least in part, from the growing social and political unrest that marked the country as it faced the Civil Rights movement and the turmoil of the Vietnam War. In fact, the violent images that appeared in American living rooms through televised scenes of Vietnam provided a "real-life" corollary to the fictional violence of the spaghetti western.

Another version of the western countered that violence by negating the traditional emphasis on outlaws, lawlessness, and aggression. In place of these features, the domestic version of the Wild West myth placed the family—or social unit—at center stage, depicting the importance of American values, social responsibility, and the need to overcome natural and interpersonal adversities. Television shows like *The Big Valley, Bonanza*, and even *Gunsmoke* were able to cross from the adult to the domestic western, thereby remaining on the air for an extended period of time. Each series emphasized family ties, social values, and the need of families—whether biologically or socially defined—to work and stay together. One of the most popular of the domestic westerns was *Little House on the Prairie* (1974), a television show based on the books of Laura Ingalls Wilder. Not only did the story revolve around a young girl, as opposed to a cowboy, but her family included only one man, her "Pa." This feminine world was depicted as vulnerable and precious, and the plot worked through each episode to introduce and fend off dangers to the domestic world. Michael Landon's change of venue from the Ponderosa in *Bonanza* to the banks of Plum Creek in the *Little House* series also illustrates the easy transition that television and film personalities could make between one western program and another.

Politically Correct Westerns

As the United States entered the end of the twentieth century, an interest grew in addressing minority groups, such as African Americans, Native Americans, and women, more fairly in western-oriented arts. The trend toward political correctness initiated revisions in language, workplace behavior, and film and television depictions of underrepresented groups. The movement proved a special challenge for the genre of westerns that had traditionally relied heavily on stereotypical characters—such as the cowboy, the Indian, the prostitute—and formulaic representations of them. The impact political correctness had on the western, however, led to a surprising and undeniable revival of the genre. For just as the emphasis on politically correct jargon, images, and roles demanded new interpretations of the American West, so did the American public respond favorably to these new versions of its frontier history.

The 1980s proved a relatively dry period in the production of either television or motion picture westerns. Despite the fact that Ronald Reagan, who had acted in westerns, was now one of the most popular presidents of the century, there was little interest in the western as a genre, either in Hollywood or the realm of network entertainment. Even more surprising, as J. Fred MacDonald argues, was the failure of the cowboy to catch the imagination of the 1980s public, especially since the cowboy's virtues mirrored the political climate of Reaganism: a "strong, assertive, and resourceful [individual]; dedicated to the concept of individualism and its economic corollary, the free enterprise system; and nationalistic, even jingoistic, in his support for the United States."[37] John Wayne was even awarded a medal by Reagan for representing these tenets so well in films.[38] Despite what seemed like a fruitful climate for the production of western films or television shows, few were made and few were successful. One reason may be that the basic tenets of the western were transposed during the 1980s decade to Vietnam War movies such as *Platoon* (1986) and *Born on the Fourth of July* (1989), which resonated more urgently with the image of a wild, uncivilized, and unlawful locale than did the now "tamed" West. Alternatively, the star of the western, the cowboy, may have metamorphosed into the more sophisticated secret agent or police detective in such programs as *Hill Street Blues*, *Miami Vice*, and *NYPD Blue*.[39] Whatever the reason, only a few films proved successful with the American public, and these examined the relationship between urban and frontier, or rural, life.

Urban Cowboy (1980) redefined the cowboy as an inhabitant of the American city as opposed to the American plains. In doing so the film brought the influence of the cowboy—his rugged individualism, self-reliance, and sense of right and wrong—into urban life. In contrast, *City*

Slickers and *City Slickers II*, produced in the late 1980s and early 1990s, took a slightly different spin on the urban cowboy myth. Rather than the cowboy bringing his rugged individualism to the city, where the corrupt world of business acquired a new sense of purpose from his presence, in the *City Slickers* series the men, submerged in modern life, seek refuge in the West. Drawing on one of the most deeply ingrained of all American frontier myths, in *City Slickers* the return to the land means a return to real manhood. *Crocodile Dundee* (1985) and *Quigley Down Under* (1990) took a different approach to this theme by combining the Australian outback with the symbolism of the Wild West.

In contrast to the 1980s, during the 1990s Hollywood and the networks produced several popular westerns, each of which revised the classic western in light of the politically correct climate of the times. In Kevin Costner's *Dances with Wolves* (1990), not only do Native Americans play a crucial and sympathetic role, but the actors who portray them are of Native American heritage and speak the Lakota language in the film. *Dances with Wolves* comments on the failure of White Americans to live in concord with the natural world around them which is marked, in the film, by their waste, from manufactured objects to slaughtered buffalo left to rot on the prairie. In contrast, the Native Americans in the film take only what they need from the environment, serving as role models for what the United States may have lost in its voracious use of the land.[40]

While *Dances with Wolves* offered moviegoers a more balanced, if at times idealized, look at the relationship between Native and White Americans, the television show *Dr. Quinn, Medicine Woman* took this charge one step further by having the program's main character be not only a woman, but a doctor as well. Featuring British actress Jane Seymour, *Dr. Quinn* provided an hour's worth of family-oriented morality in which prejudices are challenged and lessons are learned. That the source of this knowledge is a pioneer woman, with her own career nonetheless, reflects the efforts made to adapt the western to late-twentieth-century concerns about representing characters other than White males. Other popular shows and films included the miniseries adaptation of Larry McMurtry's best-selling novel, *Lonesome Dove* (1985), and the TNT network's re-make of *The Virginian* (2000), which also found new ways to express the history of the frontier as more complex and inclusive, while still maintaining many of the basic tenets of the western.

THE TWENTY-FIRST CENTURY AND THE WILD, WILD WEST

The last western movie to be produced in the twentieth century was *The Wild, Wild West* (1999), starring Will Smith. The film's failure to achieve popularity, and its disjointed plot and awkward action features, reflect a break in the popularity of the classic western plot. An updated version of the 1970s television show by the same name, the movie-makers seemed consciously aware that the western must be revised in order to draw audiences, resulting in a creation that combines the conventional characteristics of the western with twentieth-century technology.

A pair of late 1990s films recorded the incompatibility between the frontier and technology that audiences witnessed in *The Wild, Wild West*, namely Disney's *Toy Story* (1995) and *Toy Story 2* (1999). Starring computer-animated figures as opposed to live actors, *Toy Story*'s hero is a cowboy named Woody. Bearing all of the stereotypical characteristics of the American cowboy—chaps, cowboy boots, cowboy hat—Woody is a frontier-style, law-and-justice cowboy whose adventures made the film one of the most popular of the decade. It is *Toy Story 2*, however, that unwittingly illustrates the fate of the western film. In the second Pixar-animated blockbuster, the story of Woody's life is revealed. Before ending up in his current home, Woody was a member of a series of toys based on a television program called *Woody's Roundup*.

Much like the juvenile westerns of the 1950s, *Woody's Roundup* featured Woody, his horse Bullseye, his friend Jessie, and a prospector, Stinky Pete. The program, the audience is told, was extremely popular, and depicted Woody and his friends as they ventured through the Wild West. Yet the show began to lose its fans as the growth of the space and technology industries started to capture the American imagination. The fans' interest in *Woody's Roundup*—not to mention its action figures—gradually faded. As a result, Woody and his toy pals were split up, some ending up in the hands of a vintage toy collector who becomes the basis of the *Toy Story 2* plot. The subplot thoughtfully records the cultural shift from a widespread love of all things western to a newfound fascination with the novelty of technology or space. As Stinky Pete tells Woody in response to the cowboy's question about the fall from popularity, "I've got two words for you: Sputnik."[41]

What Americans find entertaining in the realm of the performing arts tends to be closely related to the social, cultural, and political issues of the historical moment in which they live. The period of westward expansion illustrates this relationship by defining popular performance as an event that simultaneously entertained and "civilized" the inhabitants of the American frontier. As the frontier disappeared, and performance became an integral part of western towns, the West itself became the subject of American theater, radio, television, and film. With the evolution of new technologies, the West continued to be the fodder of popular entertainment throughout the twentieth century.

11

Travel

When Horace Greeley urged "Go West, Young Man, Go West," he could hardly have known how aptly the phrase would capture the sentiment of westward expansion.[1] From the moment that reports of gold in California made their way into the popular press, routes to regions west of the Mississippi became filled with eager emigrants. On foot, on horseback, or by covered wagons, early travelers made their way over rough roads that, in places, were little more than narrow trails. As "California fever" took hold, the scene changed from small parties of pioneers to wagon trains that stretched for miles as they slowly moved across the plains. Innovative approaches to bridging the distance between East and West included the use of camels and the Pony Express. When there was little land left to settle, the West continued to draw travelers who were interested in sightseeing and touring the national parks, small towns, and varied landscapes of the old frontier. Other advances, including the completion of the transcontinental railroad, the invention of the automobile, and the development of industries meant to sustain and promote tourism, furthered the fascination with traveling through the American West. From the nineteenth-century prairie schooner to the twentieth-century recreational vehicle, Horace Greeley's charge of "Go West" has remained a mantra at the heart of American life.

THE TRAILS OF WESTWARD EXPANSION

From the earliest days of the explorers and trappers, the trails to the West were marked by adventure, danger, and reward. Tales of a land of plenty drew early travelers across the deserts and through the mountains, but it was the announcement that gold had been found in California that brought the first rush of settlers into the West. Known as the argonauts, or the forty-niners, the pioneers who set out in search of fortune changed the West forever. The surge of travelers was unprecedented and established a westward movement that seemed intent on fulfilling the tenets of Manifest Destiny.

Steamboats and Tom Sawyer

Travel to the western part of what is now the United States was initially completed by water. River steamboats were critical in the first part of the nineteenth century as they transported both goods and passengers along the Missouri and Mississippi rivers and provided access to, and communication with, the frontier. As memorialized by Mark Twain's novel *Tom Sawyer* (1876), as well as by painters and illustrators of the period, river travel was a romanticized form of transportation, the stepping-off point for adventurers and explorers. In addition to river travel, steamboats also sailed around South America, past Cape Horn, and landed in California and Oregon. Intent on reaching the gold mines as quickly as possible, and not willing to wait for the western trails to be cleared of snow the following spring, the first wave of argonauts chose the water routes as the fastest and most direct course available during the winter of 1848–1849. Ships that had made the voyage, but were unfit for further travel, were sometimes docked next to shore and converted to living spaces and places of business, saving gold seekers the time and money required to construct new buildings.[2] The journey by water was lengthy, however, and travelers increasingly opted for overland passages. As the weather cleared, the cross-country trails became more occupied.

Covered Wagons: Conestogas and Prairie Schooners

While emigrants traveled overland by a variety of vehicles, the form of transportation most commonly associated with westward expansion was the covered wagon. A generic term used to describe the Conestoga wagon, the prairie schooner, and other related vehicles, the covered wagon was easily recognized by its high-sided wooden carriage and rounded cloth cover. The Conestoga, originally manufactured in Pennsylvania, was the prototype for most covered wagons and was characterized as a four-wheeled vehicle topped with slender, arc-shaped strips of wood upon which the wagon cover was draped and fastened. The cover was made of canvas or other heavy fabric that could protect travelers from the sun, rain, wind, and snow they inevitably encountered on their journey. Wagons were often decorated with red, white, and blue

The pioneers (1908). Courtesy of the Library of Congress.

paint that gave them a simple, but festive, air. The popular prairie schooner, also known as the "steamboat of the plains," was widely adopted
for travel across the frontier and acquired its name because its white
cover looked like a sail as the wagon moved across the rolling land.

In preparation for emigration, wagons were outfitted with food, bed-
ding, clothing, furniture, and any other items that could fit. No one setting off across the plains would venture forth without reading at least
one guidebook, dubious texts that spent pages informing potential emigrants of what they needed to bring and how much to pack for the trip.
Inside some wagons, false floors were constructed to store extra supplies,
and the interior space was furnished as comfortably as possible for the
long journey. Inscriptions on wagon covers were quite common. Travelers wrote the longitude and latitude of their destination, and names
such as "Lone Star," "Rough and Ready," and "Gold Hunters" or other
popular phrases like "Go West, Young Man," were inscribed on the otherwise plain cloth. Doing so created a spirit of camaraderie among travelers, as well as a way to identify and distinguish one emigrant party
from another as wagons trains set off across the country.[3]

Jumping-Off Places and Stopping Places

The spirit of westward expansion, in particular during the rush periods of 1849 and 1859, was clearly enthusiastic as men, women, and
children from all walks of life set out to make their fortunes in the rich
land of the West. The excitement and camaraderie were furthered by the
existence of "jumping-off places," central locations where emigrants

would gather before starting on their westward journeys. Strategically located on the boundary between the "civilized" East and the "uncivilized" frontier, jumping-off places boasted outfitting stores that sold equipment and supplies needed for the trip. The wagon trains which departed from such locations were often long, slow progressions composed of newly acquainted adventurers bound together by a single goal: to make a fortune, or settle some land, in the American West.

The journey west has often been represented by the image of a solitary wagon traveling through oceans of golden wheat, but in reality the trails were often overpopulated and the routes haphazard. Some of the customs that developed around the journey, which helped to cultivate social interaction among the long trains of pioneers, included the practice of "nooning," as the relatively lengthy midday lunch break was familiarly called. While some emigrants rode in the wagons, many walked for parts of the trip, joining with fellow travelers for conversation, gossip, and the opportunity to commiserate. At night, the wagon trains would circle up, or corral, to protect themselves from attacks and to keep horses, mules, or oxen from wandering off or being preyed upon by other animals. The popular term "circle up the wagons" derives from this practice and refers to the need to join forces against an outside danger. A traditional evening event, the campfire was used not only for cooking dinner, but for talking with friends and family, resolving the inevitable differences that arose between travelers under stressful conditions, or simply singing songs that reminded travelers of the homes they had left behind.

Seasickness, Mirages, and Ophthalmia

As the very name of the prairie schooner reflects, the American plains were so distinct in their geography, and so unfamiliar to the emigrants who crossed them, that they were repeatedly compared to the ocean. The comparison extended beyond the similarities between the rolling fields and the rolling ocean, however. Much like the open waters of the sea, in which there is nothing to visually orient the sailor, the prairies lacked visual markers. There were no trees, rocks, houses, or other objects to break up the landscape. As a result, travelers found themselves falling victim to motion sickness or vertigo as they crossed this region of the country. Another visual problem pioneers encountered was the appearance of mirages on the landscape. Finally, some emigrants suffered so extensively from the burning sun and dry dust that they donned green goggles to counter the effects of what was called opthalmia [sic], or eye infection, by one traveler.[4]

Travel Diaries, Independence Rock, and the Trail of Discarded Things

A typical going-away gift for those traveling west was a travel diary or journal, and many pioneers dutifully recorded the details of their trips. Some diaries served simply as daily records of the miles traveled, the weather experienced, the food eaten, and the events that took place during the voyage. Many such journals recorded heart-wrenching or life-changing events—a child's death under the wheels of a carriage or the birth of a baby along the trail—in the most basic terms, suggesting that daily survival was a struggle and the focus of life on the trail. Some diarists took great pains to describe personal feelings of homesickness, fear, and excitement about the adventure undertaken. Journals of western emigrants were published during the nineteenth-century in order to fuel the curiosity of potential pioneers, and they emphasized the real-life adventures of the trip. In more recent times, western diaries have been used to create cable television shows about the West and to keep the events of westward expansion alive in American culture.

One of the most common references made in travel diaries was to natural monuments, especially Independence Rock, located near current day Casper, Wyoming. Legend has it that the rock derived its name from pioneers who believed that if they reached Independence Rock by Independence Day they would know that they were on schedule for crossing the country before the weather made mountain travel impossible. What made the site of even greater interest was the fact that it was covered with the names of other travelers who had passed by there. Tradition held that travelers would add their own names as they passed by the large granite landmark. The rock, which lifted out of the otherwise flat ground, could be seen from miles away. Travelers not only wrote their names on the rock, but left messages for friends and loved ones who were behind them on the trail.

Other messages were left along roadsides and at places along the trail as a form of communication between parties, friends, and family members. Written on thin boards, paper, and even bones, and left on conspicuously placed piles of rocks or hung from branches of trees, these messages formed a primitive communication system. If the information was for everyone following on the trail behind the writer, the note was left for others to see. If it was intended for a single traveler, the message was picked up and kept. A note passed along the line of a wagon train could take significant time to arrive at its destination, the last wagon in the train often being weeks behind the front of the caravan. Newspapers and other materials were also sometimes left for other travelers to read, creating an innovative form of the circulating library where none existed. The trails west, in other words, were far from the empty stretches of

Independence Rock—Sweetwater River and Devil's Gate (1929).
Courtesy of the Library of Congress.

land represented in many books and films on the subject. It was not uncommon to see hundreds of wagons in a single train, leaving evidence of their passage in the places over which they moved and stopped for the night, changing the landscape of the frontier by their sheer presence.

The number of items left behind on the westward trails was not limited to ordinary objects that were discarded after use or because they malfunctioned. Diaries of the trip reported that travelers who had ambitiously loaded their wagons with furniture, extra clothing, books, china sets, and even a piano or two were often forced to abandon their belongings along the road. As the trip went on, and the mountains or desert loomed closer, people and animals alike became so sick or weary that they could no longer haul or carry excess baggage. The result was a trail of discarded things, left behind to decay. While the sentiment of the jumping-off places was optimistic and enthusiastic, the feeling experienced by virtually all travelers who reached California was relief to have survived with the clothes on their backs.

Water Crossings and Corduroy Roads

Getting across bodies of water that interrupted the trail, or negotiating broken, impassable sections of the route, required innovation and creativity. Water crossings were dangerous, but these places also became the centers of trade and commerce. While many crossings were completed by floating the wagon and swimming the animals across the water, this option was frequently dangerous—if not impossible—to complete. Crossings were complicated by the fact that a river deemed passable in a guidebook that was written during a drought could prove impossible to cross during heavy rains or flood season. In response, traders and Native Americans offered pioneers the use of makeshift vessels, including canoes, scows, and rafts that would more effectively—in most cases—carry people, animals, and wagons across the rivers. There was a price for such services, however, and emigrants found themselves making unexpected payments to move their parties safely through such junctures.

Just as the obstacles of water were creatively faced, so were the impassable sections of the trail. Whether due to mud or rocks, trails became impossible to use at different points in the journey. One of the most common solutions was the "corduroy road" or "corduroy sole," made "by cutting down trees and strewing their trunks on the bottom," thereby creating a type of bridge over which wagons could pass.[5]

The California Trail and the Donner Party

The California trail was first crossed in 1841 by the Bartelson-Bidwell party, a group of early emigrants who were led by John Bartelson and John Bidwell. The party split up, however, as many emigrant parties were bound to do on the long journey, and Bidwell led the first team into California. The successful completion of the journey across the treacherous Sierra Nevada Mountains led to future efforts to travel the same route, including those by well-known explorers such as John C. Frémont and Lansford Hastings.

It was the Donner group, however, who brought the California Trail into the vocabulary of men and women across the American continent. The Donner party, named after its two leaders, George and Jacob Donner, set out for California in the summer of 1846 with eighty-nine people in their caravan. Following Lansford Hasting's controversial, because inaccurate, guide to the trail, *Emigrant's Guide to Oregon and California*, the party chose to take a "cutoff," as the innumerable shortcuts from the more heavily traveled routes were called. The choice put them on the path to disaster by delaying their ability to cross the mountains. As the party headed toward the Sierras in October, they found themselves snowbound in the mountains. Quickly creating makeshift shelters out of their wagons and wagon covers, the group fully expected to be able to wait out the stormy weather and continue on to safety. The snow did not cease, however, covering up the shelters and becoming too deep for animals to walk through. Some members of the party died. Faced with near starvation, bitter cold, and little hope, other members of the ill-fated group roasted the flesh of the dead bodies, and ate it in an effort to stay alive. Survivors at the original campsite, located at what is now called Donner Lake on Donner Pass in the Sierra Nevada Mountains of California, resorted to cannibalism. Many of those who lived through the terrible conditions were emotionally undone and barely able to communicate the distress they had experienced.

Word of the Donner party's ordeal spread like wildfire among westerners and reached easterners who were eager to hear about the dangers inherent in the westward journey. Newspapers carried article after article about the events that led up to the winter captivity and the incidents of cannibalism. As a result, travel on the California Trail became less common until the gold rush of 1849, during which so many emigrants used the route that grass and clean water became scarce. Many argonauts chose to brave the route taken by the Donner party, but the story still haunted the Donner Trail for others, who therefore sought a longer way around. Even today tourists visit Donner Lake with a combination of horror and fascination about the events that took place there.

Handcarts, the Mormon Trail, and Other Innovative Vehicles

Whereas the story of the Donner party's fateful travel across the California Trail created a fearful picture of westward emigration, in which nature overpowered ordinary people, the tale of the Mormon journey across the Oregon Trail was inspirational to the religious community. Previously settled in Missouri and Illinois, the Mormons were confronted with tension and violence as a result of their economic success, political power, and religious beliefs. In response, Brigham Young, the Mormon leader, organized and enacted a mass emigration to the region around the Great Salt Lake in Utah. Through a systematic process of sending groups of settlers ahead to establish stopping places along the route for other, weaker, travelers, Young was able to move thousands of his community members to their new home, the new Zion, in the Salt Lake Valley. The route they traveled on was named the Mormon Trail, and one of the most inventive of all forms of western travel came across it. In order to help the poorest of Mormons make the trip to Salt Lake, handcart companies were established at jumping-off places. At such companies, travelers who were unable to transport themselves and their belongings by way of the costly covered wagons, were able to make their own handcarts in which they could push their possessions across the country.[6]

Other vehicles could also be spotted making the trip, including oxcarts, chihuahua wagons on the Sante Fe Trail, and wheelbarrows. Emigrants walked or rode horses, and were always in search of an easier, quicker way to cross the country. In 1849 an inventor claimed to have created

The way they go to California (1849). Courtesy of the Library of Congress.

an aerial steamboat which would, for the price of one hundred dollars, transport travelers to California by air. While the vehicle ultimately did not work, its inventor, Rufus Porter, was ahead of his time in imagining what would eventually become the primary form of western travel, the airplane.[7] In general, the most important aspect of travel during the gold rush was to reach the destination point as quickly as possible. The methods by which emigrants did so were as varied, and as fantastic, as could be imagined, and the range of contraptions by which travelers thought they could make the trip was parodied in cartoons by the popular press.

Stagecoaches and Express Companies: Connecting the West

Aside from the covered wagon, the stagecoach is a familiar icon of westward travel. Distinctly shaped, the stagecoach included a front seat upon which the driver would sit, a rear platform that could hold baggage or travelers, and a central, slightly bow-shaped cabin, which could support, on average, nine adult passengers. The most widely used and well built of American stagecoaches was the Concord coach, developed by the Abbot-Downing Company in Concord, New Hampshire. Not only were Concord coaches roomier than their British predecessors, but they were made of the sturdiest woods and strongest irons. The coaches were beautifully decorated in bright coats of paint, sparkling varnish, and gilt lettering. Landscapes were occasionally painted on the doors and cushions were often placed on the seats to make the ride more comfortable.

Prevalent images of the stagecoach are more romantic than true, including the stagecoach that is pulled at top speed by a team of runaway horses, the stagecoach that, due to the speed of travel, careens off the side of the road, and the stagecoach that, moving through unsettled land, is attacked by Native Americans. Whether these tales originated in the dime novels of the 1800s, in the memoirs of early travelers, or in the paintings of frontier artists, the popular image of the American stagecoach bears only a slight resemblance to the real experience of traveling in one. Yet the stagecoach's hold on the popular imagination may have had as much to do with its symbolic presence as with its actual function. In a rugged land that lacked the familiar signs of life back in "the States," the stagecoach, with its bright paint, laquered wood, and gold lettering represented civilization in the wilderness. As it traveled the roads of the West the stagecoach stood for the advance of eastern culture and the inevitable cultivation of the land.[8]

Wells, Fargo & Company

Stagecoach service in the West had its origins in the entrepreneurial men who drove stages between mining towns, transporting mail in one direction and gold in the other. As the need for organized, widespread western communication systems grew, express companies sprang up to meet the demands for mail, packages, and other items that needed to be sent from the eastern states as well as between western communities. Due to the miners' need to deposit or cash in their gold, express companies also became an early form of western banking, providing a wide range of financial services to miners and other settlers. Stagecoaches were used to operate the express companies of Adams and Company, The Pioneer Stage Company, Wells, Fargo & Company, and Ben Holladay's Overland Express Company. For a time, each company vied for control of the industry, but Wells, Fargo & Company eventually dominated the other express lines, operating a combination of stagecoach and pony express services to reach even the remotest towns. As Wells, Fargo & Company became the leading service, the company designed and used its own coaches and placed the company name in full view above the door, thereby popularizing an early brand name in full-service travel. When the railroad and the automobile began to replace the need for stagecoach service, Wells Fargo continued to operate as a bank in western states like California. The company still uses its history as a stagecoach operator in contemporary advertisements, lending its image as a pioneer in transportation to its desire to attract and keep its financial customers.[9]

Stagecoach and Wells Fargo office (1866). Courtesy of the Library of Congress.

Camels, the Great American Desert, and the Pony Express

The Pony Express, which made its first trip between St. Joseph, Missouri, and Sacramento, California, on April 3, 1860, was a transportation marvel by nearly all accounts. "The Pony," as it was affectionately called, evolved from one of the major challenges facing westerners, namely the need for regular communication with the eastern states. Settlers argued that the trails they had traveled to California, Utah, Oregon, and other western states would make good, if still rough, routes for mail delivery, but the government's response to their desire for mail and other news was lukewarm at best.

The problem of opening and supporting the most direct route west, known as the Central Overland route, was in part due to the common misconception of the Southwest as dangerously uninhabitable. Tales of

The Camel Corps (1857). Courtesy of the Library of Congress.

travelers who had died of thirst on their way through the region reinforced this belief and led, in part, to the federal government's decision
to import camels. The understanding that the land was sandy desert,
and that therefore camels would make travel across the area more fea-
sible, led Congress to approve funds to purchase the animals and transport them to the Southwest. The first camels arrived in San Antonio in
1856 and were taken to various sites in an effort to help them adapt to
their new life. The experiment was a failure, however, as the camels'
hoofs, used to soft sand, developed cuts and sores. In response, their
hoofs were, at least temporarily, shod in leather boots. Such protective
footwear did not help the camels adjust to the new geography, and the
belief that they would provide a swift, strong, and durable form of transportation across the region was soon abandoned. Legend has it that visitors to the "Great American Desert" can catch glimpses of camel ghosts
that haunt the region, longing to return to their natural habitat.[10]
    The Pony Express was the privately funded answer to the communi-
cation problem that the government struggled to resolve. The idea had
its origins in the numerous express companies that evolved during the
1849 gold rush. While most men and women rushed west to try their
hand at gold mining, others saw that the need for letters and information
from the East could be turned into a lucrative business. Using mules that
could make their way through the mountain roads, single-man express
companies charged miners to receive and to deliver pieces of mail. They
also cashed in on the miner's need to have his gold transported to central
banks, a service that could cost the miner up to 5 percent of the total
price of his gold. Some express operators were even more inventive,

providing miners with their own specialized stationery, including an envelope whose corner included a specially designed imprint of the courier's choosing. The most common design, that of a pony, or a pony and a rider, traveling at breakneck speed, evolved into the trademark of the Pony Express.[11]

Though the government financially refused to support the opening of this route as the main link between the East and the West, a private company known as Russell, Majors & Waddell decided to try its luck. Consisting of close to 200 stations strategically located ten to fifteen miles apart, the Pony Express established new outposts in unsettled regions of the West. The success of the Pony Express was based on speed. As one writer reported, each rider galloped "125 miles before halting for the night. . . . Their actual time in the saddle was seventy-six hours, and their average was eleven miles an hour."[12] Riders were hired and hosted in hotels where they attended dances in their honor and dressed in the Pony Express uniforms that would distinguish them as they rode. Blue pants, a red shirt, decorative boots, and a buckskin coat made up the distinctive outfit. Pony Express riders were expected to sign a pledge stating, among other promises, that "I will under no circumstances use profane language; that I will drink not intoxicating liquors; that I will not quarrel or fight with other employees of the firm."[13]

The Pony Express fell out of use when the government signed a contract with the Overland Mail Company to provide mail service on a daily basis, and gave it the financial backing the Pony Express sorely lacked. The end of the Pony Express resonated symbolically with the growing settlement of the West, the displacement of the Native Americans, and the decline in the number of open ranges on which animals could roam. Despite its relatively short life, the Pony Express was quickly incorporated into the popular mythology of the West. Souvenirs of the Pony Express, including the animals themselves, were popular during the service's prime. The first pony to start the run had to be returned to the stable when bystanders started snatching pieces of her mane and tail that were turned into souvenir rings and watch chains. The newspapers that bore the headline "By Pony Express" brought some of the excitement and adventure of the West to eastern readers, who could imagine their news being carried at record speed across the continent by brave Pony Express riders. Wild West Shows included a Pony Express race that lives on in rodeo relay competitions, and dime novels such as Beadle's *The Pony-Express Rider* (1891) took the Pony as their subject.[14]

TOURISM IN THE WEST: TRAINS, AUTOMOBILES, AND CABLE CARS

As the West became more accessible, and as it also became more affordable, travel was increasingly common and was undertaken in a variety of forms. Beginning with pleasure trips on the railroads, and continuing with early automobiles and eventually recreational vehicles, western tourism has remained a major industry in the United States.

The Transcontinental Railroad

Whereas the Pony Express, with its ability to transport information so rapidly, was seen as a small miracle of western travel, a transcontinental railroad was beyond the wildest dreams of most frontier men and women. When surveys were authorized by Congress to establish possible routes for a cross-country train, the concept seemed far from reality. Yet it remained intriguing and, after the Civil War, when the construction of the Union Pacific route from the East, and the Central Pacific rail from the West, was under way, the country became fascinated by the possibilities inherent in the project's success. Newspapers, magazines, and books followed the progress of the two routes as they inched toward one another.

When the two rails met at Promontory Point in Utah on May 19, 1869, the first transcontinental route was completed, changing western travel forever. The entire country celebrated. The picture of railroad workers toasting the moment is one of the most commonly reproduced of all western photographs, as it symbolized the new unity between the east-ern states and western territories.[15] Yet the railroad's completion was not entirely positive. In addition to removing Native Americans further from their land, the railroad changed the landscape of each area it passed through. Through aggressive advertising campaigns, entire towns were built solely because of their proximity to the railroad, drawing emigrants to regions they may not have traveled to otherwise. Television westerns incorporated this experience as part of their standard plot by depicting speculators who, using insider information, would buy up apparently worthless land only to have it turn out to be the land through which the railroad would pass. The story line raised issues of ethics as unknowing westerners were shown selling their properties at low prices, only to see it worth great sums weeks later.[16]

Pullman Cars, Guidebooks, and Western Tourism

Tourism by train brought people into contact with the West in un-precedented ways. No sooner had the transcontinental railroad been completed than enterprising businessmen created ways to draw travelers to it. Most notable of these was George Pullman, whose invention of the Pullman car made rail travel all the rage. Far from the discomfort of the stagecoach, the Pullman car was luxury on wheels. Plush seats, carved wood, elegant draperies, and stained glass characterized the interior design of the Pullman, which came as close to a hotel on wheels as was possible. The cars reflected the elaborate decorating trends of the Victorian era, providing travelers with a sense of highly civilized living as they crossed the still relatively unsettled plains of mid-America. Dining cars were similar in style and luxury, featuring china dishes and silver utensils to mimic the atmosphere of dining in a fine restaurant.

Pullman car travelers were certain to have their guidebooks handy in order to see as many of the sights as they could during their trip. George A. Crofutt's *Transcontinental Tourist Guide*, published in the 1870s, was the most popular guidebook, but dozens of such manuals were available to travelers. Guidebooks like Crofutt's told tourists to be on the lookout for uniquely western sights, for instance prairie dogs, antelope, and buffalo, not to mention "real" Native Americans. Aware of the draw Europe had for wealthy American tourists, the books approached the relationship between the old and new worlds in two distinct ways. Some constantly compared the American landscape to that of Europe, drawing parallels between, for instance, the Rocky Mountains and the Swiss Alps. Other guidebooks argued that American geography was unique and should be taken on its own terms rather than compared to other places. In both instances, the effort was made to provide travelers with a context and an interpretation of what they saw out the windows of their train cars as they traveled, day and night, across the continent.[17]

Despite the guidebook authors' best efforts to make the transcontinental trip enjoyable, the fact remained that the miles of prairie that caused visual disorientation to earlier pioneers now caused boredom. Activities were developed to counteract the tedium of the trip, including games, music, singing, and reading. In fact, the luxurious interior of the cars helped travelers to focus inside rather than out, thereby distracting tourists from the less interesting legs of the trip. One pastime of the early railroad journey was the practice of shooting buffalo from the train. The activity seemed novel to those participating in it, but the massacres further reduced the numbers of buffalo and reflected the lack of understanding early travelers had for the fragile environment over which they passed.[18] Despite this "game," most travelers found that what took place inside the train or at depot stops along the way was of more interest than the endless landscape viewed from the train window.

Harvey Houses, Harvey Girls, and the Sante Fe Railway

In the early twentieth century, the popularity of train travel produced the need for restaurants and hotels that were conveniently located along the railways and that complemented the tourist's desire for new and unique experiences. Fred Harvey answered this call by providing tourists traveling along the Sante Fe Railway with fine dining and hospitality.

Slaughter of Buffalo on the Kansas Pacific Railroad. Courtesy of the
Library of Congress.

As a writer in *Collier's* magazine reflected, "If the .45 revolver was the peacemaker of the Southwest, Fred Harvey, founder of the empire, was its civilizer. Working with the vast, longest-in-U.S. Sante Fe railroad—some say the Santa Fe made Harvey, others stoutly declare Harvey made the Sante Fe—he carried Delmonico food standards west of the Mississippi."[19] The popular chain of Harvey Houses operated not only at the Grand Canyon, but at the highly regarded La Fonda, Alvarado, and El Tovar hotels. Meals at Harvey Houses were reasonably priced and served in clean, comfortable surroundings. Travelers on the Sante Fe route would disembark for lunch and find their meals waiting for them. The information about the "number of diners on the train was wired ahead, and a whistle blown a mile from the stop as a signal for the waitresses to put the first course on the table. Ample time was given to eating and few diners felt hurried or left hungry."[20]

The distinguishing feature of Harvey Houses was not their location or food, however, but their waitresses, known as Harvey Girls. When a young woman agreed to work as a Harvey Girl, she accepted more than just a job. Overseen by a matron, Harvey Girls were told where to live, how to dress, when to go to bed, and even whom to date. They wore immaculate uniforms—typically in black and white—and were paid well for their good treatment of customers. From the early 1880s to the 1950s approximately one hundred thousand Harvey Girls traveled west to work in Harvey restaurants. While they have been mythologized in stories as well as in the 1940s film "The Harvey Girls" starring Judy Garland, these women were early pioneers of women's independence and self-reliance.[21]

Although the mission of Harvey Houses and Harvey Girls was intricately related to meeting the needs of weary travelers along the Sante Fe route, the Harvey conglomerate also promoted the southwestern tourist industry itself through a variety of marketing strategies. As one writer put it, Harvey "sold enough Indian curios to put a touch of Navajo in every U.S. home."[22] From his deck of cards entitled "The Great Southwest Souvenir Playing Cards," which depicted images of the Southwest on their backs, to books such as *The Great Southwest Along the Sante Fe* (1914), Harvey brought the Southwest to Americans in ways that still appear in popular culture. Side trips were promoted as part of the "Indian detour" series of Harveycar Motor Cruises, an offshoot of Harvey's hotels and restaurants that promised tourists access to less traveled, more authentic southwestern sites.

In the Southwest Harvey hotels also carried books about the region, and, always responding to mass demand for a particular product, the Harvey company published its own catalog listing the titles. In order to provide railroad passengers with reading material for the long journey west, the train stations connected with the Harvey company were known for their finely kept bookshops and ability to tap into the popular taste in reading. *Publishers Weekly*, which watched Harvey bookstores with interest, published an article in 1925 that attributed Harvey with the development of the "Take Along a Book" idea of travel.[23] If the Harvey establishments were responsible for initiating the association between travel and reading, the trend has only become further ingrained in American culture since the early 1900s. Airport and railroad bookstores provide travelers with a range of popular, easy-to-read books that can be "taken along" to read in order to make the journey pass more quickly.

Autocamping and the Rise of the Motel

The popularity of western railroad travel was eclipsed in the early twentieth century with the appearance of the automobile. While Americans continued to be drawn to the West as tourists and travelers, they shifted rather quickly to using their own cars. Whereas train travel meant spending days and even weeks among other passengers, who were most likely strangers, the automobile allowed tourists to travel the country alone or with people of their own choosing. Tourists decorated their cars in ways reminiscent of the prairie schooners—with signs stating " 'Kansas City to Los Angeles,' [or] 'Ocean to Ocean.' "[24] When the car was completely covered in dust, slogans like " 'Just a Little Dusty' [would

Wigwam Hotel, Bardstown, Kentucky (1940). Courtesy of the Library of Congress.

appear] scrawled on the rear of a road-weary Model T or the polite but proud 'Pardon My Dust' " would illustrate that the drivers had explored locations that were far from the mainstream of western life.[25] Cars were also named after the West, for instance the Montana Special produced in 1911, and were marketed by staging events such as driving up western landmarks like Pikes Peak, to prove the car's endurance and power.[26]

Free camping was a short-lived luxury, however, and by the mid-1920s campsites began to charge for the use of their facilities and new forms of shelter for travelers evolved. One invention was the travel cabin, a spin-off of the traditional campsite that offered motorists more privacy, convenience, and protection from weather than did the basic tent. While some of the campground cabins were simple clapboard structures, others were designed around western themes, for instance mission- or tepee-style cabins. In the 1930s, Americans combined the drive-in convenience of the autocamp with the privacy of the cabin in yet another automotive invention, the trailer, which was parked in trailer camps across the West. In the 1940s Americans traveled west in their own cars, yet they stayed at modern motor inns or motels which provided them with private rooms, showers, and toilets. Some motels even boasted an on-site restaurant.

The West has been explored by men and women on foot and bicycle, by plane and motorcycle, by bus and by car. One of the most noticeable contemporary means of popular travel, however, remains the recreational vehicle, or RV. A kind of "home on wheels," the RV is often derided as a quintessential example of American excess and waste. The cumbersome, gas-guzzling vehicles are used to transport travelers in a fashion that helps them feel as though they never left home. Indeed, the kitchens, bathrooms, bedrooms, and living rooms that are built into the RV make for a snug home. Yet the RV may be more American than even its critics think, for as these large conveyances lumber west, they remind us of nothing less than the more primitive form of the RV: the Conestoga wagon that transported early pioneers to what they considered the promised land.[27]

Cable Cars

The San Francisco Cable Car was the inspiration of Andrew Hallidie, a British wire-rope manufacturer who helped to build suspension bridges and developed mechanisms by which large amounts of ore could be hauled out of the ground in mining carts. The cable technology that Hallidie used in his work was the same technology on which he based the cable car system. Moving at only about nine miles per hour, the first cable car was in place in 1873, moving up and down the steep San Francisco hills with surprising ease and safety. When cable cars fell out of use as the primary form of public transportation, they became a major feature of interest for western travelers. Their image was widely broadcast in 1958 with the appearance of printed advertisements and television commercials for Rice-A-Roni, a rice and pasta dish which used the cable car as its icon. The catchy jingle, "Rice-A-Roni, the San Francisco Treat," clinched the association between the San Francisco cable car and American popular culture as it played alongside the video of happy cable-car riders. Today, the cable cars are among the most popular tourist attractions in San Francisco and have spawned every imaginable souvenir and reproduction, appearing on anything from key chains and paperweights to dishcloths and plates.[28]

National Monuments, Parks, and Other Travel Destinations

Since the discovery and naming of Yellowstone Park, the natural wonders of the American West have captured the imagination of travelers, both at home and abroad. Whether pack trips to Pikes Peak or day trips to see the California "Big Trees," better known as the redwoods, western tourism has flourished around national parks and other historic sites. From the Grand Canyon to Yosemite, Death Valley to Monument Valley, the sites that are now national parks are also deeply embedded in the mass culture of the United States. Symbols of the promise the West held for the forty-niners, many parks and sites have drawn travelers because of their beauty. For instance, Yosemite and Yellowstone were both destinations for early tourists who were eager to see for themselves the natural wonders of the West. Other locations, such as Death Valley and Mount Rushmore, however, developed popular legends that added to the mystique and lure of the West and which, not unexpectedly, were taken up by advertisers and producers as legends of the Old West.

Death Valley, Borax, and the Twenty-Mule Team

In stark contrast to the rest of the West, which has been depicted by the popular press as the land of plenty, a place that restores health and from which a bounty could be reaped, Death Valley has been viewed as a fearful, hellish place that created insanity and led to painful death by starvation, dehydration, and heatstroke. The desolate conditions of Death Valley created the natural substance known as borax, a material used to make cleaning agents. What made the story into a legend was the fact that teams of men and mules braved the elements and carted load after load of borax out of the desert. The twenty-mule teams, as they came to be known, faced the scorching heat and blistering sun day after day. Many of the mules died (some reports say that as many as four of the twenty would die on each trip) and, as the tale goes, their bleached bones can still be seen in Death Valley.

In light of their unusual mission, the twenty-mule teams came to stand for endurance and hard work, both of which were conveniently positive characteristics to be associated with one of borax's main products, Borax soap. The marketing of Borax soap depended on the mythology that had sprung up around the twenty-mule team, and canisters of the product featured the familiar line of mules harnessed to a freight wagon. The word "borax" took on another meaning when it was used to refer to inexpensive, low-quality merchandise. The association may have been the result of the marketing ploy used by some manufacturers of cheap furniture, who tried to make sales by luring customers with free soap. The television series *Death Valley Days* was originally produced to promote the 20 Mule Team Borax products by dramatizing tales of the region. Numerous hosts, including Ronald Reagan, worked to create close to 600 episodes, which opened with the familiar bugle call and clips of the mules.[29] The legend of the twenty-mule team remains, and the original borax wagons made their final appearance during the 1999 Rose Bowl Parade in Pasadena, California.[30]

The Black Hills, Mount Rushmore, and Area 51

One of the West's most unique tourist attractions is the Black Hills region, home to numerous Old West monuments. The town of Deadwood, South Dakota, with its infamous reputation for outlaws and gambling, is a National Historic Landmark and prime tourist site. Gambling continues to be one of the town's major industries, and casinos are housed in western-style buildings. The most famous of these attractions is the site where Wild Bill Hickok was killed, in Old Style Saloon No. 10, and the town regularly reenacts the events of the murder for the entertainment of visitors. One of the most creative sites in the Black Hills region is Mount Rushmore National Memorial, which draws visitors to its granite peak to view the sixty-foot tall faces of four American presidents carved there: George Washington, Thomas Jefferson, Theodore Roosevelt, and Abraham Lincoln. The faces appear in a range of popular culture venues, from Alfred Hitchcock's *North By Northwest* (1959) to the animated comedy *The Simpsons*. Mount Rushmore's carved wonders can only be surpassed by the curiosities surrounding another western site, Area 51, located about ninety miles outside of Las Vegas, Nevada. A restricted, government-operated location, Area 51 has been used to test aircraft, but it is better known for the rumors of UFO sightings and alleged government cover-ups that are supposed to have taken place there. Along with Roswell, New Mexico, Area 51 has been the focus of an entire pop culture genre that includes films like *Independence Day* (1996) and *Men in Black* (1997), as well as television series such as *The X-Files*.[31]

The great national parks and monuments of the American West have been readily incorporated into American life, from the souvenir shops through which visitors are inevitably guided to the advertisements, tours, and other commercial avenues of tourism. In addition to the expected postcards and ceramic mugs, the landmarks of the West appear in other ways as well. The Grand Canyon has been the subject, and title, of films like *Grand Canyon* (1992), and scenes from Monument Valley are indelibly linked with classic westerns, including the opening scenes of *Stagecoach* (1939). Tourism of the West, in other words, takes place in the movie theater as often as it does in person, suggesting that the travel "fever" that early pioneers claimed drew them across the continent remains alive and well in American popular culture.

12

Visual Arts

Most Americans recognize—even from an early age—the figure of the Native American or the cowboy, the buffalo or the covered wagon. Whether a landscape painting in a national museum or an illustration on a book jacket, the visual arts have created some of the most lasting impressions of the American frontier. The roots of these representations lie in the nineteenth century, when painters, illustrators, and photographers headed west to document the vast land of the expanding United States. The decision to record such images, and the manner in which these artists did so, was a result of the culture in which they lived and their own understanding of that historical moment. As a result, the art they created suggested the values, beliefs, and conflicts central to the period of westward expansion. Such early art forms were not only popular in their own time, but provided the basis for future visual images of the American West.[1] More specifically, the visual representations of the frontier recorded the transformation of American history into American commercialism. For nearly every image central to the history of the West became, at or around the beginning of the twentieth century, an image tied to the marketplace of popular culture.[2]

COWBOYS, INDIANS, AND PIONEERS

One of the most beloved western images is that of the American cowboy. His image permeates popular culture as the hero of young children and as the embodiment of American manhood. The heroism with which the cowboy has been invested differs sharply from the lived experience of frontier life. However, the cowboy hero has been a staple of western mythology with roots in the visual representations set forth by two of the most recognized artists of the West, Frederic Remington and Charles M. Russell.[3]

The works of Frederic Remington and Charles M. Russell reflected the American idea of the Old West, of cowboys and horses, of men who lived in the saddle and were in conflict with Indians, the land, and each other. Frederic Remington spent his childhood in upstate New York where he learned to sketch at an early age. After dropping out of Yale Art School, and surviving an initial rejection from the woman he wanted to marry, Remington ventured to Montana where he experienced the life of the West for the first time. Captivated by the region, in 1883 he invested his small inheritance in a Kansas sheep ranch where he lived for a brief time herding sheep and riding horses. When he sold the ranch Remington traveled throughout the West, sketching cowhands, Indians, and western scenes which he tried to publish in eastern magazines. He had little success but continued to sketch and travel until, in 1886, *Harper's Weekly* used his illustration of *Indian Scouts on Geronimo's Trail* on its cover.

After that, it was only a matter of time before Remington's illustrations—primarily of cowboys and other types of men astride horses—were published in the most popular journals of the period. *Outing, Harper's Weekly, Youth's Companion* were among his venues, as were calendars and other popular literature. One of his best-known works, called by titles as different as *Cowboys Shooting Up a Western Town, Comin' Through the Rye*, and *Off the Trail*, was transformed into a huge statue that stood prominently at the 1904 St. Louis World's Fair. The statue depicted cowboys, guns in hands that were raised high above their heads, mounted on charging horses. Capturing the movements and actions that were expected of cowboys, the statue memorialized a way of life that many saw as fading into memory as the century wore on.[4]

Remington's mounted men—primarily cowboys but also scouts, military men, and Native Americans—were the basis for many twentieth-century ideas of the wild, wild West. Indeed, John Ford and Howard Hawks, both producers of western films, based much of the scenery and action in their movies on images handed down by Remington. This was not surprising given how prolific the artist was, especially toward the end of his life.[5] Yet Remington's image of the cowboy is worth examining, for in it the West is always in the process of being won—a land to be tamed, Indians to be conquered. The popularity of Remington coincided directly with the period in which it became clear that American resources were limited, that the West had borders, and that wilderness areas would eventually be settled. Perhaps as a result, his illustrations represented a nostalgia for a period in American history that was disappearing even as Remington recorded it. More important, his work

Calendar for 1898 by Frederic Remington.
Courtesy of the Library of Congress.

stood for the values with which the West had been invested—grit, hard work, and action. Reflecting the virtues of manhood promoted by his contemporary, Theodore Roosevelt, Remington's cowboys were the stuff of American myth, a myth in which the West was civilized by individuals willing to make the last stand for their country.

Remington's artistic counterpart, Charles M. Russell, was born only a few years after Remington in St. Louis, Missouri. Known as the Cowboy Artist, Russell in fact worked for a time as a cowboy, sketching some of his experiences and sculpting figures out of clay. He also lived among the Blackfeet Indians of Canada and learned their language. Russell was concerned about the welfare and the vanishing culture of the Indians, and he took advantage of his time with them to sketch what he could of their lifestyle. Russell did not set out to make money by way of his art, and he was better known for giving or throwing away his sketches than for selling them. However, during the last decade or so of the nineteenth century his work began to catch the attention of the American public, and Russell found his art to be of monetary value. When he married Nancy Cooper in 1896, Russell gave up his life as a wanderer and, in partnership with his new wife, began to focus more deliberately on his paintings and drawings, for which he began to receive ample pay.

While in many ways Remington and Russell tackled similar subject matter in their art, Russell's portrayal of Western horsemen was different from Remington's in significant ways. Whereas Remington's cowboys appear to be wrestling with the West, Russell's seem to be more at one with it. Perhaps this was the result of the artists' different relationships to the frontier. Russell had lived and worked for some time on the land, as a cowboy and among the Indians. In contrast, Remington, though he had lived and traveled briefly in the West, had only limited firsthand experience of the places and people he depicted. In fact, many of his paintings were based not on real incidents but on posed models in his New York studio. This distance from his subject may have allowed Remington to create a more stereotypical image of the cowboy, one that taps into his perception of the American cowhand as the true hero of westward expansion.[6]

Despite their differences, the artists' depictions of the American West had a tremendous influence on twentieth-century visual representations of the cowboy and other frontiersmen. In advertising, the Marlboro Man—perhaps the quintessential cowboy—can be seen everywhere, in magazines and on life-sized billboards. In movies, too, the image of the cowboy is pervasive. Early films about the Old West represented the cowboy as a man of few words and great courage, leading the way to justice in an unsettled, often unlawful, land. Early radio and television shows such as *The Lone Ranger, Hopalong Cassidy,* or *The Tom Mix Show* also borrowed from the images initiated by Russell and Remington. A wave of television shows in the 1950s, including *Gunsmoke* and *Bonanza,* focused on the post–World War II desire for entertainment which easily distinguished between good and evil. Many of these programs led to a proliferation of other commercial material, including comic books, posters, and dolls based on the programs' characters. As a visual image central to the American myth of male identity and American individualism, the cowboy as recorded in fact or fiction is alive and well in the American imagination.

Indian Galleries, George Catlin, and Darley Sketches

Since the time the first settlers caught sight of Native American peoples, Native Americans have been the focus of intense and mixed emotion in the American mind. As tribes and communities were forced further west during the nineteenth century, and as settlers pursued their own sense of destiny in establishing towns and lives west of the Mississippi, the Native American also became the subject of drawings, sketches, and early photographs. At times, these images accurately portrayed the men, women, and children on which they focused. At others, they represented Native Americans as stock figures that quickly evolved into the stereotype of the American Indian as stoic and savage in nature. Accurate or not, the artistic renderings of Native Americans during the second half of the nineteenth century were popular with the American people. They have also provided valuable records of a period in history now completely past.

Some of the earliest attempts to draw the people who occupied the land west of the Mississippi resulted in what were called Indian Galleries, traveling shows that exhibited paintings and drawings of Native American life. Extremely popular on both the national and international fronts, the most prominent Indian Galleries were created by George Catlin, John Mix Stanley, Karl Bodmer, and Paul Kane. Indian Galleries represented Indians as individuals who were at once fearsome and primitive, giving rise to the popular view of the Indian as a noble savage. This interpretation of Native American culture corresponded with the early stages of western exploration and settlement, an era when Native Americans were relatively mysterious to frontiersmen who saw them as uncivilized but not necessarily dangerous. Over time this sentiment transformed into a darker image of Native American peoples, and the visual arts reflected those changes.[7]

George Catlin began to incorporate Indians as subjects into his art soon after coming into contact with some western Indians at the Peale Museum of Natural History in Philadelphia. After briefly studying Native Americans in the East, Catlin traveled to the West with the intention of learning more about tribal life. He did so with the belief that Native American culture was disappearing and that he would document what he could of it before doing so was no longer possible. His early travels were done in association with William Clark who, after his exploration with Meriwether Lewis, served in the Missouri territory as a superintendent of Indian affairs.[8]

In 1841 Catlin published his visual study of Native American life in a two-volume collection entitled *Letters and Notes on the Manners and Customs and Conditions of the North American Indians*, a book which almost immediately caught the public's attention. The book documented the Indian diet, ceremonies, and daily activities and included numerous portraits of Indian men, women, and children. Catlin began to show his collection of almost 500 paintings, sketches, and artifacts—which he called an "Indian Gallery"—in 1837, traveling around the country and eventually across the Atlantic Ocean to Paris. It was in France, and in reference to Catlin's work, that the term "Wild West" was first coined according to the French colloquialism *le Wild West*, connecting Indian

Galleries directly to the popular phrase that has most prominently shaped the image of the American West. Catlin's paintings and sketches represented Native Americans as individuals who were different from White Americans, somewhat frightening in their unfamiliar lifestyle, but to be respected nonetheless.

While some artists worked to preserve an image of American Indians that was respectful, others reinforced the more popular idea that the Native American was to be feared and therefore contained.[9] Carved into the Capitol's rotunda in Washington, DC, is Enrico Caisici's bas-relief sculpture, *Daniel Boone Struggling with the Indian*.[10] The sculpture was intended to represent an actual moment in Boone's life when his party of settlers was attacked by a group of Indians. Yet the sculpture is significant in its representation of the "Indian warrior . . . as an ogre, savagery incarnate, with bulging eyes and a bloodcurdling snarl on his face."[11] This visual image of the Native American as threatening was also seen in works by other artists, who represented kidnappings of pioneers, attacks by fierce-looking Native American warriors, and other reflections of the Indian as fearsome and in need of being subdued.

While some artists reached their audience by exhibiting Native American images in traveling shows and by dramatic oil paintings, others found recognition through the medium of book and magazine illustrations. Felix O.C. Darley, for instance, was influenced by Catlin, and his sketches most likely reached an even larger audience. Darley first became known with the publication of *Scenes in Indian Life* (1843), for which he served as the illustrator. But his mark was truly made when his illustrations began to appear in James Fenimore Cooper's popular Leatherstocking novels, and other books such as Francis Parkman's *The California and Oregon Trail* (1849). Over the course of his life, Darley illustrated approximately 300 books, many of which were considered best-sellers. A good number of those illustrations were reproduced as prints that could be framed and hung on household walls, making Darley's artwork a standard in nineteenth-century households. As a result, Darley's illustrations of the West became inextricably connected to the ways in which non-western readers imagined the West to be.[12]

The link between Darley's illustrations and prevailing ideas about the West was somewhat problematic, however. For unlike Catlin, who had traveled extensively among Indian tribes, Darley never ventured far from the East Coast. As a result, Darley's sketches were often inaccurate. The error most frequently commented on is Darley's drawing of the Plains Indians' tepee, which he depicted as having only one ear, or point, at the top. As with much of the visual arts during the period of westward expansion, the images were created from secondhand, and sometimes even thirdhand, information. Driven by the popularity of the West as subject matter for books and magazines during the second half of the nineteenth century, the priority of publishers was to include as many illustrations of the West as possible in their texts. Accuracy was not as important as the ability to quickly and vividly produce drawings of the West as it was thought to be.

Colossal Indians and *The End of the Trail*

While illustrations and paintings reduced the Native American to the size of a book page or a canvas, popular sculptures did the opposite. The 1893 Columbian Exposition commemorated the disappearing frontier by exhibiting oversized sculptures of its figures. Phimister Proctor's immense figure entitled simply *The Indian* featured an Indian scout posed upright on his horse, his hand shielding his eyes as he peers into the distance, perhaps on the lookout for an undetermined danger. Both horse and Indian appear ready for action, and the statue's sheer size embodies the vastness of the frontier, the immensity of the movement west. Ironically, this somewhat heroic image of the Indian was displayed at the same event at which Frederick Jackson Turner claimed that the frontier was closed, that the movement west had been completed, that Manifest Destiny had been fulfilled. In this light, Proctor's colossal Indian stood for what had already been accomplished. The Indian was only heroic once he had been controlled.[13]

A more realistic representation of the Native American experience at the end of the century could be seen in another, quite different, statue at a different world's fair. James Earle Fraser was born in Minnesota and experienced the frontier firsthand. While growing up, he was particularly struck by the stories of Indians who were being removed from their land and, quite literally, running out of space in which to live. This concern was the inspiration for Fraser's most famous sculpture, entitled *The End of the Trail*. Featuring an Indian astride his horse, the statue includes both man and animal in a weary, hunched-over pose. The horse's hind legs are flexed as if halting at the edge of a cliff. A clear metaphor for the final displacement of the American Indians, *The End of the Trail* won Fraser immediate recognition in Paris and was exhibited at the 1915 Panama-Pacific Exposition where it won a prize. Since its creation, the statue has been reproduced in photographs and souvenirs ranging from "miniature . . . ashtrays to a calendar cover bearing the legend '*Thus ever it is in this world of ours / The brightest light will fail / Then a tear in the eye and an aching heart / When we come to the "End of the Trail."* ' "[14] The posture of the horse and its rider evoked the truth about the impact westward expansion had on the American Indian. Yet the proliferation of the image in the form of souvenirs, photographs, and keepsakes revealed the deep resonance the end of the frontier had within American culture. As if to further reinforce that connection, the stance of *The End of the*

"The End of the Trail," sculpture by James Earle Fraser. Courtesy of the Library of Congress.

Trail became the final pose at the end of rodeos, the contained visual image of the Wild West.[15]

Buffalo Nickel, Indian Head Penny, and Sacagawea Dollar

Despite its popular success, Fraser's statue was never placed at the edge of San Francisco Bay—the literal end of the trail and the end of the frontier—as Fraser had hoped. Instead, the plaster model from the 1915 exposition now stands in the National Cowboy Hall of Fame at Oklahoma City. Fraser, who never copyrighted the image, has been called "the most famous unknown artist" for his lack of both visibility and name recognition.[16] Yet Fraser is also responsible for another representation of the American Indian: he designed the Buffalo Nickel, first issued in 1913. The artist's idea was to design a piece of currency that reflected the uniqueness of American culture, and the result was a coin that featured an Indian profile on one side and a buffalo profile on the other. The significance of those two figures—both primary symbols of the frontier—marked the particular relationship between American art and the period of westward expansion. For just as the period of expansion drew to an end, so did images of that period appear throughout American culture as recognized symbols of the era—the Buffalo Nickel and the Indian Head Penny being key examples. The coin was larger than previous five-cent pieces, and slot machines across the country had to be changed to accommodate the new coin. The Buffalo Nickel was in circulation for twenty-five years, until 1938, when it was replaced with the five-cent piece used today. In 1986, Andy Warhol memorialized the Buffalo Nickel in a series of his signature prints, further reinforcing the persistent image of the Indian and the buffalo within American popular culture.

The Buffalo Nickel was not the first American coin to suggest the image of the American Indian, however. Just four years before the Buffalo Nickel went into circulation, the Indian Head Penny finished a fifty-year life span as the country's one-cent piece. From 1859 to 1909 the American government issued the copper coin known as the Indian Head Penny, yet the name has been persistently misleading. For the penny's imprint is not of an Indian but of Lady Liberty wearing an Indian headdress. The confusion reflects the nineteenth-century relationship between the visual arts and the American Indian. Liberty, a symbol of America, has been confused with the Indian, just as over the course of the nineteenth century Americans equated their freedom to claim the land west of the Mississippi with the right to displace Native Americans. That Liberty has adopted the Indian headdress reflects the way in which pioneers viewed Native Americans—and their customs—during the continuous march across the country. Native Americans were not a separate population whose customs were to be respected, but rather were a group whose symbols—like the headdress—could be co-opted in the process of removing tribes from the land. Moreover, the years in which the penny was minted mark the most significant phase in the period of westward expansion, from just after the gold rush until the frontier was officially closed. In other words, Indian Head pennies both symbolically and literally marked the period of western settlement, enabling pioneers to purchase goods that symbolized "civilization" with a coin that visually represented the price of that civilizing process.

At the beginning of the twenty-first century, a new twist in the use of Indian images appeared in the form of the Sacagawea dollar. In an effort to move into circulation a coin form of the dollar bill, the U.S. Treasury created the dollar with the imprint of Sacagawea, the Indian woman who tirelessly accompanied explorers Lewis and Clark on their first journey across the western United States. There is no existing picture of Sacagawea, so it is impossible to know what she actually looked like. This mystery was used to market the coin, and the woman who was chosen to pose as Sacagawea's likeness was the subject of numerous television and radio interviews when the coin was first released. In addition, intent on ensuring the public's adoption of the dollar—which would ideally supplement or even replace the existing paper bill that has a shorter life span—the Treasury chose Wal-Mart stores as the major outlet for the first release of the coins. Sacagawea dollars were also available as surprise gifts in some boxes of Cheerios cereal, illustrating the deep connections between Indian images and American commercialism.

The Cigar Store Wooden Indian

The relationship between American money and the frontier suggested by the Buffalo Nickel and Indian Head Penny point to a larger trend in which the American Indian became a regular feature in American consumerism. For instance, the stock figure of the Indian that is so typical in American art is reflected in the cigar store Indian, the carved wooden figure that advertised tobacco shops during the nineteenth century and into the early twentieth century. Created from sections of ships' masts by the same men who carved the figureheads on ships' bows, the cigar store Indian embodied, in three-dimensional form, the pervasive stereotypes. Dressed in headdress, feathered skirt, and assorted jewelry, the standard cigar store Indian turned the image of Native Americans into an advertising icon. Standing guard at cigar shops across the country, the wooden Indian came to represent tobacco products to American consumers.[17]

While the wooden Indian fell out of use as other forms of advertising took its place, the cigar store Indian continues to make appearances in popular culture, even materializing in an episode of the popular sitcom *Seinfeld* in which the political correctness that dominated the late twentieth century was challenged. The episode poked fun at the prohibition placed on such terms as "Indian giver" and "scalper" because of the alleged disrespect for Native American culture. The wooden Indian, as a form of folk art that borders on kitsch, was central to the *Seinfeld* episode as it satirized the appropriateness of embracing even the ideologically troubled aspects of American history or sanitizing language and culture to decrease its offensiveness to minority groups.

The figure of the cigar store Indian as an icon of the stereotypical Native American can be seen in other visual forms throughout the twentieth century. In the early 1900s, American Indians appeared on postcards, greeting cards, and advertisements.[18] As early as the 1920s, the Native American appeared on the cover of *Clason's Touring Atlas of the United States and Canada*, a popular guide for Americans who were able

A cigar store Indian, Denison, Iowa (1936).
Courtesy of the Library of Congress.

to purchase the newly affordable automobile in which to explore the country. On one Clason's guide the Indian, in full headdress, waves to the passengers as an automobile passes a scenic lake and mountains. Here the Native American is a symbol of welcome to the American West, where the uncivilized has been tamed by roadways and friendly natives. In an almost opposite image, the Cleveland Indians baseball team logo caricatures the smiling Indian in a cartoon-like figure that wears a single feather. While the logo is meant to be a positive representation of the Indian, it simultaneously stands for the fighting spirit of the national baseball team. Finally, in almost any popular visual representation of the frontier—whether book jackets, movies, advertisements, or product labels—Indians are depicted in one of two ways: either in physical conflict with cowboys or other horsemen, or as faithful companions, as popularized by series like *The Lone Ranger*.[19]

While the visual representation led to a stock figure that signified the ultimate removal of the Native Americans from "American" land, in some instances the arts have embraced the Native American as a symbol of what white Americans lost in their struggle for dominance. In the 1970s, a commercial about the rampant problem of littering in America featured an Indian who returned to find his beloved land ruined. A tear ran down his face at the end of the ad, marking his profound sadness at the changes in the American landscape. The commercial used the Indian as a symbol of what had been lost as a result of American carelessness and waste. While this representation of Native Americans might be seen as relatively positive, the fact that the actor who played the role was not Native American only added to the sense that Indians as symbols were being capitalized on without respect for them as individuals.[20]

In the late twentieth century, Indian art made its way into mainstream culture. Dream catchers, for instance, were part of the new-wave emphasis on spirituality. Indian tapestries, paintings, and other art became desirable commodities in the late 1980s. Artists like R.C. Gorman produced watercolors of American Indians from the Southwest, depicting them not as stoic or threatening, but as exotic and often maternal.

PIONEERS

While the visual representation of the American Indian during westward expansion was complicated by the belief that in order for America to grow in size the Indians had to be removed from the land, the artistic representation of pioneer men, women, and children was much more sentimental and sympathetic. Seen primarily as brave, hardworking folk who took the long journey west at their own peril, pioneers were another familiar subject for nineteenth-century artists who were determined to capture the images of the frontier.

The Journey West

The covered wagon, the rugged landscape, the horses, and perhaps the campfire have been typical features in visual representations of the pioneer voyage. These images reflect not only the hardship of westward emigration, but also the belief in the inevitability of westward expansion. Visual images of the westward journey reinforced the belief in Manifest Destiny, assuring Americans that God willed them to civilize the land. George Caleb Bingham's *Daniel Boone Escorting Settlers Through the Cumberland Gap* (1851–52), for instance, and Albert Bierstadt's *Emigrants Crossing the Plains* (1862), illustrated the primitive circumstances of traveling west, while also suggesting the rewards—both spiritual and material—that would come to those who undertook the mission. *American Progress* (1872), one of the most familiar of frontier images, reflects the concept of Manifest Destiny, of the inevitable, God-given mandate that

American Progress (1873). Courtesy of the Library of Congress.

the country would be settled. W.H.D. Koerner's *Madonna of the Prairie* (1921), featured on the cover of *The Saturday Evening Post* in 1922, idealized the transcontinental crossing by featuring a pioneer woman seated on a wagon with the white canvas of the wagon cover framing her head like a halo. The image of the pioneer in the process of crossing the country in horse-drawn covered wagons has been a staple of American popular culture, as is evident in any popular documentation of the period. The opening sequence to the popular 1970s program, *Little House on the Prairie*, captured the idealized image of the pioneer family who travels the country in its covered wagon, the model of family values and self-reliance.

Photographs and Daguerreotypes

Visual representations of the journey's end also served to assure those people who remained "back in the States" of the prosperity that pioneers who made the trip enjoyed upon their arrival. Some of the most captivating images of pioneers were made by the photographers who took daguerreotypes, a form of photography first discovered in 1839, which produced sepia-toned pictures. The majority of photographers turned to portraiture, taking daguerreotypes of families and individuals throughout the West, especially during the gold rush years of the 1850s. Such pictures helped to record the lifestyles of the pioneers and were sent to relatives in the East who were interested in seeing pictures of family members who had emigrated west. Photographers often became the center of attention in western towns, providing a desired service to the newly established settlers. Dressed in their best clothes, families, businessmen, and groups of friends would gather in the photographer's studio to pose for a picture. The photographer usually had a screen background against which the subjects stood in typical unsmiling fashion. Other pioneers chose to be photographed outside or in front of their frontier homes, sometimes surrounded by their most valuable possessions.

Early photographs of pioneers provide valuable records of life in the Old West. In particular, candid pictures, or those taken outside of the studio, captured scenes from western life that other visual forms could not. At the same time that such prints recorded frontier existence, they also served a secondary purpose, namely to demonstrate to non-westerners that the West was a civilized place. Posed photographs taken in studios were especially aimed at this ideal yet they have been transformed in contemporary American culture. Indeed, mock Old West photography studios are prevalent in tourist spots throughout the country, where visitors can dress up in western clothing and pose for the camera. Perhaps tapping into the widespread idealization of the time period, these pseudo-western photographs serve a different purpose than their predecessors. Rather than reassuring their viewers that the West was civilized, contemporary versions of the daguerreotype typically include women dressed in costumes reminiscent of bar-girls while men invariably sport guns and sheriff's badges. In these instances, the popular culture of the western daguerreotype allows individuals to depict themselves as part of a time when men and women lived just outside the norms of civilization. For it is the combination of the tame and the wild that makes the myth of the West so appealing.[21]

Landscapes

Although the people who existed on and traveled through the frontier were central to popular images of the West, the land itself became the focus of many artists. The great landmarks of America—including Niagara Falls, the Rocky Mountains, and Yellowstone National Park—became the subjects of popular art, not only on canvas but in other forms as well. Thomas Cole, for instance, painted Niagara Falls as early as 1830, and by 1834 wallpaper was available with woodblock impressions of the Falls printed on it. Similarly, the image of Niagara Falls was reproduced on postcards and on small prints suitable for framing. The western land-scape, in other words, was available for purchase and could be brought directly into the American home.[22]

Perhaps the most familiar images of the West were created by Albert Bierstadt, the highest-paid painter of his time. Most popular in the 1860s and 1870s, Bierstadt was a New Englander who had emigrated to America from Germany. In 1859 he joined a government expedition which was supposed to make improvements to parts of the Oregon Trail. During this period Bierstadt recorded the magnificent land around him by using his sketchbook and a stereoscope, an instrument that took primitive, but nonetheless useful, pictures. Upon his return to New York, Bierstadt began to paint his own versions of what he had seen in the West. In 1864 he exhibited one of the most popular, and memorable, of these paintings, *The Rocky Mountains,* which was completed on a canvas that measured sixty square feet in size. In it, animals and people were dwarfed by the trees and mountain peaks that dominate the majority of the painting, reinforcing the standard lore about the West's ability to overwhelm human existence. In general, Bierstadt's dramatic paintings featured towering mountains, dazzling sunlight, brooding shadows, and brilliant waters. None of his art was based on real places, however, but rather represented the composite features of the West as a promised land, an American Eden. One exception was the 1867 painting *Donner Lake from the Summit,* another large canvas that tapped into the public's knowledge of the horrific deaths and cannibalism of the Donner party two decades earlier. Widely publicized, the Donner party's fate symbolized the risks of emigrating West. Yet in Bierstadt's painting, not only was the lake and scenery peaceful, but in the distance the civilizing markers of safety in the form of railroad snow sheds can be seen. Given his ability to represent, simultaneously, both the glamour of the western landscape and the reassurance of civilizing forces, Bierstadt's success corresponded with the era in which pioneers moved steadily into the relatively unexplored frontier. As the land became known and settled, the public's desire for mythic images of the land began to weaken. Yet Bierstadt's representations of this unspoiled land remained central to the popular American image of the frontier prior to its settlement.[23]

Another landscape artist whose work shaped the familiar image of the West was Thomas Moran, an Englishman who arrived in the United States in 1844. Trained as a wood engraver, Moran joined an expedition to Yellowstone Park in 1871 as an illustrator for *Scribner's* magazine. It was there that Moran found the material on which he would focus for the majority of his career. He produced not only sketches and paintings but also the more quickly reproduced chromolithographs and watercolors that were published in popular magazines like *Scribner's.* Indeed, Moran's illustrations of the West, and of Yellowstone in particular, would help to establish Yellowstone as a National Park in 1872, in part because his sketches were used as evidence in persuading Congress to pass the Yellowstone Park bill. *The Grand Canyon of the Yellowstone* (1872) and *The Chasm of the Colorado* (1874), two of Moran's most recognized oil paintings, were hung in the Senate lobby in Washington, DC. Both paintings depicted the West as wild and unpopulated, reinforcing the belief in an indeterminate amount of space waiting to be settled by emigrants.

Perhaps one of most curious of Moran's paintings focused on a popular western destination and landmark, Colorado's Mountain of the Holy Cross. As a result of snowfall that formed a gigantic cross on its face, the mountain was considered a divine miracle, perhaps even evidence that settling the West was God's will for American emigrants. In 1874, Moran traveled to see the mountain for himself and later painted its image in one of his most acclaimed works. Together with other landscape painters, Moran and Bierstadt aimed to bring the West to the viewer in all of its mythic grandness and beauty, and with the symbolic assurance that the West was indeed to be settled.

Panoramas

Although oil paintings like those by Bierstadt and Moran aimed to capture the vastness of the American West, another popular form of visual art, known as the panorama, sought to reproduce that vastness in a form even closer to true size. The aim of an artist using the panorama as a medium was to bring the viewer as close to the real experience of the land as possible. This effort was focused on a combination of the landscape painting and other, more interactive, mediums such as lighting, narrative, and even acting. Most panoramas moved, a result of the canvas being wound upon a roller that was then turned throughout the viewing. As the scenes changed, a narrator explained them to the audience. The most popular subjects of American panoramas included the history of the Mormons by Carl Christian Anton Christensen, the Sioux uprising of 1862 by John Stevens, and the Overland Trail by James Wilkins. Half art and half performance, the panoramas were traveling exhibits shown in cities across the country during the mid-1800s. Audiences attended the shows in high numbers. For instance, reports of attendance at Wilkins' "Moving Mirror of the Overland Trail," exhibited in Peoria, Illinois in 1850, claimed that the panorama was shown to a full house for its entire stay. The artwork impacted viewers, making them feel as if they were actually in the land around them:

I had never travelled it myself; but the green prairies, the sandy deserts, the huge masses of rock, the rushing and the gentle rivers, the snow caped [*sic*] mountains, and the emigrants winding up the steep acclivity, and descending the almost perpendicular hills with their oxen and mules, and covered wagons, are all in the mind's eye as distinctly and fresh as though I had often travelled to California. . . . Mind, sense, all seemed wrapped up in the great Panorama before us; and anyone with a little imagination, would actually believe that he was on his way to California, instead of viewing the route.[24]

In many ways, the panorama's popularity could have arisen only during the period of westward expansion. An American public eager to be part of the movement to the West, combined with the growing lore around the land, gave the panorama a built-in audience, one which longed to experience the vastness of the frontier without necessarily enduring its hardships. And while the panorama's popularity was short-lived, in many ways the form anticipated some of the earliest of American movies that were, not surprisingly, known as westerns.[25]

Reproductions and Photographs

Although paintings and panoramas help to inform the twentieth-century image of western land, nineteenth-century Americans were more likely to see lithographs or other reproductions than the real paintings. For while paintings such as Moran's *The Grand Canyon of the Yellowstone* did appear in traveling exhibitions, everyday Americans could easily see them—in the form of an engraving, lithograph, or print—in magazines such as *Harper's*, *Scribner's*, or *Frank Leslie's Weekly*. The process of creating an engraving based on the original work would begin as soon as a painting, such as Bierstadt's *The Rocky Mountains*, had been completed. An engraving took time to complete, and a comparison between the original artwork and the printed newspaper or magazine image often revealed differences between the two. As a result of such changes, the images familiar to most Americans were often based on, but not identical to, the original. Reproduced illustrations, however, were sometimes exaggerated, or even satirical commentaries on the events they depicted. Certainly, they influenced the public's ideas about the West more immediately and persistently than did the watercolors or oil paintings which inspired them.[26] A prolific producer of western images was Currier & Ives, whose lithographs were pictured in magazines and made available for framing and displaying at home. Of particular success was the company's reproduction of *Westward the Course of Empire Takes Its Way* and *The Prairie Hunter* series, both by Fanny F. Palmer and Alfred L. Tait.[27]

If panoramas and landscape paintings tried to capture the sheer vastness and beauty of the American West, the photograph was able to capture the land's details. Used on government surveying expeditions, photographic equipment was heavy, awkward, and fragile, causing numerous problems every step of the journey. The best-known photographer of the West was William Henry Jackson, who worked in photography studios and, after serving in the Union army, headed west to Nebraska where he set up his own studio. In 1871 Jackson was offered a job as the official photographer on a government-sponsored expedition to Yellowstone. The invitation came from the chief geologist, Ferdinand Vandeveer Hayden, who worked for the U.S Geological and Geographical Survey of the Territories. Over the next years, Hayden and Jackson documented uncharted regions of the West and Jackson's photographs, in their ability to accurately show what the West was truly like, added to the growing idea that the West was a mythic and majestic place. One of Jackson's most popular photographs was of the legendary Mountain of the Holy Cross, first painted by Thomas Moran. The photograph, which proved that the cross did exist, only further fueled the popular belief that the frontier was God's land.[28]

Ansel Adams and the Sierra Club

Photographic images of the West remain central to American popular art, as can been seen in Ansel Adams' familiar pictures of western landscapes. Best known for his black-and-white photographs, Adams was born in San Francisco at the beginning of the twentieth century. There he visited Yosemite National Park, which became a primary subject throughout his career. Like Bierstadt and Moran, Adams depicted the West as land untouched by humans and majestic in size and shape. His photographs have received critical acclaim, and their popularity has been unmatched by other twentieth-century photographers. They have been reproduced in calendars and affordable prints that decorate office walls and homes across the country. Adams' photos are especially interesting because they depict areas of the West that have remained unsettled, reminding viewers that while the frontier may be closed, the West is not completely domesticated. Other groups, such as the Sierra Club established in 1892, have helped to protect the western landscape by selling calendars and date books that contain photographs of western landmarks such as the redwood tree.[29]

National Parks, Tourism, and Postcards

If visual representations have shaped conventional ideas of what the West looked like prior to being settled, the establishment and popularity of the National Parks has provided a way to experience the West in relatively unchanged form. A form of popular culture in their own right, national parks like Yosemite, the Grand Canyon, and Yellowstone have allowed tourists to come into direct contact with the western landscape.

This experience occurs, however, most often from the safety of resort hotels, group tours, and supervised outings. Other western landmarks have been literally marked with images of America, for instance Mount Rushmore, which features the sculpted faces of four American presidents. The souvenir shop is a staple of many of these parks, where visual images of the West can be purchased in the form of postcards, dish towels, plates, and other items that tourists can bring home with them as reminders of their trip. These images also appear as the background for a multitude of product advertisements, especially cars and trucks, and as scenery in Hollywood movies, further demonstrating the extent to which popular culture has absorbed and relied upon the images of the western landscape.

BUFFALO AND OTHER BEASTS

From the start, exploration of the West involved documenting the plants and animals that existed there. In early expeditions, mysterious and unknown birds, mammals, fish, and other beasts were trapped and sent to the East—either living or not—for study and analysis. Pioneer journals recorded first sightings of buffalo and unfamiliar animals which added an interesting backdrop for the drama of the westward movement.

Buffalo, the Audubon Society, and *The Far Side*

Not only is the landscape vast and towering, but, in the popular mythology of the West, the living things on that land are also larger than life. From the realities of giant redwood trees to the stories of soil so rich it gave rise to extraordinary crops, the West has been associated with, or thought to produce, oversized things. Legitimate examples of oversized western objects, however, also gave rise to popular lore about the size of fish, vegetables, and even people. In the twentieth century in particular, these exaggerated depictions of the West were popular, resulting in, for example, postcards illustrating giant salmon and oversized corn. Larger-than-life mythical characters such as Paul Bunyan and his ox Babe, fit this category, as does the "World's Largest Buffalo" located outside Frontier Village in Jamestown, North Dakota. Each of these figures reflects the popular notion that the West is still a place of plenty, of things and ideas on a grand scale, and the frontier is a primary source for America's image of itself as vast and great.

While the World's Largest Buffalo marks a twentieth-century interpretation of the animal, during the period of westward expansion images of buffalo were also significant. In addition to the circulation of the Buffalo Nickel, paintings and illustrations of the buffalo revealed the deep

Paul Bunyan monument, Bemidji, Minnesota (1939). Courtesy of the
Library of Congress.

connection between the animal and the popular image of the West. More
specifically, paintings such as Alfred Bierstadt's *The Last Buffalo* (1889)
illustrated the significance that the slaughter of the buffalo had for the
frontier. Not only did the animal symbolize the free-ranging existence of
the West, but buffalo capture and kill by pioneers and hunters demon-
strated the economic stakes at play in conquering western lands. The
buffalo appears throughout popular culture in two primary forms: running freely over the plains or being bloodily slaughtered. Both images
were portrayed in the Academy Award-winning film *Dances with Wolves*
(1990), which used the buffalo to stand for the loss that accompanied
civilizing the West.

John James Audubon, the illegitimate son of a French merchant and a
Haitian chambermaid, was an illustrator best known for his record of
American wildlife, particularly species of American birds. Working as a
taxidermist out of Cincinnati, Ohio, in the 1820s, Audubon studied his
subjects by shooting them. He then wired the bird to a board and drew
it in great detail. Audubon's legacy to the study of American wildlife
was *Birds of America* which, published in 1838, contained 1,055 life-sized
images of birds. Although Audubon did not find great success in his

own lifetime, his illustrations were reproduced as engravings and lithographs and have been hung in homes across the country. Audubon's name has also become synonymous with the protection of wildlife, and Audubon Society calendars and date books are standard fare in American bookstores.[30] Gary Larson's *The Far Side* cartoons provide a different perspective on western wildlife, imbuing cows and horses with an intelligence and humor that their human counterparts lack.[31]

HOME DECORATION

While the people, places, and things of the West were the subject of many visual arts of the period, the objects people hung in their own homes as they settled down in western towns were sometimes quite different. For, in addition to a fascination with the West, Americans were also participants in the trends of Victorianism that celebrated sentimental, idealized images of animals, children, and other loved ones. Also popular were romantic scenes of nature, for instance ice-skaters or horse-drawn sleds, images in which nature had been fully domesticated. Pioneers who did not bring such pictures with them, or who had to abandon them on the rigorous journey, could purchase similar items through mail-order catalogs. As the 1897 Sears Roebuck catalog claims, bargains were to be had if one would simply purchase "the World's most Famous Paintings at Enormous Reductions in Prices."[32] Moreover, catalogs themselves could serve as wall decorations simply by tearing pages of pictures from the catalog and hanging them on the wall.

COMMERCIAL ART

The popularity of western figures—cowboys, Indians, pioneers, landscapes, and animals—reflects the ease with which images of the West can be recognized and the lengths to which they have been integrated into the history and myth of the United States. The commercial art of the frontier can be characterized by the simple symbols that were used to denote the product. Whether placed on storefronts, maps, advertisements, flyers, or book covers, the majority of images used to sell products in the West took the shape of easily recognized figures. Above the sign for the "Meat Market," for instance, might be painted a black profile of a bull. On a tin of Mojave Coffee, a woman astride a horse might be holding a cup of coffee. Other straightforward associations between the product and its labels included crates of fruit from the West that were marked by bright illustrations of the products they held. Western images of the railroad, the Indian, the American eagle, and groups of pioneers also appeared on land plot certificates as well as on the homemade paper currency that was printed in Kansas and Nebraska during the 1850s. The latter, created in an effort to increase the amount of money in circulation, featured western images including Indians overlooking a growing western town, a man drinking from a wilderness stream, and a farmer cutting wheat with a scythe.[34]

The use of simple words and pictures to publicize goods, services, and events may have arisen from an effort to communicate to the large and diverse populations who were migrating west. No matter what language the pioneers spoke, they could recognize the town's market by the solid black picture of the bull over its front door. Whatever the reasons, this form of visual art was extremely common in western towns and has been reproduced in nearly every western film or television show that focuses on the frontier. The style has continued throughout the twentieth century, gaining a renewal in the 1990s when "old-fashioned" products became fashionable again. U.S. license plates also incorporate these types of visual images. For example, the Wyoming license plate features a silhouette of a cowboy riding a rearing horse, and the Oregon plate highlights a pioneer wagon.

While the stark simplicity of commercial art is a trademark of the Old West, another form of visual representation was also popular during the period of westward expansion. Posters advertising the circus, Wild West Shows, and other forms of entertainment were elaborate lithographs that used multiple colors, fonts, and figures. Typically such announcements contained a background illustration that covered the entire page and upon which numerous smaller images were placed. The multiple images reflected the types of events that were being advertised: a variety of acts, performances, or shows which viewers could watch. The intricate, multifaceted, brightly colored posters mirrored the events themselves, acting as a prelude to the entertainment westerners so eagerly sought.

Yet another common form of visual arts was the woodblock that was used to decorate the covers of dime novels, one of the best-selling literary genres of the second half of the nineteenth century. The mass-marketed books had distinctive orange covers that were easily recognized by their formulaic layouts. The top third of the cover listed the series title—*The Deadwood Dick Library, Beadle's Frontier Series,* or *The New York Detective Library,* for instance—while the bottom two-thirds included the volume's title and a woodblock illustration of a scene from the book. The pictures were typically sensational representations of masked and armed men, charging horses, and dead villains. The woodblock style was the dime novel's signature and, because it was easy to reproduce, helped to keep the books inexpensive and readily available to mass audiences.

The period of westward expansion was rife with visual images of the newly explored land. From cowboys and Indians to covered wagons and pioneers, the visual representation of the western experience promoted the urgency and inevitability of American emigration. The images recorded by painters, illustrators, and photographers during the second half of the nineteenth century shaped the way the West has since been represented in the popular visual mediums of film, television, advertising, and comic books. The accuracy of those representations is debatable, just as the personal and national issues surrounding the settlement of the West is complex. However, the visual symbols endure as part of popular culture and the American psyche, illustrating the gains and losses that went hand in hand with the process of taming the wild, Wild West.

Cost of Products[1]

Conestoga Wagon[2]	$1,500.00
Levi's Jeans[3]	$1.00
Lamp	$.75
Arbuckle's Ariosa Coffee	$.35/pound
Eggs	$.03–.06/dozen
Hat	$1.35
Boots	$3.60
Molasses	$.40/gallon
2 bowls	$.24
Butter	$.06–.08/pound
Yoke of cattle	$90.00
Cattle and wagon	$100.00
Hotel lodging	$.25/night or 3.50/week
Hotel meal	$.35/meal
Rent on a house in Kill Creek, Kansas	$3.00/month
Farmhand salary, Osborne, KS	$12/month

[1] Prices varied greatly during the period of westward expansion. They also differed from town to town, and even from day to day, depending on factors such as weather and availability of goods. With the exception of the Conestoga Wagon and jeans, this list gives a snapshot of the prices of goods during the year 1877 in the state of Kansas. They were recorded by Howard Ruede in *Sod House Days: Letters from a Kansas Homesteader, 1877–1878*, ed. by John Ise (New York: Cooper Square Publishers, Inc., 1966).

[2] Howard R. Lamar, ed., *The New Encyclopedia of the American West* (New Haven: Yale University Press, 1998), 910.

[3] The Levi-Strauss company lost its archival records in 1906. However, Lynne Downey, the company historian, states that the approximate price of a pair of Levi's would have been about one dollar.

Notes

INTRODUCTION

1. In *The Frontier in American History* (New York: Dover Publishers, 1996), Frederick Jackson Turner makes his claim that the frontier is officially closed as of 1890.

CHAPTER 1

1. Donald F. Danker, *Mollie: The Journal of Mollie Dorsey Sanford in Nebraska and Colorado Territories, 1857–1866* (Lincoln: University of Nebraska Press, 1959), 3.

2. For an excellent overview of everyday life outside the realm of popular culture, see Mary Ellen Jones, *Daily Life on the Nineteenth-Century American Frontier* (Westport, CT: Greenwood Press, 1998).

3. Howard R. Lamar, ed., *The New Encyclopedia of the American West* (New Haven: Yale University Press, 1998), 815–816.

4. Patricia Nelson Limerick, "Of Forty-Niners, Oilmen and the Dot-Com Boom." *New York Times*, 7 May 2000, Business page, 4.

5. Sheryl Gay Stolberg, "Internet Prescriptions Boom in the 'Wild West' of the West." *New York Times*, 27 June 1999, 1.

6. Jones, *Daily Life on the Nineteenth-Century American Frontier*, 98.

7. For a sampling of different religions and their influence in the West see George W. Ranck, *The Traveling Church* [n.p.] (1891); Ross Pahres, *Bible in Pocket, Gun in Hand: The Story of Frontier Religion* (Garden City, NY: Doubleday, 1967); and John Gilmary Shea, *History of the Catholic Missions Among the Indian Tribes of the United States, 1529–1854* (New York: Arno Press, 1969); Wallace Stegner, *The Gathering of Zion: The Story of the Mormon Trail* (Lincoln: University of Nebraska

Press, 1992); and "The Frontier Church," in Joanna L. Stratton, *Pioneer Women: Voices from the Kansas Frontier* (New York: Simon and Schuster, 1981), 171–183.

8. For more on frontier medicine see: Anton Paul Sohn, *A Saw, Pocket Instruments, and Two Ounces of Whiskey: Frontier Military Medicine in the Great Basin* (Spokane, WA: Arthur H. Clark Company, 1998), and Elizabeth Van Steenwyk, *Frontier Fever: The Scary, Superstitious—and Sometimes Sensible—Medicine of the Pioneers* (New York: Walker and Company, 1995).

9. Robert F. Karolevitz, *Doctors of the Old West* (New York: Bonanza Books, 1967), 85.

10. Nannie T. Alderson and Helena Huntington Smith, *A Bride Goes West* (Lincoln: University of Nebraska Press, 1942), 145.

11. Samuel Hopkins Adams, *The Great American Fraud: A Series of Articles on the Patent Medicine Evil, reprinted from Collier's Weekly* (New York: P.F. Collier, 1905) and Adelaide Hechtlinger, comp., *The Great Patent Medicine Era; or, Without Benefit of Doctor* (New York: Grosset & Dunlap, 1970).

12. Thermopolis: World's Largest Mineral Hot Springs. http://www.thermopolis.com (10 July 2001).

13. See Norton H. Moses, *Lynching and Vigilantism in the United States: An Annotated Bibliography* (Westport, CT: Greenwood Press, 1997), R.E. Mather and F.E. Boswell, *Vigilante Victims: Montana's 1864 Hanging Spree* (San Jose, CA: History West Publishing Company, 1991), and Nathanial P. Langford and Dave Walter, *Vigilante Days and Ways* (Helena, MT: Farcountry Press, 1995).

14. James Mackay, *Allan Pinkerton: The First Private Eye* (New York: John Wiley & Sons, Inc., 1996).

15. Harold Rabinowitz, *Black Hats and White Hats: Heroes and Villains of the West* (New York: Metro Books, Inc. 1996), 75–79.

16. Duncan Aikman, *Calamity Jane and the Lady Wildcats* (Lincoln: University of Nebraska Press, 1927).

17. See Michael A. Lofaro, ed., *Davy Crockett: The Man, the Legend, the Legacy, 1786–1986* (Knoxville: The University of Tennessee Press, 1985), and Michael A. Lofaro and Joe Cummings, eds., *Crockett at Two Hundred: New Perspectives on the Man and the Myth* (Knoxville: University of Tennessee Press, 1989).

18. Allen Barra, *Inventing Wyatt Earp: His Life and Many Legends* (New York: Carroll & Graf Publishers, 1998), and Richard E. Erwin, *The Truth about Wyatt Earp* (Carpinteria, CA: O.K. Press, 1992).

19. Robert M. Utley, *Billy the Kid: A Short and Violent Life* (Lincoln: University of Nebraska Press, 1991).

20. Rabinowitz, *Black Hats and White Hats*, 45. See also James Ross, *I, Jesse James* (Lake Geneva, WI: Dragon Publishing Corp, 1989).

21. See M. Paul Holsinger, "Indian Wars West of the Mississippi, 1862–1890," in M. Paul Holsinger, ed., *War and American Popular Culture* (Westport, CT: Greenwood Press, 1999), 148–177.

22. Stephen E. Ambrose, *Crazy Horse and Custer: The Parallel Lives of Two American Warriors* (New York: Anchor Books, 1976), and Edward Kadlecek, *To Kill An Eagle: Indian Views on the Death of Crazy Horse* (Boulder: Johnson Books, 1983).

23. Robert M. Utley, *The Lance and The Shield: The Life and Times of Sitting Bull* (New York: Ballantine Books, 1994).

24. Lamar, *The New Encyclopedia of the American West*, 425.

25. Odie B. Faulk, *The Geronimo Campaign* (New York: Oxford University Press, 1969, repr. 1993), and C.L. Sonnichsen, ed., *Geronimo and the End of the Apache Wars* (New York: Brompton Books, 1990).

26. See M. Paul Holsinger, "The Spanish-American War and the Philippine Insurrection," in Holsinger, *War and American Popular Culture*, 178–193.

27. See Keith Melder, *Hail to the Candidate: Presidential Campaigns from Banners to Broadcasts* (Washington, DC: Smithsonian Institution Press, 1992), and Roger A. Fischer, *Tippecanoe and Trinkets Too: The Material Culture of American Presidential Campaigns 1828–1984* (Urbana: University of Illinois Press, 1988).

28. Fischer, R., *Tippecanoe and Trinkets Too*, 83.

29. Fischer, R., *Tippecanoe and Trinkets Too*, 85.

30. See Herman Hagedorn, *Roosevelt in the Bad Lands* (Boston: Houghton Mifflin Company, 1921); H. W. Brands, *T.R.: The Last Romantic* (New York: Basic Books, 1998); and Paul Russell Cutright, *Theodore Roosevelt: The Making of a Conservative* (Urbana: University of Illinois Press, 1985).

31. For more on the Rough Riders see Theodore Roosevelt's *The Rough Riders* (New York: Charles Scribner's Sons, 1899), and Dale L. Walker, *The Boys of '98: Theodore Roosevelt and the Rough Riders* (New York: Forge, 1999).

32. Holsinger, *War and American Popular Culture*, 188–189.

33. Holsinger, *War and American Popular Culture*, 191.

34. Fischer, R., *Tippecanoe and Trinkets Too*, 169.

35. Irwin Silber, *Songs American Voted By* (Harrisburg, PA: Stackpole Books, 1971), 185.

36. See Melder, *Hail to the Candidate*, 130–131, and "Teddy Bear Origins," Mountain Green Country Sampler, 2001, http://www.mountaingreen.com/teddy_bear_origins.html (10 July 2001).

37. Melder, *Hail to the Candidate*, 130.

38. For more examples of Roosevelt's campaign songs see Silber, *Songs America Voted By*.

39. For the complete speech see John Fitzgerald Kennedy Library, 6 June 1996, http://www.jfklibrary.org (22 December 2001).

40. Patricia Limerick Nelson explores Kennedy's use of the frontier metaphor in her essay "The Adventures of the Frontier in the Twentieth Century," in James R. Grossman, ed., *The Frontier in American Culture* (Los Angeles: University of California Press, 1994). See especially pages 80–85.

41. Fischer, R., *Tippecanoe and Trinkets Too*, 256.

42. Melder, *Hail to the Candidate*, 188.

43. Fischer, R., *Tippecanoe and Trinkets Too*, 289.

44. Jim Yardley, "Vicarious Consumption: Boots Made for Walking on Pennsylvania Avenue," *New York Times*, Sunday Money and Business, 13 May 2001, 12.

CHAPTER 2

1. The phrase is taken from Elliott West's book by the same name, *Growing Up with the Country: Childhood on the Far Western Frontier* (Albuquerque: University of New Mexico Press, 1989).

2. Elliot West's *Growing Up with the Country* provides an excellent overview of the issues facing children during the period of westward expansion. See also Elliott West and Paula Petrik, eds., *Small Worlds: Children and Adolescents in America, 1850–1950* (Lawrence: University Press of Kansas, 1992), especially "Children on the Plains Frontier," 26–41. Finally, see "A Prairie Childhood" in Joanna L. Stratton, ed., *Pioneer Women: Voices from the Kansas Frontier* (New York: Simon and Schuster, 1981), 144–156.

3. Hamlin Garland, *Boy Life on the Prairie* (New York: Frederick Ungar Publishing Co., 1959), 23. See also 26.

4. For more on parenting see Elliott West, "Beyond Baby Doe: Child Rearing on the Mining Frontier," in Susan Armitage and Elizabeth Jameson, eds., *The Women's West* (Norman: University of Oklahoma Press, 1987), 179–192.

5. Paul W. Rodman, *A Victorian Gentlewoman in the Far West: The Reminiscence of Mary Hallock Foote* (San Marino, CA: Huntington Library, 1972), 290.

6. See Lillian Schlissel, ed., *Women's Diaries of the Westward Journey* (New York: Schocken Books, 1982), 130–132.

7. West, *Growing Up with the Country*, 15.

8. Elise Duback Isley, *Sunbonnet Days* (Caldwell, ID: Caxton Printers, 1935), 86–87.

9. Liahna Babener, "Bitter Nostalgia: Recollections of Childhood on the Midwestern Frontier," in West, *Small Worlds*, 303.

10. Elliott West, "Children on the Plains Frontier," in *Small Worlds*, 33.

11. Two excellent sources on frontier education include Andrew Gulliford's *America's Country Schools* (Washington, DC: Preservation Press, 1984), and Mulliford's essay, "Fox and Geese in the School Yard," in Kathryn Gover, ed., *Hard at Play: Leisure in America, 1840–1940* (Amherst: University of Massachusetts Press, 1992), 188–209.

12. Horace Mann, *A Few Thoughts on the Power and Duties of Women* (Syracuse: Hall, Mills, and Company, 1853).

13. Catherine Beecher, *The Duty of American Women to Their Country* (New York: Harper & Brothers, 1845).

14. John Steinbeck, *East of Eden* (1952; repr., New York: Penguin Books, 1981), 169.

15. Owen Wister, *The Virginian* (1902; repr., New York: MacMillan Company, 1960), 53.

16. Wister, *The Virginian*, 53.

17. Quoted in Stratton, *Pioneer Women*, 165–166.

18. Garland, *Boy Life on the Prairie*, 27.

19. Edwin Lewis Bennett, *Boom Town Boy* (Chicago: Sage Books, 1966), 40.

20. Garland, *Boy Life on the Prairie*, 27.

21. See Gulliford, *America's Country Schools*, 76–77.

22. Gulliford, "Fox and Geese in the School Yard," 200.

23. Gulliford, "Fox and Geese in the School Yard," 200.

24. Garland, *Boy Life on the Prairie*, 49.

25. Bennett, *Boom Town Boy*, 68.

26. For more on the history of game books see Bernard Mergen, "Made, Bought, and Stolen: Toys and the Culture of Childhood," in West, *Small Worlds*, 86–106.

27. Garland, *Boy Life on the Prairie*, 132.

28. For more on frontier toys, Bernard Mergen, "Made, Bought, and Stolen: Toys and the Culture of Childhood," in West, *Small Worlds*, 86–107.

29. Rodman, *A Victorian Gentlewoman in the Far West*, 134.

30. The role of dolls in nineteenth-century play is explored in Miriam Formanek-Brunell, "Sugar and Spite: The Politics of Doll Play in Nineteenth-Century America," in West, *Small Worlds*, 107–124.

31. Christiane Fischer, ed., *Let Them Speak for Themselves: Women in the American West, 1849–1900* (Hamden, CT: Archon Books, 1977), 287.

32. Mountain Green Country Sample, 2001, http://www.mountaingreen.com/teddy_bear_origins.html (10 July 2001).

33. Elliott West, *Growing Up in the Twentieth Century: A History and Reference Guide* (Westport, CT: Greenwood Press, 1996), 18.

34. For more on life in the 1950s see David Halberstam, *The Fifties* (New York: Willard Books, 1993); Karal Ann Marling, *As Seen on TV: The Visual Culture of Everyday Life in the 1950s* (Cambridge: Harvard University Press, 1986); and William M. Tuttle, Jr., "The Homefront Children's Popular Culture: Radio, Movies, Comics—Adventure, Patriotism, and Sex-Typing," in West, *Small Worlds*, 143–163.

35. Paul F. Anderson, *The Davy Crockett Craze: A Look at the 1950s Phenomenon and Davy Crockett Collectibles* (R.G. Productions, 1996), and Michael A. Lofaro and Joe Cummings, eds., *Crockett at Two Hundred: New Perspectives on the Man and the Myth* (Knoxville: University of Tennessee Press, 1989).

36. For more on the history of Disneyland, see justdisney.com, 1999, http://www.justdisney.com (22 December 2001).

37. Bennett, *Boom Town Boy*, 19.

38. www.americangirlstore.com/html/kirsten/meet/k_meet.html.

39. Janet Beeler Shaw, *Meet Kirsten: An American Girl* (Madison, WI: Pleasant Company 1986).

CHAPTER 3

1. For more on the history of nineteenth-century American advertising, see Christina Mierau, *Accept No Substitutes: The History of American Advertising* (Minneapolis: Lerner Publishing Co., 2000); Jackson Lears, *Fables of Abundance: A Cultural History of Advertising in America* (NY: Basic Books, 1994); and Juliann Sivulka, *Soap, Sex, and Cigarettes: A Cultural History of American Advertising* (Belmont, CA: Wadsworth Publishing Company, 1998).

2. Dale Morgan, ed., *Overland in 1846: Diaries and Letters of the California-Oregon Trail* (Lincoln: University of Nebraska Press, 1993), 481.

3. Howard R. Lamar, ed., *The New Encyclopedia of the American West* (New Haven: Yale University Press, 1998), 493.

4. Reuben J. Ellis, "The American Frontier and the Contemporary Real Estate Advertising Magazine," *Journal of Popular Culture* 27, no. 3 (Winter 1993): 119.

5. Sandra L. Myres, ed., *Ho for California! Women's Overland Diaries from the Huntington Library* (San Marino: Huntington Library, 1980), 118.

6. For an example of the gold rush font, see J.I. Biegeleisen, *Handbook of Type Faces and Lettering* (Arco Publishing Co., 1982), 242.

7. W.F. Rae, *Westward by Rail* (New York: Promontory Press, 1974), 199.

8. Rae, *Westward by Rail*, 200–201.

9. Quoted in Mierau, *Accept No Substitutes*, 34.

10. For more on patent medicine and patent medicine advertisements see Lears, *Fables of Abundance*; Mierau, *Accept No Substitutes*; and Sarah Stage, *Female Complaints: Lydia Pinkham and the Business of Women's Medicine* (NY: W. W. Norton & Company, 1979).

11. For examples of patent medicines see Adelaide Hechtinger, *The Great Patent Medicine Era* (New York: Grosset and Dunlap, Inc., 1970).

12. Arrell M. Gibson, "Medicine Show," *American West* 4, no. 1 (February 1967): 34–79.

13. Almost every history of American advertising includes discussions of P.T. Barnum. See especially Lears, *Fables of Abundance*, and Sivulka, *Soap, Sex, and Cigarettes*. Cody's ads were posted on tall fences, the sides of barns and other buildings. A standard ad measured twenty-eight-by-forty-two inches and Cody ordered as many as 500,000 of them a year as part of his advertising campaign.

14. *Sears, Roebuck and Co. Catalog*, 1897.

15. J. Valier Fifer's *American Progress* (Chester, CT: Globe Pequst Press, 1988) explores the history of American tourism and spends a good deal of time on the promotion of early western travel.

16. See for instance, Lawrence R. Borne's *Dude Ranching: A Complete History* (Albuquerque: University of New Mexico Press, 1983).

17. Philip Ashton Rollins, *The Cowboy* (New York: Charles Scribner's Sons, 1922), 235.

18. Rollins, *The Cowboy*, 243.

19. For more on brand name products, see Arnold B. Barach, *Famous American Trademarks* (Washington, DC: Public Affairs Press, 1971), and Hannah Campbell, *Why Did They Name It . . . ?* (New York: Fleet Publishing Company, 1964).

20. Elliott West's essay, "Selling the Myth: Western Images in Advertising" is an excellent overview of the West and advertising. In Richard Aguila, ed., *Wanted Dead or Alive: The American West in Popular Culture* (Urbana: University of Illinois Press, 1996), 269–292.

21. See also "Giant Size Remington Reproductions become Marlboro Outdoor Boards," *Advertising Age* 40 (20 January 1969), 32; the ad can be found in Sivulka, *Soap, Sex and Cigarettes*, 105.

22. The ad can be found in the illustrations section of James R. Grossman, ed., *The Frontier in American Culture* (Berkeley: University of California Press, 1994). See especially Richard White, "Frederick Jackson Turner and Buffalo Bill," pp. 7–66.

23. The Jordan Playboy ad is mentioned in many histories of advertising. See, for instance, James S. Norris, *Advertising*, 4th edition (Englewood Cliffs, NJ: Prentice Hall, 1990); Lears, *Fables of Abundance*, and Mierau's *Accept No Substitutes*.

24. A thorough analysis of the cowboy presence in marketing is Alf H. Walle's *The Cowboy Hero and Its Audience: Popular Culture as Market Derived Art* (Bowling Green, OH: Bowling Green University Press, 2000).

25. Leo Burnett, "The Marlboro Story," *The New Yorker*, 15 November 1958.

26. Burnett, "The Marlboro Story."

27. The ad ran in the January 1957 issue of *Life*.

28. Information about the Marlboro Man can be found in Burnett "The Marlboro Story"; Bruce A. Lohof, "The Higher Meaning of Marlboro Cigarettes," *Journal of Popular Culture* 3 (1969): 441–450.

29. National Public Radio's program "On the Media" ran a segment entitled "Commercial Closet," which discussed the Kellogg's Nut 'N' Honey commercial. The interview can be heard at on the media, http://www.onthemedia.org (22 December 2001).

30. For more examples of ads and icons in American advertising see Warren Dotz and Jim Morton, *What a Character! 20th Century American Advertising Icons* (San Francisco: Chronicle Books, 1996).

31. For examples of the Lady Stetson ad, see www.lib.washington.edu/exhibits/FRONTIER/Image/ (17 March 2002).

32. The ad can be found in Anne M. Butler, "Selling the Popular Myth," in *The Oxford History of the American West*, edited by Clyde A. Milner, Carol A. O'Connor, and Martha A. Sandweiss, p. 796 (New York: Oxford University Press, 1994).

33. The ad can be found in Sivulka, *Soap, Sex and Cigarretts*.

CHAPTER 4

1. The following books provide good overviews of popular American architecture: Mary Mix Foley, *The American House* (New York: Harper Colophon Books, 1980); Alan Gowans, *Images of American Living* (Philadelphia: J. B. Lippincott Company, 1964); David P. Handlin, *The American Home: Architecture and Society, 1815–1915* (Boston: Little, Brown and Company, 1979); Fred W. Peterson, "Vernacular Building and Victorian Architecture: Midwestern American Farm Homes," *Journal of Interdisciplinary History* 12, no. 3 (winter 1982): 409–427; and Dell Upton, "Ordinary Buildings: A Bibliographical Essay on American Vernacular Architecture," *American Studies International* 19 (winter 1981): 57–75.

2. Sources include Everett Dick, *The Lure of the Land* (Lincoln: University of Nebraska Press, 1970), and John Opie, *The Law of the Land: Two Hundred Years of American Farmland Policy* (Lincoln: University of Nebraska Press, 1987).

3. Huston Horn, *The Pioneers* (New York: Time-Life Books, 1974), 199.

4. Sarah Royce, *A Frontier Lady: Recollections of the Gold Rush and Early California*, ed. Ralph Henry Gabriel (Lincoln: University of Nebraska Press, 1932), 89.

5. For more on dugouts see Mary Ellen Jones, *Daily Life on the Nineteenth-Century American Frontier* (Westport, CT: Greenwood Press, 1998): 196–197; Angel Kwolek-Folland, "The Elegant Dugout: Domesticity and Moveable Culture in the U.S., 1870–1900," *American Studies* 25, no. 2 (fall 1984): 21–37; and Foster-Harris's chapter, "Free Grass and Barbed Wire," in *The Look of the Old West* (New York: Viking Press, 1955), 258–301.

6. James Maurer, "Prairie dugouts to underground dream houses: If the pioneers could see them now," *American West* 6 (1981): 35. See also Stu Campbell, *The Underground House Book* (Charlotte VT: Garden Way Publishing, 1980).

7. For more on this distinction see Terry G. Jordan and Matti Kaups, *The American Backwoods Frontier: An Ethnic and Ecological Interpretation* (Baltimore: Johns Hopkins University Press, 1989), 175–177.

8. See "Backwoods Folk Architecture," in *The American Backwoods Frontier*, 179–210.

9. H. H. [Helen Hunt Jackson], "To Leadville," *Atlantic Monthly* 43 (May 1879): 575.

10. A thorough overview of the log house is available in Foley's *The American House*, especially chapter 3.

11. Nannie T. Alderson and Helena Huntington Smith, *A Bride Goes West* (Lincoln: University of Nebraska Press), 24.

12. Clifford Edward Clark, *The American Family Home: 1800–1960* (Chapel Hill: University of North Carolina Press, 1986), 116.

13. For more on Molesworth see *"Cowboy High Style" Thomas Molesworth to the New West* by Elizabeth Clair Flood (Layton, UT: Gibbs Smith Publisher, 1995).

14. See also Henry D. McCallum, *The Wire That Fenced the West* (Norman: University of Oklahoma Press, 1965).

15. As Edgar N. Mayhew and Minor Myers, Jr., describe, in August 1895 an article by R. Davis Benn entitled "Why Not a Wigwam Style" appeared on page 65 of *The Decorator and the Furnisher*. See *A Documentary History of American Interiors from the Colonial Era to 1915* (New York: Charles Scribner's Sons, 1980).

16. Quoted in Clyde A. Milner, Carol A. O'Connor, and Martha Sandweiss, eds., *The Oxford History of the American West* (New York: Oxford University Press, 1994), 788.

17. See, for instance, the Buffalo Bill Historical Center in Cody, Wyoming, not to mention numerous campsites and museums throughout the state.

18. Clifford Edward Clark's *The American Family Home* is an excellent source for information about popular Victorian trends in architectural styles and interior design.

19. Hal Cannon, ed., *Utah Folk Art: A Catalog of Material Culture* (Provo, UT: Brigham Young University Press, 1980), 41.

20. Quoted in Cannon, *Utah Folk Art*, 116.

21. See Cannon, *Utah Folk Art*, especially the chapter on symbols, for more about the beehive and the all-seeing eye in Mormon culture.

22. Cannon, *Utah Folk Art*, 113.

23. See "Modernizing the House and the Family" in Clark, *The American Family Home*; Thomas S. Hines, *Irving Gill and the Architecture of Reform* (New York: Monacelli Press, 2000) and Neil Levine, *The Architecture of Frank Lloyd Wright* (Princeton, NJ: Princeton University Press, 1996).

24. H. Allen Brooks provides a good overview of the movement in *The Prairie School: Frank Lloyd Wright and His Midwest Contemporaries* (Toronto: University of Toronto Press, 1972).

25. Robert Winter, *The California Bungalow* (Los Angeles: Hennessey and Ingalls, 1980); L. D. Thomson, "The Rampant Craze for the Bungle-oh," *Country Life in America* 22 (July 1912): 20–21; Harold Kirker, *California's Architectural Frontier: Style and Tradition in the Nineteenth Century* (New York: Russell and Russell, 1960); and Charles V. Boyd's two articles, "An American Bungalow," *Woman's Home Companion* 46 (October 1919): 54; and "The Popular Low-Cost Bungalow," *Ladies Home Journal* 24 (October 1907): 35.

26. See "The Bungalow Craze," in Clark, *The American Family Home*, 181.

27. Mary Mix Foley gives a brief history of the ranch in *The American House*.

For more on the architecture of California, see Harold Kirker's *California's Architectural Frontier*.

28. "Eastward Ho: California Home Styles Invade the Rest of the U.S.," *Life* 32 (17 March 1952): 131–132; "The Story of the Western Ranch House," *Sunset* 121 (September 1958): 74; "What's Been Happening to That Easy-Going Western Favorite . . . the 'Ranch House'?" *Sunset* 112 (February 1955): 54–59; "From the Rancho, a Contemporary Style," *Life* 40 (16 January 1959): 58–59; Will Mehlhorn, "Ranch Houses Suit Any Climate," *House Beautiful* 89 (January 1947): 60–69; and "A Clean and Handsome Example of the West's Ranch House," *Sunset* 10 (April 1953): 74–75.

29. See Lee Silliman, " 'As Kind and Generous a Host as Ever Lived': Howard Eaton and the Birth of Western Dude Ranching," *American West* 16 (July/August 1979): 18–31; Michael Wallis, *The Real Wild West: The 101 Ranch and the Creation of the American West* (New York: St. Martin's, 1999).

30. "Livin' Large in Montana," *People* 36, no. 14: (14 October 1991): 116.

31. Katherine A. White, *A Yankee Trader in the Gold Rush*: The Letters of Franklin A. Buck (Boston: Houghton Mifflin Company 1930), 93.

32. For an account of one boom town see Gilbert A. Stetler, "The Birth of a Frontier Boom Town: Cheyenne in 1867," *Annals of Wyoming* 39, no. 1 (April 1967): 5–34.

33. Gabriel, *A Frontier Lady*, 130–131.

34. A comprehensive guide to ghost towns can be found in Bill O'Neal, *Ghost Towns of the American West* (Lincolnwood, IL: Publications International, Ltd., 1995).

35. Quoted in Stratton, *Pioneer Women*, 191.

36. Gabriel, *A Frontier Lady*, 100.

37. Howard R. Lamar, ed., *The New Encyclopedia of the American West* (New Haven: Yale University Press, 1998), 1094.

38. Quoted in Elliott West, *The Saloon on the Rocky Mountain Mining Frontier* (Lincoln: University of Nebraska Press, 1979), 35.

39. West, *The Saloon on the Rocky Mountain Mining Frontier*, 47.

40. West, *The Saloon on the Rocky Mountain Mining Frontier*, 40.

41. Some sources on buildings meant to house travelers include: Paton Yoder, *Taverns and Travelers: Inns of the Early Midwest* (Bloomington: Indiana University Press, 1969), and Richard A. Van Orman, *A Room for the Night: Hotels of the Old West* (Bloomington: Indiana University Press, 1966).

42. See David Naylor and Joan Dillon, *American Theaters: Performance Halls of the Nineteenth Century* (New York: John Wiley & Sons, Inc., 1997).

43. *Early Architecture in New Mexico* (Albuquerque: University of New Mexico Press, 1976).

44. The categories of Territorial style were borrowed from Bainbridge Bunting's book, *Early Architecture in New Mexico* (Albuquerque: University of New Mexico Press, 1976). While Bunting focuses specifically on New Mexico, his categories are useful in examining the Southwest more broadly defined.

45. Robert Venturi, Denise Scott Brown, and Steven Izenour, *Learning from Las Vegas: The Forgotten Symbolism of Architectural Form* (Cambridge, MA: MIT Press, 1998), 50–51.

46. Venturi, *Learning from Las Vegas*, 80.

47. Other information about the architecture of Las Vegas can be found in Allan Hess, *Viva Las Vegas: After Hours Architecture* (San Francisco, CA: Chronicle Books, 1993).

48. See Venturi, *Learning from Las Vegas* for more about the way signs function.

49. Sources about Disneyland and its founder include: Marc Eliot, *Walt Disney: Hollywood's Dark Prince* (Secaucus, NJ: Carol Publishing Group, 1993), and Eric Smoodin, *Disney Discourse: Producing the Magic Kingdom* (New York: Routledge, 1994).

50. See also Harold Kirker, *California's Architectural Frontier*.

51. Stratton, *The Pioneers*, 184.

CHAPTER 5

1. For a thorough study of the clothing worn in the old West see Foster William Harris, *The Look of the Old West* (New York: Viking Press, 1955); Ernest Lisle Reedstrom, *Historic Dress of the Old West* (New York: Blandford Press, 1986); and Joan Severa, *Dressed for the Photographer: Ordinary Americans and Fashion, 1840–1900* (Kent, OH: Kent State University Press, 1995).

2. Dale Morgan, ed., *Overland in 1846: Diaries and Letters of the California-Oregon Trail* (Lincoln: University of Nebraska Press, 1993), 486.

3. Quoted in Sally I. Helveston in *Feminine Response to a Frontier Environment as Reflected in the Clothing of Kansas Women: 1854–1895* (Ph.D. diss., Kansas State University, 1985), 127.

4. Katherine A. White, ed., *A Yankee Trader in the Gold Rush: The Letters of Franklin A. Buck* (Boston: Houghton Mifflin Co., 1930), 50.

5. White, *A Yankee Trader in the Gold Rush*, 52.

6. Helveston, *Feminine Response to a Frontier Environment*, 69.

7. Joanna L. Stratton, *Pioneer Women: Voices from the Kansas Frontier* (New York: Simon and Schuster, 1981), 68.

8. Elise Isley, *Sunbonnet Days* (Caldwell, ID: Caxton Printers, 1935), 75–76.

9. Isley, *Sunbonnet Days*, 76.

10. Sandra L. Myres, ed., *Ho for California! Women's Overland Diaries from the Huntington Library* (San Marino, CA: Huntington Library, 1980), 141.

11. Quoted in Dee Brown, *The Gentle Tamers: Women of the Old Wild West* (Lincoln: University of Nebraska Press, 1958), 134.

12. Brown, *The Gentle Tamers*, 134.

13. Brown, *The Gentle Tamers*, 136.

14. Quoted in Helveston, *Feminine Response to a Frontier Environment*, 130–131.

15. For a brief history of bloomers see Shelly Foote, "Bloomers," *Dress* 5 (1980): 1–12.

16. Quoted in Lillian Schlissel, ed., *Women's Diaries of the Westward Journey* (New York: Schocken Books, 1982), 105.

17. Schlissel, *Women's Diaries of the Westward Journey*, 141.

18. Brown, *The Gentle Tamers*, 145–146.

19. As one pioneer woman described it, Godey's was a major source of information about fashion trends that helped pioneer women to remain connected to eastern styles. She writes that to her wedding in Kansas she wore "a wool and

silk dress with black and wine-colored checks, trimmed with a lace collar. The skirt was worn over hoops which were the fashion then as decreed by Godey's *Lady's Book*." Isley, *Sunbonnet Days*, 112.

20. The role fashion played in the West has been explored by Helveston, *Feminine Response to a Frontier Environment* and Maria B. McMartin, "Dress of the Oregon Trail Emigrants: 1843–1855" (Master's thesis, Iowa State University, 1977).

21. Helveston, *Feminine Response to a Frontier Environment*, 15.

22. Christiane Fischer, ed., *Let Them Speak for Themselves*: Women in the American West, 1849–1900 (Hamden, CT: Archon Books, 1972), 214.

23. For more on the popular styles worn by men see "Civilians out West," in Foster-Harris, *The Look of the Old West*, 93–116.

24. For more on guns see "Cold Steel and Hot Lead" in Harris, *The Look of the Old West*, 117–150, and John E. Parsons, *The Peacemaker and Its Rivals* (New York: William Morrow and Company, 1950).

25. Brown, *The Gentle Tamers*, 137.

26. Quotes in Brown, *The Gentle Tamers*, 143.

27. Margaret Walsh offers an overview of dress pattern history in "The Democratization of Fashion: The Emergence of the Women's Dress Pattern Industry," *Journal of American History* 66, no. 2 (September 1979): 299–313.

28. For more on western stores see Lewis E. Atherton's *The Frontier Merchant in Mid-America* (Columbia: University of Missouri Press, 1971).

29. Debby Bull's *Hillbilly Hollywood* (New York: Rizzoli, International Publications, 2000) traces, in detail, the popularity of western wear in the twentieth century.

30. See Stetson, http://www.stetsonhat.com/history (22 December 2001), for more on the history of Stetson.

31. See Harris, "Hoof Trails and Wheel Tracks," in *The Look of the Old West*, 191–224.

32. Tyler Beard gives a detailed description of the changes in style from the 1930s through the 1970s. See "1930–1970: Nashville Meets Hollywood: The Golden Years of Western Wear," in *One Hundred Years of Western Wear* (Salt Lake City: Gibbs-Smith Publisher, 1993), 30–111.

33. Beard, *One Hundred Years of Western Wear*, 72.

34. Peter McQuaid's "The Cowboy Couturier," *New York Times Magazine*, 3 March 2000, 94.

35. Kathleen Madden, "Why Not the West? Range-style Dressing Takes Over." *Vogue*, September 1978, 152, 166.

36. Jim Yardley, "Boots Made for Walking On Pennsylvania Avenue," *New York Times*, 13 May 2001.

37. See S.S. Fair's "The Buckaroo Stops Here," *New York Times Magazine*, 18 June 2000, 69–77; Peter McQuaid's "The Cowboy Couturier," 85–94. Western clothing stores like Sheplers market themselves as "The World's Largest Western Stores and Catalog," providing customers with contemporary westernwear. See www.sheplers.com.

38. Levi Strauss & Co., 2001 http://www.levistrauss.com/index_about.html (22 December 2001).

39. See Iain Finlayson, *Denim: An American Legend* (New York: Simon and Schuster, 1990) for more on the mid-twentieth-century changes in denim.

40. Quoted in Finlayson, *Denim: An American Legend*, 25.

41. Fischer, *Let Them Speak for Themselves*, 216.

42. For more on the influence popular culture had on Indian dress see John C. Ewers, "The Emergence of the Plains Indian as the Symbol of the North American Indian," *Annual Report of the Board of Regents of the Smithsonian Institution* 1964: 531–544.

43. Craig Bates, "Dressing the Part: A Brief Look at the Development of Stereotypical Indian Clothing Among Native Peoples in the Far West," *Journal of California and Great Basin Anthropology* 4 no. 2 (1982): 57.

CHAPTER 6

1. Joseph E. Ware, *The Emigrants' Guide to California* (New York: De Capo Press, 1972). Reprinted from the 1849 edition with Introduction and Notes by John Caughey, p. 6.

2. Kenneth L. Holmes, ed., *Covered Wagon Women*: Diaries and Letters from the Western Trails (Lincoln: University of Nebraska, 1983), 237.

3. Owen Cochran Coy, *The Great Trek* (Los Angeles: Powell Publishing Company, 1931), 293.

4. Coy, *The Great Trek*, 293.

5. Sandra L. Myres, ed., *Ho For California! Women's Overland Diaries from the Huntington Library* (San Marino, CA: Huntington Library, 1980), 119.

6. See Julia Brier's account of her trip in Cathy Luchetti's *Home on the Range: A Culinary History of the American West* (New York: Villard Books, 1993), 50.

7. Luchetti, *Home on the Range*, 47.

8. Luchetti, *Home on the Range*, 41.

9. B. Byron Price's *National Cowboy Hall of Fame Chuck Wagon Cookbook* (New York: Hearst Books, 1995) provides a combination of historical facts about cowboys and chuck wagons with recipes from past and present cowboy cooks.

10. For more see Price, *National Cowboy Hall of Fame Chuck Wagon Cookbook*.

11. Price, *National Cowboy Hall of Fame Chuck Wagon Cookbook*, 22.

12. Quoted in Price, *National Cowboy Hall of Fame Chuck Wagon Cookbook*, 26.

13. Scott Gregory, recipe excerpt from *Sowbelly and Sourdough: Original Recipes from the Trail Drives and Cow Camps of the 1800s* (Caldwell, ID: Caxton Printers, 1995), 11; for names of meals see Lon Walters, *The Old West Baking Book* (Flagstaff, AZ: Northland Publishers, 1996).

14. Price, *Cowboy Hall of Fame Chuck Wagon Cookbook*, 121.

15. Price, *Cowboy Hall of Fame Chuck Wagon Cookbook*, 121. For more on Arbuckle's coffee see pp. 118–122.

16. W.F. Rae, *Westward by Rail* (New York: Promontory Press, 1974), 231–232.

17. Waterman Ormsby, in Lyle H. Wright and Josephine M. Bynum, eds., *The Butterfield Overland Mail*, (San Marino, CA: Huntington Library, 1942/1972), 93–94.

18. Walker D. Wyman, *Frontier Woman* (University of Wisconsin-River Falls Press, 1972), 19.

19. For more on the history of canned foods see Waverely Root and Richard de Rochemont, *Eating in America: A History* (New York: William Morrow & Co., Inc, 1976), especially chapter 23, "Beef and Buffalo."

20. Nannie T. Alderson and Helena Huntington Smith, *A Bride Goes West* (Lincoln: University of Nebraska Press, 1942), 40.

21. Barbara Swell, *Log Cabin Cooking: Pioneer Recipes and Food Fore* (Ashville, NC: Native Ground Music, Inc., 1996), 9.

22. Swell, *Log Cabin Cooking*, 7.

23. Luchetti, *Home on the Range*, xxviii–xxix.

24. Holmes, *Covered Wagon Women*, Vol. 1, 203.

25. For examples of pioneer recipes, including that for Molasses-on-Snow, see Barbara M. Walker, *The Little House Cookbook* (New York: Harper & Row, 1979).

26. Hannah Campbell, *Why Did They Name It . . . ?* New York: Fleet Publishing Company, 1964), 66. See also the following Web site, Dr Pepper, http://www.drpeppermuseum.com/history.html (22 December 2001).

27. Dr Pepper, http://www.drpeppermuseum.com/history.html (22 December 2001).

28. Several books address the ethnic diversity at the heart of popular United States cuisine. See, for instance, Luchetti, *Home on the Range*; Richard Pillsbury, *No Foreign Food: The American Diet in Time and Place* (Boulder, Co: Westview Press, 1998); and Waverley Root and "The Tepid Melting Pot," in Richard de Rochemont, *Eating in America* (New York: William Morrow & Co., 1976), 276–312.

29. William Kelly, *An Excursion to California*, Over the Prairie, Rocky Mountains, and Great Sierra Nerda. (New York: Arno Press, 1973), 244.

30. See "Cooking in wide open spaces," in Price, *National Cowboy Hall of Fame Chuck Wagon Cookbook*, 166.

31. Campbell, *Why Did They Name It . . . ?*, 25

32. Tom Daykin, *Milwaukee Journal Sentinel*, 13 March 2000.

33. Campbell, *Why Did They Name It . . . ?*, 13.

CHAPTER 7

1. Elise Isley, *Sunbonnet Days* (Caldwell, ID: Caxton Printers, 1935), 177.

2. Everett Dick discusses the problem of water in the West in "Water: A Frontier Problem," *Nebraska History* 49 (1968): 215–245.

3. Isley, *Sunbonnet Days*, 202.

4. This action is not unlike that of Yukon Cornelius in the popular Christmas program *Rudolph the Rednose Reindeer* who throws down his pick axe in the hopes of striking gold.

5. See "To Hunt the Shining Dust," in Duncan Emrich, *It's an Old Wild West Custom* (New York: Vanguard Press, 1949).

6. Will C. Barnes, *Arizona Place Names*, rev. and enl. by Byrd H. Granger (Tucson: University of Arizona Press, 1960), 82.

7. Burnes, *Arizona Place Names*, 83.

8. Emrich, *It's an Old Wild West Custom*, 28.

9. Sarah Royce, *A Frontier Lady: Recollections of the Gold Rush and Early California*, ed. Ralph Henry Gabriel (Lincoln: University of Nebraska Press, 1932), 80.

10. More examples of naming can be found in Emrich, *It's an Old Wild West Custom*; Barnes, *Arizona Place Names*; and T. M. Pearce, ed., *New Mexico Place Names: A Geographical Dictionary* (Albuquerque: University of New Mexico Press, 1965).

11. Owen Cochran Coy, *The Great Trek* (Los Angeles: Powell Publishing Company, 1931), 51.

12. *A Dictionary of Americanisms on Historical Principles*, edited by Mitford M. Mathews, is a good reference for words with an American origin (Chicago: University of Chicago Press, 1951).

13. Robert K. DeArment, *The Knights of the Green Cloth: The Saga of the Frontier Gamblers* (Norman: University of Oklahoma Press, 1982), 11.

14. Mary Ellen Jones, *Daily Life on the Nineteenth-Century Frontier* (Westport, CT: Greenwood Press, 1998), 129.

15. Mary Ellen Jones, *Daily Life on the Nineteenth-Century Frontier*, 129.

16. Coy, *The Great Trek*, 54.

17. Robert M. Wright, *Dodge City: The Cowboy Capital and the Great Southwest* (New York: Arno Press, 1975), 164.

18. Wright, *Dodge City*, 164.

19. For detailed description of social events see "A Little Light Diversion," in Dee Brown, *The Gentle Tamers: Women of the Old Wild West* (Lincoln: University of Nebraska Press, 1958) and Dary, *Seeking Pleasure in the Old West* (New York: Alfred A. Knopf, 1995), 30.

20. Stratton, *Pioneer Women*, 141.

21. The Pinedale Rendezvous is hosted by the Museum of the Mountain Man. See Museum of the Mountain Man, http://www.pinedaleonline.com/museum (22 December 2001).

22. Danker, *Mollie*, 41.

23. Dee Brown, *The Gentle Tamers*, 152–154.

24. Dennis, Lee, *Warman's Antique American Games, 1840–1940.* (Elkins Park, PA: Warman Publishing Co., Inc., 1986).

25. Ruede, *Sod-House Days: Letters from a Kansas Homesteader, 1877–78* (New York: Cooper Square Publishing, Inc., 1937), 231.

26. Brown, *The Gentle Tamers*, 154. For more on frontier jokes and humor see Mody C. Boatright, *Folk Laughter on the American Frontier* (New York : Macmillan, 1949), and David Dary, *Seeking Pleasure in the Old West.*

27. Wright, *Dodge City*, 242.

28. For more on humor and the west see Mody C. Boatright, *Folk Laughter on the American Frontier*; Peter Hertzog, *Frontier Humor* (Sante Fe, NM: Press of the Territorian, 1966); David Dary, "When Fish Grew Big in Kansas," *Kansas City Star Magazine*, 4 February 1973, 16, 18; Dary, *Seeking Pleasure in the Old West*; and Emrich, *It's an Old Wild West Custom.*

29. The interest in Davy Crockett spanned two centuries. See Paul F. Anderson, *The Davy Crockett Craze: A Look at the 1950s Phenomenon and Davy Crockett Collectibles* (R.G. Productions, 1996), and Michael A. Lofaro and Joe Cummings, eds., *Crockett at Two Hundred: New Perspectives on the Man and the Myth* (Knoxville: University of Tennessee Press, 1989).

30. William Kelly, *An Excursion to California Over the Prairie, Rocky Mountains, and Great Sierra Nevada* (New York: Arno Press, 1973), 64.

31. Katherine A. White, ed., *Yankee Trader in the Gold Rush* (Boston: Houghton Mifflin Co., 1930), 68.

32. Christiane Fischer, ed., *Let Them Speak for Themselves: Women in the American West, 1849–1900* (Hamden, CT: Anchor Books, 1972), 28.

33. Kelly, *An Excursion to California*, 231–232.

34. Royce, *A Frontier Lady*, 113.

35. Dary, "Along the Rails" in *Seeking Pleasure in the Old West*, 224–239.

36. Fred and Jo Mazzulla, *Brass Checks and Red Lights: Being a Pictorial Pot Pourri of Prostitutes, Parlor Houses, Professors, Procuresses and Pimps* (Denver: Fred and Jo Mazzulla, 1996), 49.

37. Mazzulla and Mazzulla's *Brass Checks and Red Lights* is an interesting compilation of the names and lifestyles of western prostitutes.

38. Fischer, *Let Them Speak for Themselves*, 131.

39. Nannie T. Alderson and Helena Huntington Smith, *A Bride Goes West* (Lincoln: University of Nebraska Press), 269.

40. Alice Beck Kehoe, *The Ghost Dance: Ethnohistory and Revitalization* (Austin, TX: Holt, Rinehart & Winston, 1997).

41. White, *a Yankee Trader in the Gold Rush*, 120.

42. Fischer, *Let Them Speak for Themselves*, 274.

43. For more on various sports involving animals, see Dary, *Seeking Pleasure in the Old West*.

CHAPTER 8

1. These characteristics are general trends seen in the majority of literature about the American West. For more detailed discussion and analysis of such trends, see Christine Bold, *Selling the Wild West: Popular Western Fiction, 1860–1960* (Bloomington: Indiana University Press, 1987); John G. Cawelti, *Adventure, Mystery and Romance* (Chicago: University of Chicago Press, 1976), and *Six-Gun Mystique* (Bowling Green, OH: Bowling Green University Popular Press, 1971); Henry Nash Smith, *Virgin Land: The American West as Symbol and Myth* (Cambridge, MA: Harvard University Press, 1950).

2. Perry Miller's *Errand into the Wilderness* is an exploration of this subject (Cambridge, MA: Belknap Press of Harvard University Press, 1956).

3. Richard Aquila offers an excellent and concise overview of popular early American writings about the frontier. See his "Introduction" to Richard Aquila, ed., *Wanted Dead or Alive: The American West in Popular Culture* (Urbana: University of Illinois Press, 1996), 1–16.

4. For more on Pocahontas see Robert S. Tilton, *Pocahontas: The Evolution of an American Narrative* (Cambridge: Cambridge University Press, 1994).

5. Captivity narratives are central to early American literature. See Gordon M. Sayre ed. *"American Captivity Narratives."* Selected Narratives with Introduction/Olavdah Equiano, Mary Rowlandson, and others. (Boston: Houghton Mifflin, 2000).

6. Leslie Fiedler explores this male-centric vision of the world in *Love and Death in the American Novel* (New York: Criterion Books, 1960), arguing that the basis of American literature is a flight from the domestic world that women

inhabit and symbolize. In contrast, Annette Kolodny explores the consequences of associating the land with the feminine or female in *The Lay of the Land* (Chapel Hill: University of North Carolina Press, 1975). See Chapter 4, "Singing Her Past and Singing Her Praises" for discussion of the West and in particular of Cooper.

7. Ray Allen Billington, *Land of Savagery, Land of Promise: The European Image of the American Frontier* (1981).

8. Katherine A. White, *A Yankee Trader in the Gold Rush: The Letters of Franklin A. Buck* (Boston: Houghton Mifflin Co., 1930), 165.

9. See Barbara Cloud, *The Business of Newspapers on the Western Frontier* (Rens: University of Nevada Press, 1992), and David Dary, *Red Blood and Black Ink: Journalism in the Old West* (New York: Knopf, 1998).

10. By one account, "a survey of fifteen publishers, revealed that approximately 75 percent [of all dime novels] dealt with frontier subjects, with a majority of these depicting the West beyond the Mississippi." Bill Brown, ed., *Reading the West: An Anthology of Dime Westerns* (Boston: Bedford Books, 1997), 16.

11. See Brown, *Reading the West*.

12. Bill Brown, "Reading the West: Cultural and Historical Background," in *Reading the West*, 21.

13. Christine Bold compares the *Seth Jones* series to Cooper in her essay "Malaeska's Revenger; or, The Dime Novel Tradition in Popular Fiction, in Aquila, *Wanted Dead or Alive*, 21–42.

14. Aquila, *Wanted Dead or Alive*, 25.

15. Aquila, *Wanted Dead or Alive*, 27

16. Aquila, *Wanted Dead or Alive*, 309.

17. Christine Bold, *Selling the Wild West: Popular Western Fiction, 1860–1960* (Bloomington: Indiana University Press, 1987).

18. See also John A. Dinan, *The Pulp Western: A Popular History of the Western Fiction Magazine in America*, I.O. Evans Studies in the Philosophy and Criticism of Literature no. 2 (San Bernardino, CA: Borgo Press, 1983), and Tony Goodstone, ed., *The Pulps: Fifty Years of American Popular Culture* (New York: Chelsea House, 1970).

19. Some useful books about comics include: Mike Benton, *The Comic Book in America: An Illustrated History* (Dallas, TX: Taylor Publishing, 1989) and Maurice Horn, *Comics of the American West* (New York: Winchester Press, 1977).

20. For more on cowboy poetry see David Stanley and Elaine Thatcher, eds., *Cowboy Poets and Poetry* (Chicago: University of Illinois Press, 2000).

21. David Stanley describes the traditional (and variations on the traditional) rhyme and meter of cowboy poems in his essay "Form and Tension in Cowboy Poetry," in Stanley and Thatcher, *Cowboy Poets and Poetry*.

22. For more on the connections between poems and songs see Charlie Seemann's "Hitching Verse to Tune: The Relationship of Cowboy Song to Poetry," in Stanley and Thatcher, *Cowboy Poets and Poetry*.

23. For more on western literature and the authors mentioned here, see *A Literary History of the American West* (Fort Worth, TX: Texas Christian University Press, 1987).

24. William Bloodworth, "Writers of the Purple Sage: Novelists and the American West," in Aquila, *Wanted Dead or Alive*, 45.

25. Zane Grey, *The Last Trail* (New York: Tor Books, 1998), 42.

26. See Christine Bold's discussion of L'Amour in "The Last Few Spaces," in *Selling the Wild West*, 143–154.

27. For more on Laura Ingalls Wilder see Fred Erisman, *Laura Ingalls Wilder* (Boise, ID: Boise State University Press, 1994), and John Miller, *Laura Ingalls Wilder's Little Town: Where History and Literature Meet* (Lawrence, KS: University Press of Kansas, 1994).

28. AmericanGirl.com,2001,http://www.americangirlstore.com/html/kirsten/meet/k_meet.html (22 December 2001).

29. These writers have been loosely described as the authors of "new westerns," "revisionary westerns," and similar terms meant to underscore their departure from the conventional western plot and themes. See William Bloodworth, "Writers of the Purple Sage," and Michael L. Johnson, *New Westers: The West in Contemporary American Culture* (Lawrence; KS: University Press of Kansas, 1996).

30. C. L. Sonnischsen's anthology of humorous Western literature, *The Laughing West* (Athens: Ohio University Press, 1988), provides good examples of the genre.

CHAPTER 9

1. Michael L. Johnson gives a thorough overview of western music, especially contemporary western music, in his chapter "Garth and Friends: Resinging the West, Dancing to the Cowboy Beat." In *New Westers: The Western in Contemporary American Culture* (Lawrence: University Press of Kansas, 1996): 260–302. Two historically based analyses of western music are Richard Aquila's "A Blaze of Glory: The Mythic West in Pop and Rock Music," and Kenneth J. Bindas's "Cool Water, Rye Whiskey, and Cowboys: Images of the West in Country Music." Both are in *Wanted Dead or Alive: The American West in Popular Culture*, edited by Richard Aquila (Urbana: University of Illinois Press, 1996).

2. Sandra L. Myres, ed., *Ho for California! Women's Overland Diaries from the Huntington Library* (San Marino, CA: Huntington Library, 1980), 21.

3. Lillian Schlissel, *Women's Diaries of the Westward Journey* (New York: Schocken Books, 1982), 181.

4. Mary Ballou, " 'I Hear the Hogs in My Kitchen': A Woman's View of the Gold Rush" in Archibald Hanna, ed. (New Haven: Yale University Press; printed for Frederick W. Beinecke, 1962). In Christiane Fischer, ed., *Let Them Speak for Themselves: Women in the American West 1849–1900* (New York: E.P. Dutton, 1977), 43.

5. Robert M. Wright, *Dodge City: The Cowboy Capital and the Great Southwest* (New York: Arno Press, 1975), 320.

6. Dee Brown, *The Gentle Tamers: Women of the Wild West* (Lincoln: University of Nebraska Press, 1958), 152.

7. Brown, *The Gentle Tamers*, 153.

8. N. Howard Thorp, *Songs of the Cowboys* (New York: Clarkson N. Potter, Inc., 1966), 88.

9. Eleanora Black and Sidney Robertson, eds. *The Gold Rush Song Book* (San Francisco: Colt Press, 1940), iv–v.

10. Dwyer, Richard A., and Richard E. Lingenfelter, *The Songs of the Gold Rush* (Berkeley: University of California Press, 1964), 166.

11. Black and Robertson, *The Gold Rush Song Book*, 23.

12. Dwyer and Lingenfelter, *The Songs of the Gold Rush*, 43.

13. Dwyer and Lingenfelter, *The Songs of the Gold Rush*, 48.

14. John A. Lomax, ed., *Cowboy Songs and Other Frontier Ballads* (New York: Macmillan Company, 1938), xvi.

15. "Jack" Thorp, "Banjo in the Cow Camps," in Thorp, *Songs of the Cowboys*, 13.

16. Thorp, "Banjo in the Cow Camps," 15.

17. See, for example, Lomax, *Cowboy Songs*, and Thorp, *Songs of the Cowboys*.

18. Thorp, *Songs of the Cowboys*, 123.

19. Thorp, *Songs of the Cowboys*, 114–115.

20. Lomax's *Cowboy Songs* contains the first record of the phrase "Git along, little dogies." For a history of the expression, see "The Editor Again," page xx.

21. The impact was significant. As Douglas B. Green writes, "The most obvious barometer . . . [of the] change of attitude is the *Billboard* charts, where the term "hillbilly" was eventually (and mercifully) dropped as a means of categorizing the music and replaced with the more dignified "folk," then "country and western," attaching the attendant integrity and glamor of the movie cowboy and the romantic West to the basically rural, southeastern country songs that always dominated the charts. See *Country Roots: The Origins of Country Music* (New York: Hawthorne Books, Inc, 1976), 107.

22. For more on the relationship between country music and western images see Green, *Country Roots*, especially the chapter "Singing Cowboys."

23. See David Rothel, "Collecting Gene Autry Memorabilia," in *The Gene Autry Book* (Madison, NC: Empire Publishing Co., 1988), 202–224.

24. See the chapter on "Singing Cowboys" in Green, *Country Roots*, 87–108.

25. Guthrie's autobiography *Bound For Glory* (New York: E. P. Dutton & Co., 1943) describes his impressions of the rich California land and of the migration West that occurred during the 1930s by those in search of work.

26. Arlonet (21 November 2001), http://www.arlo.net/lyrics/this-land.shtml, (22 December 2001).

27. For more on Montana, as well as the development of female style in country-western music, see Mary A. Bufwack, "Girls with Guitars—and Fringe and Sequins and Rhinestones, Silk, Lace, and Leather," *South Atlantic Quarterly* 94 (winter 1995): 173–216.

28. For more on the rise of the cowgirl image see Robert K. Oermann, "Mother, Sister, Sweetheart, Pal: Women in Old-Time Country Music," and Robert K. Oermann and Mary A. Bufwack, "Patsy Montana and the Development of the Cowgirl Image," *Journal of Country Music* 8 (1981): 18–32.

29. For more on Wills and western swing see Green, *Country Roots*.

30. Country Beat (1996–2001. Rev. 8/28/2001), http://www.countrybeat.com/ElectricSlide.html (22 December 2001).

31. Jimmie N. Rogers gives a thorough overview of the predominant themes of country-western music in *The Country Music Message: All About Lovin' and Lovin'* (NJ: Prentice-Hall, 1983).

32. Kenneth J. Bindas's overview of this period in western music is excellent. See "Cool Water, Rye Whiskey, and Cowboys," in Aquila, *Wanted Dead or Alive*.

33. Kirke Mechem, "Home on the Range," *Kansas Historical Quarterly* 17 (November 1949): 313.

34. Kirke Mechem reflects on this word change in his history of the song "Home on the Range." See his article "Home on the Range."

35. http://www.50states.com/songs.

36. See Gerald Bordman's *American Musical Theater* (New York: Oxford University Press, 1995).

37. For an exhaustive account of western images in pop music see Richard Aquila, "A Blaze of Glory: The Mythic West in Pop and Rock," in *Wanted Dead or Alive*. The footnotes are especially detailed.

38. For more on Black Lodge Singers see their Web site: http://www.glrain.net/black2.htm.

39. For a history of the cowboy image in popular music, see William W. Savage, Jr., *The Cowboy Hero: His Image in American History and Culture* (Norman: University of Oklahoma Press, 1979).

40. For more on outlaw musicians, see Michael Dunne's "Romantic Narcissism in 'Outlaw' Cowboy Music," in George H. Lewis, ed., *All that Glitters: Country Music in America* (Bowling Green, OH: Bowling Green State University Popular Press, 1993), 226–238; and Michael Bane, *The Outlaws: Revolution in Country Music* (New York: Doubleday Dolphin, 1978).

41. Kenneth J. Bindas, "Cool Water, Rye Whiskey, and Cowboys," in Aquila, *Wanted Dead or Alive*, 231.

42. Bindas, "Cool water, Rye Whiskey and, Cowboys," 231.

43. For Black's work with QVC see "Advertising," *New York Times*, 20 June 1995, 144, p. D11. His appearance on cereal boxes is discussed in "Kellogg cereals take singer Clint Black to heart," *Brandweek* 30 September 1996, 37, 5.

44. For more on Riders in the Sky, see "Too Slim, Ranger Doug and Woody Paul," in *Riders in the Sky* (Salt Lake City: Peregrine Smith Books, 1992).

45. The tendency has been to produce slightly different versions of a hit song—one for country radio stations and another for Top-40 audiences.

46. See Bufwack, "Girls with Guitars."

47. For more on contemporary musicians see Aquila, "Blaze of Glory," and Johnson, "Garth and Friends."

48. See Bob Paxman's article, "Country vs. Pop," in *Country Week* 4 April 2000, 30–34.

CHAPTER 10

1. The dates in the following discussion are approximate; the forms of entertainment from each period overlapped with others. However, the general trend of each era is the point of this chapter.

2. For more on western theater, see Dunbar H. Ogden, ed. *Theatre West: Image and Impact* (Amsterdam: Atlanta, GA: Rudopi Press, 1990); Richard A. Van Orman, "The Bard in the West," *Western Historical Quarterly* 5, no. 1 (1974): 29–38; Melvin Schoberlin, *From Candles to Footlights: A Biography of the Pike's Peak Theatre, 1859–1876* (Denver, CO: Old West Publishing Company, 1941); and Margaret G. Watson, *Silver Theatre: Amusements of the Mining Frontier in Early Nevada, 1850–1864* (Glendale, CA: Arthur H. Clark Company, 1964).

3. Prior to eastern influences, the primary form of drama in the West was the miracle play, integral to Catholicism and included at religious festivals.

4. Campton Bell, "The Early Theatres, Cheyenne, Wyoming, 1867–1882," *Annals of Wyoming* 25 (1953): 3–21.

5. See Glenn Hughes, *A History of the American Theatre 1700–1950* (London and Toronto: Samuel French, 1951), 309.

6. Hughes, *A History of American Theater*, 168.

7. Clarissa Young Spencer, *One Who Was Valiant* (Caldwell, ID: Caxton Printers, 1941), 140.

8. Hughes, *A History of American Theatre*, 301.

9. Richard A. Van Orman, "The Bard in the West," 33.

10. For more on Shakespeare in the West see Esther Cloudman Dunn's *Shakespeare in America* (New York: Macmillan Company, 1939).

11. See Hughes, *A History of American Theatre*, 218. Robinson is also mentioned extensively in Robert Glass Cleland, ed., *Apron Full of Gold* (San Marino, CA: Huntington Library, 1949), 41–42.

12. Cleland, *Apron Full of Gold*, 73.

13. See, for instance, James C. Malin's "Dodge City Varieties—A Summer Interlude of Entertainment, 1878," *Kansas Historical Quarterly* 22 (1956): 347–353.

14. See Arrell M. Gibson, "Medicine Show," *American West* 4, no. 1 (February 1967): 34–39 and 74–79.

15. For more on frontier melodrama see Rosemarie Bank's "Frontier Melodrama," in Dunbar H. Ogden, ed., *Theatre West: Image and Impact*, 151–160.

16. Paul Reddin's *Wild West Shows* (Urbana and Chicago: University of Illinois Press, 1999) traces the history of Wild West Shows.

17. William F. Cody, *The Life of Buffalo Bill* (first published in 1879; New York: Indian Head Books, 1991). See also Joy S. Kasson, *Buffalo Bill's Wild West: Celebrity, Memory, and Popular History* (New York: Hill and Wang, 2000).

18. Howard R. Lamar, ed., *The New Encyclopedia of the American West* (New Haven: Yale University Press, 1998), 1260.

19. Glenda Riley's chapter "The Legend," in *The Life and Legacy of Annie Oakley* (Norman: University of Oklahoma Press, 1994), 206–230, is especially useful in understanding the impact of Annie Oakley on popular culture.

20. Another way that such personalities blurred the line between the myth and reality of the Old West was by using their real names to market their fictional programs.

21. In "Shootout at Universal Studios," James Bierman describes the popular appeal of the Stunt Show. In Dunbar H. Ogden, ed., *Theatre West: Image and Impact*, 229–235. See "Screen: 'Lone Ranger' Rides Again," *New York Times*, 11 February 1956, sec. 12, p. 1.

22. Kristine Fredricksson, *American Rodeo: From Buffalo Bill to Big Business* (College Station: Texas A & M University Press, 1985).

23. For more on western radio shows see Jim Harmon, *The Great Radio Heroes* (Garden City, NY: Doubleday, 1967).

24. Alanna Nash, "Into the Sunset Ride An Era's Heroes," *New York Times*, 13 February 2000, sec. 2, p. 35.

25. For a list of the most successful westerns and the most rented westerns,

see Phil Hardy, *The Western* (New York: William Morrow and Company, Inc., 1983), 364–365.

26. For more on westerns see Ian Cameron and Douglas Pye, eds., *The Book of Westerns* (New York: Continuum Publishing Company, 1996); John G. Cawelti, *The Six-Gun Mystique* (Bowling Green, OH: Bowling Green University Popular Press, 1984); Jane Tompkins, *West of Everything: The Inner Life of Westerns* (New York: Oxford University Press, 1992); and Will Wright, *Sixguns and Society: A Structural Study of the Western* (Berkeley: University of California Press, 1975). The categories discussed below are based on those described by J. Fred Mac-Donald in *Who Shot the Sheriff? The Rise and Fall of the Television Western* (New York: Praeger, 1987) and Phil Hardy, *The Western*. MacDonald discusses television westerns, but his distinctions can be used in reference to films as well.

27. Hardy, *The Western* 18.

28. Hardy, *The Western*, 104.

29. J. Fred McDonald's *Who Shot the Sherriff?* includes information about ratings, number of episodes, dates and other statistics helpful in understanding the wide popularity of the juvenile western.

30. MacDonald, *Who Shot the Sheriff?*, 22.

31. MacDonald, *Who Shot the Sheriff?*, 22.

32. MacDonald, *Who Shot the Sheriff?*, 23.

33. MacDonald, *Who Shot the Sheriff?*, 24.

34. Hardy, *The Western*, 188.

35. MacDonald, *Who Shot the Sheriff?*, 55.

36. Christopher Frayling, *Spaghetti Westerns: Cowboys and Europeans from Karl May to Sergio Leone.* (Boston: Routledge & Kegan Paul, 1981), xi.

37. Frayling, *Spaghetii Westerns*, 10.

38. Reagan also awarded a medal to one of the most popular writers of western literature, Louis L'Amour.

39. For more on the relationship between the western and the Vietnam films that populated the 1980s, see Michael Walker, "Dances with Wolves" in Cameron and Pye, *The Book of Westerns*, 284–293.

40. See Walker, "Dances with Wolves" for further analysis of the film.

41. The tension between the western and technology can also be seen in the original *Toy Story*. Woody the cowboy competes with Buzz Lightyear, the astronaut, for attention and popularity.

CHAPTER 11

1. Although Greeley has been credited with coining the "Go West, Young Man, Go West" phrase, scholars have claimed that it was actually John L.B. Soule who made the statement first in an 1851 editorial published in Indiana's *Terre Haute Express*. The exact phrase has not been located in the newspaper's pages, however, and the phrase's origins are still undocumented. See *The Oxford Dictionary of Quotations*, 3rd edition (Oxford: Oxford University Press, 1990) for notes on the *Terre Haute* attribution.

2. Oscar Lewis's *Sea Routes to the Gold Fields* (New York: Alfred A. Knopf, 1949) chronicles the journey by sea. Oscar O. Winther's *The Transportation Frontier* (New York: Holt, Rinehart & Winston, 1964) is another source.

3. For more on the covered wagon see George Shumway and Howard C. Frey, *Conestoga Wagon 1750–1850*. 3rd edition (York, PA: Trimmer Printing, Inc., 1968), and Winther's, *The Transportation Frontier*.

4. William Kelly, *An Excursion to California* Over Praire, Rocky Mountains, and Great Sierra Nevada (New York: Aeno Press, 1973), 279.

5. Kelly, *An Excursion to California*, 56.

6. See LeRoy R. Hafen and Ann W. Hafen, *Handcarts to Zion: A Story of a Unique Western Migration, 1856–1860* (Glendale, CA: Arthur H. Clark Company, 1960).

7. Owen Cochran Coy, *The Great Trek*, (Los Angeles: Powell Publishing Company, 1931), 284.

8. See Ralph Moody's *Stagecoach West* (New York: Thomas Y. Crowell Company, 1967).

9. For more on the history of Wells Fargo, see their Web site, http://www.wellsfargo.com (22 December 2001).

10. See Jefferson Davis, *Report of the Secretary of War Respecting the Use of Camels for Military Transportation*. 34th Cong., 3rd sess. (Senate Executive Document No. 63, 1857), and Eva Jolene Boyd, *Noble Brutes: Camels on the American Frontier* (Plano, TX: Republic of Texas Press, 1995).

11. Examples of such stamps and stationery can be found in H.C. Needham and Victor M. Berthold's *Hand-stamped Franks Used as Cancellations on Pony Express Letters, 1860–61, and the Pony Express Stamps and Their Use* (reprinted from the Collector's Club Philatelist, New York, 1927).

12. Quoted in Arthur Chapman, *The Pony Express: The Record of a Romantic Adventure Business* (New York: Cooper Square Publishers, Inc., 1971), 88–89.

13. Chapman, *The Pony Express*, 98.

14. Chapman makes some of these connections in *The Pony Express*, 308.

15. Stephen E. Ambrose's *Nothing Like It in the World: The Men Who Built the Transcontinental Railroad, 1863–1869* (New York: Simon & Schuster, 2000) provides an excellent history of the railroad's creation.

16. For more on the impact of the railroad on the West, see "Tunnel Vision: The Spectacle of the Transcontinental Railroad, 1850–1869," in Anne Farrar Hyde's *An American Vision: Far Western Landscape and National Culture, 1820–1920* (New York: New York University Press, 1990), 53–106.

17. For more on understanding the American landscape, see Anne Farrar Hyde's *An American Vision*, especially chapters 3–6.

18. See *Harper's Weekly Magazine* 11 (December 1876): 797, for a full account of shooting buffalo in this fashion.

19. Dickson Hartwell, "Let's Eat With The Harvey Boys," *Collier's* 9 April 1949, 30.

20. Richard A. Van Orman, *A Room for the Night: Hotels of the Old West* (Bloomington: Indiana University Press, 1966), 120.

21. Lesley Poling-Kempes's *The Harvey Girls: Women Who Opened the West* (New York: Paragon House, 1989) and Marta Weigle and Barbara A. Babcock, eds., *The Great Southwest of the Fred Harvey Company and the Sante Fe Railway* (Phoenix: Heard Museum, 1996), provide good introductions to the topic.

22. Hartwell, "Let's Eat With The Harvey Boys," 30.

23. See David Farmer, "The Fred Harvey Company—Bookseller to the South-

west," 60–64, and "Introduction," 1–8, in Weigle and Babcock, eds., *The Great Southwest of the Fred Harvey Company and the Sante Fe Railway.*

24. Warren James Belasco, *Americans on the Road: From Autocamp to Motel, 1910–1945* (Cambridge: MIT Press, 1979), 34. The first three chapters of Belasco's book address the early history of autocamping.

25. Belasco, *Americans on the Road*, 34.

26. Curt McConnell. *Great Cars of the Great Plains* (Lincoln: University of Nebraska Press, 1995).

27. Roger B. White's *Home on the Road: The Motor Home in America* (Washington, DC: Smithsonian Institution Press, 2000) looks at trailer homes and RV's as popular culture. See also Belasco, *Americans on the Road*, especially the last two chapters.

28. Information about Rice-A-Roni and cable cars can be found at http://ricearoni.com/history/cablecar.html (22 December 2001). Rice-A-Roni jingle is available at http://www.rice-a-roni.com/jingle/flash/index.html.

29. See Death Valley Days (2001) http://www.deathvalleydays.com (22 December 2001).

30. Nick Eggenhofer's *Wagons, Mules and Men* (New York: Hastings House Publishers, 1961) discusses the twenty-mule teams. See pages 93–99.

31. Many Web sites have been dedicated to unraveling the mysteries of aliens and unidentified flying objects in the West. See, for instance, Report of Air Force Record Regarding the "Roswell Incident" July 1994, http://www.af.mil/lib/roswell.html (22 December 2001) and http://www.txdirect.net/~area51/ (22 December 2001).

CHAPTER 12

1. Some reviews of western art, including popular art, include Richard Aquila, "The Pop Culture West," in Richard Aquila, ed., *Wanted Dead or Alive: The American West in Popular Culture* (Urbana: University of Illinois Press, 1996): 1–16; James K. Ballinger and Susan P. Gordon, "The Popular West: American Illustrators 1900–1940," *American West: Its Land and Its People* 19 (July/August 1982): 36–45; Howard R. Lamar, "An Overview of Westward Expansion," in William H. Treuttner, ed., *The West as America: Reinterpreting Images of the Frontier, 1820–1920* (Washington: National Museum of Art, 1991): 1–26; and Robert Taft, "The Pictorial Record of the Old West," *Kansas Historical Quarterly* 19 (August 1951): 225–253.

2. See Nancy K. Anderson, " 'The Kiss of Enterprise': The Western Landscape as Symbol and Resource," in Marianne Doezema and Elizabeth Milroy, eds., *Reading American Art* (New Haven: Yale University Press, 1998), 208–231; and Anne M. Butler, "Selling the Popular Myth," in *The Oxford History of the American West* Clyde A. Milner, Carol A. O'Connor, and Martha A. Sandweiss, eds., (New York: Oxford University Press, 1994), 771–801.

3. An excellent source on the significance of cowboys in American culture is William W. Savage, Jr., *The Cowboy Hero: His Image in American History and Culture* (Norman: University of Oklahoma Press, 1979).

4. See Karal Ann Marling, "Anxiety, Nostalgia, and World Fairs," in *The Co-*

lossus of Roads: Myth and Symbol along the American Highway (Minnesota: University of Minnesota Press, 1984): 17–30.

5. According to one source, Remington "produced more than 2,700 paintings and drawings, his illustrations appearing in forty-one different periodicals and 142 books. He also wrote several volumes of stories." See Howard R. Lamar, ed., *The New Encyclopedia of the American West* (New Haven: Yale University Press, 1998), 955.

6. For more on the differences between Remington and Russell see Robert Hughes, *American Visions* (New York: Alfred A. Knopf, 1997); and Butler, "Selling the Popular Myth."

7. For more on Indian Galleries see William Truettner, *The Natural Man Observed: A Study of Catlin's Indian Gallery* (Washington DC: Smithsonian, 1979); and Julie Ann Schimmel, "John Mix Stanley and the Imagery of the West in the Nineteenth Century" (Ph.D. diss., New York University, 1983).

8. The full citation for Catlin's original publication is *Notes to the Manners, Customs and Conditions of the North American Indians* (1841).

9. See Hughes, *American Visions*, for a full discussion of the "Noble Savage" and "Demonic Indian" distinction.

10. Not surprisingly, western art has been popular throughout the nation's capital. Ronald Reagan, in particular, insisted that the White House be decorated with art depicting the American frontier. This association is also present in popular films about the White House. For instance, in the 1998 movie *Wag the Dog* the Robert de Niro character claims that the young girl who accuses the president of inappropriate behavior "picked up a Remington bust" before the president approached her. See also Clement E. Conger with William G. Allman, "Western Art in the White House," *American West: Its Land and Its People* 19 (March/April 1982): 34–41.

11. Hughes, *American Visions*, 185.

12. John C. Ewers, "Not Quite Redmen: The Plains Indian Illustrations of Felix O.C. Darley," *American Art Journal* 3 (Fall 1971): 88–98.

13. See Marling, "Anxiety, Nostalgia, and World Fairs."

14. According to a *New York Times Magazine* article by Aline Loucheim (13 May 1951, p. 24), the receipts from sales of pictures of the statue at the Exposition stood at $150,000.

15. For more on *The End of the Trail*, see Aline B. Louchheim, "Most Famous Unknown Sculptor," *New York Times Magazine*, 13 May 1951, 24; and Marling, "Anxiety, Nostalgia, and World Fairs."

16. Louchheim, "Most Famous Unknown Sculptor," 24.

17. For recent exhibitions of cigar store Indians see Wendy Noonan, "Cigar Store Indians on Parade," *New York Times* 21 November 1997, p. E45; and "Rose Phyllis, "Folk Art Carved Out of Masts and Stereotypes," *New York Times*, 17 September 1997, sec. 2, p. 93.

18. Patricia C. Albers and William R. James, "Post Card Images of the American Indian: The Collectible Sets of the Pre–1920s Era." *American Postcard Journal* 7 (1982): 17–19.

19. See Robert F. Berkhofer, Jr., "The Western and the Indian in Popular Culture." In *The White Man's Indian from Columbus to the Present* (New York: Alfred A. Knopf, 1978), 96–104. The Clason guide can be found on plate 10 in James R.

Grossman, ed., *The Frontier in American Culture* (Los Angeles, CA: University of California Press, 1944).

20. For more about this commercial see Stuart Elliott, "An Environmental Campaign Is 'Back by Popular Neglect,' " *New York Times* 22 April 1998, sec. D, p. 6.

21. For more on early photography and the West see: Karen Current, *Photography and the Old West* (New York: Harry N. Abrams, 1978) and Nelson B. Wadsworth, *Set in Stone Fixed in Grass: The Mormons, the West, and Their Photographers* (New York: Signature Books, 1996).

22. For more on the popular culture of Niagara Falls, see Elizabeth McKinsey, *Niagra Falls: Icon of the American Sublime* (Cambridge: Cambridge University Press, 1985). Because there was no copyright law, images of the Falls were liberally reproduced in a variety of forms and with no credit given to the artists who originally created the image.

23. One of the best discussions of western art is Robert Hughes' chapter, "The Wilderness and the West," in *American Visions* (New York: Alfred A. Knopf, 1997), 137–205.

24. John Francis McDermott, "Gold Rush Movies," *California Historical Society Quarterly* 33 (March 1954): 29–38.

25. For more on panoramas see Kevin J. Avery, " 'The Heart of the Andes' Exhibited: Frederic E. Church's Window on the Equatorial World," *American Art Journal* 18 (1986): 52–72; John L. Marsh, "Drama and Spectacle by the Yard: The Panorama in America," *Journal of Popular Culture* 10 (Winter 1976): 581–590; McDermott, "Gold Rush Movies"; Henry M. Sayre, "Surveying the Vast Profound: The Panoramic Landscape in American Consciousness," *Massachusetts Review* 24 (Winter 1983): 723–742.

26. Martha A. Sandweiss, "The Public Life of Western Art," in Jules David Prown, et al., *Discovered Lands, Invented Pasts: Transforming Visions of the American West* (New Haven: Yale University Press, 1992), 117–133; and Brucia Witthoft, "The History of James Smillie's Engravings after Albert Bierstadt's *The Rocky Mountains*," *American Art Journal* 19 (spring 1987): 40–51.

27. See also: Peter C. Marzio, *The Democratic Art: Pictures for a Nineteenth-Century America: Chromolithography, 1840–1900* (Boston: David R. Godine, 1979).

28. A number of excellent sources on American landscape photography include Weston J. Naef, *Era of Exploration: The Rise of Landscape Photography in the American West, 1860–1885* (Buffalo: Albright Knox Gallery and The Metropolitan Museum of Art, 1975).

29. See Ansel Adams, *Ansel Adams: An Autobiography* (New York: Little, Brown and Co., 1996).

30. Audubon (2001) http://www.audubon.org/ (22 December 2001).

31. The Far Side (2001) http://www.thefarside.com (22 December 2001).

32. Fred L. Isreal, ed., 1897 Sears, Roebuck catalogue [reprint] (New York: Chelsea House Publishers, 1968), 670.

33. Keith Wheeler, *The Townsmen*, part of Hedley Donovan, ed., *The Old West* New York: Time-Life Books, 1975), 104.

34. Ibid., 148–49.

Further Reading

Aikman, Duncan. *Calamity Jane and the Lady Wildcats*. Lincoln: University of Nebraska Press, 1927.

Ambrose, Stephen E. *Nothing Like It in the World: The Men Who Built the Transcontinental Railroad, 1863–1869*. New York: Simon & Schuster, 2000.

Anderson, Nancy K., and Linda S. Ferber. *Albert Bierstadt: Art and Enterprise*. New York: Brooklyn Museum in association with Hudson Hills Press, 1991.

Aquila, Richard, ed. *Wanted Dead or Alive: The American West in Popular Culture*. Urbana: University of Illinois Press, 1996.

Avery, Kevin J. " 'The Heart of the Andes' Exhibited: Frederic E. Church's Window on the Equatorial World." *American Art Journal* 18 (1986): 52–72.

Ballinger, James K., and Susan P. Gordon. "The Popular West 1900–1940." *American West: Its Land and Its People* 19 (July/August 1982): 36–45.

Bane, Michael. *The Outlaws: Revolution in Country Music*. New York: Doubleday Dolphin, 1978.

Barnes, Will C. *Arizona Place Names*. Rev. and ed. by Byrd H. Granger. Tucson: The University of Arizona Press, 1960.

Bates, Craig D. "Dressing the Part: A Brief Look at the Development of Stereotypical Indian Clothing Among Native Peoples of the Far West." *Journal of California and Great Basin Anthropology* 4, no. 2 (1982): 55–66.

Beard, Tyler. *100 Years of Western Wear*. Salt Lake City: Gibbs-Smith Publisher, 1993.

Beck, Ken, and Jim Clark. *The All-American Cowboy Cookbook: Home Cooking on the Range*. Nashville: Rutledge Hill Press, 1995.

Belasco, Warren James. *Americans on the Road: From Autocamp to Motel, 1910–1945*. Cambridge, MA: MIT Press, 1979.

Bennett, Edwin Lewis. *Boom Town Boy*. Chicago: Sage Books, 1966.

Billington, Ray A. "Books That Won the West." *American West* 4 (1967): 25–32, 72–75.

Black, Eleanora, and Sidney Robertson, eds. *The Gold Rush Song Book*. San Francisco: Colt Press, 1940.

Black, Mary. *American Advertising Posters of the Nineteenth Century*. New York: Dover Publications, Inc., 1976.

Bloom, Harold, ed. *Native American Writers*. Philadelphia, PA: Chelsea House Publishers, 1998.

Boatright, Mody C. *Folk Laughter on the American Frontier*. New York: Macmillan, 1949.

Bold, Christine. *Selling the Wild West: Popular Western Fiction, 1860–1960*. Bloomington: Indiana University Press, 1987.

Borne, Lawrence R. *Dude Ranching: A Complete History*. Albuquerque: University of New Mexico Press, 1983.

Brown, Bill, ed. *Reading the West: An Anthology of Dime Westerns*. Boston: Bedford Books, 1997.

Bull, Debby. *Hillbilly Hollywood*. New York: Rizzoli International Publications, 2000.

Bunting, Bainbridge. *Early Architecture in New Mexico*. Albuquerque: University of New Mexico Press, 1976.

Burnett, Leo. "The Marlboro Story: How One of America's Most Popular Filter Cigarettes Got That Way." *The New Yorker*, 15 November 1958, 41–43.

Butler, Anne. M. *Daughters of Joy, Sisters of Misery: Prostitutes in the American West, 1864–1890*. Urbana: University of Illinois Press, 1985.

———. "Selling the Popular Myth." In *The Oxford History of the American West*, ed. by Clyde A. Milner, Carol A. O'Connor, and Martha A. Sandweiss, 771–801. New York: Oxford University Press, 1994.

Cameron, Ian, and Douglas Pye, eds. *The Book of Westerns*. New York: Continuum Publishing Company, 1996.

Cannon, Hal, ed. *Utah Folk Art: A Catalog of Material Culture*. Provo, UT: Brigham Young University Press, 1980.

Cawelti, John G. *The Six-Gun Mystique*. Bowling Green, OH: Bowling Green University Popular Press, 1984.

Chapman, Arthur. *The Pony Express: The Record of a Romantic Adventure in Business*. New York: Cooper Square Publishers, Inc., 1971.

Clark, Carol. *Thomas Moran, Watercolors of the American West*. Austin: University of Texas Press/Amon Carter Museum of Western Art, 1980.

Clark, Clifford Edward. *The American Family Home: 1800–1960*. Chapel Hill: University of North Carolina Press, 1986.

Cleland, Robert. *Apron Full of Gold*. San Marino, CA: The Huntington Library, 1949, p. 4.

Cody, William F. *The Life of Buffalo Bill*. First published in 1879. New York: Indian Head Books, 1991.

Cole, George. *A Complete Dictionary of Dry Goods*. Chicago: J.B. Herring Publishing Co., 1984.

Conger, Clement E., with William G. Allman. "Western Art in the White House." *American West: Its Land and Its People* 19 (March/April 1982): 34–41.

Connor, Seymour V., and Jimmy M. Skaggs. *Broadcloth and Britches: The Sante Fe Trade*. College Station: Texas A & M University Press, 1977.

Danker, Donald F., ed. *Mollie: The Journal of Mollie Dorsey Sanford in Nebraska &*

Colorado Territories, 1857–1866. Lincoln: University of Nebraska Press, 1959.

Dary, David. *Seeking Pleasure in the Old West*. New York: Alfred A. Knopf, 1995.

DeArment, Robert K. *The Knights of the Green Cloth: The Saga of the Frontier Gamblers*. Norman: University of Oklahoma Press, 1982.

Denning, Michael. *Mechanic Accents: Dime Novels and Working-Class Culture in America*. New York: Verso, 1987.

Dennis, Lee. *Warman's Antique American Games, 1840–1940*. Elkins Park, PA: Warman Publishing Co., Inc., 1986.

Dotz, Warren, and Jim Morton. *What a Character! Twentieth Century American Advertising Icons*. San Francisco: Chronicle Books, 1996.

Dunlop, Richard. *Doctors of the American Frontier*. New York: Doubleday & Company, Inc., 1965.

Dunn, Esther Cloudman. *Shakespeare in America*. New York: Macmillan Company, 1939.

Dwyer, Richard A., and Richard E. Lingenfelter, eds. *The Songs of the Gold Rush*. Berkeley: University of California Press, 1964.

Elazar, Daniel J. *Cities of the Prairie: The Metropolitan Frontier and American Politics*. New York: Basic Books, Inc., 1970.

Ellis, Reuben. "The American Frontier and the Contemporary Real Estate Advertising Magazine." *Journal of Popular Culture* 27, no. 3 (Winter 1993): 119–133.

Emrich, Duncan. *It's An Old Wild West Custom*. New York: Vanguard Press, 1949.

Etulain, Richard W. "Art and Architecture in the West." *Montana: The Magazine of Western History* 40 (Autumn 1990): 2–11.

———. *Re-imagining the Modern American West: A Century of Fiction, History, and Art*. Tucson: University of Arizona Press, 1996.

———. *Telling Western Stories: From Buffalo Bill to Larry McMurtry*. Albuquerque: University of New Mexico Press, 1999.

Ewers, John. C. "The Emergence of the Plains Indian as Symbol of the North American Indian." *Annual Report of the Board of Regents of the Smithsonian Institution* (1964): 531–544.

———. "Not Quite Redmen: The Plains Indian Illustrations of Felix O.C. Darley." *American Art Journal* 3 (Fall 1971): 88–98.

Fabian, Ann. *Card Sharps, Dream Books, & Bucket Shops: Gambling in 19th-Century America*. Ithaca: Cornell University Press, 1990.

Fair, S.S. "The Buckaroo Stops Here." *New York Times Magazine*, 18 June 2000, 70–77.

Fifer, J. Valier. *American Progress*. Chester, CT: The Globe Pequot Press, 1988.

Finlayson, Iain. *Denim: An American Legend*. New York: Simon & Schuster, 1990.

Fischer, Christy. "Wrangler Makes Brand Imprint Via Rodeo Scene." *Advertising Age* 63 (1992): 33, 38.

Fischer, Roger A. *Tippecanoe and Trinkets Too: The Material Culture of American Presidential Campaigns, 1828–1984*. Urbana: University of Illinois Press, 1988.

Foote, Shelly. "Bloomers." *Dress* 5 (1980): 1–12.

Frayling, Christopher. *Spaghetti Westerns: Cowboys and Europeans from Karl May to Sergio Leone*. Boston: Routledge & Kegan Paul, Ltd., 1981.

Frederick, J. V. *Ben Holladay: The Stagecoach King*. Glendale, CA: Arthur H. Clark Company, 1940.

Fredriksson, Kristine. *American Rodeo: From Buffalo Bill to Big Business*. College Station: Texas A & M University Press, 1985.

Gale, Robert L. *Louis L'Amour*. Rev. ed. New York: Twayne Publishers, 1992.

Gard, Wayne. *Frontier Justice*. Norman: University of Oklahoma Press, 1949.

Garland, Hamlin. *Boy Life on the Prairie*. New York: Frederick Ungar Publishing Co., 1959.

Garner, Mark L. *Wagons for the Sante Fe Trade*. Albuquerque: University of New Mexico Press, 2000.

Gibson, Arrell M. "Medicine Show." *American West* 4, no. 1 (February 1967): 34–79.

Goldman, Marion. *Gold Diggers and Silver Miners: Prostitution and Social Life on the Comstock Lode*. Ann Arbor: University of Michigan Press, 1981.

Gordon, Jean, and Jan McArthur. "Interior Decorating Advice as Popular Culture: Women's Views Concerning Wall and Window Treatments, 1870–1920." In *Making the American Home: Middle-Class Women and Domestic Material Culture, 1840–1940*, ed. by Marilyn Ferris Motz and Pat Browne. Bowling Green, OH: Bowling Green University Press, 1988.

Green, Douglas B. *Country Roots: The Origins of Country Music*. New York: Hawthorne Books, 1976.

Gregory, Scott. *Sowbelly and Sourdough: Original Recipes from the Trail Drives and Cow Camps of the 1800s*. Caldwell, ID: Caxton Printers, Ltd., 1995.

Grossman, James, ed. *The Frontier in American Culture*. Los Angeles: University of California Press, 1994.

Grover, Kathryn, ed. *Hard at Play: Leisure in America, 1840–1940*. Amherst: University of Massachusetts Press, 1992.

Gulliford, Andrew. *America's Country Schools*. Washington, DC: Preservation Press, 1984.

Hafen, LeRoy R., and Ann W. Hafen. *Handcarts to Zion: A Story of a Unique Western Migration, 1856–1860*. Glendale, CA: Arthur H. Clark Company, 1960.

Harmon, Jim. *The Great Radio Heroes*. Garden City, NY: Doubleday, 1967.

Harris, Foster William. *The Look of the Old West*. New York; Viking Press, 1995.

Helveston, Sally I. *Feminine Response to a Frontier Environment as Reflected in the Clothing of Kansas Women: 1854–1895*. Ph.D. diss., Kansas State University, 1985.

Hertzog, Peter. *Frontier Humor*. Sante Fe, NM: Press of the Territorian, 1966.

Holsinger, M. Paul, ed. *War and American Popular Culture: A Historical Encyclopedia*. Westport, CT: Greenwood Press, 1999.

Howard, Thomas Frederick. *Sierra Crossing: First Roads to California*. Berkeley: University of California Press, 1998.

Hughes, Glenn. *A History of the American Theatre 1700–1950*. London and Toronto: Samuel French, 1951.

Hungerford, Edward. *Wells Fargo: Advancing the American Frontier*. New York: Random House, 1949.

Hyde, Anne Farrar. *An American Vision: Far Western Landscape and National Culture, 1820–1920*. New York: New York University Press, 1990.

Isley, Else. *Sunbonnet Days*. Caldwell, ID: Caxton Printers, 1935.

Ives, Halsey C. Introduction to *The Dream City, a Portfolio of Photographic Views of the World's Columbian Exposition*. St. Louis, MO: N.D. Thompson Publishing Company, 1893.

Johnson, Byron A., and Sharon P. Johnson. *Gilded Palaces of Shame: Albuquerque's Redlight Districts, 1880–1914*. Albuquerque, NM: Gilded Age Press, 1983.

Johnson, Michael L. *New Westers: The Western in Contemporary American Culture*. Lawrence: University Press of Kansas, 1996.

Johnson, Susan Lee. *Roaring Camp: The Social World of the California Gold Rush*. New York: W. W. Norton & Company, 2000.

Jones, Daryl. *The Dime Novel Western*. Bowling Green, OH: Popular Press, 1978.

Jones, Mary Ellen. *Daily Life on the Nineteenth-Century American Frontier*. Westport, CT: Greenwood Press, 1998.

Jordan, Terry G., and Matti Kaups. *American Backwoods Frontier: An Ethnic and Ecological Interpretation*. Baltimore: Johns Hopkins University Press, 1989.

Karpenstein, Katherine. "Illustrations of the West in Congressional Documents, 1843–1863." Master's thesis, University of California, 1939.

Kimball, Arthur G. *Ace of Hearts: The Westerns of Zane Gray*. Fort Worth, TX: Texas Christian University Press, 1993.

Kirker, Harold. *California's Architectural Frontier: Style and Tradition in the Nineteenth Century*. New York: Russell & Russell, 1970.

Kolodny, Annette. *The Lay of the Land*. Chapel Hill: University of North Carolina Press, 1975.

Larsen, Lawrence H. *The Urban West at the End of the Frontier*. Lawrence: Regents Press of Kansas, 1978.

Lears, Jackson. *Fables of Abundance: A Cultural History of Advertising in America*. New York: Basic Books, 1994.

LeBlanc, Beverly. *The Cowboy's Cookbook*. Philadelphia: Courage Books, 1998.

Lewis, George H., ed. *All that Glitters: Country Music in America*. Bowling Green, OH: Bowling Green University Popular Press, 1993.

Lewis, Lloyd, and Henry Juston Smith. *Oscar Wilde Discovers America*. New York: Harcourt, Brace and Company, 1936.

Lewis, Oscar. *Sea Routes to the Gold Fields*. New York: Alfred A. Knopf, 1949.

Lohof, Bruce A. "The Higher Meaning of Marlboro Cigarettes." In *The Popular Culture Reader*, ed. by Jack Nachbar, Deborah Weiser, and John L. Wright. Bowling Green, OH: Bowling Green University Press, 1978.

Lomax, John A., ed. *Cowboy Songs and Other Frontier Ballads*. New York: Macmillan Company, 1938.

Louchheim, Aline B. "Most Famous Unknown Sculptor." *New York Times Magazine* 13 May 1951, 24.

Luchetti, Cathy. *Home on the Range: A Culinary History of the American West*. New York: Villard Books, 1993.

MacDonald, J. Fred. *Who Shot the Sheriff? The Rise and Fall of the Television Western*. New York: Praeger, 1987.

Mackay, James. *Allan Pinkerton: The First Private Eye*. New York: John Wiley & Sons, Inc., 1996.

Marling, Karal Ann. *The Colossus of Roads: Myth and Symbol along the American Highway*. Minneapolis: University of Minnesota Press, 1984.

Marsden, Michael T. "The Modern Western." In *The American Literary West*, ed. by Richard W. Etulain. Manhattan, KS: Sunflower University Press, 1980.

Marsh, John L. "Drama and Spectacle by the Yard: The Panorama in America." *Journal of Popular Culture* 10 (Winter 1976): 581–590.

Marzio, Peter. *The Democratic Art: Pictures for a Nineteenth-Century America*: Chromolithography, 1840–1900. Boston: David R. Godine, 1979.

Mazzulla, Fred, and Jo Mazzulla. *Brass Checks and Red Lights: Being a Pictorial Pot Pourri of Prostitutes, Parlor Houses, Professors, Procuresses and Pimps*. Denver: Fred and Jo Mazzulla, 1996.

McConnell, Curt. *Great Cars of the Great Plains*. Lincoln: University of Nebraska Press, 1995.

McDermott, John Francis. "Gold Rush Movies." *California Historical Society Quarterly* 33 (March 1954): 29–38.

———. *The Lost Panoramas of the Mississippi*. Chicago: University of Chicago Press, 1958.

McDonald, Archie P. *Shooting Stars: Heroes and Heroines of Western Film*. Bloomington: Indiana University Press, 1987.

McDonald, Douglas. *The Legend of Julia Bulette and the Red Light Ladies of Nevada*. Las Vegas: Nevada Publications, 1983.

McMartin, Maria B. "Dress of the Oregon Trail Emigrants: 1834–1855." Master's thesis, Iowa State University, 1977.

McQuaid, Peter. "The Cowboy Couturier." *New York Times Magazine*, 19 March 2000: 86–94.

Melder, Keith. *Hail to the Candidate: Presidential Campaigns from Banners to Broadcasts*. Washington, DC: Smithsonian Institution Press, 1992.

Mierau, Christina. *Accept No Substitutes: The History of American Advertising*. Minneapolis: Lerner Publishing Co., 2000.

Montana, Monte, Jr. *Buffalo Bill's Wild West Cowboy Cuisine*. Springfield, CA: Buffalo Bill's Wild West, 1996.

Moody, Ralph. *Stagecoach West*. New York: Thomas Y. Crowell Company, 1967.

Murdoch, David H. *The American West: The Invention of a Myth*. Reno: University of Nevada Press, 2000.

Naylor, David, and Joan Dillon. *American Theaters: Performance Halls of the Nineteenth Century*. New York: John Wiley & Sons, Inc., 1997.

Novak, Barbara. *Nature and Culture: American Landscape and Painting, 1825–1875*. New York: Oxford University Press, 1980.

Ogden, Dunbar H., ed. *Theatre West: Image and Impact*. Amsterdam; Atlanta, GA: Rodopi Press, 1990.

O'Neal, Bill. *Ghost Towns of the American West*. Lincolnwood, IL: Publications International, Ltd., 1995.

Ormsby, Waterman L. *The Butterfield Overland Mail*. Edited by Lyle H. Wright and Josephine M. Bynum. San Marino, CA: Huntington Library, 1942.

Ostendorf, Berndt. "Western Icons and Myths in American Advertising." In *The American West as Seen by Europeans and Americans*, 384–396. Amsterdam: Free University Press, 1989.

Overstreet, Daphne. *Arizona Territory Cook Book*. Phoenix: Golden West Publishers, Inc., 1997.

Paden, Irene D. *The Wake of the Prairie Schooner*. New York: Macmillan Company, 1943.

Palmer, Joel. *Journal of Travels Over the Rocky Mountains to the Mouth of the Columbia River; Made During the Years 1845 and 1846: Containing a List of Necessary Outfits for Emigrants*. Vol. 30 of *Early Western Travels*. Cleveland: Arthur H. Clark Co., 1905.

Parkman, Francis. *The Oregon Trail*. Boston: Little, Brown, and Company, 1872.

Parsons, John E. *The Peacemaker and Its Rivals*. New York: William Morrow and Company, 1950.

Perl, Lila. *Hunter's Stew and Hangtown Fry: What Pioneer America Ate and Why*. New York: Seabury Press, 1977.

Peters, Harry T. *Currier and Ives: Printmakers to the American People*. Garden City, NY: Doubleday, Doran, 1942.

Pillsbury, Richard. *No Foreign Food: The American Diet in Time and Place*. Boulder, CO: Westview Press, 1998.

Poling-Kempes, Lesley. *The Harvey Girls: Women Who Opened the West*. New York: Paragon House, 1989.

Pomeroy, Earl. *In Search of the Golden West: The Tourist in Western America*. New York: Alfred A. Knopf, 1957.

Prassel, Frank Richard. *The Great American Outlaw: A Legacy of Fact and Fiction*. Norman, OK: University of Oklahoma Press, 1993.

Price, B. Byron. *National Cowboy Hall of Fame Chuck Wagon Cookbook*. New York: Hearst Books, 1995.

Rabinowitz, Harold. *Black Hats and White Hats: Heroes and Villains of the West*. New York: Metro Books, 1996.

Reddin, Paul. *Wild West Shows*. Urbana and Chicago: University of Illinois Press, 1999.

Reed, Ethel. *Pioneer Kitchen: A Frontier Cookbook*. San Diego: Frontier Heritage Press, 1971.

Riley, Glenda. *The Life and Legacy of Annie Oakley*. Norman: University of Oklahoma Press, 1994.

Rodman, Paul W., ed. *A Victorian Gentlewoman in the Far West: The Reminiscence of Mary Hallock Foote*. San Marino, CA: Huntington Library, 1972.

Root, Waverley, and Richard de Rochemont. *Eating in America: A History*. New York: William Morrow & Company, 1976.

Rothel, David. *The Gene Autry Book*. Madison, NC: Empire Publishing Company, 1988.

Ruede, Howard. *Sod-House Days: Letters from a Kansas Homesteader, 1877–78*. New York: Cooper Square Publishing, Inc., 1937.

Rundell, Walter, Jr. "The West as Operatic Setting." In *Probing the American West: Papers from the Santa Fe Conference*, ed. by K. Ross Toole, et. al. Santa Fe, NM: Museum of New Mexico Press, 1962.

Saunders, Richard H. *Collecting the West: The C.R. Smith Collection of Western American Art*. Austin: University of Texas Press, 1988.

Savage, William W., Jr. *The Cowboy Hero: His Image in American History and Culture*. Norman: University of Oklahoma Press, 1979.

Sayre, Henry M. "Surveying the Vast Profound: The Panoramic Landscape in American Consciousness." *Massachusetts Review* 24 (winter 1983): 723–742.

Schechter, Harold, and Jonna G. Semeiks. "Leatherstocking in 'Nam: *Rambo, Platoon*, and the American Frontier Myth." *Journal of Popular Culture* 24, no. 4 (spring 1991): 17–25.

Schimmel, Julie Ann. "John Mix Stanley and the Imagery of the West in the Nineteenth Century." Ph.D. diss., New York University, 1983.

Schoberlin, Melvin. *From Candles to Footlights: A Biography of the Pike's Peak Theatre, 1859–1876.* Denver, CO: Old West Publishing Company, 1941.

Schorin, Gerald A., and Bruce G. Vanden Bergh. "Advertising's Role in the Diffusion of Country-Western Trend in the U.S." *Journalism Quarterly* 62 (1985): 515–522.

Severa, Joan. *Dressed for the Photographer: Ordinary Americans & Fashion, 1840–1900.* Kent, OH: Kent State University Press, 1995.

Shumway, George, and Howard C. Frey. *Conestoga Wagon 1750–1850.* 3rd ed. York, PA: Trimmer Printing, 1968.

Silber, Irwin. *Songs America Voted By.* Harrisburg, PA: Stackpole Books, 1971.

Sivulka, Juliann. *Soap, Sex, and Cigarettes: A Cultural History of American Advertising.* Belmont, CA: Wadsworth Publishing Company, 1998.

Slotkin, Richard. *The Fatal Environment: The Myth of the Frontier in the Age of Industrialization, 1800–1890.* New York: Atheneum, 1985.

———. *Gunfighter Nation: The Myth of the Frontier in Twentieth-Century America.* Norman: University of Oklahoma Press, 1992.

———. *Regeneration Through Violence: The Mythology of the American Frontier 1600–1860.* Middletown, CT: Wesleyan University Press, 1973.

Smith, Henry Nash. *Virgin Land: The American West as Symbol and Myth.* Cambridge, MA: Harvard University Press, 1950.

Sohn, Anton Paul. *A Saw, Pocket Instruments, and Two Ounces of Whiskey: Frontier Military Medicine in the Great Basin.* Spokane, WA: Arthur H. Clark Company, 1998.

Stage, Sarah. *Female Complaints: Lydia Pinkham and the Business of Women's Medicine.* New York: W. W. Norton & Company, 1979.

Stanley, David, and Elaine Thatcher, eds. *Cowboy Poets and Poetry.* Chicago: University of Illinois Press, 2000.

Stetler, Gilbert A. "The Birth of a Frontier Boom Town: Cheyenne in 1867." *Annals of Wyoming* 39, no. 1 April 1967: 5–34.

Stewart, George R. *Ordeal By Hunger: The Story of the Donner Party.* Boston: Houghton Mifflin Company, 1988.

Stratton, Joanna L. "A Prairie Childhood." In *Pioneer Women: Voices from the Kansas Frontier,* 144–156. New York: Simon & Schuster, 1981.

Sullivan, Larry E., and Lydia Cushman Schurman, eds. *Pioneers, Passionate Ladies, and Private Eyes: Dime Novels, Series Books, and Paperbacks.* New York: Haworth Press, 1997.

Swell, Barbara. *Log Cabin Cooking: Pioneer Recipes and Food Lore.* Asheville, NC: Native Ground Music, Inc., 1996.

Taft, Robert. *Artists and Illustrators of the Old West, 1850–1900.* New York: Charles Scribner's Sons, 1953.

Taft, Robert. "The Pictorial Record of the Old West: XIV. Illustrators of the Pacific Railroad Reports." *Kansas Historical Quarterly* 19 (November 1951): 359.

Taylor, Joshua C. *America As Art.* New York: Harper & Row/Icon Editions, 1976.

Thayer, Stuart, and William L. Slout. *Grand Entrée: The Birth of the Greatest Show on Earth, 1870–1875*. San Bernardino, CA: Borgo Press, 1998.

Thorp, N. Howard. *Songs of the Cowboys*. New York: Clarkson N. Potter, Inc, 1966.

Tompkins, Jane. *West of Everything: The Inner Life of Westerns*. New York: Oxford University Press, 1992.

Truettner, William. *The Natural Man Observed: A Study of Catlin's Indian Gallery*. Washington DC: Smithsonian, 1979.

Turner, Frederick Jackson. *The Frontier in American History*. New York: Dover Publishers, 1996.

Tyler, Ron, et al. *American Frontier Life: Early Western Painting and Prints*. New York: Abbeville, 1987.

Van Orman, Richard A. "The Bard in the West." *Western Historical Quarterly* 5 no. 1 (1974): 29–38.

Van Steenwyk, Elizabeth. *Frontier Fever: The Scary, Superstitious—and Sometimes Sensible—Medicine of the Pioneers*. New York: Walker and Company, 1995.

Venturi, Robert, Denise Scott Brown, and Steven Izenour. *Learning from Las Vegas: The Forgotten Symbolism of Architectural Reform*. Cambridge, MA: MIT Press, 1988.

Walker, Barbara M. *The Little House Cookbook*. New York: Harper & Row, 1979.

Walker, Paul Robert. *Great Figures of the Wild West*. New York: Facts on File, 1992.

Walle, Alf H. *The Cowboy Hero and Its Audience: Popular Culture as Market Derived Art*. Bowling Green, OH: Bowling Green University Press, 2000.

Wallis, Michael. *The Real Wild West: The 101 Ranch and the Creation of the American West*. New York: St. Martin's, 1999.

———. *Route 66: The Mother Road*. New York: St. Martin's Press, 1992.

Walsh, Margaret. "The Democratization of Fashion: The Emergence of the Women's Dress Pattern Industry." *Journal of American History* 66 (1979): 299–313.

Walters, Lon. *The Old West Baking Book*. Flagstaff, AZ: Northland Publishing, 1996.

Watson, Margaret G. *Silver Theatre: Amusements of the Mining Frontier in Early Nevada, 1850–1864*. Glendale, CA: Arthur H. Clark Company, 1964.

Weier, Ped., ed. *Bring Warm Clothes: Letters and Photos from Minnesota's Past*. Minneapolis: Minneapolis Star and Tribune Co., 1981.

Weigle, Marta, and Barbara A. Babcock, eds. *The Great Southwest of the Fred Harvey Company and the Sante Fe Railway*. Phoenix, AZ: Heard Museum, 1996.

West, Elliott. "Beyond Baby Doe: Child Rearing on the Mining Frontier." In *The Women's West*, ed. by Susan Armitage and Elizabeth Jameson, 179–192. Norman: University of Oklahoma Press, 1987.

———. *Growing Up in the Twentieth Century: A History and Reference Guide*. Westport, CT: Greenwood Press, 1996.

———. *Growing Up with the Country: Childhood on the Far Western Frontier*. Albuquerque: University of New Mexico Press, 1989.

———. *The Saloon on the Rocky Mountain Mining Frontier*. Lincoln: University of Nebraska Press, 1979.

West, Elliott and Paula Petrik, eds. *Small Worlds: Children and Adolescents in America, 1850–1950*. Lawrence: University Press of Kansas, 1992.

White, Roger B. *Home on the Road: The Motor Home in America*. Washington, DC: Smithsonian Institution Press, 2000.

William, George. *The Red-Light Ladies of Virginia City, Nevada*. Dayton, NV: Tree By the River Publishing, 1984.

Winther, Oscar O. *The Transportation Frontier*. New York: Holt, Rinehart & Winston, 1964.

Wright, Will. *Sixguns and Society: A Structural Study of the Western*. Berkeley: University of California Press, 1975.

Yoggy, Gary A. *Riding the Video Range: The Rise and Fall of the Western on Television*. Jefferson, NC: McFarland & Company, Inc., 1995.

Young, Agnes. *The Recurring Cycles of Fashion*. New York: Harper & Bros., 1937.

Index

journey west, 170–173; and rock
and roll, 185–187; sheet music, 179;
themes in, 178–179

Names, 135–137
National Monuments, 231
National Parks, 252–253
Native Americans, and fashion, 108
New Frontier, The, 22
Newspaper, as wallpaper, 73, 158–159
Nooning, 112
Nudies, 102–103

Oakley, Annie, 199–201
Outlaw musicians, 186–187

Panoramas, 250–251
Patent medicine, 9; advertisements, 50–51
Penny candy, 125
Performing arts: in the old West, 191–197; West as American myth, 197–198
Photographs, 247–248
Picnics, 125–126
Pinkerton detective agency, 10–11
Pioneers, art, 246–248
Political campaigns, and the West, 18–23
Pony Express, 224–225
Postcards, 252–253
Practical jokes, 141
Prairie School, The, 77–78
Prostitution, 144–145
Pullman car, 226–227
Pulp magazines, 162

Radio, 201–203
Railroads, promotions for, 46–47
Ranchhouses, 78–79; and Hollywood, 79
Rawhide, 207
Reagan, Ronald, presidential campaign, 23
Remington, Frederic, 236–238
Rendezvous, 138
Restaurants, 126
Rice-a-Roni, 129

Rodeo, 201
Rolling cabins, 68
Roosevelt, Theodore, 17–18, 19–22;
Clifford Berryman cartoon, 21; campaign paraphernalia, 21–22; teddy
bear, 20–21
Rough Riders, 19–22
Russell, Charles M., 236–238

Sacagawea dollar, 243–244
Saloon, 84–85; food, 118–119; free
lunch, 118–119
Sawyer, Tom, 214
School, 29–34; books, 32; recess, 32–34;
schoolteacher, 29–34; women as
teachers, 29–31
Schweppes, 66
Shakespeare, William, 193
Show tunes, 185
Sierra Club, The, 252
Singing cowboy, 180–182
Singing cowboys, clothing, 101–102;
Patsy Montana, 182–183; new cowgirl singers, 188–189
Sitting Bull, 16
Soddy, 69–71
Soiled doves, 144–145
Songs of the forty-niners, 176–177
Spanish-American War, 17
Sports, 149–150
Stagecoach, 205, 221–222
Sunbonnets, 92–93
Surprise parties, 138

Taco Bell, 86–87
Tar-paper shacks, 68
Teddy bear, 20–21, 37
Tepees, 75
Theater, 192–193; local, 195–196
Tommy knockers, 134–135
Tourism, 225–233
Toy Story, Toy Story 2 (film), and
Woody and Buzz Lightyear, 42, 211
Toys, rag dolls, stick horses, 36–37
Trade cards, 54
Trails, 213–214
Trains, watching as pastime, 140
Transcontinental railroad, 226

About the Author

SARA E. QUAY is Associate Dean of Arts and Sciences at Endicott College in Massachusetts.